Discovering Vietnam's Ancient Capital

Discovering Vietnam's Ancient Capital

The Archaeology and History of the Imperial Citadel of Thăng Long–Hanoi

Edited by

Andrew Hardy and Nguyễn Tiến Đông

NUS PRESS
SINGAPORE

© 2024 Andrew Hardy and Nguyễn Tiến Đông

Published by:

NUS Press
National University of Singapore
AS3-01-02, 3 Arts Link
Singapore 117569

Fax: (65) 6774-0652
E-mail: nusbooks@nus.edu.sg
Website: http://nuspress.nus.edu.sg

ISBN 978-981-325-229-5 (paper)
ePDF ISBN: 978-981-325-230-1
ePub ISBN: 978-981-325-231-8

National Library Board, Singapore Cataloguing in Publication Data
Name(s): Hardy, Andrew (Andrew David), 1966– editor. | Nguyễn, Tiến Đông, editor.
Title: Discovering Vietnam's ancient capital: the archaeology and history of the imperial citadel of Thăng Long–Hanoi / edited by Andrew Hardy and Nguyễn Tiến Đông.
Description: Singapore: NUS Press, 2024. | Includes bibliography and index.
Identifier(s): ISBN 978-981-325-229-5 (paperback) | 978-981-325-230-1 (ePDF) | 978-981-325-231-8 (ePub)
Subject(s): LCSH: Imperial Citadel of Thăng Long (Hanoi, Vietnam) | Hanoi (Vietnam)--History. | Hanoi (Vietnam)--Civilization.
Classification: DDC 959.702--dc23

Cover image: Lý-dynasty terracotta dragon, symbol of the emperor, exhibited at the Thăng Long Imperial Citadel on-site museum (110 cm × 87 cm) (Photo: Institute of Archaeology).
Facing title page (Fig. 1): Lý-dynasty terracotta phoenix, symbol of the empress, exhibited at the Thăng Long Imperial Citadel on-site museum (53 cm × 62,5 cm) (Photo: Institute of Archaeology).

Printed by: Integrated Books International

CONTENTS

LIST OF MAPS AND FIGURES

Maps

Figures

ACKNOWLEDGEMENTS

Photographs credited to the Institute of Archaeology were taken by Nguyễn Hữu Thiết, except Figure 6, which is by Lê Thị Liên. Photographs credited to the École française d'Extrême-Orient (EFEO) were taken by Andrew Hardy.

Federico Barocco drew Maps 20–22 of the Thăng Long Imperial Citadel and Hanoi Citadel.

The chapter by Phan Huy Lê is the edited translation of an article previously published in *Khảo cổ học* no. 1, 2006: 5–27. A different translation was published under the title 'Structure of Thang Long Capital City and Location of Forbidden City over Historical Periods' in the journal *Vietnam Social Sciences*, No. 1 (177), 2017: 33–82. For the illustrations to this chapter, we thank the Institute of Hán-Nôm Studies.

For the maps and photographs illustrating Olivier Tessier's chapter, we thank the EFEO, the Musée national des arts asiatiques—Guimet in Paris, the Bibliothèque de l'ancien Musée des colonies (Paris), housed at the Université Côte d'Azur and the Archives nationales d'outre-Mer (ANOM) in Aix-en-Provence.

Nguyễn Tuyết Nga and Andrew Hardy translated the chapters by Tống Trung Tín, Lê Thị Liên, Nguyễn Hồng Kiên, Nguyễn Văn Anh, Đỗ Danh Huấn, Nguyễn Tiến Đông and Phạm Văn Triệu; Trần Thị Lan Anh and Andrew Hardy translated the chapter by Phan Huy Lê; Andrew Hardy translated the chapters by Nguyễn Văn Sơn, Olivier Tessier and Đào Hùng.

The editors would like to express their warm thanks to Bùi Thu Phương for her help with documentation, and to Vũ Thị Mai Anh for her research.

FOREWORD

The Imperial Citadel of Thăng Long had a thousand-year history as the capital of Đại Việt and, as the seat of its independent ruling dynasties the Lý, Trần and Lê, lay at the heart of the civilisation that underpins today's nation of Vietnam. This history is a source of considerable pride for Vietnamese people.

Despite this, until the early twenty-first century, the citadel was known to us only through a small number of historical records found in books and maps, and a smattering of place names, legends, and historical sites. It is no exaggeration to say that the archaeological excavation at 18 Hoàng Diệu Street, carried out in 2002–04 by the Institute of Archaeology, was an event of immense importance for scholars' understanding of the Imperial Citadel. The cultural layers of the site's stratigraphy reveal a complex of vestiges dating from pre-Thăng Long times through the Thăng Long period to the modern era of the city of Hanoi. The discoveries excited admiration from members of the academic community, but also from the leaders of Vietnam's Communist Party and government, the Vietnamese people, and many foreigners, including some heads of state. Amid the ruins of palaces and pavilions, as the priceless artefacts crafted centuries before our time were uncovered, all gazed with veneration upon the cultural heritage of Thăng Long.

Preliminary results of the archaeological research into the site have already been published in books and articles, some of them authored by contributors to this volume. The present book, edited by Andrew Hardy and Nguyễn Tiến Đông, takes a more historical approach, exploring the discovery's history from two perspectives. In the first, the discovery is

Fig. 2. Ly-dynasty terracotta phoenix, symbol of the empress, unearthed at 18 Hoàng Diệu Street, Hanoi (Photo: Institute of Archaeology).

deemed an event of sufficient historical importance to warrant its own record: Part I of the book seeks to present an insider view of the excavation written by its archaeologists. The second shows how the results of the excavation have given scholars new insights into the narrative of Hanoi's past: Part II presents research into the site's history since the archaeological discovery.

In these two ways, the book sheds light on the backstory to the archaeological park created at the site in 2010 and inscribed in the same year on UNESCO's register of World Cultural Heritage. In my view, it is also a form of homage to the generations of Vietnamese who built and lived in the citadel and whose creations appeared under the archaeologists' trowels during one of the most remarkable archaeological excavations in our country's history.

Nguyễn Gia Đối
Former Director
Institute of Archaeology (*Vietnam Academy of Social Sciences*)

Map legends:

Map 1. Hồng Đức Map of Đông Kinh, the Forbidden City (Institute of Hán-Nôm Studies, A.2499), part of the mapping exercise ordered by King Lê Thánh Tông, most likely compiled in 1490. Oriented to the North.

Map 2. 'Plan annamite d'Hanoi' in the collection of the Bibliothèque Nationale de France, collected between 1876 and 1883. (Département Cartes et plans, GE A-395 (RES). Public domain.)

Map 3. Hanoi, 1873, at 1:8,800 scale.

Map 4. Hanoi, 1885, as seen in 'Environs de Hanoï, dressés par le service topo-graphique de l'état-major du corps expéditionnaire du Tonkin'. The map's military character is clear (the map is in different collections, including Bibliothèque nationale de France, GEC-521. Public domain).

Map 5. Hanoi, 1902, at 1:10,000 scale, detail of 'Plan de la ville de hanoï / levé sur le terrain et déssiné par le sergent Lecureur du Service géographique'. This map of Hanoi shows the city after the most intense period of colonial remaking: the walls of the citadel torn down, new avenues sketched out, and a railway line running through the city. (Service geographique de l'indochine. Public domain.)

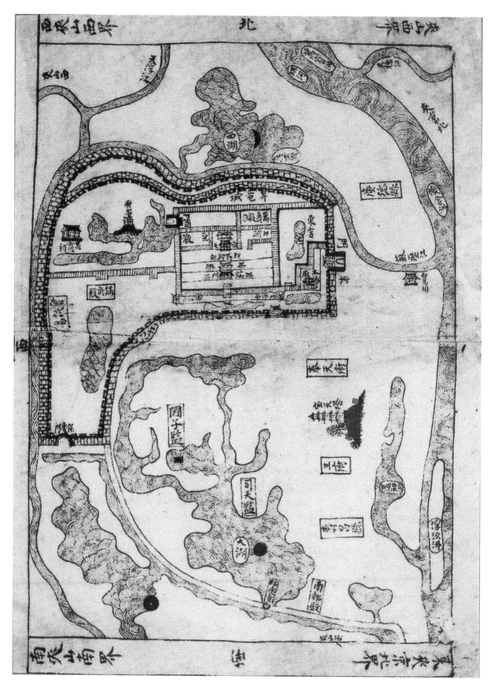

Map 1

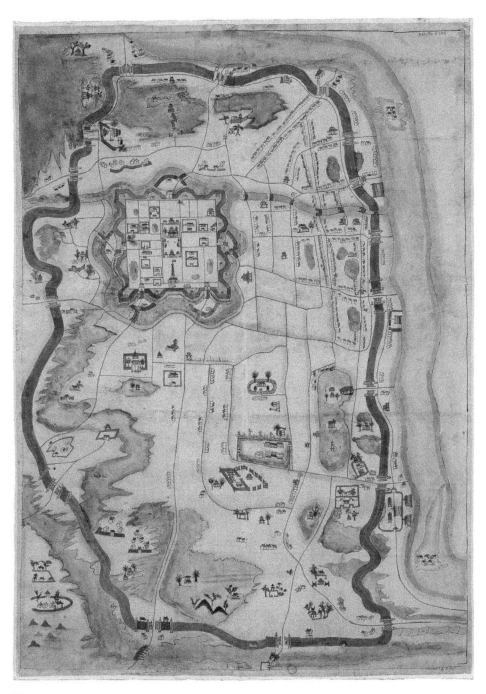

Map 2

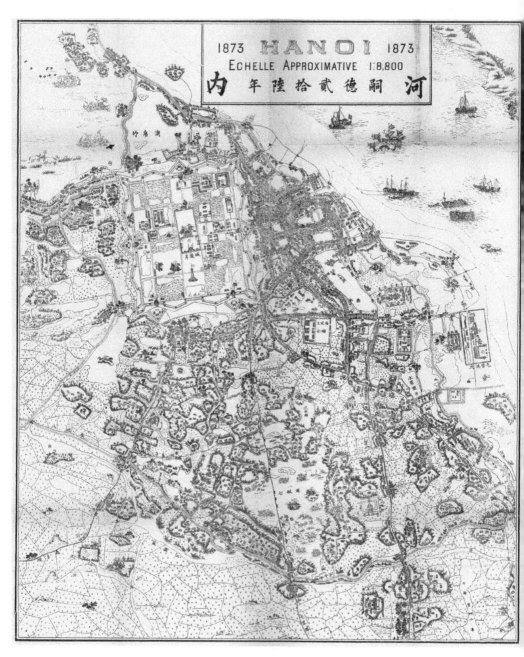

Map 3

Map 4

Map 5

The Discovery of Thăng Long Imperial Citadel: Archaeological Dig and Historical Event

Andrew Hardy

Passer-by, before this first monument of Paris, reflect that the town of the past is also the city of the future and that of its hopes.

Jean Paulhan[1]

1. BACKGROUND

In 1995, a maze of market stalls occupied the streets on the western edge of Hanoi's old commercial quarter. They lined Phùng Hưng Street, beside the old French-built railway. They passed under the iron bridge, where market noises and loudspeaker instructions were periodically drowned by the whistle of approaching steam trains—still running in those days—and a deafening roar as the locomotive rattled the bridge's girders. Here, the stalls spilled into Cửa Đông Street. I didn't know it when I rented a room there that year: the stalls were only a temporary interruption to the area's normal routine. They had moved there after the Đồng Xuân market burnt down some months earlier. It was fully two years before the stalls returned to Đồng Xuân, where a modern market hall now stands behind the old colonial façade, beautifully restored. It was then possible to see how Cửa Đông Street was quite unlike the other thoroughfares of the 'thirty-six streets and wards' of the old quarter.

It took me a year to learn my way around the old quarter. Each turn increased my disorientation. One narrow street led into another, each distinguishable only by its name on shop signs, still referring to the merchandise sold there centuries before: oriental medicines on Lãn Ông Street (named after an eighteenth-century doctor), aluminium in Hàng Thiếc Street (lit. 'tin street'), and so on. The names and wares had to be learned, and I was long mystified by the fact that Hàng Thiếc and Lãn Ông were, in a sense, exceptional. Both had names recalling a merchandise and were lined with shops selling that merchandise; the shops on only a very few streets sold the goods advertised in its name. I found bamboo sold on Hàng Vải (cloth street), beer on Hàng Hương (perfume street), ceremonial paraphernalia on Hàng Than (coal street). It was as though only the commercial culture—the habit of selling the same goods on the same street—had survived the historical ups and downs of the commerce itself.

The trick, I found at first, was to remember a few often-travelled routes. Turn right under the railway bridge, up Đường Thành Street, past the Hàng Da market, left into Chân Cầm Street, then right and past the cathedral. This route took me to Tràng Thi Street, where I was working at the time. In this way, like other new residents of Vietnam's capital, I gradually built up a mental map of the city's routes and ways. I also took an interest in their names: one street, Tràng Thi, for example, evoked the camp where Confucian examinations were held before their abolition during the colonial era. The same street led east towards the Opera House; this section took the name Tràng Tiền, the mint. In the late nineteenth century, this became the city's first *'rue française'* (*phố tây*), linking the French concession by the river with the gate on the south side of the citadel. It thus divided the commercial district from the French quarter, a grid of broad tree-lined avenues that covered the area south of the Hoàn Kiếm Lake (Papin 2001: 221–3, 236; Mangin 2001: 103).

Strangely, Cửa Đông resembles one of these French-style avenues more than a street of the old quarter. Its pavements are broad and spacious. Its shops sell no particular merchandise. After the market stalls left in 1997, a few cafés took their place, their owners negotiating with police over a new law ordering the sidewalks' clearance for pedestrians. I could visualise then what I had long known from its name: Cửa Đông means east gate and, like the name of nearby Đường Thành (rampart road), recalls an association with the city's ancient seat of power: the Imperial Citadel of Thăng Long.

A gate still stands at the western end of Cửa Đông. In 1995, yellow letters on a red sign spelled the words 'Barracks of the Vietnam People's Army' (*Doanh trại Quân đội Nhân dân Việt Nam*). A sentry box was manned by uniformed guards. No ramparts surrounded this area west of the old quarter, but it remained a military zone surrounded by a wall. This meant that when I wanted to visit friends living up at the West Lake, I had to make a long detour: up Lý Nam Đế Street, which follows the eastern edge of the military zone, then via Quán Thánh Street to the lake. The return route was along Phan Đình Phùng, an avenue lined with sumptuous colonial villas now occupied by government agencies and officials' families. Halfway along Phan Đình Phùng, which also bounds the military zone, an old brick citadel gate still bears the marks left by French cannons in their nineteenth-century assault. This is the nineteenth-century citadel's North Gate. A nearby street also bears its name: Cửa Bắc (north gate).

On each trip to the West Lake, I chafed at the need for such a long detour. I was also struck by the military zone's incongruity: in the late twentieth century, an army barracks still operated in the heart of the city. The site's function had remained unchanged since the days of the ancient citadel evoked by these place names. And a decade later—after the events described in this book—my surprise found a new object. An excavation conducted at 18 Hoàng Diệu Street, which bounded the modern military zone on its western side, showed that a wealth of royal architecture had accumulated here over a period of more than a thousand years; it was now coming to light under the archaeologists' trowels. I was not alone in my surprise. As the historian Đào Hùng relates in his chapter, the memory that royal architecture had ever existed in this place had all but disappeared from the city of Hanoi.

This loss of memory contributed to the emotional reception given to news of the archaeologists' findings, not only among historians and other specialists, but also among the city's population and indeed Vietnamese people throughout the country. This book's aim is to complement previous publications (which include Phan Huy Lê 2004, Tống Trung Tín 2006, Phan Huy Lê 2010a, Trương Quang Hải 2010, Tống Trung Tín & Bùi Minh Trí 2010, Phan Huy Lê et al. 2014, Tống Trung Tín & Nguyễn Văn Sơn 2014, Nhật Minh 2015, Tống Trung Tín 2020) by recording the moment of discovery and some of the emotions that accompanied it. Studying the results of the 2002–04 excavation is a challenge faced by Vietnam's archaeologists and historians: the work will take many years.

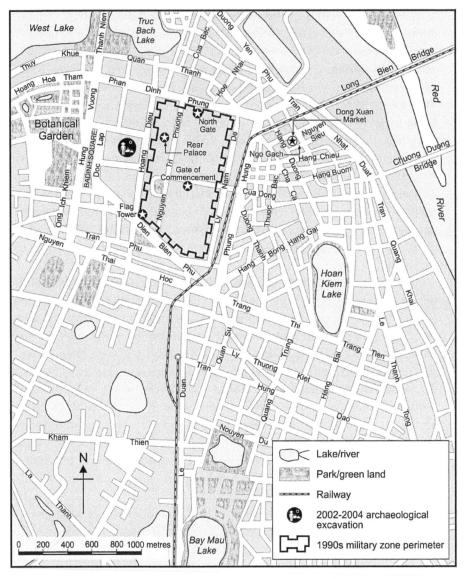

Map 6. Street map of Hanoi, c. 2000 (Cartographer: Lee Li Kheng).

But the archaeological dig was itself a historical event of great significance and merits its own record.

In every city, there exists a tension between the desire to conserve traces of its history and the loss of sites of memory that inevitably accompanies modernisation and development. But the memory loss that took place in Hanoi is exceptional. Before the 2002–04 excavation, we knew surprisingly little of the city's early history. In the year 2000, a specialist in architectural heritage summarised the state of our knowledge as follows.

> It is a significant fact that in Hanoi there is not much that is old, apart from religious buildings and some tumuli to the west of the old sector. Although the Ly, Tran, Later Le and, to a lesser extent, the Nguyen built extensively in the city, little of Hanoi's pre-colonial architecture remains. Successive invasions and internal conflict led to the destruction of most of their works. Those that have survived date mostly from the mid-seventeenth century or later. Of the Imperial Citadel's architecture, only very few vestiges remain today; in fact, only the Mirador Tower and the Cua Bac, or North Gate, are accessible to the general public. Most of the former citadel area is controlled by the Vietnamese army and closed to visitors. There are, however, other relics of the past—a dragon staircase among them—hidden from view. Presumably curatorial attention is being paid to them by the army and when, as has been promised, the army relinquishes the citadel site over the next decade, these relics will again be available as part of the people's heritage. (Logan 2000: 59–60)

The loss of memory owes much to the view that the site of a monument is more important than the actual monument itself. In recent years, the replacement of structurally sound old temples and pagodas is living testimony to this tradition; the rebuilding of Yên Phụ communal house, beside Hanoi's West Lake, is a nearby example. But the extent of memory loss in Hanoi has also been due to Vietnam's high turnover of political regime over the last two hundred years.

In the first change of regime, in 1802, the city lost its name and its status as capital. By the eighteenth century, the Lê-dynasty court's lustre had faded: the country was ruled not by the king but by two competing aristocratic dynasties. From their capital at Phú Xuân (today's Huế), lords of the Nguyễn family governed a region that extended south from a network of dividing walls in today's Quảng Bình province. North of these walls was the domain of the Trịnh family, who ruled from Thăng Long but not from the Imperial Citadel. The Trịnh lords had their own complex of palaces located outside the royal enclosure.[2]

After the destructions of the Tây Sơn Rebellion, the Nguyễn seized power over the whole country in 1802. The new dynasty's first king, Gia Long, established his court in Huế, relegating Thăng Long to the status of regional centre. The city's elegant name was similarly downgraded. In 1805, the pronunciation of Thăng Long did not change, but the name's regal characters, 升龍 (soaring dragon), were replaced with the more prosaic 昇隆 (rising prosperity). Then, in 1831, Gia Long's successor, Minh Mạng, renamed the city Hà Nội (河內)—'inside the river'—a banal geographical reference of northern Chinese inspiration (Papin 2001: 197–8). Gia Long and Minh Mạng also rebuilt the citadel, reducing the height of its ramparts in a deliberate policy of status reduction. The Nguyễn rulers' legitimacy was thus underlined; memories of the Lê dynasty's royal dignity were erased.

In the second change, the French conquest, the city lost its material fabric. In the years after 1883, the gates and ramparts of the Nguyễn citadel—here referred to as the Hanoi Citadel—were levelled. Many historical sites disappeared as a network of avenues and buildings took the shape of French Haussmann-style modernity. By the turn of the century, the original landscape of Thăng Long–Hanoi had been substantially transformed. The Indochina Union's first governor-general, Paul Doumer, halted the process: he restored Hanoi's status as capital (1902), transferred his offices from Saigon and took steps to ensure the preservation of remaining monuments.[3] But immense damage had already been done and the city did not recover its ancient name. These processes are charted in detail in the chapters by Đào Hùng and Olivier Tessier.

Finally, when the French left in 1954, much of Hanoi's social memory followed. Under the terms of Article 14d of the Geneva Agreements that partitioned Vietnam at the seventeenth parallel, many of the city's inhabitants moved south. Its new residents were people from the nearby provinces who had no inherited knowledge of ancient Thăng Long.

Written documents compensate little for these losses. They do inform us that the site was chosen by Gao Pian (高骈 Vietnamese: Cao Biền), the Chinese governor there in 865–68 (see Franciscus Verellen's chapter). They report its establishment as Vietnam's capital by the first king of the Lý dynasty. But in his *Histoire de Hanoi*, published just before the 2002–04 excavations commenced, Philippe Papin underlined the paucity of the historical record. In the following extract, we may observe him valiantly building a narrative from the available documentary fragments, even as he remained aware that only archaeology would provide the necessary materials.

[Gao Pian] first had a new rampart built, 9 m high and 8 m wide, which rested on a stone foundation and included 55 watchtowers, 6 small arched lateral gates and 5 great gates topped with a balcony. Then he surrounded it with an earth embankment, lower in height and about 6000 m in circumference. It was for this reason that the city took the name 'great exterior rampart' (Đại La Thành).

The fortifications of Đại La have long disappeared, but in the 19th century, numerous land registers (*địa bạ*) of the villages and quarters of Hanoi still referred to it. To locate Đại La, perhaps we should return to the legends. The *Collection of the Prodigies of Gao Pian* affirms that 'the Nùng mound constitutes the exact centre of Đại La'. However, certain bricks have been found at the foot of this mound. While we await the completion of excavations, we must content ourselves with the indications given by the emperor Lý Thái Tổ in 1010: 'Đại La, the ancient capital of Prince Gao, is located between Heaven and Earth, at the place where the Dragon curls and the Tiger sits.' (Papin 2001: 46, citing *Việt Sử Lược*)

The imperial text mentioned here is *The Edict for the Transfer of the Capital*, written in the spring of 1010. By this decree, Lý Công Uẩn (Lý Thái Tổ), the founder of the Lý dynasty, ordered the capital's return from Hoa Lư to the site chosen by the Chinese governor.[4] Papin also relates the legendary explanation of the choice of name for the city: the king consciously sought to establish a political tradition by which the dynasty's legitimacy and power was closely associated with this specific place.

In the first year of his reign, in the seventh lunar month of 1010, after receiving the approbation of the court, Lý Thái Tổ thus had the capital transferred. As the imperial cortege arrived in view of Đại La, the sovereign saw an amber-coloured dragon rise in the sky and, interpreting it as an excellent omen, he gave the town the name it would conserve for nine centuries, Thăng Long, the 'city of the rising dragon'. But in Vietnam as in China, the dragon was also the symbol of the emperor: in the shadow of a legend forged to justify its use, the city's name referred to the rise of a new dynasty. (Papin 2001: 64)

Historical documents also reveal that the city of Đại La–Thăng Long was defined by two main ramparts. Indeed, parts of the outer rampart survived to the late twentieth century. During a 1992 visit to Hanoi, I had the good fortune of meeting a historian of Hanoi who asked if I would like to see it. Nguyễn Khắc Đạm led me to Đại Cồ Việt Street; the newly built road, he said, marked the city wall's former line. Then, in front of the Kim Liên Hotel, he pointed to a low earth embankment beside the road: a vestige of the rampart, he said. Further up, between rows of small houses with tiled roofs, we cycled along a narrow lane on the top of an embankment; this was a street called Đê La Thành (lit. 'outer rampart dike'). He didn't take me as far as Bưởi village, where the dike turned north. Instead, a short cut led us up Liễu Giai Street. This avenue had just been built and we rode up it through vegetable gardens, marshland and lotus ponds to Hoàng Hoa Thám Street, which also followed an embankment.

Until the 1990s, much of the embankment—known as *thành ngoài* (the outer rampart) or Đại La rampart—lay beyond the inhabited city. Although it was rebuilt, modified and extended by successive dynasties, part of the line I followed in 1992 dated from the Trần dynasty.[5] For much of its existence, it would have been a simple dike or line of bamboo hedge.

The 'inner rampart' (*thành nội*), known as the Imperial Citadel of Thăng Long, was a wall surrounding the third, innermost enclosure, the Forbidden City.[6] In the late twentieth century, neither social memory nor archaeological evidence existed to compensate for the imprecision of historical and cartographical data on this area. At that time, there was no consensus among Vietnamese historians on the Imperial Citadel's exact location, or indeed that of the Forbidden City. By contrast, the nineteenth century Hanoi Citadel, built by the Nguyễn dynasty, was relatively well documented: its North Gate, Flag Tower and other monuments still stand. A theory of the older Imperial Citadel's location here had long been voiced by a section of the academic community, led by the historian Trần Quốc Vượng. It competed, however, with a second theory situating it further to the west. The location of the citadel and its ramparts is discussed here in the chapters by Tống Trung Tín, Đào Hùng, Phạm Văn Triệu and, especially, Phan Huy Lê.

Before the late 1990s then, no firm evidence linked the Nguyễn-dynasty Hanoi Citadel with the documentary descriptions of the ramparts, palaces, and royal gardens of the older Imperial Citadel of Thăng Long.

2. THE 2002–04 EXCAVATION

Hoàng Diệu Street, where the excavation took place, ran along the western edge of the military zone. Around the time the dig started, I began to travel along this street quite often, on my way from the old French quarter up to the West Lake. Back in the 1990s, I had rarely used this route, preferring to pass the villas of Điện Biên Phủ Street, the Ministry of Foreign Affairs in its elegant Indochina-style building, and Ba Đình

Square with the National Assembly, Vietnam's first post-independence major work of architecture (1959). This was an imposing structure located beside the War Memorial and opposite the Ho Chi Minh Mausoleum. Before I turned the corner at the end of Độc Lập Street, I could see the diving board in the Central Sports Club (the 1930s French *cercle sportif*) and then, after the turn, the yellow and red-painted walls of the former Lycée Albert Sarraut, today the headquarters of Vietnam's Communist Party. A vista opened towards another French period building, the former governor-general's residence, now the President's Palace. A further turn took me up Hùng Vương Avenue towards the causeway that separates the West Lake from the smaller Trúc Bạch Lake to its east. To my left, hidden beyond the trees of the gardens, was the wooden house where Ho Chi Minh lived the last years of his life as Vietnam's President.

I always enjoyed this section of the journey, partly for its architecture and green space and partly for the sense it gave of passing through the heart of things. This was the centre of Vietnam's government: all the most important institutions, both symbolic and functional, both past and present, were here. I changed my route because of the traffic, preferring now the broad empty lanes of Hoàng Diệu Street, the shade of its towering trees, and the architecture of Cửa Bắc Church at the far end. Then I became aware that behind the high wall at No. 18 an excavation was taking place.

Rumours of it started filtering out in 2003. Colleagues at the Academy of Social Sciences talked of extraordinary discoveries made by the team from the Institute of Archaeology. They recommended I visit. On my weekly trips to the West Lake, I noticed that some of the young couples who normally congregated on the West Lake causeway to gaze into each other's eyes had taken to parking by the high wall on Hoàng Diệu Street. I saw them there as I passed, standing on their mopeds, peering into the archaeological site. What was in there, I wondered, that could so dramatically refocus their attention? I arranged a visit and saw the site early in 2004.

It was a cold clear morning. The gate opened and to my right a yawning hole stretched for several hundred metres into the distance. The colour struck me first, a brilliant orange-red lit by the winter sun contrasting with the familiar green-grey tones of the city. Further on, a second deep red pit stretched parallel to the first as far as the enclosing wall. Between these two enormous 'trenches', the ground had not been touched. The far end was encumbered by huge piles of earth that grew by the minute as lines of workers moved in pairs carrying new deposits.

Fig. 3. Nguyễn Tiến Đông guiding visitors around the site (Photo: EFEO 2004).

Both rectangular pits and the central strip seemed to be living things; there were people everywhere, most of them moving, busy, some of them seated, drawing, absorbed. 'You see that central strip?' One of the archaeologists, Nguyễn Tiến Đông, had met us at the gate: 'We think it's an ancient river.' I barely heard him, understanding now why those mopeds had been parked against the wall.

The Institute of Archaeology had invited us to join a group of forty or more schoolteachers for a tour. Nguyễn Tiến Đông, explaining the site through a megaphone, stood in the pit. Standing at ground level, I was struck how far down he was: four to five metres at its lowest point, I learned. His explanations were lively and clear. They had to be: at first sight the ruins were, to say the least, perfectly bewildering.

'This is a length of guttering,' he pointed to a couple of metres of channel built with bricks and terracotta tiles. 'It drained the water from the palace into that drain over there,' indicating a broader channel, another course of red bricks, several metres off.

'This stack of pebbles here,'—a square area of small stones—'was probably the foundation for a wooden pillar.' He then pointed to other similar pebble squares, showing how they lined up, asking us to imagine a building supported by pillars, with each pillar placed on its own individual foundation of tightly rammed stones.

'Do you see this stone plinth, shaped like a lotus flower?' The plinth lay beside its foundation and would in turn have supported a pillar. Explained in this way, the association of pebble foundation–stone plinth–wooden pillar became clear. That day I did not know that just a few months earlier this association had deeply puzzled the archaeological team (see the chapter by Nguyễn Hồng Kiên).

'These pillars supported the palace roof, which was covered with items like these,' he pointed to fragments of curved roof tiles, strewn across the area. At one spot the giant head of a terracotta phoenix remained, untouched, where it had been found: 'This would have adorned the end of a palace roof.'

'We think this was a Trần-dynasty palace—and do you see here?' He pointed to a set of ruins lying at a lower level: 'These are part of the Lý-dynasty cultural layer.'

'How do you know?' one of the teachers asked. 'By the type of brick, mainly,' the answer swiftly came, 'and by the decorative motifs. This, for example, is a Lý-dynasty brick, re-used here in a Trần-dynasty building.'

* * *

My main memory of that morning is a series of flashes of understanding, given by these explanations, amidst great clouds of confusion. I struggled to grasp the grammar of archaeology: the way one thing fitted with another in multiple overlapping 'cultural layers'. I recall a piece of wooden pillar, still standing, now protected with canvas: 'the building's original support'. A blackened horizontal line in the earth: 'evidence that the city was burnt, but we're not sure when'. A mass of broken and intact ceramics: 'dumped here in the water, below the bank of the ancient river'. Discarded mollusc shells: 'our ancestors were much like ourselves, they too liked to eat seafood'. A long area of strewn gravel more than a metre wide: 'we think this was a path leading down to the ancient river—do you see how it picks up again on the far side? They probably crossed by boat, or perhaps there was a bridge'. At the time I had no idea of the extent to which the archaeologists, despite their specialist training, shared this sense of bewilderment as they worked (see the chapter by Lê Thị Liên).

The language of history was almost as confusing. Up to that time, my historical research had focused exclusively on Vietnam's twentieth century and my grasp of the preceding centuries was shaky. Certainly, I knew that the Lý dynasty (eleventh to twelfth centuries) was the first of Vietnam's first long-lasting independent dynasties and that it was followed by the Trần (thirteenth to fourteenth centuries). I knew about the Tây Sơn Rebellion, which overthrew the Lê dynasty, captured Thăng Long in 1789, and was in turn replaced by the Nguyễn in 1802.

But the Lê dynasty itself was more difficult. This was partly because there were two Lê dynasties: a short-lived Early Lê or Former Lê (late tenth century) and a much longer late Lê (fifteenth to eighteenth centuries). Then, within the late Lê dynasty, there were several periods. There was the Early Lê period of the fifteenth century, dominated by the dynasty's founder, Lê Lợi, and its greatest king, Lê Thánh Tông. There was the period of the Mạc dynasty, that ruled in the northern delta for most of the sixteenth century before its retreat to Cao Bằng in 1592. And there was the Lê Restoration period that occurred when the Lê family was restored to the capital at Thăng Long but not to actual power, divided now between the Trịnh and Nguyễn lords in the north and south (seventeenth to eighteenth centuries).

The period just before the Lê was not much easier. I learned how the Trần dynasty had been overthrown in 1400 by one its own generals, Hồ Quý Ly—who established the Hồ dynasty and moved the capital to Thanh Hóa—and how this general who had routed the armies of

Champa failed to defeat an invasion from the north. As a result, from 1407–28, Vietnam was ruled from Thăng Long by governors sent from Ming-dynasty China.

I knew nothing at all of the centuries before the Lý dynasty, or the rapid succession of families that preceded the accession of Lý Thái Tổ. There was Ngô Quyền, who declared independence from China with the collapse of the Tang dynasty and established the capital at Cổ Loa on the north side of the Red River (939). There was Đinh Bộ Lĩnh, who proclaimed himself king in 968 and established the capital at Hoa Lư (today's Ninh Bình province). Then there was that short-lived Early Lê dynasty that ruled from Hoa Lư until the accession of Lý Thái Tổ. I had no idea what the 'Đại La period' might be, but this term in particular kept coming up as we toured the site. Nguyễn Tiến Đông finally explained when we stopped at a well with red bricks superimposed on grey bricks. 'The grey bricks are Chinese style, so we can say the well dates from the Đại La period, when China ruled Vietnam from this site. In those days, Hanoi was called Đại La. The bricks date from the seventh to ninth centuries. The red ones, which resemble the bricks of Champa, were added at a later date, to raise the level of the well.'

Then there were the things that the archaeologist himself could not explain. In a further trench (in Section B), molluscs had been carefully laid out in a regular pattern across a broad area: it looked like a courtyard tiled with shells. But are courtyards ever paved with fragile shells? Such 'mysteries', I later learned, confronted the excavation team on a daily basis, as the archaeologists Lê Thị Liên and Nguyễn Văn Anh relate with great frankness in their chapters.

During our visit, several of the schoolteachers asked questions. I myself couldn't see where one question might finish and the next begin, and kept silent. But towards the end I did ask one, a question that seemed rather off the subject, but nonetheless puzzled me. 'Why has that area been left untouched?' I was pointing to a column of earth in the middle of the vast excavated trench nearest to the street; I later learned that this area was Section A. The 'column' was formed of a block of unexcavated ground, topped by a low building a few m^2 in area, standing plumb in the middle of the excavated trench. I was surprised by the answer, which had nothing to do with history or archaeology. In fact, the explanation reflected recent changes in Vietnam's land ownership laws.

The land at 18 Hoàng Diệu Street had formerly been a residential area within the army barracks, where modest houses provided accommodation for officers and troops. Like the farmland in rural areas, it was privatised in the 1990s, during the early period of Vietnam's *Đổi mới* reforms, and land title was given to the army families who lived there. Then the land's use for construction of new National Assembly and Convention Centre buildings on this site was approved, it was repossessed, and its owners compensated. Once they had left, the two-hectare site was occupied by the archaeologists, who were given six months to conduct a rescue excavation under the provisions of Vietnam's 2001 Law on Cultural Heritage. The snag was: one army captain refused to leave his tiny house in the barracks. And so the archaeologists, pressed for time, had to respect his ownership of that patch of land. They dug around his house, leaving the building and the ground it stood on undisturbed. The army captain couldn't live there, but turned up from time to time, so I learned, to chat with the guards and look from the gate across the deepening hole in the ground at his house as it became gradually stranded and began to tower over the vast expanse of red ruins. Here too was a man attached to the past.[7]

I went home amazed and a little anxious; the ruins were extraordinary and certainly merited the rumours now circulating the city. From this short visit, I could see that the site was of great beauty and exceptional historical significance. Yet despite my ignorance of archaeology, even I could see this it was archaeologically extremely complex. And if it was preserved in the future (many of the rumours said that it should be), did Vietnam possess the technical expertise to manage it? Did *anyone* have the expertise to manage the conservation of such a vast area, in a climate where the air was so humid and the rains torrential. This challenge was in the minds of all concerned, as some of the chapters in this book indicate.

3. AFTERMATH

The first months of 2004 were, for me, a period of learning. I returned regularly to the site and heard the team present their work, both in their modest office and around the site. I listened to colleagues, visited archaeological sites elsewhere in Vietnam and the other vestiges in the citadel area, most of which dated from the Nguyễn dynasty. They had been within the modern military zone, under army control, and had recently been handed over to the Hanoi city authorities. I learned how the North Gate, the ruins of the Kính Thiên Audience Hall, the Rear Palace (Hậu Lâu), the Gate of Commencement (Đoan Môn) or South Gate, and the

Flag Tower formed the citadel's central axis. I discovered how a turning point in our knowledge came in the late 1990s, when archaeological research (related in detail in Tống Trung Tín's chapter) revealed new information about these monuments.

Firstly, an excavation at the Gate of Commencement proved that although most of the existing monuments were built during the nine-teenth century, the site itself had been in use as early as the Lý period. Secondly, it showed that the monuments' spatial configuration along the north–south axis had remained unchanged since the Lý dynasty (though see below for debate on this). Thirdly, it suggested that the Kính Thiên site, which lay at the axis' centre, had been the most important building in the palace complex: it was here that the king held audience. The site remained important in the twentieth century. Deep in the ground under the ruined palace, the Democratic Republic of Vietnam's war against the USA was commanded from bunker D67, built for Party Secretary Lê Duẩn, General Võ Nguyên Giáp and other leaders. In short, this research, conducted in the late 1990s, supported the hypothesis that the Nguyễn dynasty's Hanoi Citadel was built on the site of the ancient Imperial Citadel of Thăng Long, founded by Lý Thái Tổ.

The research also showed the relation of the north–south axis with vestiges discovered across the road at 18 Hoàng Diệu Street: the ruined palaces found in 2002–04 were located directly west of the central axis. The archaeologists then thought that they had served as living quarters for the royal family and other high-ranking members of the court. Later research suggests that, at least in the nineteenth century, this was a storage area. Certainly, the site had different functions in different historical periods (see Phan Huy Lê, 2006). Its proximity to the core of political power and the long and almost unbroken period of its royal occupation—approximately 1000 years[8]—gave it immense historical value (see the chapter on the Forbidden City by Phan Huy Lê).

By the summer of 2004, the École française d'Extrême-Orient (EFEO) had set up a project to assist the Academy of Social Sciences with tech-nical expertise. In the project document, the site's historical value was assessed as follows:

> It presents two original features. The first is the concentration of the vestiges, as thirteen centuries of history are 'compressed' in a layer of ground less than five metres thick. The stratum of Đại La (9th cen-tury) is followed by the successive strata of the Lý, Trần, Lê, Hồ, Mạc, Nguyễn and French eras (19th century). The continual use of this

Fig. 4. French President Jacques Chirac visited the excavation in 2004, the first foreign head of state to do so (Photo: EFEO).

place, cause of the vestiges' concentration, is the second original feature. There are certainly older and better conserved sites elsewhere, but the whole interest of this one lies in the fact that it manifests the historical longue duree: it is here that Vietnam's political heart has been established for more than a millennium. Moreover, it remains so today as around the archaeological area may be found the National Assembly, the Ho Chi Minh Mausoleum, the palace of the President of the Republic, the seat of the Communist Party and the place chosen by President Ho Chi Minh for his proclamation of independence on 2 September 1945.[9]

In August 2004, this position was reiterated during a conference held in Hanoi, at which the Vietnamese specialists sought the advice of foreign colleagues.[10] Experts from France, Italy, Japan, Korea, Norway, Spain and elsewhere joined their Vietnamese colleagues in voicing their recognition of the site's historical and heritage value. Two months later, French President Jacques Chirac made an official visit and recorded the following words in the site's visitors' book: 'To the Academy of Social Sciences and the EFEO's experts, in testimony of my recognition of the admirable historical work being done here and my hopes for the continued valorisation of this site, which bears witness to the history of Vietnam and honours humanity. J. Chirac, 7 October 2004'.[11]

At the same time, the discovery was enjoying broad appreciation in Vietnam. It was made public at temporary exhibitions: artefacts unearthed at the site were displayed at the Hanoi Ancient Citadel complex, which could now be entered from Nguyễn Tri Phương Street, a street newly opened to public use that year by the army. Exhibitions were also held at the Temple of Literature in Hanoi, the Museums of History in both Hanoi and Ho Chi Minh City, as well as a number of provinces. Visitors were impressed by the artefacts' great quantity and high quality, as well as by the simple fact that they were previously unknown. They gave tangible expression to a certain narrative of the Vietnamese nation, made up of the ancestors' struggles and achievements as they contributed to the 'history of building the country and defending the country'.[12] At the same time, they demonstrated the diversity of Vietnam's cultural influences and evolution over the period of the site's occupation. Imbued with Chinese characteristics from the early centuries, subsequent periods were marked by a search for independent stylistic expressions with inspiration from Southeast Asian traditions, above all from Champa (see Nguyễn Tiến Đông's chapter).

* * *

Such assessments of the site's value led the Academy of Social Sciences, whose archaeologists were responsible for the excavation, to take an audacious step. With the support of the Vietnam History Association, they filed an application for its preservation. Their aim was to transform this rescue excavation into a permanent historical monument. In so doing, they raised important questions about the future development of the city of Hanoi. This did not consist of a straightforward dilemma between cultural and economic development, with one side recalling the past and the other planning the future, although economic considerations were certainly of great importance. It turned too on alternative visions of how Vietnam's past could serve its future.

Simplified, one vision sought to use twenty-first century architecture to maintain the heart of state power and political legitimacy within the precincts of Ba Đình district. This vision held to a principle that Lý Thái Tổ had understood (when he returned the capital to Đại La) and that Hồ Quý Ly had abandoned (when he moved the capital to Thanh Hóa): a secure and flourishing future for Vietnam and its people depended on the location of its government at the 'dragon's belly button', at the most geomantically auspicious site on the 'dragon vein'. In line with the country's rising prosperity based on its *Đổi mới* reforms, this ancient principle now received contemporary architectural expression using modern construction designs, materials and technology. In proposing partial conservation of the archaeological site accompanied by the construction of new national monuments, its proponents relied on ancient political instincts. They stood within a tradition upheld by centuries of Vietnamese kings, by Paul Doumer, and by Ho Chi Minh himself. This tradition, of course, had given rise to the archaeological site itself.

The other vision saw modernity in terms of harmonious integration of historical monuments into the modern urban fabric. It proposed that the archaeological site should be protected in its entirety and the new buildings relocated. A heritage perimeter should be legally defined, allowing the development of a cultural landscape based on conservation of the vestiges and its nearby urban context. This would lead to comparison of the future Hanoi with other developed historic cities: London, Paris, Rome, and so on. According to this vision, the preservation of the entire site area and creation of an archaeological park at 18 Hoàng Diệu Street would serve as the centrepiece for a city centre characterised by its historical environment and cultural values.

The first saw modernity as founded on ancient political tradition while the second saw modernity as based on the development of cultural heritage.

* * *

News of the discovery was enthusiastically announced in the press. Glowing appreciations of the vestiges' value were published, buoyed by the public's excitement. At the same time, in 2003–04, the challenges the discovery raised were frankly discussed on the pages and screens of the country's media. In the public forum, debate focused, on the one hand, on Vietnam's need for cultural heritage development and, on the other, on understandable concerns that the country lacked the capability to conserve the ruins successfully.

The press items tell a story of their own, too long to reproduce here in full. Their titles' question marks and future tense illustrate the dilemma posed by the discovery:

- 'Will the new National Assembly be built on another site?'
- 'Temporarily fill with sand to excavate at a later date; build an open-air museum or...?'
- 'The Forbidden City opens its doors'.
- 'Does the Ba Đình site merit listing as world heritage?'
- 'A tree cannot grow without roots'.
- 'The Imperial City of Thăng Long's value will soon be affirmed'.
- 'The people continue to contribute support for the conservation of the Hanoi Imperial Citadel'.
- 'The Ministry of Culture and Information has presented the government with three options'.
- 'New arguments over the Imperial Citadel site'.
- 'On construction in the Imperial Citadel area: who is right?' [13]

A clear summary of the dilemma appeared in an article on the internet news service *Vietnamnet* (19 August 2004):

> The largest national conference ever held on the Ba Đình site was opened this morning in Hanoi, to assess its value and make recommendations about the protection and development of its values. This conference will be decisive, as it will determine the content of the Report presented to the Prime Minister about this time next month, on the basis of which the destiny of the Imperial Citadel of Thăng Long–Hanoi will be decided. [...]
>
> According to research results discussed and presented this morning at Panel 1 (presided by Professor Phan Huy Lê), it is possible to conclude: the Ba Đình site lies within the area of the Forbidden City, that is to say the central part of the Imperial Citadel. [...]
>
> Should the entire site be preserved or a part of it?
>
> Up to now this question remains unanswered. Researchers' opinions fall into two groups. The first group of opinions firmly demand that the entire site be protected. According to this view, the entire site just discovered, the sites related to the Imperial Citadel of Thăng Long area and the sites related to the period of resistance wars against France and the USA and, recently, the construction of socialism should be preserved. No construction should be done here. The area should be turned into a cultural park and given over to archaeological research. (...)

HƯỚNG THAM QUAN

THE WAY TO VISIT

→

The second group of opinions maintains that only a number of important sections should be protected, while construction should be permitted on the remaining sections to serve the country's socio-economic development needs. In general, the opinion urging partial preservation mainly argues from analysis of the inadequacy of present-day Vietnam's finances, management potential, specialist knowledge, conservation technology, climatic conditions and the multi-layered characteristics of the archaeological site.[14]

From 2004–08, the dilemma was resolved with a compromise within which both visions of modernity found their place: the 'second group of opinions' mentioned above. The decisions taken give us a clear idea of the role played by the past in the future shape of Hanoi. The first step was the relocation of the National Convention Centre project to the suburb of Mỹ Đình (construction was completed in 2006). This freed part of the archaeological site for the preservation of the ruins. In accordance with the aim of cultural heritage development, the vestiges were designated a national monument (2007) and an application was filed with UNESCO for world heritage recognition (2008) (see the chapter by Nguyễn Văn Sơn). Secondly, a neighbouring area of land on Ba Đình Square was chosen for construction of the National Assembly. The site of the old National Assembly (demolished in 2008) was chosen for the new parliament building (completed in 2014), thus upholding the political tradition founded by Lý Thái Tổ.

In 2010, as Thăng Long–Hanoi celebrated its millennium, UNESCO inscribed the site on the World Heritage List, under the title *Central Sector of the Imperial Citadel of Thăng Long–Hanoi*. The same year, the city opened a new archaeological park at the site, where the public may now see how the archaeologists' efforts restored an important part of the city's past to its present. The site was given the following summary description, reflecting UNESCO's recognition of its values of intercultural exchange, political continuity and a succession of events marking 'the formative and development process of an independent nation over more than a thousand years'.

The Thang Long Imperial Citadel was built in the 11th century by the Ly Viet Dynasty, marking the independence of the Dai Viet. It was

Fig. 5. Built in 2014, Vietnam's new National Assembly Building is located within the archaeological park (Photo: EFEO, 2014).

constructed on the remains of a Chinese fortress dating from the 7th century, on drained land reclaimed from the Red River Delta in Hanoi. It was the centre of regional political power for almost 13 centuries without interruption. The Imperial Citadel buildings and the remains in the 18 Hoang Dieu Archaeological Site reflect a unique South-East Asian culture specific to the lower Red River Valley, at the crossroads between influences coming from China in the north and the ancient Kingdom of Champa in the south.[15]

The UNESCO designation, as the chapter by Nguyễn Văn Sơn suggests, was not only the culmination of years of intense archaeological and historical research, but also of an immense political effort to ensure the conservation and development of the heritage.

* * *

As the UNESCO description indicates, the citadel's value as heritage rests on two features of its history. One is the site's longevity. Uniquely in East and Southeast Asia, Thăng Long was a centre of regional power for many centuries, predating and outlasting by a millennium Vietnam's other historical capital at Huế. This earned the city a reputation as the heartland of the Vietnamese empire and 'cradle' of the modern nation. Scholarship has nuanced this view: Vietnamese expansion is better understood as an episodic process involving regional challenges to the imperial centre that periodically resulted in the southward recentring of power (Taylor 1998). Yet the longevity of Thăng Long as an imperial capital and the transition to Hanoi's colonial and post-colonial primacy complicate that revisionist narrative. The vestiges show that it remains relevant to tell stories of the Đại Việt empire and the Vietnamese nation from the vantage point of this city in the Red River Delta.

Secondly, as the UNESCO paragraph states, the vestiges reflect a unique culture located at a meeting point between two other empires: China to the north and Champa to the south. Imperial interactions are reflected in the very colours of the archaeological site. The red bricks of the Lý–Trần period are evidence of Champa influence, when the newly independent Vietnamese kingdom sought to set itself apart from China. They contrast with the grey bricks of the periods before and after the Lý–Trần, which reflect Chinese practices of mixing ash to clay that characterised construction of the Tang and late Lê periods. Within this basic periodisation, the vestiges provide a vast quantity of material data allowing scholars to place this remarkable Vietnamese city in regional context.

The site's longevity and influences also underpin its value for historical research. In this context, it is worth repeating that this is the first time that material data have become available on a scale that allows comparative analysis. In the past, our knowledge of the construction of the city's palaces, temples, ramparts, gardens and waterways relied on the court chronicles and cartographical records dating mostly from the Lê and Nguyễn dynasties. These sources required ingenious historical analysis of the sort deployed by Phan Huy Lê in his chapter but kept our knowledge firmly within the bounds of Vietnamese history. Thanks to the work at 18 Hoang Diệu Street and other sites in Hanoi, there is an abundance of archaeological data. In his ground-breaking account of Thăng Long's history in this volume, Phan Huy Lê shows how these data can now be linked with the historical records and compared across historical periods.

The archaeological data can also be compared with data from other sites, making it possible to analyse the external influences at work in the building of Thăng Long. The most striking of these is the influence of Champa. Viewed from the Thăng Long citadel, the history of Đại Việt can no longer be written exclusively in terms of its relationship with China as a product of selected, imported, localised models from the north (Woodside 1971). The south was not just a frontier zone into which Sino-Vietnamese imperial power expanded and was transformed on its periphery; Champa impacted powerfully on Vietnamese civilisation in its heartland too. That impact is visible here, as Nguyễn Tiến Đông shows in his chapter on Cham art forms and construction technologies at Thăng Long. This creates the possibility for a new narrative of Vietnamese history, one that emphasises the importance of Đại Việt's regional connections and does so systematically over the long durée. We now have the sources we need to include Champa in the mainstream of Vietnamese history, as part of the processes of political integration and crisis, state consolidation and centralisation that were described theoretically by Lieberman (2003; 2009) and can now be studied in empirical detail at the Thăng Long archaeological site.

Comparison may be made not only of the artistic and technological details at Thăng Long, but also of the city's overall scale and urban plan. Scholars now possess the materials they need to situate Vietnamese urban civilisation in regional context, to draw comparisons with urban models from East Asia, mainland Southeast Asia (Angkor, Pagan) and the Malay World. The potential exists to make connections among Asian urban forms of the sort pioneered by Paul Wheatley (1971; 1983), and replace his Chinese urban imposition perspective on the development of the Vietnamese city (critiqued in Taylor 1986) with a more interesting theory that accounts for multiple influences.

This comparative work has not yet started; Vietnamese archaeologists are still publishing research within the chronology and conceptual frameworks of Vietnamese history (see, for example, contributions on Thăng Long in Reinecke 2015; Tống Trung Tín 2020). Indeed, the sheer quantity of archaeological data, the creative hybridity of the architecture, and the complexity of the stratigraphy present many challenges to comparative research. As the archaeologists have found, each theory developed on the basis of one set of evidence might quickly be revised in the light of another. Tống Trung Tín's chapter in this volume describes how the excavation in 1999 of a linear area paved with Tran-dynasty tiles in lemon flower shapes allowed scholars to posit the existence of a road extending from the Đoan Môn Gate to the Kính Thiên Audience Hall over a period of many centuries. The archaeologists have since reinterpreted this finding; apparently, the lemon flower designs were arranged to decorate the base of a wall built along this line. They thus disproved the existence of the road, along with their understanding of the urban plan associated with that road. Yet they were not back to square one. As the work continues, interpretations and reinterpretations of the new archaeological data will teach us about urban form in Vietnam, place Vietnam's urban development in regional context, and contribute to knowledge of comparative urbanism across the East and Southeast Asian regions.

4. STRUCTURE OF THE BOOK

From 2004, the Academy of Social Sciences and the Institute of Archaeology, which managed the archaeological site before returning it to the Hanoi city authorities in 2011,[16] benefitted from the technical expertise of several countries as well as UNESCO. This book cannot hope to account for all the Vietnamese and international projects that have contributed to the site's conservation and development. As part of the EFEO's contribution, however, a team of experts visited the site in August 2004 and submitted a number of recommendations. In addition to offering technical expertise to the Institute of Archaeology, notably for the on-site museum named 'One Thousand Years from Under the Ground' that opened in 2010, the EFEO hoped to contribute to the documentation of the discovery. This volume originated from that hope.

The book's inspiration was twofold. Firstly, we saw this archaeological discovery as a significant event of modern cultural and political history, and felt that future generations of archaeologists and historians studying the site would appreciate a contemporary account of the first excavation. Secondly, we hoped to contribute to understanding of the site by publishing results of research into its history. The excavation's director, Tống Trung Tín, welcomed the idea and agreed to write while his memory was still fresh. His colleagues followed suit. The chapters of this book were written soon after the dig by those who participated in the excavation and research, colleagues involved in the research and management aspects of the project, and a number of people who made contributions in the project's aftermath.

The result is a personal record of the event. Owing to the intimacy of the authors' accounts, the editors used a light brush, particularly regarding the chapters' subjective qualities: our aim was not only to portray a scientific experience but also the emotions it aroused. One editorial choice stands in exception to this rule, however. Almost every manuscript contained the emotive word 'priceless' applied many times to the artefacts unearthed at the site. To avoid repetition, this word has been removed unless it contributes directly to the chapter's argument. On behalf of the authors, let me instead say—once and for all—that the discoveries made at the Thăng Long Imperial Citadel are indeed of incalculable value.

The book has two parts. The first tells the story of the excavation. In 'Part I. Excavation of the Citadel as Historical Event', the archaeologists present diary-like accounts of their research experience. They report the dig's results, but also convey a sense of what the digging was like. They relate their questions and discussions, their moments of puzzlement and flashes of understanding, their despair and excitement as they descended through the layers of mud and soil, as some 'mysteries' were resolved while others emerged to frustrate their understanding.

In Chapter 1, Tống Trung Tín summarises the research that preceded the 2002–04 excavation and gives a detailed account of the dig. He concludes with an assessment of the historical significance of the archaeological materials. This is followed in Chapter 2 by a set of insights into 'life in the trenches' by a senior archaeologist at the site: Lê Thị Liên, who relates the uncovering of lake, river, palace and kitchen sites to describe the day-by-day challenges faced by the archaeologists and their teams of workers. The next chapters zoom in on different technical aspects of the work. In Chapter 3, Nguyễn Hồng Kiên recalls how the findings transformed his understanding of Vietnamese historical architecture. In Chapter 4, Nguyễn Văn Anh describes the problems he encountered with the site's stratigraphy and the identification of three layers corresponding to the site's three main historical periods. In Chapter 5, Đỗ Danh Huấn— a young historian drafted into the excavation trenches due to a shortage of archaeologically trained personnel—describes his attempts to grapple with archaeological and historical issues raised by the brick building materials at the site. The final contribution to Part I turns to the aftermath of the dig. Chapter 6 is an account of the conservation and development work that led to the citadel's inscription on UNESCO's World Heritage list and the creation of an archaeological park, written by the site's then director Nguyễn Văn Sơn.

The second part of the book—'Part II. Research into the History of the Citadel'—presents the results of historical research conducted into the site. Chapter 7 is an essay by the historian Đào Hùng (1932–2013) that explains why so few memories of the imperial court at Thăng Long subsisted among the population of late twentieth-century Hanoi. Chapter 8 turns to the early period in the site's history, when it was part of the Tang dynasty empire: Franciscus Verellen presents a historical account of the ninth-century Chinese governor who rebuilt a city here and was subsequently celebrated as its founder. Chapter 9, by the historian Phan Huy Lê (1934–2018), studies the evolution of the citadel's three ramparts and locates the excavation site within the Forbidden City of the Lý, Trần and Lê dynasties (eleventh to eighteenth centuries). The next two chapters adopt a comparative approach to the historical analysis of archaeological data. In Chapter 10, Nguyễn Tiến Đông documents the influence of Champa on Đại Việt, as evidenced in a comparitive study of materials unearthed in Hanoi with Cham artefacts of the same period. In Chapter 11, Phạm Văn Triệu describes his early efforts at reconciling data from old maps and chronicles with archaeological findings. In the closing contribution, in Chapter 12 Olivier Tessier uses court chronicles and colonial archives to document the nineteenth-century downgrading of the citadel by the Nguyễn dynasty and the downgraded citadel's final destruction by the French.

Notes

1.   Inscription (1951) at the entrance to the Arènes de Lutèce Roman amphitheatre, Paris ('*Passant songe devant ce premier monument de Paris que la ville du passé est aussi la cité de l'avenir et celle de ses espoirs*').

2. Papin (2001: 148) locates this site in the area bounded by today's Lý Thường Kiệt, Quán Sứ, Nguyễn Gia Thiều and Quang Trung Streets.

3. The site he chose for the Governor-General's Palace (the Palais Puginier, today's Phủ Chủ Tịch or President's Palace) was in close proximity to the ancient royal enclosure. On Paul Doumer, the palace, and the Hanoi Citadel, see Logan (2000: 86–8).

4. The edict text in Chinese characters has been published with Vietnamese and English translations in Bùi Tuyết Mai (2004: 22–3).

5. This is the Đê La Thành Street section, according to Papin (2001: 70).

6. A small central area within the inner rampart formed the Forbidden City, where the king's palaces, temples and audience hall were located. The land excavated in 2002–04 lay within the central area, the exact perimeter of which remains unknown. See Phan Huy Lê's chapter.

7. Today this 'earth column' remains untouched, although the captain's tiny house was destroyed in 2006.

8. In the centuries after Gao Pian established his headquarters here in 865, the capital was *not* located at Đại La–Thăng Long–Hanoi for only three periods: 939–1010 (the capital was at Cổ Loa, then Hoa Lư), 1400–07 (Thanh Hoá) and 1805–1902 (Huế).

9. 'La cité impériale de Thang-Long (Hà-Nôi): Projet archéologique et historique présenté par l'École française d'Extrême-Orient', pp. 2–3. The project was set up on the initiative of the EFEO's director Franciscus Verellen and run by Andrew Hardy (2004), Philippe Papin (2004–05) and Olivier Tessier (2006–12).

10. 'International Expert Consultation Meeting on the Ba Dinh Archaeological Site and Thang Long Imperial City', organised by UNESCO, the Vietnam National Commission for UNESCO and the Vietnam Academy of Social Sciences, Hanoi, 10-11 August 2004.

11. 'À l'Académie des Sciences sociales et aux experts de l'EFEO en témoignage de reconnaissance pour l'admirable travail historique qui est fait ici et avec mes vœux de poursuite de mise en valeur de ce site, [témoignage] de l'histoire du Viet-Nam et qui fait honneur à l'humanité. J. Chirac, 7 octobre 2004'. Reproduced in the Vietnamese press: Hoàng Ngọc Chau, 'Tổng thống Pháp Jacques Chirac chiêm ngưỡng di tích Hoàng thành Thăng Long', *An ninh Thủ đô*, 8/10/2004, p. 5.

12. '*Lịch sử dựng nước và giữ nước*'—this is a key term in the vocabulary of Vietnamese nationalist historiography and public discourse.

13. 'Sẽ chuyển địa điểm xây nhà Quốc hội mới?' (*Vietnamnet* 27/10/2003); 'Tạm lấp cát để khai quật sau; xây bảo tàng ngoài trời hay...?' (*Vietnamnet* 11/11/2003); 'Cấm thành giờ mở cửa' (*Vietnamnet* 28/4/2004); 'Khu di tích Ba Đình có xứng đáng là di sản thế giới?' (*Lao động* 11/8/ 2004); 'Một cái cây không thể lớn lên nếu thiếu gốc rễ" (*An ninh Thủ đô* 19/8/2004); 'Giá trị Hoàng thành Thăng Long sẽ sớm được khẳng

định' (*An ninh Thủ đô* 20/8/2004); 'Nhân dân tiếp tục đóng góp ủng hộ tôn tạo Hoàng thành Hà Nội' (*An ninh Thủ đô* 8/9/2004); 'Bộ Văn hóa-Thông tin đã trình Chính phủ 3 phương án' (*Văn hóa* 21-23/9/2004); 'Tranh cãi mới về khu di tích Hoàng thành' (*Vietnamnet* 16/10/2004); 'Về việc xây dựng tại khu vực Hoàng thành: Ai đúng?' (*An ninh Thủ đô* 18/5/2006).

14. 'Kết luận mới nhất về Hoàng thành Thăng Long', *Vietnamnet* 19/8/2004. Consulted on 23/3/2005 at http://vietnamnet.vn/service/printversion?article_id=501650.

15. See http://whc.unesco.org/en/list/1328 (consulted 11 September 2013).

16. In 2011, the site was handed over to the Hanoi city authorities and managed by the Thăng Long–Hanoi Heritage Conservation Centre.

PART I

Excavation of the Citadel as Historical Event

The Excavation Starts

Project leader Tổng Trung Tín describes the tense first days: 'drizzle cutting our faces and bitterly cold ground water constantly flooding our trenches. Many of the worker teams could not stand it and left. Seeing this endless water and sodden mud, some of the staff said: "I don't suppose there's anything down there".'

Fig. 6. Much of the work was done by farmers, artisans, school-leavers and soldiers unused to the archaeologist's trowel. Gradually they became enthused about Thăng Long's history as it unfolded before their eyes (Section D) (Photo: Institute of Archaeology, 2003).

Fig. 7. Soldiers and workers reach a cultural layer of Trần-dynasty remains (Section B), examined and discussed here by historian Trần Quốc Vượng (left) and archaeologists Tổng Trung Tín and Nguyễn Đăng Cường (centre) (Photo: Institute of Archaeology, 2003).

Fig. 8. The finds were of incredible complexity with multiple overlapping cultural layers, each bearing material evidence of a different period in the site's 1,300-year history (Section B) (Photo: Institute of Archaeology, 2003).

Fig. 9. The weather improved and trenches deepened, raising as many questions as they resolved. Here, a courtyard paved with cockle shells is being unearthed (Section B) (Photo: Institute of Archaeology, 2003).

The Excavation Team

The excavation was conducted by the Institute of Archaeology (Vietnam Academy of Social Sciences), with assistance from the University of Social Sciences and Humanities (Hanoi National University) (Photos: Institute of Archaeology, 2003).

Figs. 10 & 11. The team, pictured here on site and in conference, was led by the archaeologist Tống Trung Tín (top, front row, fifth from left) and advised by the archaeologist Hà Văn Tấn (bottom, first from left), and historians Trần Quốc Vượng (top, front row, sixth from left) and Phan Huy Lê (bottom, right).

Palace Architecture

Complex vestiges of palace architecture were unearthed: bricks, roof and paving tiles, drains, plinths and foundations for pillars, decorative features. New palaces were built on the ruins of old, materials were used and reused.

Fig. 12. Each pillar was placed on a plinth supported by its own foundation of gravel and rubble. Here, rows of square pillar foundations mark the site of two buildings, a Trần-dynasty palace built on the site of a collapsed Lý-dynasty palace (Section D). Behind, the swimming pool of the old Ba Đình Club (removed in 2006) (Photo: Institute of Archaeology, 2004).

Fig. 13. Palaces and courtyards were paved with terracotta tiles. Here (Section D), foundations of a Lý-dynasty octagonal pavilion (upper right) are surrounded by paving of three periods: early Lý dynasty (lower left), later Lý dynasty (right) and Trần dynasty (upper left) (Photo: Institute of Archaeology, 2004).

Figs. 14 & 15. The roof of a large and prestigious Lý-dynasty palace here (Section A) was decorated with bodhi leaves and dragon and phoenix heads in terracotta (Photo: Institute of Archaeology, 2003).

Fig. 16. A large Lý-dynasty palace (Section A). To help visualise the site, each person is standing in the place of one of the palace's pillars (Photo: Institute of Archaeology, 2003).

Fig. 17. The excavation trenches from the 2002–04 dig are now open to the public. Lanterns represent the original wooden pillars of this palace of the Lý–Trần period (Section B) (Photo: EFEO, 2016).

Water on the Site: Rivers, Wells and Drains

Ancient lakes and rivers were integral to the site's structure and yielded rich harvests of archaeological material, thrown into the water by previous generations.

Fig. 18. Archaeologist Lê Thị Liên describes Lê-dynasty artefacts unearthed in an ancient river in Section D: 'we seemed lost in a bed of treasure: countless varieties of terracotta jars, pots and vessels of many different sizes; high-footed cups; jars decorated with areca branch images; bowls, dishes, vases and bottles, decorated with blue and white designs, brown or white glazes, designs raised in relief or set under glaze...' (Photo: Institute of Archaeology, 2004).

Fig. 19. Sorting through the debris on the bed of the ancient river between Sections A and B. Top right: huge mounds of excavated earth piled up in this central sector (Photo: Institute of Archaeology, 2003).

Many wells, lined with brick or stone, were discovered in the excavated area, providing further evidence of the area's extensive inhabitation in the past.

Fig. 20. A Đại La-period well (Section B) (Photo: Institute of Archaeology, 2003).

Fig. 21. A Trần-dynasty well (Section A) (Photo: Institute of Archaeology, 2003).

38

Elaborate drainage systems were built with bricks and tiles of vibrant red, reflecting eleventh-century masons' adaptation of Champa technologies of terracotta manufacture. Drains of all shapes and sizes were unearthed in every sector.

Fig. 22. Archaeologist Bùi Văn Liêm (far right) in discussion with Nishimura Masanari (third from right) and other Japanese colleagues about a Trần-dynasty drain largely built with reused materials (Section A) (Photo: Institute of Archaeology, 2003).

Fig. 23. A Trần-dynasty drainage system intersects with a courtyard of the same period. Later, on the same site, foundations of gravel and brick rubble (left and right) supported the plinths and pillars of a Lê-dynasty building (Section A) (Photo: Institute of Archaeology, 2003).

Paths, Roads and Galleries

Fig. 24. Bricks arranged in lemon flower patterns were used by the Trần dynasty as paving in the Forbidden City. Archaeologists initially thought the paving here (Section D) was a road, before concluding that the lemon flower patterns were used to decorate the foot of a wall (Photo: Institute of Archaeology, 2005).

Fig. 25. Re-used and imperfect materials identify this as a Trần-dynasty road (Section B). A drain (centre) and a pillar foundation (right) were built over the road later in the same dynasty. A hole for tipping rubbish was dug during the colonial period: at the bottom were found a quantity of French wine bottles (centre left) (Photo: Institute of Archaeology, 2003).

Outreach

Rumours of the discoveries circulated the city through 2003, and quickly the archaeologists realised they needed to show the site to members of the community.

Fig. 26. Phoenix heads and bodhi leaves in terracotta lie where they were unearthed. Project director Tống Trung Tín presents the debris of a collapsed Lý-dynasty palace roof to visiting politicians (Section A) (Photo: Institute of Archaeology, 2004).

Fig. 27. University students listen to archaeologist Nguyễn Tiến Đông's presentation of Lý- and Trần-dynasty vestiges (Section A) (Photo: Institute of Archaeology, 2004).

CHAPTER 1

Archaeological Research and Discoveries at the Thăng Long Imperial Citadel Site, 18 Hoàng Diệu Street, Hanoi

Tống Trung Tín

The Thăng Long Imperial Citadel site at 18 Hoàng Diệu Street was discovered in 2002–03. It received official recognition at two conferences organised by the Vietnam Academy of Social Sciences in September 2003 and August 2004. Scientists from France, Britain, Spain, Japan and Korea participated in research at the site and paid tribute to its national significance and international stature.

The site's study, protection and development are long-term undertakings, which will occupy scholars for many years, even generations. Today, however, scholars working at the site and others who have shown an interest have—when they look back—accumulated a quantity of memories. Time has passed quickly; the chaos of more work awaits us ahead. Although quite recent, many of the exciting events surrounding the work on Thăng Long Imperial Citadel are gradually fading into the past. I am delighted to take this opportunity to record some of the main aspects of our research on Thăng Long Imperial Citadel site, to record for posterity a few of these momentous events.

We may say that the discovery of Thăng Long Imperial Citadel was a stroke of luck, but it was also the inevitable result of a long process of research and reflection by Vietnamese historians and archaeologists on the location, structure, scale and appearance of Thăng Long Citadel. It was equally the result of the effective implementation of Vietnam's Law on Cultural Heritage, regarding the study and protection of cultural and historical sites.

The origins of research on Thăng Long Citadel may be traced to the late nineteenth and early twentieth centuries, when the city of Hanoi's westward expansion led to the discovery of abundant remains, dating over a period of thousands of years, at sites such as Quần Ngựa, Hữu Tiệp, Vạn Phúc, Cống Vị and Bách Thảo. At that time, French scholars such as Henri Parmentier thought that these were evidence of palaces built by the different generations of Vietnam's kings and lords. Then, during the second half of the twentieth century, Vietnam's most learned scholars turned their attention to the history of the capital and discussed the location and scale of Thăng Long. Their debates focused on the location of Thăng Long Imperial Citadel.

Opinions were divided on this question, but they may be classified into two basic types. According to the first, represented by Trần Huy Bá, the Imperial Citadel's location during the Lý and Trần periods was in western Hanoi, in the area between the Botanical Garden (Bách Thảo) and the Racecourse (Quần Ngựa). According to the second, represented by Trần Quốc Vượng, throughout the Lý, Trần and Lê periods the citadel's central area did not move and was located on the site of the Lê dynasty's Kính Thiên palace, in the centre of today's Ba Đình district.

That debate took place when I was very young, before I studied history at university, before I chose to specialise in archaeology. I first read the articles that contributed to the debate after graduating, when I went to work at the Institute of Archaeology. I realised that one definite conclusion could be drawn from the opinions expressed: that the location of Thăng Long Imperial Citadel could be confirmed only by the results of archaeological excavation.

During my time at university, I knew of no vestiges of Thăng Long capital city or of Thăng Long Imperial Citadel. During my studies at Hanoi University's Department of History (1972–76), the course on archaeology made no mention of historical archaeology: we learned only about prehistory. Apart from an appendix listing a few historical sites dating from the period of Chinese rule, there was no mention of historical archaeology at all.

At the Institute of Archaeology, however, there was a Department of Historical Archaeology, headed by Phạm Huy Thông. In those days it was called the Feudal Archaeology Section, or Feudal Section for short.

When I left university and joined the Institute (1977), I was appointed to the Feudal Section, then headed by Đỗ Văn Ninh. For me, historical archaeology was to become a sort of destiny, the destiny of my life in research. This is partly because I have been closely associated with the field ever since. It is also because I had the opportunity of working at the Thăng Long citadel site.

Just a year after I joined the Institute of Archaeology, together with the members of the Feudal Section and staff of the National Museum of History, I encountered underground vestiges of the capital at Thăng Long for the first time.

1. MY FIRST CONTACT WITH VESTIGES OF THE CAPITAL AT THĂNG LONG, 1978–80

This was in the course of participating in research at the Racecourse (Hanoi) and Ly Cung (Thanh Hóa) sites and in the discovery of vestiges under the ground at the crossroads of Hàng Đường and Ngõ Gạch Streets.

On the subject of the archaeology of Thăng Long–Hanoi, I have already mentioned the Racecourse site, which became famous after the French made discoveries there during the expansion and construction of the city's western districts. These findings were meticulously documented by Parmentier and Mercier in an article entitled 'Éléments architecturaux au Nord Vietnam' (1952). The authors recognised the sophistication of the Lý- and Trần-period sculptures discovered there and understood that they came from Lý- and Trần-dynasty palaces.

In 1978–79, the city authorities decided to build the Hanoi Children's Palace in the Racecourse area and thus allowed archaeologists to conduct investigations there. The research was organised as a cooperation between the Hanoi Department of Culture and Information, the Museum of Vietnamese History and the Institute of Archaeology. At that time, I was busy preparing my trial-year report for the Institute so I could only join the excavation for a few days, after which my participation mainly took the form of visits. I knew the participating institutions planned to use this work to seize the opportunity provided by the government's decree on heritage protection to test the controversy surrounding the location of Thăng Long Imperial Citadel. When I examined most of the excavated trenches there, I felt that the cultural layer was very thin and the artefacts were quite simple, mainly belonging to the Lê period.

The investigation's results were published in the annual gazettes of the Museum of History (Bảo tàng lịch sử Việt Nam 1979) and the Institute of Archaeology (Institute of Archaeology 1979). The National Museum of History then held a seminar on Thăng Long Imperial Citadel, at which Phạm Quốc Quân presented an overview of 'The Archaeology of the Racecourse and the Question of Thăng Long Imperial Citadel' (Phạm Quốc Quân 1979). In this paper, he argued that the Racecourse area had been a settlement inhabited by ordinary people and that further study on the location of Thăng Long Imperial Citadel should be pursued in the area of the Hanoi Citadel of the Nguyễn period. Đỗ Văn Ninh referred to this assessment in his book on Vietnamese ancient citadels (*Thành Cổ Việt Nam*, 1983).

Although I did not directly work on the Racecourse excavation, I was able to attend this seminar and present data from an excavation at Ly Cung (Thanh Hóa province), a site dating from the Trần and Hồ dynasties. Why was data from Ly Cung, located far to the south in Thanh Hóa, able to make a contribution to the study of Thăng Long?

The site we studied at Ly Cung was Bảo Thanh Palace, built by Hồ Quý Ly in 1397 to prepare for his struggle for control over the court against the Trần dynasty. In 1979, Phạm Như Hồ and I were sent to excavate this site. With the Institute's agreement, we spent a total of five excavation seasons working there.

Our excavation was successful, with the discovery of architectural foundations and a collection of fine architectural artefacts. During my study of this collection, I paid particular attention to various types of bricks decorated with diverse dragon images that showed a clear evolution from a graceful and sophisticated style to a simpler and more ventilated manner of expression. Many other artefacts, decorative motifs and materials showed a similar evolution. The remarkable thing was that this evolution took place during the Trần period, the thirteenth to fourteenth centuries. Yet the annals clearly dated the Ly Cung site to the year 1397.

This raised the following question: Why did so many artefacts with different Trần-period dates appear at Ly Cung in the same cultural layer? Had the materials possibly been transported to Ly Cung from somewhere else?

To answer this question, I consulted the annals and collected a wide range of data relating to Trần art for the purposes of comparison. At that time, I had no knowledge of the archaeology of the Trần period, so I had to start my research from scratch: I worked on it continuously for a number of years. During those years, I visited almost all the Lý, Trần and Lê sites in provinces such as Hà Tây, Nam Định, Thái Bình, Hải Dương, Hưng Yên, Haiphong, Quảng Ninh, Vĩnh Phúc, Bắc Ninh and Bắc Giang, as well as provincial and national museums. This work enabled me to gather a large quantity of material on the sites and sculptures of the Lý, Trần and Lê dynasties, some of which I then swiftly turned into my doctoral thesis in history, defended in 1990.

While examining Thăng Long artefacts displayed at the National Museum of History, I realised that terracotta pieces bearing dragon motifs from Thăng Long resembled some of the artefacts discovered at Ly Cung. I became increasingly convinced that some of the Trần materials at Thăng Long Citadel had been transferred to Ly Cung.

This assumption was confirmed by my reading of the chronicles, notably the Complete Annals of Đại Việt (*Đại Việt sử ký toàn thư*) which record a particularly important change in the architecture of the capital. In or around the year 1397, Hồ Quý Ly ordered the mandarin Nguyễn Bửu to remove bricks, tiles and timbers from Thụy Chương and Thiền Anh Palaces (in Thăng Long) and send them to Từ Liêm and Nam Sách districts for transportation to a new capital (the Western Capital in Thanh Hóa). The books also record that more than half the materials were lost, sunk in a storm.[1]

It became clear that, during the transfer of the capital from Thăng Long to Thanh Hóa, Hồ Quý Ly had ordered the removal of some of the palaces at Thăng Long. These were transported to the new capital, to ensure its rapid completion and a swift end to the political upheaval of dynastic takeover. As we have seen, more than half the transferred materials were lost in a storm. This also means that nearly half survived and appeared in the new capital. As a result, magnificent Thăng Long artefacts may be found at the Ly Cung citadel and the Hồ dynasty Nam Giao Shrine (Thanh Hóa), where they lie beside locally produced items.

I published the results of this research in an article entitled 'Sculptures from Ly Cung' (Tống Trung Tín 1981). In the article, I argued that towards the end of the Trần period the most central and important of all the capital's palaces was demolished and its materials collected and transported to Ly Cung. This was Thiên An Palace. Research on Thăng Long materials at Ly Cung thus allowed me to make two comments on Thăng Long Imperial Citadel under the Trần dynasty:

• Firstly, that the architecture at Thăng Long Imperial Citadel was decorated with finesse, sophistication and grandeur.
• Secondly, that in 1397 some Trần-dynasty buildings at Thăng Long Imperial Citadel were demolished and their materials collected for transportation to the Western Capital in Thanh Hóa. These included

Thiên An Palace, the dynasty's most important palace at Thăng Long Imperial Citadel. If any vestiges of that palace remain, they will consist only of its foundations.

In 1980, another remarkable find was made, which contributed to my study of Thăng Long Imperial Citadel. In January of that year, a worker installing water pipes phoned the Institute to inform us of the discovery of ancient bricks at the crossroads of Hàng Đường Street and Ngõ Gạch Street. The head of my section, Đỗ Văn Ninh, immediately sent me to check the site.

After receiving my instructions, I cycled over to the site. When I arrived, I saw a trench of about 2 m^2 to 3 m^2 dug across the asphalt road, containing a large quantity of clear water. In the trench there were some large bricks dating from the Lê period. The workers told me that to repair the water pipes they had opened the ground to a depth of 1 m, whereupon they came across a large green stone lying in their way. When they broke it up, they found a layer of large bricks; some had already been removed and thrown up to the road. Workers who understood the objects' cultural value then informed the Institute. That was the state of the trench when I arrived.

I went down inside the trench to investigate. It was full of water, so I had to rely on touch to assess the state of the relics. Clearly these were architectural relics from a Lê-dynasty building and remained in fairly good condition. In the upper layer, there were large green stones (at least three of them); the layer below consisted of large tightly joined bricks. I told the workers that if it was not necessary to destroy them, the bricks should be left in place with the water pipes laid on top, the trench filled in and the road surface restored.

I reported these results to Đỗ Văn Ninh. He listened and said: 'So, the ground surface of old Hanoi was much lower than it is today. Today's surface has been raised considerably.' He took notes and wrote a report. He even made the following humorous remark: 'In the future, when we're getting on in years, if you attend a conference on Thăng Long, you'll earn a good deal of prestige from talking about this event, as you now have direct knowledge of an underground site from the Lê period which few others know about.'

I reported the site's discovery at the institute's 1980 Archaeological Discoveries Conference. Some researchers told me this might be Cầu Đông, a famous site on the eastern side of the Lê-period Thăng Long citadel. At that time, I was not sure about this idea.

In the early years of the twenty-first century, further repairs were carried out in this part of the city and large bricks turned up again. On this occasion, however, the Institute was not informed. I found out about it through Dương Trung Mạnh (a former member of the Institute's staff) who told us that his brother, Dương Trung Quốc, had collected some old bricks there. Trần Quốc Vượng and I took the Thăng Long research group over to Dương Trung Quốc's house to see. They were the same large bricks I had seen twenty years before.

Nowadays, the whole site still lies quietly under the ground. Above, the city bustles by; few people are aware that there is an archaeological site below. For me, although this was a modest discovery and has not yet been surveyed or excavated, it made a deep impression: these were vestiges of Thăng Long under the ground of inner-city Hanoi. At a depth of 1 m under a paved road in the old quarter of thirty-six streets, we had found a site that is relatively intact, in good condition. Other remains of the capital must also exist. I became convinced that Trần Quốc Vượng's theory was right. I started to believe that, given the chance to dig in central Hanoi, we would unearth many other vestiges of Thăng Long. The only problem was how to conduct an excavation at a time Vietnam had no experience of historical archaeology or urban archaeology: the cost would be unbelievably prohibitive. At that time, even the most imaginative archaeologist could not have dreamed of conducting an archaeological excavation in central Hanoi.

None of these excavations and investigations led to any great discovery. They were, however, of immense value in orienting our later archaeological excavation towards the heart of the city. Meanwhile, most research institutes and government bodies agreed that, if the occasion presented itself, archaeological investigation of central Hanoi was necessary. The opportunity arose during preparations for the 990th anniversary of the foundation of Thăng Long–Hanoi (1010–2000).

2. EXPLORATION OF THE THĂNG LONG AND HANOI CITADELS' CENTRAL AXIS, 1998–2000

The central axis of Thăng Long–Hanoi Citadel is aligned north–south, and extends from the Flag Tower, through the Gate of Commencement, past Kính Thiên Palace and the Rear Palace, as far as the North Gate. The North Gate and Flag Tower are monuments of the Nguyễn dynasty's Hanoi Citadel, while the Gate of Commencement and Kính Thiên Palace were part of the Lê dynasty's Thăng Long citadel. Most historians and archaeologists believe that the Lê-period Kính Thiên Palace was built on the site of the Lý–Trần-period Thiên An Palace (also called Càn Nguyên Palace). The Nguyễn-period Flag Tower was built on the site of the former Tam Môn gate, dating from the Lê period.

All this means that Hanoi Citadel in the Nguyễn period shared the same central axis as Thăng Long Imperial Citadel in the Lý, Trần and Lê periods. Our exploration there was extremely useful, allowing us to verify our assumptions about the location, scale and structure of the Imperial Citadel and the capital city of Thăng Long.

Excavation at 5 Hoàng Diệu Street

Prior to excavations conducted in central Hanoi on the occasion of the 990th anniversary of Thăng Long–Hanoi, the Institute of Archaeology, the National Museum of History and the Hanoi Department for the Management of Historical and Scenic Sites jointly conducted a test excavation at 5 Hoàng Diệu Street. This may be the first time an archaeological excavation was conducted in the heart of Hanoi. Phạm Quốc Quân and I carried out the excavation under the leadership of Trịnh Cao Tưởng.

After digging through the modern layer to a depth of 1 m, we found a concentration of large bricks and ceramics from the Lê period. Delighted, we continued digging until we encountered an intractable problem: a strong current of ground water filled up the excavated trenches. We had no experience of this sort of flooding. From a depth of 3 m, we had to dig down, evacuate water and search for artefacts at the same time. It was dangerous, as sometimes the trench wall collapsed. At some points we could not reach the sterile layer, out of concern for the safety of the staff and workers.

For these reasons, the survey's results were not entirely satisfactory, even though a cultural layer measuring 4 m in depth had been uncovered for the first time. This signalled the city centre's far greater potential by comparison with the Racecourse area. On the other hand, the survey raised a question that archaeology in central Hanoi would face in the future: how to deal with the ground water? We would only be able to conduct a successful excavation once this water was brought under control. In the end, for reasons that were sensitive in those days, the excavation was kept under wraps; the results were not made public and no other scientists were invited to the site. The excavation lapsed into silence. We were unable to fulfil our intention of conducting a more extensive dig here.

Excavation at the Rear Palace

In 1998, two years before the 990th anniversary, the Vietnamese state transferred the management of three sites—the Gate of Commencement, the North Gate and the Rear Palace—to the Hanoi city authorities. Formalities for the transfer of the Rear Palace were completed first. The Institute of Archaeology and the Hanoi Department for the Management of Historical and Scenic Sites excavated the site in 1998.

This was the first time we were able to excavate a relatively large surface on the central axis, more than 200 m². The trench revealed the extremely complicated evolution of the architectural foundations in this area, located behind Kính Thiên Palace.

First of all, there was the scenery. The earliest scenery of this area was identified as a large 'lake' or area of 'flowing water'. On the lake's eastern side, there was a landing stage built with various types of stone, including Lý-period stone pedestals inscribed with lotus designs. Around it, abundant high-quality porcelain and ceramic items were found, dating from the Early Lê period and bearing dragon and phoenix designs as well as the Chinese character for 'mandarin' (官 *quan*). This clearly indicated that the landing stage was in extensive operation in the fifteenth century. The excavation's location at a 'lake' meant that no traces of earlier architecture were found at this time. It is possible that the lake already existed during the Lý–Trần period and continued to be used in the early years of the Lê dynasty. Around the seventeenth to eighteenth centuries, it was filled in and levelled to form a foundation for construction. The entire area of the excavated trench contained a dense concentration of materials of various types dating from the Lý–Trần and Early Lê periods. Architectural traces from the Lê Restoration period were found in the layer above this. Within a small area, we were able to observe the rich evolution of sites that had been royal palaces.

As for the artefacts, I can say that never before had scholars been so impressed by the objects used on a daily basis in the royal palaces. Most striking was a set of translucent thin-bodied ceramics decorated with designs typical of the royal household, such as dragons, phoenixes, peonies and scrolled clouds. This collection of quality porcelain discovered in dense concentrations demonstrated the high standard of living enjoyed in the royal living quarters located behind Kính Thiên Palace. Impressed by these artefacts, I immediately wrote an article on 'High Quality Glazed Ceramics in Thăng Long's Royal Palaces' which was published that year in the Ministry of Culture and Information's newspaper *Văn hóa*. Another set of artefacts that also made a strong impression on me were the yin-yang tiles from the Lê dynasty's early period. These were large red tiles, with one end forming a near crescent shape and commonly decorated with dragons. Undoubtedly, these tiles were from a large and important former palace in the area behind Kính Thiên Palace. The Đại La, Lý and Trần artefacts also reflected the existence of the Rear Palace site over a long period of time. The use of an entire set of Lý-period lotus flower pedestals in construction during the Lê dynasty's early period suggested a dramatic evolution in Lý-period architectural traces in the area.

The Rear Palace was the first official excavation in the central axis and its results led many scholars to visit the site. They were all convinced of the immense potential of Thăng Long–Hanoi site. Trần Quốc Vượng was among the most excited. He visited the site repeatedly and said to me: 'You should continue digging, you must continue digging. This is just a start. As yet, Tín, we understand nothing.' The writer Nguyễn Quang Thân was shown around the site by the Institute of Archaeology's director Hà Văn Tấn: he went home so moved that he penned an article entitled 'Excavation of Thăng Long Citadel Leads to Discovery of Đại La Citadel'.

Excavation at the Gate of Commencement

In 1999–2000, the Institute worked with the Hanoi Department of Culture and Information and the Secretariat of the 1000th Anniversary of Thăng Long–Hanoi to conduct excavations at the Gate of Commencement and North Gate. We dug the main trench to the north of the Gate of Commencement, then extended it to the west. Another trench was dug to the east of the gate. The main trench yielded important results.

At a depth of 1.9 m, we found part of a brick road running through the middle of the gate towards Kính Thiên Palace. The road was very carefully structured: a sunk foundation had been lined and rammed with 11 layers of gravel, broken bricks and tiles, measuring more than 0.8 m thick. On top of this, the road was built with bricks. Its surface was bordered with bricks laid in squares, each square enclosing a pattern of erect bricks and tiles arranged in 'lemon flower' shapes. The bricks and tiles mainly dated from the Lý and Trần periods. This very distinctive lemon flower arrangement only existed in Trần architecture. The road surface was densely covered with building materials and ceramics of the Lý and Trần periods.

After confirming that this was indeed a Trần road, I instantly made a link with the earlier debates, believing the road to be an extremely important piece of evidence. Its stability and the meticulous technology of its construction inclined me to think it was one of the most important roads in the Trần citadel at Thăng Long. Its location in the middle of the Gate of Commencement and the direction of its course towards the Kính Thiên Palace were possible indications that the Lê-period Gate of Commencement and Kính Thiên Palace were located in the same place as the Trần-period Gate of Commencement and Thiên An Palace. While studying the road, I also saw how Lý materials had been re-used to build the Trần road. For this reason, I thought the Trần road had been built on the basis of the previous Lý road. All this suggested that the assumption that the central area of the capital city and Imperial Citadel of Thăng Long under the Lý, Trần and Lê dynasties was Kính Thiên Palace was now, for the first time, being proved correct.

The discovery rapidly attracted the attention of scholars interested in the history of Thăng Long. First and foremost, this was because it offered a preliminary identification of the central location of the Lý and Trần Imperial Citadel as Kính Thiên Palace, which had previously been assumed but could not yet be shown. This had now been proved for the Lê period by the existence of two sites: the Gate of Commencement and the foundations of Kính Thiên Palace. As for the Lý and Trần dynasties, the existence of the Gate of Commencement and Thiên An Palace— located underneath the Lê-period Gate of Commencement and Kính Thiên Palace, respectively—remained entirely a matter of speculation.

The first visitor to the road was Đỗ Văn Ninh, the head of my section. After I explained my thoughts to him, he was cautious and said nothing. He returned several times and studied the site very carefully. Some days later, he came back and told me: 'After careful consideration, I realise that your opinion is correct. All the building materials used in the road's construction support it, because they date only from the period up to the end of the Trần dynasty. The lemon flower style is also unique to the Trần.' The next visitors were Hà Văn Tấn and Trần Quốc Vượng; the road easily convinced these two senior scholars of its significance. We published the results of this research (Tống Trung Tín et al. 2000). Of course, the issue required further investigation when opportunities arose to expand our excavations and, for the moment, our point of view remained speculative.

At the Gate of Commencement, in addition to the Trần road, we found a fairly intact courtyard built with large Lê bricks, adjacent to the white stones bordering the foundations of the gate. The courtyard was large, lay above the Trần road and belonged to the Lê-dynasty cultural layer. It proved that the Nguyễn dynasty completely re-used the Lê-period Gate of Commencement building, including its foundation and lower storey. The Nguyễn simply added a tower on top of the Lê gate.

Excavation at the North Gate

At the North Gate, the exploration was carried out in two trenches to the north and south of the gate. Both trenches led to other unexpected discoveries. In the western trench, we found a fairly firm architectural foundation at a depth of 2.2 m downwards. We noted the presence of a sunk foundation of broken bricks covered with a layer of stone, which served to support the wall that bordered the building's raised foundation. This wall was built of green stones in the lowest layer, with large bricks placed on top.

In the southern trench we found traces of another part of the wall. This part had similar architecture to the first. However, it seemed to be a section of rampart, as the remains consisted of large tightly rammed bricks and tiles and were oriented north–south. At the North Gate, therefore, two structures were discovered under the ground, both dating from the Lê period. The architectural foundations were large in scale and meticulously and firmly reinforced.

However, within a very small excavated trench, it was impossible to make any clear identification of what these buildings were and what their structural relation to the Lê-dynasty Thăng Long citadel might have been. The only clear thing was that the North Gate site belonged to the Nguyễn-dynasty Hanoi Citadel and had been built on top of other large Lê-dynasty structures. The architecture of the middle part of the North Gate suggested it formed a section of the citadel's rampart. However, no wall appears at this location on the map of the Lê-dynasty Thăng Long citadel. For this reason, it is possible that Thăng Long citadel's structure during the Lê period was more complicated than it appeared on the old maps. Or, on the other hand, that the northern section of the Lê citadel might have extended beyond the Nguyễn-period location of the North Gate.

During these excavations on the central axis of Thăng Long Imperial Citadel, we were thus able to shed some initial light on the mysteries in which the central area of Thăng Long remained shrouded. For the first time, we were able to use our own eyes to examine an underground network of overlapping vestiges of Thăng Long. At the Gate of Commencement, the Nguyễn citadel was built on the Lê citadel, which was itself built on top of Trần and Lý ruins. Most significantly, it was on this occasion that we saw the Trần road for the first time. At that point in time, this was the oldest archaeological vestige of Thăng Long Citadel that anyone had ever seen. No one had dared imagine such a find.

Prior to these excavations at Thăng Long, I had been in charge of the excavation at the ancient capital of Hoa Lư (Ninh Bình) and found brick courtyards decorated with lotus and phoenix designs from the tenth-century Đinh and Early Lê periods (including foundations previously discovered by a team from the provincial museum). While preparing for the Thăng Long excavation, I said to Nguyễn Thị Dơn, an official of the Hanoi Department of Culture and Information who was working with us, that I hoped excavation of the capital at Thăng Long would yield vestiges similar to those at Hoa Lư. She agreed and said: 'The city authorities hope to find remains at Thăng Long from the Lý and Trần periods, in the same way as Đinh–Early Lê-period remains were found at Hoa Lư. Such a discovery would be perfect, even if it were no bigger in size than a mat.'

For this reason, the discovery of the Trần road at the Gate of Commencement was a great achievement. In addition to the architectural vestiges, a dense concentration of artefacts was unearthed, dating from the seventh to ninth centuries through to the late nineteenth and early twentieth centuries, in a very thick cultural layer of great value for understanding the history and culture of Thăng Long.

Those artefacts were the first confirmation of the opinion that the heart of the Thăng Long Imperial Citadel and the capital city was located at Kính Thiên Palace. The artefacts also provided the Vietnam Academy of Social Sciences with the scientific basis for a plan to conduct a great excavation at 18 Hoàng Diệu Street, where—later—a complex of Thăng Long Imperial Citadel sites to the west of Kính Thiên Palace was discovered.

3. DISCOVERY OF THĂNG LONG IMPERIAL CITADEL AT 18 HOÀNG DIỆU STREET, 2002–04

This excavation was the result of a gradual process. In 2000, during the test excavations at the Rear Palace, North Gate and Gate of Commencement sites, I started studying the surrounding area and became aware that the land at 18 Hoàng Diệu Street was about to be cleared for an important government construction project. At that time, I did not know what would be built there or how large the area was. When I saw that the houses near the gate had been removed, leaving an open space where an excavation could be conducted, I informed the Institute's director, Hà Văn Tấn, the Hanoi Department of Culture and Information and the Secretariat of the 1000th Anniversary of Thăng Long–Hanoi. At the same time, I wrote an official request to the Ministry of Culture and Information for permission to conduct an excavation. Hà Văn Tấn (who was seriously ill at the time) himself handed a handwritten letter to the acting Deputy Minister of Culture and Information, Lưu Trần Tiêu, to inform him of the need for a rescue excavation there. The Ministry could not, however, grant the permit, as the Ministry of Defence had yet not decommissioned the land.

Thus, in 2001, the excavation of the land at 18 Hoàng Diệu Street had to be postponed. Instead, we did our best to focus on investigating an area at 62–4 Trần Phú Street. There we found part of a citadel rampart made of laterite and large bricks. Those traces were judged to be the remains of the wall surrounding the Nguyễn-dynasty Hanoi Citadel (nineteenth century). Underneath, an intact cultural layer from the Trần period was found, as well as a set of Lý and Trần artefacts.

Around August 2002, Nguyễn Xuân Hải—an official of the Ministry of Construction—called and told me the news that his ministry wished to implement a government directive, requiring the Ministry of Culture and Information and the Academy of Social Sciences to conduct an excavation at 18 Hoàng Diệu Street, to prepare for a construction project there. The project was of the first importance: for the construction of the Ba Đình National Convention Centre and a new National Assembly Building. The land was about 4.8 ha in area. To discuss plans for the excavation, the Ministry of Construction then organised an inter-agency meeting, with the Institute of Archaeology, Department of Cultural Heritage, Hanoi Department for the Management of Historical and Scenic Sites, Hanoi Museum, and the Secretariat of the 1000th Anniversary of Thăng Long–Hanoi.

At the meeting, various views were expressed about how to excavate such a large area to ensure that construction could start before August 2003. Some suggested that a few small test trenches measuring 1 m²–4 m² could be opened to check the situation before construction started. Others thought that after preliminary investigation with these test trenches, people could be assigned to follow the bulldozers and gather up the artefacts. On the basis of my experience in the previous test excavations, I was determined to present a serious proposal: in principle, with ancient city sites, the whole area should be excavated and not a square metre should be left unturned; however, because we had little experience of urban archaeology and little knowledge of the vestiges we might potentially uncover, we should proceed in two stages.

Stage 1: Conduct test excavations on about 2,000 m^2 of the 48,000 m^2 area.

Stage 2: Expand the excavation on the basis of the results of Stage 1.

I also expressed my certainty that there were vestiges underground: only their potential was unknown.

On the basis of our experience of previous excavations in Hanoi and our knowledge of the typical structural characteristics of capital citadels, I proposed that the test excavation trenches should be larger than during normal excavations. If they measured 1 m^2–4 m^2, as at prehistoric settlement sites, it would be impossible to study the status of the vestiges and to dig down to the sterile layer, as the cultural strata would be thick and the ground water abundant. The trenches should measure 50 m^2–100 m^2.

This plan was agreed upon and approved. Deputy Minister Lưu Trần Tiêu signed a document requesting the Academy of Social Sciences to assign responsibility for the project to the Institute of Archaeology. Đỗ Hoài Nam, the Academy's President, signed an order establishing a Management Board to oversee the excavation and appointed me as project chairman. We immediately drew up a project, entitled 'Test Excavation Project at 18 Hoàng Diệu Street'. The project was approved by the Academy of Social Sciences, Ministry of Culture and Information, Ministry of Planning and Investment, Ministry of Finance, and the Government.

Our successful request for an excavation permit was a sign of great progress, as much remained to be said about the conditions of implementation of the Law on Cultural Heritage. After my teacher Phan Huy Lê read the news in the press—that the government had permitted the Institute to excavate 2,000 m^2 out of the 48,000 m^2—I still remember how he asked me: 'Why does your plan only cover 2,000 m^2 and not the whole area?' I replied that the heritage law was understood very differently by different institutions, so we had to plan in stages. He smiled in sympathy. After that, we made our preparations for the dig.

* * *

The excavation officially started on 17 December 2002. Trần Quốc Vượng chose the date and led the ritual for breaking the ground. I had committed myself to the opinion that vestiges would be found, so once the excavation got underway, I started worrying. I was not at all sure what results it might yield. Normally, there was no particular problem if archaeological remains were found or not. But on this occasion, I had imprudently expressed a very strong opinion to the government and several ministries: this made me very anxious. So, to be absolutely sure, we chose sites for the trenches in line with the topography and deliberately concentrated as many of them as possible close to the Kính Thiên Palace.

The first days were extremely difficult and miserable. The weather was piercingly cold, with drizzle cutting our faces and bitterly cold ground water constantly flooding our trenches. Many of the worker teams could not stand it and left. Seeing this endless water and sodden mud, some of the staff from my Institute and the Hanoi Department of Culture and Information said: 'I don't suppose there's anything down there.'

My anxiety nonetheless gradually subsided. Early on, a staff member on night duty phoned to tell me that Lê-dynasty fragments had appeared on the surface. My hopes rose, as this was an early indication of possible vestiges below. Digging continued in the trenches. Firstly, a foundation of square bricks was found in trench A7, managed by Trịnh Hoàng Hiệp, as well as a strip of bricks arranged in the lemon flower shape characteristic of the Trần dynasty. I was delighted and asked the workers to preserve those vestiges and treat them with particular care.

Then long lines of erect bricks and valuable artefacts were unearthed in trench B3, managed by Bùi Văn Liêm. A Lý-dynasty stone pedestal bearing a lotus inscription appeared in trench B5, managed by Nguyễn Tiến Đông. A border of bricks arranged in Trần lemon flower shapes was found in trench A1, managed by Phạm Như Hồ. At this point we were all thrilled, as we were now sure that the site had huge potential. Stone pedestals, building foundations, pillar foundations, gutters, and lemon flower arrangements were appearing one after the other. The situation seemed favourable and was evolving at great speed. At all the places we had chosen to explore, dense concentrations of artefacts and thick cultural layers were turning up. Traces of architectural foundations were being found in over 80% of the excavated trenches.

I briefly reported the initial results of the excavation to Đỗ Hoài Nam. He in turn reported to acting Deputy Prime Minister Nguyễn Tấn Dũng, directly responsible for the construction project. He immediately came to visit the site. I remember it was late afternoon, towards the end of the year. In the course of his short visit, he was deeply impressed by the vestiges, especially a pedestal bearing a lotus design found in trench B5, managed by Nguyễn Tiến Đông. He then quickly consulted leaders at the Academy of Social Sciences, Ministry of Construction, and

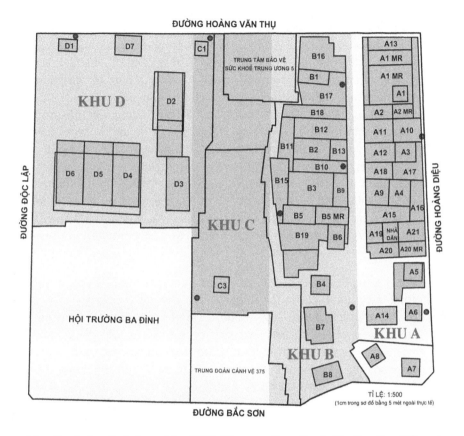

ĐƯỜNG HOÀNG VĂN THỤ

KHU D

KHU C

KHU B

KHU A

HỘI TRƯỜNG BA ĐÌNH

TRUNG ĐOÀN CẢNH VỆ 375

TRUNG TÂM BẢO VỆ SỨC KHOẺ TRUNG ƯƠNG 5

ĐƯỜNG ĐỘC LẬP

ĐƯỜNG HOÀNG DIỆU

TỈ LỆ: 1:500
(1cm trong sơ đồ bằng 5 mét ngoài thực tế)

ĐƯỜNG BẮC SƠN

Map 7. A detailed plan of the 2002–04 excavation site, indicating the different sections, or *khu*, of the dig, referred to here frequently (Institute of Archaeology).

Ba Đình Convention Centre and National Assembly Building Construction Management Board. I made a short presentation and requested his approval for an expansion of the investigation. He quickly agreed to let us draw up a plan for further excavations, and later a project for the entire site's excavation. That was a turning point for the archaeological excavation at 18 Hoàng Diệu Street, as well as for research on Thăng Long Imperial Citadel.

In March 2004, the Academy of Social Sciences implemented a directive from the Prime Minister instructing the Institute of Archaeology to stop the excavation and to start work on the scientific analysis, evaluation and development of the site. By this time, we had excavated over 19,000 m². The preliminary results were as follows.

Cultural Layers

Cultural layers are layers of earth under the ground containing cultural vestiges from different historical periods, in this case of Thăng Long–Hanoi. For archaeologists, cultural layers serve as a sort of 'passport', allowing them to conduct authentic research into the nation's past.

Cultural layers were found throughout the site, containing historical and cultural vestiges of Thăng Long–Hanoi over a period of more than 1,300 years. These cultural layers generally appeared from a depth of around 1 m below the surface and were about 2 m–3.5 m thick. In some trenches, such as A10–A11, B3–B9, and D4–D6, vestiges from different periods were observed overlapping each other. A good example is trench B3, managed by Bùi Văn Liêm and Nguyễn Gia Đối, where the following cultural transformations through the different historical periods were visible:

- From a depth of 0.9 m–1.9 m, we encountered the Lê-dynasty cultural layer (dating from the fifteenth to eighteenth centuries).
- From a depth of 1.9 m–3 m, we found the Lý- and Trần-dynasty cultural layers (eleventh to fourteenth centuries). At this point, there were also vestiges of a Trần foundation made of square bricks superimposed on a Lý foundation made of square bricks, separated by a layer of banked earth 12 cm–15 cm thick.
- From a depth of 3 m to about 4.2 m we found the Đại La cultural layer (seventh to ninth centuries).

At other locations, complex variations in the cultural layers were inevitably observed, but this example is representative of the basic pattern of the site.

Architectural Vestiges

In all the cultural layers, architectural remains were unearthed from the site's different historical periods: the pre-Thăng Long or Đại La period (seventh to ninth centuries), the Lý dynasty (eleventh to twelfth centuries), Trần dynasty (thirteenth to fourteenth centuries) and Lê dynasty (fifteenth to eighteenth centuries). They could be recognised above all through the presence of pillar bases, brick foundations, walls built around foundations, and so on. For example: The earliest architectural remains belonged to the Đại La period and included traces of building foundations constructed with grey bricks, as well as stone pillar pedestals and wooden pillars. Similar vestiges were found in trenches A5, A16, B10, B13, B16, D5, D6, and so on, especially in trenches B3–B13, where the remains of a large building were uncovered. Pillar foundations made of broken pieces of brick and tile were discovered in trench A15. A large brick drain was found in trench A20, where sections of grey brick wall, oriented east–west and built to support the foundation of a building, were clearly visible. Architectural vestiges from the Lý dynasty were most clearly identified in trench A20. Here, the foundations of two buildings were separated from each other by a courtyard paved with square bricks. It was not yet possible to estimate the size of the building because the trenches could not be extended into a nearby residential area and the foundations appeared to extend towards Hoàng Diệu Street.

Characteristic of both buildings was their construction with red bricks to support verandas and stone pedestals bearing lotus designs. The vestiges show verandas (measuring 47 cm high and 88 cm wide) bordered with nine rows of supporting bricks. The bricks (measuring 40 cm × 19.5 cm × 4.5 cm) were light red; some were inscribed with Chinese characters on the side.

Ten stone pedestals bearing lotus designs were found placed on very solid pillar foundations made of gravel and bricks. The pedestals (measuring 65 cm–73.5 cm × 65 cm–74 cm) were square, with round surfaces (41 cm–49 cm in diameter) bearing carvings around the edge of designs of fourteen slender lotus petals with graceful features. They resemble the pedestals at Tường Long Tower (Haiphong, 1057) and Chương Sơn Tower (Nam Định, 1107).

Within the area of this building's foundations, we found decorative elements dating from the Lý and Trần periods, suggesting that it already existed under the Lý and continued to be used under the Trần. Trench A1 revealed remains of a large building (60 m long and 17.65 m wide), with more than 40 square pillar bases (1.30 m × 1.30 m) strengthened by a foundation of gravel and broken pieces of brick and tile, similar to the building found in Trench A20. This building apparently existed through the Lý and early Trần periods.

In Section B, we found many architectural vestiges, including a fairly complete building from the Lý period (over 60 m long and 9 m wide), with more than 42 gravel pillar foundations dividing it into eleven compartments and two wings. This is the most complete architectural vestige at the site. Section C, while not yet extensively excavated, revealed the presence in trench C3 of square pillar bases (1.4 m × 1.4 m) strengthened by a foundation of gravel and square bricks, dating from the Lý period.

Trench D7 revealed a foundation built with bricks inscribed with the Chinese characters 李家第三帝龍瑞太平四年造 (*Lý gia đệ tam đế Long Thụy Thái Bình tứ niên tạo*). This translates as 'made in fourth year of the third Lý king's reign period Long Thụy Thái Bình' and means that the bricks were manufactured in 1057 during the reign of King Lý Thánh Tông.

In Sections A and B, we found vestiges of a type of building made with seven pillar bases, with a square base in the middle and six round bases set around it. The seven pillar bases thus formed the ground plan of a round building (3.74 m in diameter). Some researchers thought these were the remains of hexagonal riverside structures, as the vestiges were located near an ancient river. Eleven sets of such pillar bases have so far been found along that river, in addition to a large building with many compartments discovered in trench A1. All the buildings were fitted with drains. Some were small gutters for single buildings, while others were larger drains for draining entire areas. All the channels evacuated water into rivers or lakes.

Architectural vestiges from the Trần dynasty were clearly visible in trenches A1 and B3, as well as Section D. They consisted of foundations made of bricks arranged in the lemon flower shapes typical of the Trần, and they all lay above architectural remains dating from the Lý. In trench B16, we also found the foundations of a building with stone pedestals decorated with lotus designs dating from the Trần.

Archaeological vestiges from the Lê dynasty were extensively damaged because they were in the upper layer. In some locations, however, vestiges appeared with pillar bases built with large bricks on top of Lý and Trần architectural vestiges. The best example was found in trench A1.

Apart from the remains mentioned above, eleven water wells were discovered (two Đại La, two Lý, two Trần, three Lê and two Lê–Nguyễn) and a complex and overlapping network of ponds and lakes. Human skeletons were discovered in cultural layers from around the Trần period, and from the late Lê and Nguyễn periods. The most remarkable are two skeletons in trench B16, found at a depth of 2.1 m under a Trần stone pedestal with lotus designs. They were of children aged about eight to ten, with their heads oriented east but off by about 20^0–30^0 to the north. Their dating and anthropological features are under study.

Artefacts

In terms of quantity, the artefacts discovered—including broken pieces, intact objects and broken items that can be reconstructed—may be

Fig. 28. Impressed bricks, Đại La period (Photo: Institute of Archaeology 2003).

estimated in the millions. The majority are bricks, tiles and ceramics. Each period yielded objects with their own particular characteristics.

The Đại La period (seventh to ninth centuries) yielded abundant bricks and tiles. Grey bricks inscribed with three Chinese characters 江西軍 (*Giang Tây quân*), meaning 'Jiangxi army', or 江西塼 (*Giang Tây chuyên*), meaning 'Jiangxi brick', are characteristic of this period. From time to time, a red brick was unearthed. The figure of a crocodile swimming in waves appears in relief on the surface of some square paving bricks. Tile caps are decorated with varied designs: the faces of sacred animals, clown faces, lotuses. Ceramics characteristic of this period include glazed jars with six knobs and high-bodied celadon glazed pots. A number of small lion statues were also discovered.

The Đinh–Early Lê period (tenth century) yielded red bricks inscribed with characters 大越国軍城塼 (*Đại Việt quốc quân thành chuyên*), meaning 'bricks for building the military citadel of the country of Đại Việt'. This type of brick is commonly found in buildings of the Đinh–Early Lê period at the capital at Hoa Lư (Ninh Bình). Tubular roof tiles were also found, with statues of loving duck pairs attached to the tiles' surfaces. There were also earthenware items, some decorated with wave designs, some not, and various types of flared-mouth round-bottomed pots decorated with the cord designs that had become traditional since the Đông Sơn culture.

The Lý dynasty (eleventh to twelfth centuries) yielded various types of brick and tile that showed a higher level of development than seen in any previous period. Both square and rectangular bricks were found. Among the more remarkable were the rectangular construction bricks (measuring 38 cm × 23 cm × 5.6 cm) bearing Chinese characters in relief 李家第三帝龍瑞太平四年造 (*Lý gia đệ tam đế Long Thụy Thái Bình tứ niên tạo*), meaning 'made in fourth year of the third Lý king's reign period Long Thụy Thái Bình'. Some square paving bricks show sophisticated decorative designs of lotus and chrysanthemum flowers.

Roof tiles include a tubular type and a yin-yang type, as well as tiles with lotus-shaped ends. At some locations, tile caps and tile surfaces were found with a bodhi leaf design attached, decorated with dragon, phoenix, lotus or chrysanthemum figures, in hundreds of variants. A large number of dragon and phoenix heads were found. We also discovered staircases, door hinges and pedestals all made of stone and inscribed with dragons, phoenixes, flowers and leaves. Artefacts also included large quantities of glazed ceramics from the Lý period, including bowls, dishes, pots, basins, models of towers, boxes, etc., with fine celadon, white, blue, yellow and brown-inlaid glazes and magnificent designs, demonstrating that production during this period reached a very high standard.

During the Trần dynasty (thirteenth to fourteenth centuries), artistic endeavour built upon and developed the achievements of the Lý period. Trần artefacts thus reflect continuity with Lý traditions, yet also changed dramatically over time. This may be seen in the large number and broad variety of architectural decorative materials found in the trenches, including statues of dragon and phoenix heads, tile caps with attached bodhi leaves or off-centre bodhi leaves decorated with dragon figures, and square paving bricks bearing chrysanthemum and peony designs. Characteristic of the Trần are construction bricks with the characters 永寧場 (*Vĩnh Ninh trường*) in relief, meaning 'Vĩnh Ninh area', and tiles with lotus-shaped ends. Trần ceramics are richer and more diverse than under the Lý, with the appearance of ceramics with blue-and-white and iron-brown motifs. Under the Trần, however, ceramics were more simply decorated than during the previous period.

The Lê dynasty (fifteenth to eighteenth centuries) lasted for nearly three centuries and for the periodisation of its artefacts may be divided

Fig. 29. Impressed brick, Lý dynasty (Photo: Institute of Archaeology 2003).

into three stages: the Early Lê, the Lê-Mạc and Lê Restoration periods. In the first, characteristic artefacts include large bricks, as well as large yin-yang tiles, which are found in red or grey, or glazed in green or yellow, decorated with dragons or flowers and leaves. Blue-and-white ceramics and high-quality thin white ceramics were also unearthed. Many of the large bricks are inscribed with Chinese characters indicating the number of a unit within the Lê army.

Tubular tile caps decorated with dragon figures in relief continue to be found from the Lê-Mạc period. The dragon figure of this period is similar to that found on Mạc terracotta lampstands. On ceramic items, dragons were drawn simply, with less refinement and sophistication than observed during the Early Lê period. Medium-sized and small bricks were used during the Lê-Mạc and Lê Restoration periods. Various types of tubular tiles, yin-yang tiles, and tiles with lotus-shaped ends, as well as statues of 'crocodiles' decorating the roof edges of buildings, were also found.

Lê Restoration ceramics are abundant and diverse, although their quality, style and decoration lacked the refinement of previous periods. In addition to these objects discovered in great quantity, other types of artefacts were discovered, including objects in metal (cannons, swords, knives, arrowheads and bronze coins), Chinese ceramics (seventh to nineteenth centuries), Islamic ceramics (ninth century) and Japanese ceramics (late seventeenth century). The sites and artefacts that emerged from the excavation reflect the characteristics of a capital citadel and cover a period of history lasting more than a thousand years.

4. SIGNIFICANCE OF THE FINDINGS

In August 2003, the excavation's deadline was nearly upon us. Aware that I had to present its results, I started thinking about the significance and value of the vestiges. I quickly imagined and sketched out the site's significance—which was huge—under the following headings.

The Citadel's Continuous History

This is the first time a set of abundant and complicated vestiges and artefacts from a central section of the Thăng Long Imperial Citadel and Hanoi Citadel was unearthed. The remains demonstrate a continuous evolution from the Đại La period (seventh to ninth centuries) and Đinh–Early Lê period (tenth century) through the Lý and Trần dynasties and the Early Lê, Lê-Mạc and Lê Restoration periods (eleventh to eighteenth centuries). The site may be identified as part of the central section of Thăng Long Imperial Citadel under the Lý, Trần and Lê dynasties for several reasons.

Firstly, in many trenches we found architectural remains and artefacts dating from the Lý, Trần and Lê dynasties overlapping architectural remains and artefacts from the Tống Bình and Đại La periods. These findings prove that King Lý Thái Tổ's words in the 'Royal Edict for the Transfer of the Capital' refer to the removal of the capital from Hoa Lư to Đại La and name the Lý dynasty's capital Thăng Long.

Secondly, the architectural vestiges include the foundations of dozens of solidly constructed buildings and many large edifices covering thousands of square metres. They belonged to the central section of Thăng Long Imperial Citadel under the Lý, Trần and Lê dynasties. This is demonstrated through the comparison of the location of Kính Thiên Palace with historical records. According to the chronicles, the Lý, Trần and Lê dynasties ordered the construction of many palaces, towers and temples around the central palace (named Càn Nguyên and Thiên An under the Lý and Trần, and Kính Thiên under the Lê) to serve as a place for the court to work and the royal family to enjoy entertainment and recreation.

Under the Lý, for example, according to *Việt sử lược*, Thăng Long Imperial Citadel was built by King Lý Thái Tổ in the following plan. Càn Nguyên Palace was located at the centre. Tập Hiền Palace and Phi Long Gate were placed to its east, with Giảng Võ Palace and Đan Phượng Gate to its west. Cao Điện Palace and Long Trì Courtyard were built to the south, with galleries on both sides. To the north (to the rear of Thiên An Palace), Long An Palace and Long Thụy Palace were built, with Nhật Quang Palace on the left (to the east), Nguyệt Minh Palace on the right (to the west), and Thuý Hoa Palace to the rear. Hưng Thiên Temple and Ngũ Phượng Pavilion were also built. Thái Thanh Palace, Vạn Tuệ Temple and Quảng Trần Phúc Scriptures Library were then built in 1011 (*Việt sử lược* 1960: 70–1).

In 1017, after an earthquake at Càn Nguyên Palace, Lý Thái Tổ gave audience in the palaces to the east. In the same year, the eastern palaces were struck by lightning, and the king gave audience in the palaces to the west (*Việt sử lược* 1960: 74). According to the chronicles, in the same year the king built three more palaces to the west. In 1029, the king ordered the restoration and reconstruction of Thiên An and other palaces there:

Tuyên Đức Palace stood to the east, Thiên Phúc Palace stood to the west, Long Trì was to the front with Văn Minh Palace to its east and Quảng Vũ Palace and two bell towers to its west, Phụng Thiên Palace stood to the south with Chính Dương Tower in front, and Trường Xuân Palace and Long Các Palace stood to the north (*Việt sử lược* 1960: 79).

In 1203, King Lý Cao Tông built a new palace complex to the west. It consisted of several buildings, including Thiên Thụy Palace in the middle, with Dương Minh Palace to the east, Thiên Quang Palace to the south, Chính Nghi Palace to the south, and Kính Thiên Palace and Lệ Giao Terrace in front. Vĩnh Nghiêm Gate was built to the south, Việt Thành Gate to the west, Thắng Thọ Palace to the north, with Thánh Thọ Tower in front, and Nhật Kim Tower to the east. To the west was Nguyệt Bảo Tower, Lương Thạch Building, Dục Đường House, Phú Quốc Tower, Thấu Viên Gate, and Dưỡng Ngư Lake, beside which Ngoạn Y Temple was built 'with fragrant flowers and exotic grasses growing around three of its sides, lake water flowing into the river, skilful temple carvings and decorative features including beautiful woodwork of unprecedented quality' (*Việt sử lược* 1960: 165–6).

These are just some examples of Imperial Citadel architecture under the Lý, before building work of the Trần, Lê and Nguyễn periods is even mentioned. Given this historical evidence of a concentration of palaces, towers and temples to the west of Kính Thiên Palace during the Lê period (Thiên An Palace under the Lý and Trần), the dense vestiges of well-built, elaborate and splendid-looking buildings found at 18 Hoàng Diệu Street must be the remains of the palaces, towers and temples of the former Imperial Citadel at Thăng Long.

Thirdly, the connection of the site to the Lý, Trần and Lê dynasties is also demonstrated by analysis of the artefacts discovered. They include building materials, such as stone pedestals bearing lotus designs, various types of tile and brick, statues and bas-reliefs of dragon and phoenix figures, all of which were symbols used in the decoration of royal architecture. They also include high-quality ceramics bearing sophisticated designs, including Lê porcelain bearing the characters *quan* and *kính* and decorative features, including phoenixes and five-clawed dragons, demonstrating that they were items reserved for the king and queen's daily use.

Identification of the names and function of all the architectural vestiges by comparison with historical records will be time consuming, especially for an archaeological excavation of this scale. However, on the basis of the data we possess today, we may be certain that the architectural vestiges belong to part of the architectural complex of the Lý–Trần–Lê-period Thăng Long Imperial Citadel located to the west of Kính Thiên Palace.

The Citadel's Scale and Location

The second reason for the site's significance is that the vestiges and artefacts allow us to visualise the location, scale and physiognomy of the Lý–Trần–Lê-period Thăng Long Imperial Citadel and the Nguyễn period Hanoi Citadel. According to research by the Institute of Archaeology, the inner rampart of Thăng Long Imperial Citadel (as it appears on Lê-dynasty maps) had the following rough outline:

- Its northern boundary was in the area of today's Phan Đình Phùng Street
- Its southern boundary was in the area of Trần Phú Street
- Its eastern boundary was in the area of Thuốc Bắc Street, and
- Its western boundary was beyond Ông Ích Khiêm Street (this citadel's location in this direction has yet to be identified).

The complex is estimated to have covered around 160 ha. Under the Lý and Trần dynasties, it may have covered a smaller or larger area while under the Lê it was extended to the west. During the Nguyễn period it was reduced to about 100 ha. Many types of building were built in the Imperial Citadel. The excavation shows that in the western area, those buildings were so disposed that they formed many layers that ran parallel with one another, oriented north–south. Mingled with these layers of architectural vestiges, or located between the buildings, lakes served to evacuate water and create fine scenery.

Each building was beautifully and skilfully decorated. From the Đại La period, there are lotuses and chrysanthemums, and the heads of brawny, fierce-looking sacred animals. From the Đinh–Early Lê period, there are lotuses and pairs of loving ducks. Under the Lý dynasty, the decorative arts reached a peak of perfection, while Trần decorative features were strong, becoming gradually simpler by comparison with the Lý. Under the Lê, the finest work appears during the Early Lê period of the fifteenth century, while subsequent decorations on bricks and tiles become progressively simpler.

The Citadel's Cultural Influences

Thirdly, the architectural artefacts and vestiges found in the excavated area, as well as the items for palace use, ceramics and weapons, demonstrate that Lý–Trần–Lê arts reached a high level, and reflected both Vietnamese cultural identity and multiple relations and exchanges between Thăng Long and other countries of the world. With its origins in the Đinh–Early Lê period, artistic creation under the Lý reached a peak of perfection. Trần arts were inclined to strength and free expression, while Lê arts changed rapidly, tending to increasingly simpler forms of expression. The vestiges and artefacts found at Thăng Long clearly reflect Vietnam's cultural identity. Examples include Lý and Trần dragons, which had an S-shaped crest, in contrast with Chinese dragons, and the bodhi leaves with dragon and phoenix figures that were attached to Lý and Trần roofs, in contrast with roofs in neighbouring countries.

Many types of artefact reflect relations between Thăng Long and other parts of Vietnam or other countries of the world. Trần-dynasty Thiên Trường ceramics have been found in Nam Định. From the Lê period, many ceramics produced in Thăng Long were found, but also various types of ceramics made in Hải Dương. Commercial relations meant that many Chinese ceramics—dating from the seventh to ninth centuries through to the nineteenth century—were imported to Vietnam and Thăng Long. Late seventeenth-century Japanese Hizen ceramics were also discovered, as well as fragments of ceramics coming from further afield, including Islamic pieces from the Middle East. Cham ceramics and Vietnamese bricks bearing Cham scripts in relief vividly reflect the long-standing historical relations between Vietnam and Champa.

The Citadel's Heritage Value

Fourthly, the vestiges and artefacts form part of an ensemble of priceless cultural heritage, including the Thăng Long–Hanoi Citadel and several revolutionary sites in the central area of Hanoi's Ba Đình district. The value of the vestiges and artefacts is enhanced when placed in relation with other historical sites in this area, including the Flag Tower, Gate of Commencement, Kính Thien Palace, Rear Palace, One Pillar Pagoda, the Vietnam People's Army high command, Ba Đình National Assembly Building and several sites related to Ho Chi Minh. This complex of historical sites symbolises in a unique, rich and attractive way the history of nation building in Vietnam and the history of the nation's capital.

The vestiges of Thăng Long–Hanoi Citadel merit inscription on the World Heritage List; this point of view was expressed in the Academy of Social Sciences' first report to the government in September 2003. Nowadays it is true to say that everyone recognises the site's value, as demonstrated by the submission of a dossier for consideration by UNESCO. In those days, however, not everyone understood the value of the vestiges. But we certainly did, right from the start of the excavation.

5. CONSERVING THE HERITAGE

The site's immense value was obvious to any visitor to the excavated area who was interested in Vietnam's cultural heritage. As the excavation's end approached, my awareness of its value set me thinking all the more about the site's destiny. In my role as the excavation's leader, I wondered if I should propose that part of this unusually important historical site be preserved *in situ* for the future. When I shared my thoughts to colleagues at the dig they all agreed, but no one dared imagine my proposal would be accepted. After all, the decision had already been taken at the highest levels to build the new National Assembly and Convention Centre buildings on the site. I also knew that everyone would be distressed if the vestiges had to be removed and the site handed over for construction. Nguyễn Tiến Đông said to me: 'On the day the vestiges are moved out, do you mind if I stay at home? I won't be able to come in that day.'

I nonetheless still believed the archaeological site would convince; I believed in the Consultative Council and in the country's senior leadership, once they had received the necessary information from researchers. I wondered why many of us felt inferior at the small and humble scale of Vietnam's cultural heritage compared to other world heritage sites. Now we had our own historical site of monumental scale; certainly, there was no reason not to seek to preserve it. I was determined to be fearless in proposing that the vestiges should be preserved and submitted this idea to the Consultative Council set up by the Minister of Culture and Information.

One further thing made me decide to submit the proposal: Nguyễn Văn Huy's thoughts on the matter. Trần Quốc Vượng had told him about the site and shown him around. He encouraged me—he may have been the first person who encouraged me—to submit the proposal. He also wrote his own letter to the President of Academy of Social Sciences and the Minister of Culture and Information, suggesting that Sections A and B should be preserved at all costs. The Consultative Council asked me to prepare a report and consider alternative projects for the vestiges' removal, including a proposal for their protection. At first, I wanted to request preservation of Section A in its entirety, that is, the vestiges located along Hoàng Diệu Street. But deep down, I thought the Thăng Long Imperial Citadel was valuable because it is a complete complex of sites, and that no more valuable site existed. That meant that I wanted to protect the whole site.

I recall the day before the meeting of the Council. At about 10 pm, its chairman, Phan Huy Lê, phoned me for a detailed discussion of the site's current condition and value. We also talked about the other proposals. He asked: 'Which sections and vestiges would you like to keep?' I replied that archaeologists normally love vestiges and are normally very ambitious, so I would keep all of them *in situ*. None should be removed. The structure of Thăng Long appeared there as a complete system. For these reasons, it was impossible for me to suggest what to keep and what to remove. He chuckled and said: 'I understand. I do sympathise, Tín. But it is not so easy! You bear a heavy responsibility. Tomorrow you will play a double role: one as excavation leader reporting to the Council and the other as a member of the Minister's Consultative Council presenting a proposal. Think hard! Make your presentation!'

The next morning, in the Ministry of Culture and Information's meeting room, I presented my report on the excavation's preliminary results and the initial assessment of the site's value. The discussion session was in the afternoon. I asked to speak first. I proposed the whole site should be preserved. The discussion was very lively. To my surprise, most participants supported my point of view, including Phan Huy Lê, Đỗ Văn Ninh, Hoàng Văn Khoán, Trần Đức Cường, Vũ Minh Giang, Phan Khanh and Nguyễn Văn Huy. Phan Huy Lê and Vũ Minh Giang presented an analysis of scientists' responsibility for the future of national cultural heritage. At the end, Phan Huy Lê wrapped up the meeting with a recommendation that the Ministry of Culture and Information transmit all the views expressed to higher authority.

The excavation results and scientists' recommendations were then reported to the government. Throughout 2004, scholars organised conferences and analysis, focusing on the site's value and recommendations for its protection. At those meetings, they further examined the site's value and significance. Đỗ Bang (from Huế University) was one of the first scholars to make a written recommendation for the site's submission to UNESCO for recognition as World Cultural Heritage. Based on two national conferences organised to evaluate the site, the government came to regard the excavation results and Thăng Long Imperial Citadel as extremely valuable.

President Trần Đức Lương, in his New Year's speech to the Vietnamese people, presented his assessment: 'the excavation at Ba Đình in Hanoi revealed many priceless cultural and historical vestiges of the ancient Thăng Long Imperial Citadel'. This was the first time that an archaeological event was mentioned in the Vietnamese President's New Year wishes. In October 2003, former Prime Minister Võ Văn Kiệt had visited the site and wrote in the site's visitors' book: 'This is cultural heritage of more than national interest—it is of global significance'. The scientist and revolutionary veteran Trần Bạch Đằng observed: 'the discovery of Thăng Long Imperial Citadel under the ground is the finest achievement of Vietnamese historical research'. Throughout 2004, we were busy all day long welcoming top-ranking state leaders, delegations from the National Assembly, researchers from at home and abroad, and other groups representing the public. French President Jacques Chirac and Japanese Prime Minister Junichiro Koizumi visited and were deeply impressed by the site. President Chirac wrote that Thăng Long Imperial Citadel 'is essential for Vietnam's history and does honour to Mankind'. The Secretary General of UNESCO, Koichiro Matsuura, wrote 'this is a unique site, with special significance not only for Vietnam but also for the world.'

The news spread widely in the press, with debates in Vietnam and overseas resulting in broad appreciation of the importance of the site. Then the Prime Minister expressed his opinion that the entire Thăng Long Imperial Citadel site at 18 Hoàng Diệu Street should be protected. In September 2008, he authorised the submission to UNESCO of an application for the site's recognition as World Heritage, including the area at 18 Hoàng Diệu Street and the Hanoi Citadel area (across the street), located at the centre of the ancient Thăng Long Imperial Citadel.

Amid the great pleasure of scholars at this news, I have written down these few initial notes about my research on Thăng Long Imperial Citadel. In a single paper, it is not possible to tell all the stories of the research or mention all great historical and cultural values embodied by Thăng Long Imperial Citadel. The pressure felt by my colleagues and myself during the last few years—of how to protect the site—has gradually faded. The archaeologists are now able to enjoy a little more tranquillity, to return their normal silent tasks of excavation, weighing, measuring, appraising and conducting research on the vestiges and artefacts, of making their contribution to the scientific record. Excavations continue. Sorting of the findings is underway, and will go on for years, as researchers treat the huge quantity of excavated data that form the basis for scientific assessments of the site's value. As we do this work, we deepen our knowledge of the Imperial Citadel and capital city at Thăng Long.

Note

1. See *Đại Việt sử ký toàn thư*, entry for 1397, eleventh lunar month, quyển VIII, pp. 31a–31b.

CHAPTER 2

Intriguing Mysteries from a Corner of the Imperial Citadel

Lê Thị Liên

1. THE EXCAVATION STARTS

In late 2002, the Institute of Archaeology's staff were eager for news from the Ba Đình excavation site. A few of us had been sent as 'pioneers' to dig the first test trenches. We all wanted to join in. This was not only true of archaeologists and historians: anyone who had read the pages of our country's history books wanted to see the actual evidence of that history, from inside the famous capital city of Thăng Long.

After a couple of months, several rooms of a single-storey terraced house belonging to the former army barracks—now transformed into an office and storehouse—were full of artefacts. The concrete floor of the yard and its canvas shelter, where the objects were sorted and classified, had to be extended daily. Many of those small houses with their peeling walls had just been demolished. It was extraordinary to imagine that, right under their foundations, there lay countless potsherds coloured with brown and blue designs, with celadon and white glazes—that right under their foundations, there were phoenix-shaped tiles and smooth fragments of inscribed stone. The archaeologists were astonished. When we moved, we stepped on fragments; our hands and minds sought to understand these broken vestiges of daily life in the past. Treasures emerged from the ground in great quantities. But the joys of discovery jostled with the stresses we faced, from the pressure of time and the numerous difficulties of the project's first stage.

In mid-2003, I was assigned to the excavation. I had requested a minor delay to my start date in order to attend a conference in Japan where I hoped to visit a number of archaeological sites, Nara Imperial City in particular. The institute had asked me to contact overseas scholars to learn more from their experiences in the excavation and study of ancient imperial city sites. We were especially interested in places like Nara and Xi'an (China).

I started work in June. At first, I was in charge of trench B11. Later, I moved to D5, located in the Ba Đình Sports Club tennis court area and connected to trenches D4–D6. Covering a total area of 2,100 m², this was by far the largest trench I had ever excavated. Nguyễn Văn Tiến, a young, enthusiastic, and hard-working graduate of the University of Social Sciences and Humanities' History Department, was assigned to work as my assistant. The young archaeologist Ngô Thị Lan also worked with me until the last day of the excavation; she was industrious and eager to learn. With the other members of the institute's staff there, we formed a friendly group, discussing and collaborating, and coping with problems as they arose.

The hectic pace of events at the site quickly revealed the inadequacy of my previous experience. There was the time factor: we were fascinated by the finds we were making, but the pressure of time was a constant source of stress. There was the weather. Groups of inexperienced workers from various places suffocated in the hot summer air or stewed under plastic shelters during downpours that came as unexpectedly as they went. Rain filled up the trenches, so water pumps came to the rescue! And there were problems related to the site's location: excavation in a bustling and over-populated capital city was by no means simple. The earth we removed piled up in great volumes; it was rush hour, and the trucks could not take it away!

The trenches looked like a giant chessboard on which thousands of people hurried at their tasks. We assigned their positions and monitored their work. Although the trenches were large, they were crowded with workers and dense with finds. Workers called us from left and right, informing us of unusual finds, asking us to help deal with them. Few are fortunate enough to work at an ancient royal site, especially one like Thăng Long that prospered and declined over a period of one thousand years. The piles of ruins contained multiple mysteries; it was impossible to understand immediately how one thing related to another.

On particularly busy days, hundreds of workers occupied the trenches, people from many places, of varying ages, belonging to different teams. The farmers had long years of experience with gardening and farming, yet were quite unused to holding tiny hoes, digging in the archaeologists' manner, 'scratching the earth' and scraping at its chaos of bricks and tiles. The school leavers were unnerved as they stepped into thick mud, exhausted by the unceasing labour of passing buckets filled with wet soil. As for the master carpenters and masons, their experience made them irritable when reproved for making a straight cut into the bank of an ancient body of water or the foundation of an ancient building. These were their first days of archaeological work. Everyone was confused by the sight of piles of bricks, tiles and stones that had just been cleaned with great effort, with many asking questions like: 'Those heaps of broken bricks: are they palaces? They are no better than our cattle pens,' or, 'Why do we have to scratch like this? Can't we hoe firmly to get a good cut?'

We simultaneously coped with the sun and rain, with the mud and the rubbish of past generations that had accumulated over centuries, buried in the ground. We strained our eyes to observe, our ears to listen, our minds to think. We shouted ourselves hoarse, hollering to the crowds of people, to stop them shovelling potsherds or decorated bricks into one corner, to prevent them hoeing off a foundation at another. Almost before they realised it, the workers became passionate about their work. We spent our days sharing each gulp of water and each cob of corn. During our breaks we listened to stories about their families, we told the glorious history of Thăng Long Imperial Citadel as related in the histories, explained the meaning of the objects that appeared under their hands. We soon understood each other better: close bonds were formed.

Discussion often circled around the site. A young boy cried cheerfully, 'Oh! I've been working on this area of bricks since morning, but I don't know what it was. Was it a well?' Another commented, 'Later, you can take your children to visit the on-site museum and proudly tell them that you took part in the excavation and discovery of Thăng Long Imperial Citadel.' An old man continued: 'Too right, not everyone can visit this place. We're lucky to see it being exposed day by day.'

With this new-found enthusiasm, they thought nothing of the scorching sunlight or the fact their clothes were constantly soaked with sweat or rain. One farmer barely noticed when I called break time. With his small build and skilful hands, he had quickly realised what we needed. I appointed him as a 'pioneer' in the use of our specialised tools to do the delicate work of first cleaning. He cleared the finds in a trench or the shapeless edge of a section of foundation so that other workers could lay the remains bare at speed, without digging them out by accident. I told him: 'Whenever you feel tired, just stop and rest. You should respect the site's break time. To keep our health, we need to rest. And I need you very much.'

I will be grateful to them all my life. They helped me so much at a time I was under immense stress. Anyone who has witnessed the incredible speed of such work will understand our mental state, we had to keep apace with the progress of a historic excavation. We had many emotions: delight and curiosity as countless secrets appeared before us, sadness at the necessary speed of the work, and worry about missing or losing some valuable piece of data. The Management Board suffered greatly from the pressure of responsibility. They would urge us on, saying, 'We've got to work fast, we've got to work much faster. The deadline is approaching. If we don't work any faster, we'll have to go along behind a bulldozer picking up artefacts.'

Until the end of August 2003, this was a rescue excavation: it was intended to 'free up' the land chosen for the new National Assembly Building's construction. At the same time, the Management Board was working hard to explain the significance and value of the site and its discoveries. Down in the trenches, we went on digging, hoping a time extension would be approved.

The landscape of Section D was attractive: cool trees and well-appointed roads surrounded the flat ground of the tennis court. At first it was a relief to think we no longer had to work in a place full of mud and water. However, this first impression turned out to be totally wrong. Under the tennis court, we had to clear the top layer of chaotic bricks, tiles and stones left by the power shovel. We never expected to face such a huge muddy morass with its bricks, tiles, and potsherds. It was impossible to identify what these items were and how they interrelated. Wherever our hoes came down, they touched the remains of something or other. We dug temporary ditches and drainage holes, then shifted them elsewhere: this enabled us to evacuate the water quickly and avoid breaking the artefacts in the trenches. This is, of course, dull work for archaeologists, who are more interested in making new and exciting discoveries than simple irrigation channels in narrow muddy ditches.

Our workers ceaselessly drained the water away and sheltered the site from the rain, spending many days simply scraping mud. And thanks to their efforts, a corner of the ruined citadel gradually appeared before us. Here you could see a patch of floor laid with now-damaged square bricks;

there you could see pillar foundations made of tightly packed gravel; over there, sunk foundations became visible, covered with broken bricks as well as tiles decorated with dragons and phoenixes or green and yellow glazes. Scattered here and there you could see traces of ash, black-earth holes full of potsherds, broken bones, bits of bamboo, and partly burnt timbers. These were the 'disposal areas' that archaeologists cherish more than gold: they contain historical evidence of life in past centuries. Collection and treatment of their contents requires time, effort, money, brainpower and passion, allowing us to visualise the diverse objects' original shape and beauty.

At that point, however, we had to explain, convince and encourage the workers: 'Careful you don't break anything! Don't throw anything away! They may be broken pieces, but that doesn't mean we should disparage the heritage left by our forefathers.' All this was impossible to explain to the people whose heads appeared over the fence, trying to satisfy their curiosity about what we were doing. We hoped the day would soon come when every Vietnamese would understand and revere the fragments we were trying to collect.

* * *

The 2003 session of the National Assembly came as a stroke of luck for us, as we were ordered to suspend the work. Several sections of the site were maintained for display to visitors. After the strain of several months' hot and rainy weather, we were all exhausted. The site was immensely complicated and our experience was far too limited. The imperial citadels at Xi'an in China, Nara in Japan, and Kyongju in Korea have been studied for several decades yet even there the work is far from complete. We needed more time and advice from our colleagues at home and abroad to decipher the numerous phenomena we encountered in the excavated trenches and come up with appropriate ways of treating them. In the meantime, we were already receiving visits from high-ranking leaders from various countries, newspaper and television reporters, and scholars from home and abroad. Word of the excavation was getting out.

After the National Assembly session closed, our excavation was allowed to proceed at a more reasonable pace. But other thorny questions now confronted us: With the ruined architectural layers and cultural remains from numerous periods, what should be removed and what should be left on site? How should we conduct our excavation so that a historical range of the vestiges and images from each period could remain clearly visible? The Management Board's view was that we should keep the remains of the Lý and Trần dynasties—the most glorious period of Đại Việt civilisation—for future conservation and reconstruction.

From the discoveries made in Sections A and B, we were convinced that the foundations we could see concealed further layers of pillar bases, raised foundations made of brick, black-earth holes, and so on. Our assumptions were based on the exposed traces of foundations and the lake/riverbed, and the gaps left between them where vestiges had been destroyed. We proceeded to dig narrow ditches to verify them. It is hard to describe the pleasure we felt when, as expected, we identified rows of pillar holes lying deep in pinkish-brown alluvial soil, which had been built for strengthening the foundations of pillars using different technologies. We also came across enigmatic phenomena that were much more difficult to interpret. Why was there a set of monkey bones in a black-earth hole beside the base of a wooden pillar? Those burnt patches of floor: were they traces of a kiln? How did they relate to those clay ditches we had cut through? Why did they lie right beneath the architectural layers?

Even now, as I write, we have not been able to answer all these questions. The excavation at the site has now ceased and the trenches have been back-filled. We dropped plastic bags containing small cards into the ditches and test trenches before covering them with sand; in this way, we covered the unexposed traces along with all their unanswered questions. We hope to return one day, conduct further excavations and find the answers we need.

2. MYSTERIES EMERGE FROM THE RUINS

A Half-Moon Lake

> Để anh mua gạch Bát Tràng về xây
> Xây dọc anh lại xây ngang
> Xây hồ bán nguyệt cho nàng rửa chân
> Let me buy you bricks from Bát Tràng
> I'll lay bricks up and lay bricks down
> And build a half-moon lake for you to wash your feet.

> (Vietnamese folk rhyme)

The chaotic layers in trench D5's northwest corner were wearing us out. We found Lê-dynasty bricks, some broken and some intact, arranged in separate grid patterns. A large hollow area, descending to more than 2 m below the surface, had been filled with stones used to make a tarmac road. In the northeast corner, patches of clay appeared at a depth of about 1 m. There was mud and water everywhere. Groups of workers at the two neighbouring trenches (D4 and D6) were scooping water to clean the bricks and tiles that now formed huge piles. They started making fun of other workers who were planning to dig a drainage ditch: 'Water flows to low places! You're about to find some real treasure.'[1] The water level gradually fell and in the muddy layer a patch appeared: slightly porous, it was very dark and about a finger phalanx thick. I called a stop at once and asked someone to cut a test ditch through. A similar trace appeared, lying long, dark, and flat between two layers of mud. Remembering our experience at trench B11, we were delighted: 'Great! Now remove all the mud lying on top of the dark layer. Be careful not to destroy the layer.'

Our most 'seasoned' workers were assigned to the job. The dark area gradually broadened out. It was broad and flat, certainly much broader than I expected. I guessed it was a large tree with its foliage, as we had found at B11. It extended over to the west, into the area of D6. What could it be? Perhaps a bamboo lattice covering something? The muddy layer on top contained quantities of broken bricks, tiles and potsherds. Underneath, there was a layer of fine dark grey mud, about 20 cm thick containing almost no artefacts. I chose our two most skilful workers to follow the edge of the dark trace, by no means a simple task when the layer above it was several hundred years old. We eventually identified a verge sloping in a crescent shape slightly to the west, strewn with gravel and sand. There was also a straight verge on the far side, extending about 6 m into the area of D6. On the verge, several metres to the west, we found three clusters of foundations for strengthening the feet of pillars: they were 'hexagonal building pillar foundations' consisting of six circular foundations placed around a square foundation. But it was not yet possible to say whether these had belonged to hexagonal pavilions or some other type of building.

This was a body of water. Its southern end seemed to connect to a channel running almost perpendicularly, which itself was blocked by a bank of broken bricks and tiles decorated with large lotus petals. At its northern end, the eastern verge was built with large stones, tapering off gradually with various layers of waste dating from various periods. The body of water had survived as a small gutter of the Nguyễn period. It then disappeared. We started to visualise the existence of an attractive crescent-shaped lake there. But from which period? It probably dated from the Lý period and had gradually filled in since the late Trần period.

Evidence from the different layers indicated that from the late Lê period, no lakes, trees, or fish remained here at all.

* * *

Was that all? No, a store of unexpected things lay under the lake's bed, in much the same way as those who followed the legendary Dragon King came across countless royal palaces lying under the bed of the sea. We continued digging deeper, leaving a narrow border to mark the eastern edge. The first unexpected event was the appearance of a row of pillar foundations made of a mixture of rammed gravel and clay. They lay on the same line as similar pillar foundations found in the higher layer on both the eastern and western verges, but were much 'thinner'. Had they been damaged or were they the foundations of pillars supporting a water palace? Under the muddy layer, we found fragments of dark grey yin-yang or tubular tiles. These bore clear traces of cross-hatching patterns from printing with coarse cloth and strangely decorated animal heads with glowering eyes and sticking-out tongues, while the tile edges were decorated with serrated bands or waves. These artefacts were identified as dating from the Đại La period.

Cautiously, we continued scraping off the muddy layer. The area was scattered with broken red bricks and tiles, clods of yellow and white clay; these were meticulously removed. Our sharp scrapers cleaned the lake bottom's surface. As we worked, a large reddish-brown solid area appeared before us, with the green spots of a raised foundation made of grey alluvial clay. Here and there we found square holes filled with dark grey broken bricks and tiles mixed with ash and clay, all tightly rammed. Sections of squared wooden beams lay deep within or under those holes. They reminded us of trench D6, with its wooden beams arranged in pigsty manner on a layer strengthened by broken grey bricks and tiles. They also resembled the timbers wedged under the pillars in the Đại La-period cultural layer at B17. These discoveries convinced us that this had been a great monument. Its appearance and size remained a mystery.

A River's Mystery

We extended the area of trenches D4, D5 and D6 in all four directions. Our knowledge of the crescent lake between D5 and D6 made it easy to identify sections of its sloping verge. The verge had been rammed and strewn with broken bricks and tiles or tiny pieces of gravel; at some points, we found patches of yellow sand and white gravel. The hard part was dealing with the layer of mud, the water, and the vast quantities of bricks and tiles that had to be dealt with before we could recognise holes, sections of the verge, and ancient water channels. Large bricks, countless ceramic fragments, and pieces of stoneware from the Lê period had accumulated in a metre-thick mass at the southeast corner of D4.

Then, under the layer of dark grey mud south of D5, a straight line appeared, separating the yellow clay to the north from a layer of earth mixed with dark grit to the south. We followed its edge and realised the layer of earth and dark grit was veering to the south. Broken bricks, tiles and potsherds lay over it. A concave area on the southern wall of trench D5 was clearly visible. It then blurred as it extended towards the east and west (D4 and D6 trenches). What could it be? The question occupied my thoughts until we started digging again to the south.

Our patience and confidence had increased by this point, even though the ruins were as chaotic as during the first days of the excavation. We were no longer so pressed for time. There were fewer workers and they were now used to the work. It was a cool and dry autumn, the ideal season for excavation in Vietnam's northern region. We sunk a deep ditch between the trenches and placed plastic pipes underground to evacuate the artesian water that leaked constantly from the trench walls; soon the muddy layers were drained and the hole's surface was dry, enabling us to work with greater care.

As soon as we had removed a layer of earth, a verge full of tiny broken bricks and tiles appeared meandering in an east–west direction through all three trenches. To my surprise, the hollow muddy area lay to the north of this verge. This might be the remains of a dried-up canal. Our measurement of the western and eastern trench walls suggested that it had been about 3 m–4 m wide. Numerous artefacts were scattered there: bronze coins from the Hồng Đức period, a stone bullet, and fragments of blue and white Lê- and Nguyễn-period ceramics. On the muddy layer, there was a deposit of leaves and branches from trees that commonly grow in marshy areas and along the banks of water courses. They had hollow trunks and broad leaves. There were also some thorny bamboo stems and very thin bamboo leaves. The characteristics of this layer of leaves resembled those of a layer in trench D2, opposite D4N, across the road to the east.

Carefully we removed the layers of decayed leaves. Then we took out the grey mud. A dense band of potsherds appeared and extended towards the south verge, much like the one we had found in the riverbed between Sections A and B. This really had been a 'river'! Then, suddenly, we seemed lost in a bed of treasure: countless varieties of terracotta jars, pots and vessels of many different sizes, high-footed cups, jars decorated with areca branch images, bowls, dishes, vases and bottles decorated with blue and white designs, brown or white glazes, and designs raised in relief or set under glaze. There were the dark fragments of terracotta pots and stones in great quantities.

We had found the river's north bank. Now we wondered: where was its south bank? It might extend far into the area of a present-day terrace of one-storey houses near the Ba Đình National Assembly Building, as we realised from the cross-section of verge we had cut. Later, we came to a better understanding of this 'ceramics river'. On 15 October 2003, we removed and delivered over 120 buckets of artefacts to the on-site store-house for cleaning and temporary storage. The thick, muddy layer at the bottom had yielded a plethora of diverse items: a conical hat made of palm-leaf, a long-handled bucket plaited with splints and rimmed with rattans, timbers with multiple mortises, and so on. Exposing the shapes of these tiny, apparently humble things that had lain in mud for hundreds of years required all our care and patience. Unfortunately, after taking them from the ground, we did not have adequate facilities for their con-servation. All that remain of them are the photographs we took. Above all, many of the terracotta items, jars, pots and pebbles contradicted the way we had imagined life in the royal palaces. And it is likely that many more mysteries lie down there in the river bed.

As we dug down, the muddy layer gradually became smaller. Over by the south wall it finally disappeared. We exposed further sections of verge in trenches D5N and D6N, which were full of broken bricks in some places and yellow sand in others. How wide was the river? How deep was its deepest layer? At that point, nobody could say. Unexpected things were appearing under our scrapers every day.

We removed ceramic and earthenware objects and the second muddy layer. This lay under the layer of ceramics and earthenware; the first muddy layer was above it. We then found a roughly cut stone plinth of indeterminate shape. The interesting thing about it was that it lay along the same line as four other stone plinths of the same type: the distance between each was 5 m. The line sloped down in an east–west direction, from D4 through D5N and D6N, as though it was 'diving down to the river bed'. Furthermore, over to the west of D5N and D6N, we unearthed timbers that overlapped vertically and horizontally, beside a sunk foundation of large grey bricks that, from their arrangement, we dated to the Đại La period. Meanwhile, to the east (trench D4N), thick masses of ashes appeared next to a brick ditch, not far from an area of friable grey soil. On the trench wall, conical holes of black earth contrasted with patches of brown alluvial soil as solid as pieces of meat pie. All these phenomena bearing so much data completely bewildered us. We made assumptions, discussed them, and then changed them. The past was gradually appearing before us. Some things were clear, others remained obscure.

3. THE UPS AND DOWNS OF ARCHITECTURAL MONUMENTS

Settlers of the River Plains

Who first set foot on this fertile alluvial soil? What houses did they inhabit? Those coarse potsherds with their cord beaten designs and flared or curved mouths suggested a relation with the Đường Cồ ceramics site, a late site of Đông Sơn Culture. But these mysteries remain hidden under the foundations of the ruined palaces.

The Architecture of Đại La Citadel

The crescent lake covered a relatively large area of land, and it was through this land that we dug down to verify the sterile layer. At both ends of the lake, to the north and south, the tops of two small wooden posts became visible. We thought they might be part of a row of wooden pillars. How far were they apart? We dug down to check and stretched a rope to mark the line, assuming a set number of pillars and a set distance between them. We found traces of a third hole used for strengthening a pillar. Then at the bottom of the trenches, we dug small pits where we expected to find the pillars (the excavated areas had to be narrowed to the maximum, to avoid underground water that could undermine and destabilise the architectural foundations above).

Finally, a row of five pillar holes emerged, 4 m apart and aligned north–south. Some of the pillars were still in place, some had been lost. Each had been fixed deeply in the square hole of its base. They passed through a layer of alluvium and a layer of grey clay, and were supported underneath by small pieces of wood and broken bricks. Near the top of the foundation the pillars were packed around with broken bricks.

The holes contained soil mixed with grey clay and a smaller quantity of broken bricks and tiles. Judging from the quantities of grey yin-yang tiles found there, we thought that these had been used on this building's roof. However, the building's scale remains concealed deep below the reddish-brown alluvial layer.

Rich architectural traces of the Đại La period had been found in Sections A and B, so we were not surprised by the presence of these broken grey tiles and bricks. The square holes, however, were large (measuring nearly 1 m wide and 90 cm deep) and filled with grey tiles, ash and grey clay: this puzzled us a great deal. We pondered over this technique for reinforcing the feet of pillars. It was completely different from the architecture we had found in the layers above.

We found six such holes under the crescent lake (at a depth of about 2.7 m–2.9 m). Four were arranged in a standard square formation, 2.5 m apart along their east–west axis and 2.2 m apart along their north–south axis, measured from the centre of each hole. The other two holes were located as a pair, at a distance of 8 m north of the group of four. Short sections of timber found lying across the surface, inside or at the bottom of the holes demonstrated the technique used in this swampy area to prevent the pillars from subsiding. Traces of similar holes continued to appear to the south, in D5N and D6N. Wooden pillars may have stood on them. How big and how tall were they? What did their frame structures look like? They may have belonged to a great building, perhaps a palace. Within such a complicated architectural composition, there must have been main pillars with subordinate pillars at the corners.

We found yin-yang tiles piled up in great quantities at the southeast corner of D6; many other relatively large tiles were scattered near the pillar holes. The strange style of the roof edge decoration suggests that the roof structure must have been bulky. We found odd-looking animal-head images around the site but could not identify which part of the roof they had decorated.

Broken dark grey bricks decorated with big lotus petals had been placed on a raised foundation consisting of a tightly rammed mixture of grey clay and reddish-brown alluvial soil. The exposed foundation covered an area measuring more than 18 m long and 16 m wide. Possibly over 0.5 m thick, it still lies under the lakebed. At one of those pillar holes, we found a set of monkey bones. Why were they there? Had they been left accidentally? Or was this evidence of some ancient ritual of which we know nothing today?

The multitude of details that continued to appear across a large area and at different depths testified to the complicated and highly diverse features of the architecture. In particular, there were a number of coins marked *Khai Nguyên Thông Bảo* (see below). This marking gives an indication of their date: late seventh to mid-ninth centuries. Did they belong to the Đại La-period monuments built by Gao Pian?

Heirs to Đại La Citadel

Next to a pillar hole in the deepest architectural layer, we found a unique terracotta pot. Our experts dated it to the tenth century. It lay in an area of yellow clay scattered with reddish-brown alluvial soil. There were many such areas of clay scattered around, lying deep in the alluvial layer. They resembled that type of pillar foundation made of earth rammed into conical holes in which roughly trimmed pillar plinths had been half buried. Both ends of this row of plinths disappeared, one under the raised foundation made of yellow clay to the east (trench D4), the other under the river of ceramics to the west (trench D6N). This structure's foundation had not been as 'fortunate' as buildings of the Đại La period: it had been demolished when the river and lake were created, although a few traces remained in the raised foundations of the Lý- and Trần-period palaces in the east and central areas of trench D5. Only five plinths were discovered before the excavation was suspended, but these were enough to allow us to visualise a building of monumental scale.

It was difficult to identify the tiles used on its roof. We did find exotic broken tiles, black in colour and made of similar material to the glazed tiles typical of the Lý and Trần periods. They looked like grey yin-yang tiles, apart from their unique decorative style, found nowhere else. Several pairs of plump terracotta loving ducks resembled the ducks found at the royal capital at Hoa Lư. Were they used to decorate this architectural complex? If not, what did they decorate? Who created them? These questions are impossible to answer, but we believe they date from late tenth to early eleventh centuries, precisely the period during which the Lý dynasty relocated the capital to Thăng Long.

Traces of Dazzling Palaces

Visitors to the site would find it hard to believe that traces of golden palaces lay in this vast muddy expanse dotted with black-earth holes full of ash and wreckage. But much of trench D5 and parts of D4 and D6 were occupied by the raised clay foundations of large buildings. These buildings may have been expanded and extended in successive periods. Differences in the clay used during each period and the rows of pillar foundations supporting plinths testify to multiple changes to the architectural structures found in the upper layer. Many different styles and scales were adopted for these buildings.

Because they remained relatively intact and easily distinguishable amid the chaos of the other ruins, we recognised the pillar foundations first: cube-like shapes of fresh yellow clay, decreasing in size as we dug down. Their layer contained the same type of yellow clay spotted with brown soil mixed with alluvial earth. How had they been built? After thorough study, we found that thin wooden planks (about 20 cm wide) had been attached to form square frames placed in holes dug through the brown alluvial soil. Sticky clay was mixed with a certain proportion of gravel: the frame was filled with this mixture which was then firmly pounded. At the same time, the surrounding foundation was gradually raised. Gaps between the pillar foundations made of gravel and the raised foundation of the building itself were closed with a lining of tightly rammed pure clay (about 20 cm thick). This ensured that the pillar foundations could not absorb water from the raised foundation. Seven rows of five pillar foundations were found, aligned east–west. Each pillar foundation was 2.5 m–2.8 m from the next, the rows were 5 m apart and the raised foundation covered an area of about 480 m², lying at a depth of 1 m below the modern ground surface. The interesting thing was that the different altitudes of the pillar foundations and the raised foundation surrounding them suggested they belonged to a palace complex with foundations at various levels or an architectural complex with many parts, all closely related to the nearby lake and water courses.

What about the frame and walls of this palace complex? There is no possible evidence for any particular assumption. Plinths found nearby and the system of pillars do, however, allow us to imagine that the building was made of wooden frames and pillars placed on stone plinths inscribed with lotus images. And the palace roof? It is difficult to make an accurate drawing. There remain only two sides of the building: at their longest axis, about 17 m of remains still exist, of which several pillar foundations made of gravel had been destroyed.

As for the sunk foundation, many kinds of materials were used in its construction. Apart from the burnt walls of kilns, fragments of ceramics and terracotta items, we found countless broken bricks and tiles. These were either plain or decorated with lotus and chrysanthemum designs;

there were also pieces of tubular and flat tiles and roof tiles, red and unglazed or bearing a yellow, white or green glaze. We also found fragments of tile-ends decorated with dragons, phoenixes and lotuses, and fragments of stone decorated with the image of a dragon with a round body and the fins of a fish. Under the tunnel-shaped bottom of this foundation, we discovered a thin piece of gold decorated with a dragon in the style of the Lý period.

Any assumption made about the roof structure needs to be proved by putting all the broken pieces together and comparing the information obtained. Judging from the discovered fragments, this palace complex must have been decorated with stone banisters carved in the form of dragons, splendid wooden balustrades covered with lacquered crimson and coloured frescos painted on stone.

The magnificent palaces collapsed. Broken, burnt and blistered glazed tiles were found among the fragments lying at the bottom of the crescent lake. Was it a simple fire, a raid by Champa, or some other event that caused the monuments to burn down? They were later rebuilt, possibly on a larger scale. Their clay foundations were extended to the north and raised with reddish-brown clay spotted with tiny laterite grains, which may have been brought in from afar. Broken bricks, tiles and potsherds were used to raise the foundation, which was then covered with a layer of fine clay (about 10 cm–15 cm thick). The surface was then pounded with small wooden hammers; liquid ash was used to prevent the clay from sticking. The layout and size of the compartments changed, ascertained through the study of the network of pillar plinth foundations, mainly built with broken fragments of terracotta.

These pillar foundations differed from those built with gravel. Terracotta items were broken into tiny pieces and used to fill the foundation, layer by layer. Each was about 3 cm thick and alternated with a similarly thick layer of clay. We cannot estimate the size of this building, as these pillar foundations built of terracotta fragments disappear in the north area of the site, under the swimming pool of the Ba Đình Sports Club. But we can see the main difference between the pillar foundations made of terracotta and those made of gravel: the terracotta ones appear in pairs. These foundations may have had a red upper surface, with a top decorated with beautifully inscribed bodhi leaves, dragons and phoenixes. Great dragon or phoenix heads were depicted in a strong and well-ventilated style. The decorated buildings were connected by covered walkways or paths along the banks of the lake, laid with bricks and tiles decorated with four-petal flower designs (lemon flowers).

A terrible disaster may have befallen the monuments built with terra-cotta pillar foundations. To the northwest of trench D4B, near a section of road laid with bricks arranged in lemon flower shapes, we discovered a large heap of broken bricks and tiles covered with ashes. They may have been pushed into this corner when the collapsed monuments were rebuilt. Layers of ash covered one of the ruined pillar foundations made of broken terracotta. Nearby, a large celadon vase in the shape of a blossoming daisy was found buried in the mass of broken bricks and tiles. The vase was full of fine soil mixed with ash. We no longer know what the vase was used for. So many transformations took place during the history of Đại Việt: when the Trần-dynasty king and his entourage returned after victory over the Yuan dynasty invaders from the north, they had to stay at the Guards' barracks because the palaces had been burnt down by the enemy. Later, the armies of Champa brought looting and destruction. Was this ash covering the vast quantities of broken bricks and tiles evidence of such an event? We are not yet able to answer this question.

During the Early Lê period, construction may have continued in this corner of Thăng Long citadel. The architectural foundations may have been raised once again. The broken bricks, tiles and ash were levelled and covered with greyish-yellow clay to raise new foundations for new buildings. Great architectural complexes, built on similar scales to the past, were roofed with lotus-shaped tiles and decorated with bodhi leaves, while roof edges were inscribed with dragon images. But the dragons and phoenixes were no longer meticulously carved. Their bulky images appeared on irregular bodhi leaves set along the ridge of the roof. They appeared crudely carved on the bodhi leaves attached to lotus-shape-ended tiles placed along the edge of the roof. Their construction dates are impossible to identify, although we may learn something from the ceramic fragments.

Lost in Oblivion

The golden splendour of this area gradually vanished, perhaps from the middle of the Lê period. Architectural monuments continued to be built and continued to collapse. Time passed. The tile-ends became gradually thinner, the brick road became gradually patchier. Pillar foundations appeared simpler and smaller and the compartments were becoming more humble. Then, at a much later date, this corner of the citadel was deserted and forgotten. Thăng Long citadel was downsized. During the

Nguyễn period, only the area within the Hanoi Citadel's four walls remained in use.

4. STORIES FROM THE KITCHEN WASTE DUMPS

We believe that the first people on this land farmed fields or gardens. Evidence for this appeared rarely in the excavated trenches. In the area of dark earth mixed with ash, we found the intact seeds of plant varieties such as pumpkin, melon, bitter melon and peach. In the light-coloured kitchen ash, possibly formed after the burning of straw, we found numerous darkly burnt ceramic pots. Who made them? Study of the artefacts collected from these cooking areas and rubbish dumps may offer a few clues.

During the Đại La period, when people lived in houses roofed with grey tiles, they used several types of tableware: bowls with a celadon glaze that ran in drops, shiny black-glazed dishes, and coarse ceramic plates with heavy bottoms and a very thin glaze. Large shallow bowls with sloping walls and a dark grey colour of the Việt Châu ceramics type were very common. The more luxurious items included ceramic jars with four crossed handles and a thin glaze layer. There were even the famous Tang-period coloured ceramics. Terracotta jars were more commonly used. Two kitchen areas were found, one to the north and the other to the south of the groups of architectural foundations made of brown soil mixed with grey clay. Their relationship to those buildings is unknown, except for the fact that they were of the same period. The northern kitchen area included a thick layer of ash concentrated in an area of several square metres. We found many broken bones there, including a jaw intact with its teeth. The southern kitchen area was located outside the area of brown soil, possibly in a small building. Grey bricks were arranged around a fireplace and its ash. Broken bowls, dishes and animal bones were found.

Evidence of food included the meat of animals and seafood, mainly snails with very thin shells and shiny brown backs, although other types of sea mollusc (cockles and clams) were also in evidence. Their shells had been dumped in a pile in small holes dug under the foundation, along with broken ceramic pieces. A unique 'toilet' consisted of a round hole containing ashes and tree branches cut into pieces. We found ivory dice marked with black holes. Did people entertain each other with games? Who did all these objects belong to?

At least 47 coins bearing the words *Khai Nguyên Thông Bảo* (開元通寶) were found in these kitchen areas and rubbish holes. Their size, appearance and other features indicate that they were of different types and cast at different times. Several large, beautifully cast coins were also found, with finely inscribed characters and a crescent or star figure on one face. These are comparable to coins cast during the reign of the seventh-century Tang-dynasty emperor Gaozong. The smaller coins show that, with the exception of some officially cast coins, many were imperfectly cast: their edges were uneven, and they wore out after long periods in circulation. One coin bore the character *Đàm* (潭), of the *Hội Xương Khai Nguyên Thông Bảo* (会昌開元通寶) type first cast in 845 during the reign of the Tang emperor Wuzong. The characters *Đàm* (潭), *Kinh* (京), *Việt* (越), and *Hồng* (洪) on coins often indicate place names. Can we associate them with the court officials of the Tang period, those who built and rebuilt Đại La citadel so many times? Can we say that these wooden pillars and ash-filled holes supported some of the houses built by Gao Pian in 866?

One of the most 'clearly exposed' of these rubbish holes was found towards the end of a sunk foundation, where it descended steeply towards the bottom of the crescent lake. It contained ash, animal bones, innumerable calcified seashells, terracotta vessels, glazed potsherds, broken bricks and tiles, tiles with a greyish-white glaze, and so on. The presence of terracotta wares and ceramics, especially brown-inlaid items, and the absence of blue and white ceramics lead us to conclude that this was a hole left by inhabitants of the Trần period. Cockles and clams with 20 cm shells were their preferred food. The bones of large animals seem to reflect their energetic characteristics, evident too in the designs on their favourite brown-inlaid ceramics.

Iron tools—chisels, boat nails, hoe blades perhaps, hairpins, fish-hooks, and many bronze arrows with lozenge shaped cross sections and short tails—were scattered among the dark-earth holes that remained to be fully exposed. Their stories are discernible as through a half-lit screen; the pages of their history still lie under the foundations of later palaces.

5. PORTRAYING A BRILLIANT PERIOD OF THE PAST

King Lý Thái Tổ relocated the capital from Hoa Lư to Thăng Long in 1010. That very year, he built palaces worthy of an independent nation in control of its destiny. During the reign of King Lý Thánh Tông, these were modified to become the palaces of the Imperial Citadel; in 1057, many great pagodas and temples were built within and around the citadel ramparts. Verses inscribed on steles placed at the pagodas built during this period describe the grace and splendour of those pagodas. We cannot visualise how the Lý-period palaces were built, but these inscribed descriptions somehow help us make the link with the broken items scattered around this corner of the capital's citadel, in the area of trenches D4, D5 and D6.

During the Lý period, between trenches D4 and D5, a splendid palace was raised and roofed with green- or yellow-glazed tiles covering an area of about 480 m². Its foundation was covered with square bricks bearing sophisticated daisy designs, engraved with a large daisy in the middle, four other daisies in the circle enclosing the large daisy, and gentle sprays at the corners. South of this building, a 2 m wide walkway ran beside a water channel. Its foundation was covered with plain square bricks and it gave access to the water where boat travel was possible to other palaces further east. People also reached this palace along another walkway further north, up a staircase with its stone-sculpted dragons, their fleshy bodies covered with small fish-like scales, on either side. To the east, a walkway connected the palace to a small garden with exotic flowers and grasses. Along this walkway, it was possible to reach other palaces to the northeast. Over to the west, a row of walkways of the 'floating pavilion' type stood in the water of an attractive crescent-shaped lake connected to a channel to the south and possibly another lake to the northwest. Balustrades decorated with crimson lacquer, sophisticated dragons engraved on terracotta, and the polished green glaze of the roof rendered these palaces magnificent. Other sumptuous palaces could be reached to the west.

6. HOPES FOR THE FUTURE

In March 2004, the Management Board ordered us to stop excavating. We urgently wanted to complete the work in progress. At the same time, we were puzzled, unable to decide upon the best treatment for the dark-earth holes or the clusters of artefacts we were finding. If they were filled in with sand, would the organic matter be safely preserved until our return? If we removed them for conservation in the storehouse, more artefacts, and more of the phenomena that lay under them, would then appear under our scrapers; we would have been unable to cope with the quantities unearthed. Right up to the day the site actually closed, we kept asking for a few more days of work. We walked between the gravel bases, the piles of bricks, the dark-earth holes, trying to note down what we had seen, watching in melancholy as workers poured sand into trenches, covering over the exposed traces.

The excavation stopped at the point where the basic layers of a very small area of Thăng Long's ancient citadel had been uncovered. Test ditches had been dug to study the site's cultural layers and other architectural features. The area of trenches D4, D5 and D6 most clearly revealed all three of the site's cultural periods: Đại La (seventh to ninth centuries), pre-Lý to Lý and Trần (tenth to fourteenth centuries), Lê and Nguyễn (fifteenth to nineteenth centuries). They indicate the existence of at least seven stages of major construction work. They contain traces of human life through all those periods, providing data in greater abundance and detail than given by any of the historical records of Đại La and Thăng Long.

The information gathered, while insufficient for many purposes, clearly shows that the site is of immeasurable value not only for scholars but also for the Vietnamese nation and mankind. It is evidence of the achievements made by human hands and minds over a period of more than a thousand years of history. As a Japanese scholar remarked: 'everyone who visits the site is left deeply touched'. Many of the Vietnamese who were fortunate enough to visit were moved to tears. Standing among the piles of ruins at the site today, people are truly overwhelmed by this national spirit. This in turn has the potential to awaken a sense of pride and self-confidence in the initiative and creativity of today's generation and the generations of the future. In the overall context of the Thăng Long Imperial Citadel, this is the inestimable value of the site.

However, reaching a full understanding of these pages of history, researchers, especially archaeologists, will need to expend more time and effort. Adequate preparation in terms of time, knowledge and facilities— including the necessary equipment and teams of properly trained professionals who can benefit from other countries' experiences—will be indispensable for future excavations. The selection of excavation methods will be important for the study of each separate architectural unit as well as the entire complex for each period and each stage of construction. Scientific discussions on site and at conferences will enable investigators to work together and look for common solutions. The site's extremely complicated formation requires combinations of excavation and artefact study, excavation and conservation planning, excavation and temporary preservation. It is particularly urgent to deal with vulnerable pieces, such as items in wood, bamboo, rattan, textile fabric, fruit seeds, husks, rice, bones and the remains discovered in the dark-earth holes.

The social life of ancient Thăng Long will be revealed through a combination of research methodologies. This site needs the help of researchers from many fields, as well as laboratory experts, conservators, curators and young archaeologists who have been properly trained and possess a clear scientific orientation and enthusiasm for their work.

Vietnamese people and their overseas friends long for the day they will be able to contemplate the authentic images of this magnificent citadel. In the modern social life of a thousand-year-old capital city, the nation's traditions and cultural identity may be seen with our own eyes, seized with our minds and feelings at the Thăng Long Imperial Citadel site in Ba Đình. If future generations understand the lessons of the past, with all its greatness, hardships and bitterness, people will love each other more and strive to work together for world community.

Note

1. 'Water flows to low places': Vietnamese saying [nước chảy chỗ trũng] meaning 'the rich get richer'.

CHAPTER 3

Discoveries Change Our Understanding of Vietnam's Ancient Architecture

Nguyễn Hồng Kiên

When the excavation of the Thăng Long Imperial Citadel site started at 18 Hoàng Diệu Street, I was working for another organisation doing research on ancient architecture and had yet to join the Institute of Archaeology. The particular conditions of this archaeological excavation project meant that few outsiders were allowed to enter the excavation site. However, the Institute of Archaeology sometimes called me for consultation because of my twenty years of experience in the study of Vietnamese traditional architecture.

I was immediately fascinated by the site. The archaeologists called me because of my expertise; there were nonetheless many occasions on which I was confused by what I saw and found it quite impossible to make a judgment. How many times did I have to confess, 'I have no idea about this', or 'I have never seen the like of it'? In a sense, this was normal because I was used to architectural sites that have survived to the present day: they remain standing firmly on the ground. The remains of Thăng Long Imperial Citadel, however, came from under the ground. Worse still, there were times when my honest confessions were misunderstood: people thought I was 'keeping the secrets of my trade to myself'.

The truth is that working on that excavation was a learning process. It allowed me to increase my knowledge and understanding in multiple ways. Fortunately, I was not busy at my old institute: I worked independently there, so there were no restrictions on my time. I sometimes came to the archaeological site even when I was not called. The experience greatly changed many of my former understandings of Vietnamese architecture and in this short contribution I will try to explain how.

* * *

According to my research into on-the-ground architecture, ancient Vietnamese buildings only had foundations of the 'raised raft' type. Technically speaking, this architecture used a system whereby the building's weight was supported by a frame, a wooden structure with a set of pillars as its main component. The building's heavy weight was distributed across the different pillars. And the pillars' feet were strengthened with stone plinths, which were much broader than the diameter of the pillars they supported. These plinths were then placed on the ground, which was raised higher than the surrounding area to form a raft foundation raised above the level of the ground. At that time, I did not believe that Vietnam's ancient architects understood the use of below-ground foundations.

The results of the excavation at 18 Hoàng Diệu Street opened my eyes. Many of the excavated trenches revealed square holes containing small, tightly rammed pebbles or gravel. At some spots, the pebbles were mixed with broken pieces of brick and tile. During excavation, as the earth surrounding these holes was removed, the pebble holes emerged from the surface of the trench floor; they seemed to be pillars made of pebbles. At first, neither I nor the other researchers were able to explain this phenomenon. Later, through observation and measurement, I found that these square 'pebble pillars' were associated with each other. On the basis of our memory of previous excavation results, we assumed they were the remains of a reinforcing element for stone plinths. This was just an assumption because the distance between the plinths was very great. When asked my opinion, I replied that at existing architectural sites the compartment distance (in other words, the distance between two rows of pillars) never exceeded 5 m.

One day, arriving at the excavation site, I received a phone call from my colleague, the archaeologist Nguyễn Tiến Đông. 'Come at once! In the trench being excavated by my wife, they've exposed stone plinths: they're more than 5 m apart'. I came to Bùi Thu Phương's trench and measured the distance. I was astonished: the distance between the plinths' central points was exactly 5.75 m. Some days later, after removing earth to lower

Fig. 30. A lotus flower motif decorates this Lý-dynasty plinth still standing on its foundation of gravel and brick rubble. Here (Section B), it was built on top of a Lý-dynasty drain. Probably the plinth was re-used here in the construction of a Trần-dynasty palace (Photo: Institute of Archaeology 2003).

the depth of the trench, we uncovered the plinths' bottom section (65 cm × 74 cm). Each lies on a square foundation made of pebbles (130 cm × 130 cm). This evidence, found *in situ*, allowed us to confirm that sunk foundations made of pebbles and broken pieces of brick and tile bases were used for strengthening the bases of pillars. This means that when the Việt people of the Lý period realised that the earth foundation in this area was weak, they dug holes to a depth of at least one metre where the pillars were to be located. Pebbles and broken bricks and tiles were then mixed with clay and rammed tightly into those holes.

Later, excavations conducted by the National Museum of History at Báo Ân Pagoda (Gia Lâm, Hanoi) and Lam Kinh site (Thọ Xuân, Thanh Hóa) increased my understanding of these pillar foundations. Báo Ân Pagoda is located near a river. But even in the mountainous area of Thanh Hóa province, where the earth foundation is relatively stable, we still found holes supporting stone plinths. In the other words, ancient Vietnamese architects did make use of below-ground foundations. In modern construction terms, we should say that these below-ground foundations were local or pad foundations.

As the work proceeded, almost unwittingly I became an informal member of the excavation team. I was involved in the study and evaluation of the excavation's results, and also in the struggle to protect the heritage it unearthed. Day by day—along with the project's director, archaeologist Tống Trung Tín—I carried a projector to show the results in many places. We made presentations at the Academy of Social Sciences, the History Association, the Union of Science and Technology, the Ministry of Culture and Information, the Ministry of Science and Technology, the Vietnam Communist Party's Central Department of Science and Education, and we reported to the Government and the President.

I call this a 'struggle' because at that time there were two opposing set of standpoints. One group urged the archaeologists to take anything they needed from the ground and then return the land as soon as possible to the new National Assembly and Ba Đình Convention Centre Project. The other group wanted to preserve and maintain the newly excavated area for future generations. Those who preferred to proceed with construction stressed the significance and necessity of planning the nation's political centre in the Ba Đình area. According to their calculations, preservation would be very costly; they also argued that given Vietnam's scientific and technological capacity at the time, preservation was not feasible. Those who wanted to maintain and preserve the site underlined its unique character; they argued that with all the wealth you can imagine, it is impossible to re-create a historical site.

The crucial basis for a proper decision was an assessment of the site's value. National and international conferences and workshops were held in the fields of archaeology, architecture and construction, as well as across the disciplines. Leading experts from many countries attended. At these conferences, almost all the Vietnamese and international experts expressed their very high regard for the excavation results.

Nevertheless, some people doubted these opinions and questioned the scale and dimensions of the architectural remains. At a conference held at the Institute of Architectural Studies, a professor of architecture even joked that several special species of tree must have existed in ancient times and can no longer be found today; otherwise, he asked, how was it possible to source such huge trunks of wood, long enough for the compartment distance to reach nearly 6 m? On that day, speaking to the architects on behalf of the archaeologists, I had to stress that scientists should keep up to date and accept new knowledge when they did scientific research. I also quoted the results of previous research into ancient Vietnamese architecture.

The largest monument from the late nineteenth to early twentieth centuries that survives to the present day is the Phát Diệm cathedral complex (Ninh Bình). The cathedral's main sanctuary has a compartment distance of 5.8 m–6.4 m. The distance between the main pillars (the largest pair of internal pillars is 12.4 m high) is 6.4 m; the distance between the main pillars and the secondary pillars (6.5 m high) is 3.2 m; and the distance between the secondary pillars and the veranda pillars (5 m high) is 2.6 m. The second example is Thầy Pagoda (Quốc Oai, Hà Tây). In the main sanctuary of this seventeenth-century pagoda, the distance between the main pillars is also 6.0 m. The third example is the excavation at Lạng Pagoda (Văn Lâm, Hưng Yên). At this site, an excavation conducted in 1973 revealed a compartment distance of 5.2 m and 6 m in the remains of an architectural layer dating from 1582 (Mạc dynasty). It seems that the archaeologists running that excavation did not believe that such large-scale architecture could exist at that time, so in their analysis they divided the building into two parts. However, I do believe in such architecture and will prove it is the remains of a single architectural work.

My frankness about our need to rectify old understandings had a number of troublesome consequences. In particular, the architectural community resented the fact that one of its people disagreed with its way of thinking. No longer wishing to work for my old institute, I applied for a job with the journal of Vietnam's Association of Architecture, *Kiến Trúc* (Architecture). My application, which had a strong chance of success, was ultimately turned down. This was my way of discovering that human beings find it difficult to accept change. The struggle to protect the heritage ended when the Prime Minister decided to preserve the excavated area of Thăng Long Imperial Citadel at 18 Hoàng Diệu Street. Many people who had previously opposed the site's conservation now tell each other stories and express their appreciation of the site. We, the archaeologists, look at each other and smile: this was the result we had long hoped for.

CHAPTER 4

Interpreting the Cultural Layers

Nguyễn Văn Anh

The discovery of Thăng Long Imperial Citadel provides archaeological evidence to improve our understanding of the process of formation and development of Thăng Long–Đông Đô–Hanoi. This is also the first time that international archaeologists have been able to study the Imperial Citadel. They all agree that the thick cultural strata reflecting the site's interrupted development over a period of 1,300 years is the outstanding characteristic of the site. This makes comparison possible with the world's other great imperial cities with long histories. Their judgment has underlined the site's value, which was first identified by the archaeologists directly involved in the excavation and research. By reopening the diaries of the excavated trenches, we can read the scientific assessment made of each cultural layer as it was discovered. As at other sites, each layer of earth that archaeologists call a 'stratum' contained important pieces of information.

Cultural layers are archives of information. Each layer may be likened to a page recording the formation and development of an area of ground and the life of the inhabitants who lived there. The book, however, is fragile. Rather like the book of an individual life, it can only be read once. The moment you open one archaeological 'page' is the moment you do away with the previous page. For this reason, the phenomena found at each layer are always examined with intense interest. The Thăng Long Imperial Citadel site is no exception to this general rule.

In terms of stratigraphy, three main cultural layers were found at the site. With a number of exceptions, all the excavated trenches shared the same features. The first layer was made up of brown or greyish-brown earth mixed with broken bricks, tiles and the potsherds of blue and white ceramics. These remains served as a sort of database allowing the archaeologists to identify this layer as reflecting inhabitation during the Lê period. The next layer contained reddish-yellow clay with grains of laterite. Here, dense architectural traces included palace foundations, roads and drainage ditches. These enabled us to visualise the magnificent Dragon Phoenix (Long Phượng) Citadel, dating from the Lý and Trần periods. The final layer, at an average depth of over 3 m, contained brown or reddish-brown earth mixed with ash and partially decayed flora. Diverse artefacts were unearthed, but the most numerous were tubular tiles—with one end decorated with the face of a clown or the petals of a lotus flower—and broken curved grey tiles.

The second of these cultural layers has attracted the most interest. This is not only because of the architectural traces and fine artefacts it contains but also for the reddish-brown colour of the clay found there. The same clay layer was found at previously excavated Imperial Citadel sites, such as Đoan Môn Gate (1999) and the Rear Palace (1998). At that time, it was identified as a cultural layer. This type of clay layer appeared very regularly in the trenches at the 18 Hoàng Diệu Street site and raised a number of particularly interesting questions, as outlined below.

Geologists note that Hanoi's geological formation was a long and complicated process, closely linked to the formation of the Red River Delta in Vietnam's northern region. Some tens of millions of years ago, Hanoi formed a sort of hollow: the geologists call the area 'the Hanoi hollow' or 'the Hanoi frying pan'. It was several dozen metres deeper than it is today and gradually filled up with various materials from its surroundings. After the Flandrian marine transgression reached the maximum level 5,000–6,000 years ago, the sea gradually went out and the Hanoi area and its surroundings became a landscape of lakes and marshes under the influence of the tides. The further the sea withdrew, the further the Red River extended. Today, it still carries and deposits silt to form fertile new land, excellent for agriculture. However, this is not the whole story. The river's 'angry' moods divided the plain it had just formed. These left high tongues of land along the river and oxbow lakes, as may still be seen today. It was at this time that the first humans settled and exploited this fertile land, as indicated in the Metal Age archaeological evidence dating from more than two thousand years ago.

The settlement layer of the first humans in Hanoi is thus the land formed by the Red River's alluvial deposits. At a depth of 4 m under the lowest cultural layer of the Thăng Long site, the excavation consistently revealed a reddish-brown alluvial layer, with a relatively high content of fine sand. In archaeological terminology, this is called the sterile layer.

The questions that puzzled us were the following: Why, in the second cultural layer with its yellow earth, did we keep finding a rich seam of laterite covering the third cultural layer, known to archaeologists as the pre-Thăng Long layer? Had there possibly been a geological incident? Was Hanoi and the Imperial Citadel afterwards covered with the reddish-brown layer of clay? In fact, there was no such geological incident. Even the most romantic archaeologist should never ask such a question. So, what then was the reason?

In the rapid process of Hanoi's urbanisation, small villages and rice fields on the city's outskirts are gradually being replaced by tall buildings and modern blocks of flats. Those locations have been levelled for the purpose of construction and the ground level has been raised. Fifteen-tonne trucks have transported soil from Sơn Tây and Xuân Mai along the Láng–Hòa Lạc Highway (Highway 32) to fill fields, lakes and ponds and raise the foundations for the new urban area.

This reminded me of a story Nguyễn Tiến Đông told us of construction work carried out during 1970s–1980s at the Thượng Đình industrial zone and the Thanh Xuân area of apartment blocks. At that time, the fields at Mễ Trì were filled in to prepare for building at Thanh Xuân. The infill was a reddish-brown clay with multi-grained laterite collected from Xuân Mai in Hòa Bình province. Green fields of rice and vegetables gave way to that reddish-brown clay. Then the local people stopped calling these long familiar fields by their old names. Instead, they used a completely new name: Red Clay Fields. The thought suddenly occurred to us: What if, several hundreds of years from now, experts in the discipline of industrial archaeology were to conduct an excavation here? They would certainly find the same phenomenon as we had found at Thăng Long Imperial Citadel: a layer of fine reddish-brown clay covering the previous settlement layers.

It seems that the reddish-brown clay that lies several metres thick over the pre-Thăng Long layer must be a layer of raised foundation. We may envision the following scenario. In 1010, Lý Công Uẩn moved the capital to Đại La, where he chose the central area of Prince Gao Pian's former citadel to site his palaces and temples. But he did not only build new palaces: he built them on foundations raised with clay. We may be sure that this clay did not originate from the Imperial Citadel. Archaeologists supposed that it was collected from the hills of the middle region around Hanoi. This, however, was no more than an assumption; scientific evidence is still required and that means geology. Professor Nguyễn Địch Dĩ and his colleagues from the Institute of Geology were invited to test the archaeologists' hypothesis. The managers of the excavation asked them to identify the provenance of the clay.

For this it was first necessary to study the chemical and physical properties of each type of earth at the site. The geologists and archaeologists collected clay samples from the different cultural layers. Trenches A4, A5 and B3 were chosen for the samples. The results of analysis of the second cultural layer showed that it did indeed contain the same clay type as may be found in the hills of the middle region. It also contained spotted clay originating from marine clay. As the bird flies, Hanoi is hundreds of kilometres from the sea. Why did we find this type of sea clay at this site? As mentioned above, Hanoi once formed a gulf of the sea and, when descending to a depth of 5 m, we found a layer of spotted clay. The clay in the cultural layer is the same clay as we found in the sterile layer.

The phenomenon we observed is actually very common in the northern delta: long ago, the practice of building on clay dug up from the surrounding area became traditional—part of the way people react to their natural environment—especially in the wet lowland areas. These areas of the delta were subject to flooding in the rainy season, as the river did not drain the water quickly. Living in this wet environment, the inhabitants of the Red River basin reacted, on the basis of experience, to the natural conditions. They invented the practice of *đào ao vượt thổ*: digging ponds to collect clay for raising the foundations of their houses. In so doing, they protected their houses from flooding and made ponds to raise fish for their family. The pond was also used for daily activities, such as washing, cleaning and for drainage when it rained.

In their descriptions of the northern plain's inhabitants, seventeenth-century Western visitors recorded their surprise at the Việt people's subtle capacity of adaption to their living environment. Moreover, the technique under discussion was not new, even in eleventh and twelfth centuries: it had been developed many centuries before. In their excavation at Luy Lâu—the political centre of Giao Chỉ in the second to the fifth or sixth centuries—archaeologists encountered the same practice as at the Imperial Citadel. The layer of raised foundations there is nearly 1 m thick.

This ancient tradition may also be found at the stone cathedral of Phát Diệm (Ninh Bình), where the practice of digging ponds to collect clay was applied with great flexibility to create the landscape for an architectural complex. The cathedral was built on land reclaimed from the sea.

To raise the area's ground level, the engineer decided to dig a pond in front of the building. This created the desired landscape (in line with East Asian fengshui cosmology). All the earth dug from the pond was used, of course, to raise the foundation for construction.

* * *

Let us return now to Thăng Long Imperial Citadel. The architectural vestiges, including palace foundations, roads, drainage ditches, and so on, demonstrate that the citadel had been scientifically planned and that natural features, such as trees, lakes, and ponds, were integrated into the architectural design. Some lakes were originally either natural or semi-natural, but many others were completely manmade. We had no difficulty discerning that ponds and lakes were dug and the clay that was removed was used to raise the surrounding areas. Raising the ground for construction required a large amount of earth, much of which had to be brought in from other places. Where was it brought from? How was it transported? These questions remained unanswered. The archaeologists reminded the geologists that in ancient times Vietnamese transported goods mainly by water. The hill clay at Thăng Long must have come from somewhere by water. The geologists agreed.

In November 2004, when the cold wind started blowing, the geologists conducted their first exploration. The first direction they looked was southwest of Hanoi, in an area close to the Đáy and Nhuệ Rivers in the districts of Từ Liêm, Quốc Oai, Đan Phượng, Thạch Thất and Phúc Thọ. I was fortunate enough to be invited to join the survey. The field survey and the holes dug for samples taught me a great deal of geology and helped me understand the geological data. At Quốc Oai district, we surveyed the left bank of the Đáy River collecting samples of hill clay. At one point, we decided to dig a deep hole to collect more clay from various depths. Then we met a young couple who were digging a well to collect water for their field. We asked them to let us collect samples of clay from their well. Fortunately for us, they were delighted to help. While we were taking video footage and photographs of the place where the samples were collected, other farmers from nearby fields came over and watched us. They too were enthusiastic and helped us without any conditions, apart from the request, 'Please remember to send the television and press reports to us.' They thought we were reporters. Wherever we went, the local people helped a great deal. Their help ensured that our survey of the southwest was completed sooner than planned.

Our next survey was of the area north of the city. We travelled up the Red River to explore Đông Anh district (Hanoi) and then turned north into the Đuống River. Here some hills still stand along the river, especially in Từ Sơn district (Bắc Ninh). The exploration initially showed that the clay there was similar in many respects to that at the Imperial Citadel site. More importantly, its transportation would have been more convenient than from the southwest area. Analysis and comparison of clay samples continue, and the question of the clay's origin will soon be answered. The answer will give us a fuller understanding of the construction of Thăng Long Imperial Citadel, our ancestors' architectural masterpiece. It will also provide scholars with some interesting information about ancient society.

Measurement of the Imperial Citadel's scale and its earth layers' thickness will allow us to calculate the amount of clay that had been dug up. When we know the quantity of clay used and the means of its transportation, we will be able to estimate the number of workers that would have been needed for construction. This data will help us understand how the workforce was mobilised and organised for the building of Thăng Long Imperial Citadel. At the present time, we possess sufficient evidence to prove the participation of the military in its construction during the Lê period. The numbers and designations of units of military and guards were printed on large bricks: they built the citadel. However, we do not know whether soldiers participated during the Lý and Trần periods. This information is important, adding to our stock of social and economic information of which the history books make very little or no mention. It will allow us to fill gaps in our knowledge of Vietnamese history from the eleventh to the fourteenth century.

CHAPTER 5

Our Ancestors' Bricks

Đỗ Danh Huấn

I remember a morning at the end of March 2003. It had rained during the night. There were footprints on the path. Large thick sheets of steel bounced as people trod on them. The wheels of transport trucks left marks on the road. Only by walking very carefully could you avoid getting your shoes caked with mud. From Hoàng Diệu Street there was the sound of cars hooting and mopeds passing at speed. I remember this scene of a new day at the archaeological site of Thăng Long Imperial Citadel. The working atmosphere of the excavation was bustling and serious, quite a contrast from the days when, as students, we had practiced excavation at Đình Chàng, in Đông Anh district on the outskirts of Hanoi. This was the first day I went to work at the site: 31 March 2003.

Of course, looking back, there is no way to compare the time I spent working at the site to the thousand years during which our ancestors built the Thăng Long Imperial Citadel. There is no way to compare it with even one of the days during which the ancient bricks lay in silence underground. From the peak of Ngũ Lĩnh Mountain to Cổ Loa—An Dương Vương's old capital—and onward to the Thăng Long–Đông Đô–Hanoi Citadels of the Lý, Trần and Lê-dynasty kings, here we could see the historical evolution of our country as it had been fashioned by our ancestors' hands, a product of their brains and their national consciousness. On that first day, all these thoughts took form as my eyes were confronted with new and unfamiliar sights. The excavated trenches spread out before me. The artefacts—of gigantic proportions—were so mysterious. Their features were so sophisticated and beautiful.

Fig. 31. A courtyard paved with cockle shells is being unearthed in Section B (Photo: Institute of Archaeology 2003).

Then I was assigned a task. At that time, some of the trenches had already been excavated, exposing artefacts and overlapping architectural layers: these included trenches A1 and A2, B3 and B5. I was told to work at eastern trench B2 (B2Đ), where I was to assist archaeologist Nguyễn Văn Anh, who was in charge there. By then, B2Đ had already been dug deep; bricks from palaces that had been built hundreds of years ago appeared before my eyes. The brick foundations and borders were neither linked nor distributed across a large area. They were cut into unrelated sections. Nobody knew why they were like that. Further away, at the far corner of the trench, I could see bamboo poles emerging from the ground in clusters. I asked Văn Anh: 'Were those bamboo trees?' He replied, 'No, they were the poles set to strengthen the foundations when the new building was built.' I nodded, 'That must be it.' Naively, I had thought they were bamboos our royal ancestors had planted when they were on the throne.

At our trench, we were responsible for dozens of workers, including men and women of all ages. On that first day, some of the female workers started teasing me. I decided to ignore them and pretended that nothing was going on. It was not my intention, but I must have looked as cold as stone. They whispered to each other, 'That guy seems very stuck up!'

The weather started to change. The sun blazed out of a blue sky. In term of its artefacts and architectural finds, our trench had a very interesting location compared to neighbouring trenches. We found bright red square bricks arranged tightly to form areas which must have been beautiful courtyards. The bricks had just been unearthed; they were being cleaned by the skilful hands of women workers and they were drying in the sunshine beaming into the heart of our country's capital. To my eyes, they appeared red and full of vitality. On them, I could hear the echoing sound of footsteps.

It is hard to imagine how meticulous and painstaking archaeologists must be when they handle an artefact or take it from the ground. They clean it gently and carefully, draw it, describe it, measure it, and record its dimensions. It is as though someone was extracting a thorn from your hand or foot. While working on the excavations, the management issued us all with the basic equipment necessary for our work: rulers, pens, notebooks, scrapers, trowels, and plastic bags. We used these to work on the objects as they were exposed.

As we excavated and supervised the workers, we used our free moments to observe and think about the artefacts and architectural traces emerging from the site. After looking many times at the bricks, one day I asked Văn Anh: 'Why do these bricks all bear the same crescent "motifs"?' He thought for a moment, then replied: 'Those are technical traces made when the bricks were cut during production, leaving crescent-like motifs on the brick surface.'

One day, while I was working, a short man came over to the trench. He was about 40 years old and dressed in smart jeans. I was particularly struck by his impressive moustache and the camera he had slung around his neck: it looked like a very high-quality model. He focused its lens on the carefully arranged bricks and clicked several shots, one after the other. Then he turned to speak to the head of B2 trench, saying, 'These vestiges of brick foundation—aren't they wonderful!' I had only been working at the site for a few days, and knew no one there at all. Later, I discovered this was Nguyễn Hồng Kiên, a top-notch archaeologist.

The trench beside ours was trench B2. It had been excavated earlier: rows of mysterious bricks had been exposed. Traces of brick borders were visible, but they had been interrupted by the rise and fall of time and history. Some of the bricks were broken in three pieces while others fortunately remained intact; some lay on their side and some lay sloping head down as though they had suffered under the pressure of time. But for me, the most impressive brick was a large, rectangular red one. On it

Fig. 32. A dragon in bas-relief on a brick, from trench B2 (Photo: Institute of Archaeology 2003).

was a dragon in relief. I thought to myself: 'Why do "you" lie alone here?' I stood there and stared at it for a while. A very special object, it must have been placed at some luxurious spot in the royal palace. The worker who produced this brick must have been very skilled.

Thanks to the artist's skilful hands and imagination, the dragon appears powerful and vigorous, with a swift mane, flashing convex eyes, clear fins and scales. One sturdy foot stretches forward in running position as its five bristly claws grip the road. Then I remembered the dragons that decorate the stone steles at the Temple of Literature in Hanoi and the communal houses and pagodas of my village and elsewhere. Their appearance is the same: they have the same violence and majesty, the same fins, scales and manes. The only difference is that the dragons on the steles are on flat surfaces, not raised in relief. I quickly sketched out some of this brick's basic features in my excavation diary.

Archaeological excavation diaries are quite different from personal diaries. We had to enter the scientific details, describing and outlining all the events of the day. Whatever remains were found, they had to be described in a succinct and comprehensible way. Our excavation diaries record the sophisticated and scientific nature of our search for broken fragments. These are similar to reading a set of historical books or a novel.

The brick foundations and borders unearthed in our trench were plotted clearly in our diaries, with their positions, coordinates, names, and other shorthand notes. Other people might find them impossible to understand. Our trench was no different from any other trench: in the others too, if anyone thought about a brick, whether broken or intact, they drew its shape in detail and added notes about its colour, name, and especially its 'altitude' compared to the common 'horizon'.

In the bright sunlight of the first days of summer, the draughtsmen had to bend down, their faces very close to the surface of the earth, to measure every millimetre and centimetre of each find with meticulous precision. They had to get the most accurate measurements for their drawings. As for the photographers, sometimes they stood up to focus the lens, sometimes they bent close to the earth like farmers growing rice, placing the lens right up against the brick, capturing its distinct, authentic features. Heavens! Hundreds and thousands of bricks were all recorded in the same way.

* * *

It was now the beginning of summer. The sun beat down from the sky, vapours rose from the ground and we suffocated. All the workers, especially the women and girls, covered their faces completely, except for their eyes. Drops of sweat poured from the pores of their skin, soaking the clothes on the backs and shoulders of the young staff and workers. Everyone knew it was hard working in the sun; their skin turned dark, yet they were still enthusiastic, still engrossed in the work.

At two in the afternoon, when we returned to work, the sun shone from the west. Whether bending or standing, everyone had to face the scorching sun. A bucket of water was brought over and soon drunk.

Pity the poor bricks: they had just emerged from underground after hundreds of years of silent sleep and now had to suffer such severe sun and heat that even the stones perspired. In the morning, when the mist still lay on the ground, those bricks were bright and red; from midday to afternoon, they seemed to change colour, turning a pale or light pink.

Trenches B3 and B5 were near our trench. I sometimes went over to look at the artefacts. When I got back, I said to the head of our trench, 'Our trench seems to have been badly damaged. The artefacts here are nothing compared with theirs. In B3 and B5, there are even large-scale square brick borders that seem to form the gallery or foundation of an old palace. The sections of brick wall are straight. The bricks are large and thick, grey or red in colour. There are also drainage ditches built with specialist bricks I have never seen before. There's one that measures nearly 100 cm long, 40–50 cm wide and 10 cm thick. How strange it all is. How could our ancestors have made and fired such a large thick brick, and do it so well that that the brick didn't buckle? I even saw square bricks with lotus flower, meandering chrysanthemum, or peony designs set in a large circle at the very centre of the brick. At the four corners, there are lines running along the bricks' sharp edges; the lotus and chrysanthemum petals are trimmed in a balanced, neat and sophisticated way.' I silently associated these with the image of a king from the Lý, Trần or Lê dynasty, wearing royal robes, his royal boots on his feet, pacing across those bricks as he worked out how best to build the country.

The more I visited and observed other trenches, the richer the types of brick I found. Perhaps the king and his people produced many different types of brick for each building. Previously, I had believed that our trench was the best at the site. To my surprise, that belief 'hit the deck' as soon as I saw the other trenches. Take trench A1, for example. I saw an area of bricks several hundred square metres across, made up of bricks used for building walls. They lay in no apparent order, overlapping each other: some were intact, but most were broken. Nobody knows how long they had been there and where they came from. Had they once formed the palace of some king or queen?

* * *

After a working morning, we ate and rested in a small room. There was an order book: those who wanted a lunch box entered their order in advance. Some preferred rice with bean curd cooked in tomato sauce, some liked boiled pork with shrimp sauce, others ordered fried chicken. A lunch box cost 5,000 VND and came with a plastic cup of vegetable soup. Everyone ordered their box. Some touched little while others ate like horses. There were times when midday came but the caterer had not yet arrived: all fidgety, we went in and came out, hungry and impatient. Some made use of the time to catch a quick nap. At other times, they gave us under-cooked rice, leaving us hungry and irritated. Whatever meal we got, though, we somehow remained cheerful, laughing as we ate, talking about what had been found in the trench that day. There was always someone to say that their trench was 'number one', the top trench at the site for making unique finds. The discussion continued passionately as lunch came to an end. We worked hard, ate hard, and 'polished off' those boxes of rice that contributed so little for strengthening our young bodies.

In this room, there was also a small showcase displaying a selection of the site's artefacts. Among them, I noticed three rectangular bricks used for bordering. Three Chinese characters were inscribed on each— 永寧場—but I did not immediately understand them. Lunch had finished and the others were sleeping deeply, curled up like shrimps, with their legs dangling over the edge of their chairs as though hanging from the sky. But I was still curious; I sacrificed my nap to continue looking at these bricks. They resembled those unearthed in my trench but mine were not inscribed. I compared their colour, style, and size as well as the manufacturing technique visible on the surface. At this point, I was able to read two of the characters but was not sure about the third. I asked myself why these three characters were printed on the bricks. Were they someone's name? Were they the name of a place?

That afternoon, back at the trench, I asked the head about the bricks in the showcase. He translated the inscription—*Vĩnh Ninh trường*— explaining 'They are bricks from the Vĩnh Ninh area.' I continued: 'What date?' He replied, 'Scholars think they belong to the Trần period.' A little later, he pointed to the same kind of brick in the wall of B2 trench. The brick was still lying half in the wall, half sticking out and it revealed three Chinese characters, printed with tiny, thin and well-balanced features, set completely within their frame but slightly off centre compared with the brick. I came nearer and read *Vĩnh Ninh tường* (or Vĩnh Ninh wall). I misread it because I was remembering the time I had visited the library of the Institute of Hán-Nôm Studies to read the land register of Đồng Xuân commune (Thọ Xương district, in present-day Hanoi). In the register, I found that many hamlets and precincts had a brick wall boundary. I made a connection from this memory to the brick I was holding, particularly as the area we were excavating was not far from Đồng Xuân.

After this initial period assisting the head of B2Đ trench, once the work there was under control, I was sent to trench A1 to help Doãn Văn, Phạm Văn Triệu and Nguyễn Hữu Công with their work. This trench was huge and revealed many architectural traces and valuable bricks. Away from my old place of work and the workers, who had become familiar after many days together, I had to get to know new colleagues and new workers. Because of the trench's size, it was impossible to erect any shelter at A1. We all had to work in direct sunshine, apart from the odd minute or two hiding in the cool of the shade. I was not used to this at first, but realised that at all the trenches everyone—leaders and workers alike—took their work very seriously and had a strong sense of responsi-bility. Due to particular characteristics of the work and weather, it was not easy to distinguish our staff from other workers at the trench; everyone wore dark old clothes, with trousers rolled-up to the knees and palm-leaf or bamboo hats of all kinds. We all looked like farmers in the fields.

For younger members of staff like me, A1 trench was always a theme for discussion over lunch: we claimed our trench was the best and finest of all. This was because this trench contained many borders built with a broad variety of bricks. I realised that our ancestors had made use of diverse materials. There were walls built of small bricks and borders built of long bricks, and intact or broken bricks of many kinds—rectangular and square, thick and thin, decorated and plain—all such bricks had been used. High-quality intact bricks had been placed in key positions, while smaller broken bricks were inserted into slots; their good flat surfaces faced out while the damaged sides were hidden inside. Overall, relatively few intact bricks were used in construction. Skilful hands and athletic minds had put many broken bricks to good use.

I was lucky to work at A1 because I was sometimes able to spend time assisting Hà Nguyên Điểm, a technical draughtsman. He was already getting on, but his industriousness, caution and scientific spirit inspired others to follow his example. He once told me of his work on the excava-tion at Hoa Yên Pagoda at Yên Tử (Quảng Ninh), saying that the bricks and architecture found there were very fine, but could not be compared to the bricks found at Thăng Long Imperial Citadel. He had to spend most of his time seated in the hot sun as he drew the strata of the walls. He wore a large cotton towel over his shoulders to absorb the sweat. From time to time, he would stop drawing, stroke the hair on his head and wipe away the drops of sweat running down his cheeks and neck.

At A1 we uncovered a foundation made of square bricks with other bricks inserted. I was given the task of cleaning the dirt from them before Mr. Điểm starting his drawing and description work. The foundation did not seem to have been harmed, it was quite intact. After drawing and photographing, Mr. Điểm asked, 'Can you do something for me?' I said, 'Sure!' Then he told me to climb up the trench bank, adjust the total station theodolite and read the altitude of each brick and border for him to record on the drawings. To do this, I asked another worker to hold the scale, placing it at specific points on each artefact. Up on the bank, I regulated the theodolite and then read out the altitudes to Mr. Điểm. The work was like a strange conversation: I kept my eye on the scale as I called loudly. 'One hundred and seventy-two; one hundred and seventy-six; one hundred and ninety-six...' The numbers indicated the depth (altitude) of each brick, their distance from the standard mark we had made on the present-day surface of the ground. Both myself and my helper read the numbers out repeatedly, while Mr. Điểm recorded them on his drawings until all the altitudes were correctly entered.

I remember another spot in A1, beside a long channel that was oriented north–south. Here, while we were removing broken ceramics, a small brick courtyard was revealed, built with square, evenly inserted bricks. As we discovered this courtyard, water from underground leaked out across its surface, which was covered with sharp-edged potsherds that could cut our feet at any time. The sun was setting; some of the younger members of staff and I continued working and encouraged the workers to stay a little longer before nightfall. It was rare to find a square brick intact. But there were many thousands of broken square bricks decorated with lotus petals or chrysanthemum spray designs.

In those days, many trenches were in operation and the earth we removed piled up higher and higher like a small mountain. The Management Board hired trucks to take it away. In the afternoon, when our working day was done, management asked us to help stretch cords to delineate the next trench for excavation and, at the same time, to supervise the trucks transporting the earth. Those who were not on duty could rest or review the work, entering data into the diary, recording both common and unusual artefacts.

According to summer working hours, we started at 6.30 am. At about 8.30–9.00 pm, the ten-to-fifteen-tonne trucks started arriving at the site and the earth mound gradually grew smaller. At night, the site bustled like day, the excavator roared while the trucks rumbled, and periodically a flashing light on the excavator swept the sky, illuminating a corner of the site. The trucks worked through midnight without stopping. Around one or two in the morning we all went to a small restaurant on Nguyễn Biểu Street, where two women served us a bowl of noodle soup or congee to help us keep warm. When we returned, at about three in the morning, the truck fleet stopped work, the site gate closed and silence enveloped the site for a short time.

After a long period in Section A, I was sent back to Section B. Of course, this time I was not back at B2Đ. Instead, I was assigned to a new trench: B17. During my first days at this 'new land', I expected the trench would reveal unexpected finds of rare and valuable objects, with normal bricks or bricks inscribed with Chinese characters. But after we removed the top layer, no ceramics and no architectural traces appeared at all. I then imagined the trench would yield only very poor remains. However, when we had completely removed the first layer (L1), I found many bricks. Elated, thinking this was a good sign, I took my notebook, entered the details and made a sketch at once. In the second layer, to my surprise, half the trench's area (about 80–90 m^2) contained large bricks from the Lê period of various shades of red and grey. Then there appeared a 'carpet' of bricks broken in two or three pieces, some of which bore petal or chrysanthemum spray designs. There were even bricks inscribed with characters.

Delighted, I made a detailed plan to deal with the brick carpet. I first went to ask for guidelines from the Management Board. After that, step by step, we cleaned the bricks, using small trowels to remove tiny pieces of dirt, then washed them with a soft feather brush and water. We dried them and started describing, drawing, and calculating the relative coordinates of the walls, noting all these details in the diary. After cleaning, the area brightened up: some of the bricks were positioned low, some high. Some completely emerged from surface while others lay entirely underground. There were bricks that stuck out just a little, as though they had a nose to breathe the air. The brick area at B17 contrasted with the one at A1: it was a little more 'high class'. Old Mr. Bùi Vinh, the senior archaeologist in charge of B16, looked across at B17 from his trench and said: 'What a radiant trench you have! It's the best in Section B!' His words were both tactfully encouraging and an objective assessment. I replied, 'Thank you, but that is too much praise.'

In accordance with my plan, after cleaning I called a photographer to record an overview and details of this area, especially the normal bricks. This was possibly the most successful of all the excavated trenches, in terms of our 'achievement' of unearthing a great number of bricks. I now became particularly interested in the bricks inscribed with Chinese characters. Apart from bricks bearing the characters *Vĩnh Ninh trường* or *Giang Tây quân* (江西軍), as had been found in other trenches, in B17 many other bricks were inscribed with strange characters: *Hổ Uy quân* (虎威軍), *Huyền Qua quân* (玄戈軍), *Tráng Phong quân* (壯夆軍), and *Vũ Kỵ quân* (武騎軍). As attractive as they were, they greatly fascinated me and they were all the more valuable because bricks bearing characters are rarely found in excavations. They also provide useful data for archaeologists and historians to solve many of the historical problems that have, up to now, been considered gaps in our knowledge.

Consider the bricks with the characters *Thu Vật huyện* and *Thu Vật hương*. They had already been exposed in B17 for a long period, but I could still translate only the characters 物縣 (*Vật huyện*) and 鄉 (*Vật hương*). I could not read the other character, 收 (*Thu*), nor could I find it in any dictionary. I had to wait until one afternoon when Professor Nguyễn Hải Kế visited the site. I took him to visit the trenches where traces of buildings had been found. When he saw those bricks, he immediately read *Thu Vật huyện* and *Thu Vật hương*. Bùi Văn Hiếu and I had previously discussed the matter at great length, but had never reached a conclusion about the meaning of the third character. Now, after my teacher had read it, I thought: 'So, the character I have been puzzling over is *Thu*.' With this information, I went back to the books and official histories and found that the place names *Thu Vật huyện* (Thu Vật district) and *Thu Vật hương* (Thu Vật village) were located in Yên Bình district (present-day Yên Bái).

So that's what it was! The bricks were made under the Lê dynasty, but the location Thu Vật had existed since the Trần period: this was where King Trần Nhật Duật had stationed his troops. This name persisted through the Lê and Nguyễn periods. The story is the same with the brick bearing the characters *Vĩnh Ninh trường*, later deciphered by Đỗ Văn Ninh who said it referred to a place in Vĩnh Lộc district (present-day Thanh Hóa). These bricks tell us that the construction of the capital at Thăng Long continued through the Lý, Trần and Lê periods; local people were mobilised, some to make bricks, some to make tiles, some to provide wood and stone, all to build the Đại Việt state.

Later, all the large and bordering bricks of various dates—which we called plain bricks because they bore no Chinese characters—were carefully numbered and taken to the storehouse. Later still, when it became impossible to count them, they were arranged in square piles in the open air. The inscribed bricks were collected, ordered and carefully placed for their protection in the storehouse.

One day, I was called and told to number and carefully record all the Chinese characters on the bricks; the records would form a database for research. I then started working very hard, placing each brick on a shelf in the storehouse, recording each inscribed character. Then came the day I completed my work, with a pile of hundreds of pieces of paper on which you could read the words: *Vũ Kỵ quân* (武騎軍), *Huyền Qua quân* (玄戈軍), *Tráng Phong quân* (壯夆軍), *Hổ Uy quân* (虎威軍), *Lý Gia đệ tam đế Long Thụy Thái Bình tứ niên tạo* (李家第三帝龍瑞太平四年造),

Thu Vật huyện, Thu Vật hương (收物縣收物鄉). *Tả* (左), *Hữu* (右), *Trung* (中), *Tiền* (前) *Hậu* (後), *thần Dực* (神翊), *Đệ Nhị hỏa* (第二火), *Đại Thông độ* (大通渡), *Đại Thông độ ông* (大通渡翁), *Tam Tự quân* (三字軍), *Tam Phụ quân* (三輔軍), *Dương Vũ quân* (揚武軍), *Chiêu Thắng quân* (昭勝軍), *Trung Uy quân* (忠威軍), *Sung Uy quân* (崇威軍), *Ma Lạc đô* (麻落都), and so on. All were digitalised and filed.

Whether or not they were named, whether or not they were inscribed with characters, all the bricks convey a spirit of history, of the past speaking to the present. On their shelves in the small storeroom, they lie side by side, sleeping silently, while in huge piles outside more bricks of many kinds—bordering bricks, large bricks, light bricks, dark red bricks, grey bricks, bricks of eel-skin colour resulting from their high firing temperature—all these bricks lie silently after hundreds of years under the ground. Today, these bricks and their archaeologists tell us about the past, the great and glorious momentum of our ancestors' history. More than that, they proudly proclaim that the artisans, the hard-working, passionate, home-loving craftsmen with their skilful hands and creative minds, produced what we can see today. One, two, three bricks, and then the tens, hundreds and thousands of bricks discovered at this site tell of our ancestors' strength and intelligence in the first stages of nation building. They are the foundation on which today's Vietnam took shape. With the sacred spirit of its rivers and mountains and the strength of the Vietnamese people, the nation came together on this patch of land at Thăng Long over a period of more than a thousand years.

CHAPTER 6

The Central Sector of the Imperial Citadel of Thăng Long–Hanoi: World Heritage

Nguyễn Văn Sơn

In December 2002, an archaeological excavation took place at 18 Hoàng Diệu Street whose initial aim was to retrieve artefacts and release the land for the construction of a new National Convention Centre and National Assembly Building. The work was assigned to the Institute of Archaeology (Vietnam Academy of Social Sciences), which was given approximately nine months to complete its excavation of an area estimated at 48,000 m². The archaeologists, led by the institute's vice-director Tống Trung Tín, were able to excavate 2,000 m² in the project's first phase. Preliminary results from this small area revealed rich architectural vestiges from different historical periods: Đại La, Lý, Trần and Lê.

On the basis of these results, the project's Management Committee and the academic community submitted a request to the government to expand the excavation. In 2003 and early 2004, the total area excavated rose to 19,000 m². The findings were astonishing: the site became known for a set of architectural remains and artefacts that 'dazzled' the scholarly community within Vietnam and abroad. National and international conferences were held to study and evaluate the heritage. A new understanding of the central area of Thăng Long Imperial Citadel developed; the finds shed new light on cultural values of the highest importance for the Vietnamese nation. Mass media reported on a daily basis about the scale and value of the site and artefacts unearthed. Photographs were published showing hundreds of people standing on the gravel foundations of pillar bases, as though each of them was a pillar, proving that the remains of some very large buildings were now being discovered for the first time. The publicity surrounding the results of the excavation created a sort of 'earthquake' in Vietnam at the time.

In 2004, I still worked at the People's Committee of the city of Haiphong. I was asked to contact the excavation's project management committee to organise a tour of the archaeological site for the city's top officials. I got in touch with Tống Trung Tín, who agreed to my request. The visit for Haiphong's officials took place; our group was shown around by Tống Trung Tín and Nguyễn Tiến Đông, who made detailed presentations of the excavation and its results, as well as initial assessments of the site's value. Several members of the group expressed concern when they learned that such a valuable site was in danger of removal to make way for the construction of a National Convention Centre where an APEC meeting, hosted by Vietnam, was due to be held.

At that time, many domestic and international conferences and symposiums were organised to evaluate the heritage and discuss the question of the preservation of the site or its removal to make way for the National Convention Centre. The scientific community was unanimous in its assessment of the site's great cultural value for the nation, but had nonetheless to weigh the pros and cons of conservation as opposed to development. The conferences concluded with basic agreement among members of the scientific community that a request should be submitted to the Party and Government for the conservation and protection of the heritage. The Ministry of Culture and Information was asked to produce a synthesis of the results of its consultation with ministries and other government agencies, and the scientific community's opinion, as expressed in the request already submitted. Two alternative projects were identified:

- Project 1: conservation of the entire archaeological site, covering an area of 48,000 m^2.
- Project 2: conservation of Sections A and B, covering an area of 19,000 m^2.

Very fortunately for me, in April 2005 I was assigned to work at the Department of Cultural and Social Affairs at the Office of the Government and was given responsibility for heritage. I had previously had to ask permission to visit the site, now I became a direct participant in the deliberations over its conservation.

At this point, Deputy Prime Minister Phạm Gia Khiêm, acting for the Prime Minister, approved a request from the Ministry of Culture and Information to guide provincial and city authorities in their research and writing of applications for UNESCO recognition of world heritage status for their respective sites. These included:

- The Hanoi Ancient Citadel Area (at that time, the Imperial Citadel was still known as the Ancient Citadel);
- The Cát Tiên Forest Area (in the territory of three provinces: Đồng Nai, Bình Phước, Lâm Đồng);
- The Hồ Dynasty Citadel Area (Thanh Hóa province);
- The Con Moong Caves Area (Thanh Hóa province);
- The Đinh and Lê Royal Temples Area at Tràng An (Ninh Bình province).

In implementation of this order, the Hanoi city authorities drew up plans for a heritage area that included the following sites: the Hanoi Ancient Citadel, the old commercial quarter, the temples to the four guardian deities of Thăng Long, and the Temple of Literature. After reporting to the Politburo and Party Central Committee, in March 2006 the Government issued a directive with three points:

- Conservation of the entire archaeological site at 18 Hoàng Diệu Street;
- Permission for Hanoi city People's Committee to set up an authority to manage the Hanoi Ancient Citadel and Thăng Long Imperial Citadel;
- Assignment to Hanoi city of responsibility for the urgent drafting of a heritage application for UNESCO recognition as world cultural heritage, in time for the celebrations of the Thăng Long–Hanoi millennium in 2010.

It was also very fortunate for me that in December 2006 I was transferred to work for the Hanoi city authorities and appointed as director of the Centre for Conservation of Cổ Loa and Hanoi Ancient Citadel (known today as Thăng Long–Hanoi Heritage Conservation Centre). Once again I was directly involved, this time in drafting the heritage application for the Thăng Long Imperial Citadel. The Hanoi People's Committee approved the Centre's request to establish a Steering Committee and Scientific Advisory Board for the drafting of the Thăng Long Imperial Citadel heritage application and for the conservation of the Cổ Loa and Hanoi

Ancient Citadel sites. Hanoi People's Committee Vice President Ngô Thị Thanh Hằng chaired the Steering Committee, while the Scientific Advisory Board consisted of professors and scholars, including Phan Huy Lê, Lưu Trần Tiêu, Nguyễn Quang Ngọc, Đỗ Văn Ninh, Phan Khanh, Tống Trung Tín, Lê Văn Lan and Nguyễn Vinh Phúc. The Board worked with professors from Japan, France, Australia and Italy, as well as UNESCO, including experts from the Île-de-France invited to help Hanoi draft the application.

From January 2007 to September 2008, we worked with the Advisory Board professors and overseas scholars to debate the perimeter, outstanding universal value and management plan of the heritage area, as well as the contents of the application, in line with UNESCO procedures. After many drafts, the group responsible for writing the application proposed that the core area of the heritage zone should include the central axis of the Thăng Long Imperial Citadel, bounded by Phan Đình Phùng, Nguyễn Tri Phương, Điện Biên Phủ and Hoàng Diệu Streets, and the archaeological area at 18 Hoàng Diệu Street. Regarding the outstanding universal value, the group proposed points for discussion at several conferences. The application gradually took shape: the drafting group completed it for submission to UNESCO in Paris on the day of the deadline (30 September 2008).

The application was submitted on time, but the eighteen months it took to prepare it, including the independent assessments by UNESCO specialist agencies, was a rushed and exhausting period for the Steering Committee, Scientific Advisory Board and drafting group. The International Council on Monuments and Sites (ICOMOS) sent an expert in the field of architecture to make an on-site assessment of the heritage. The World Heritage Centre then sent Vietnam a written request for explanations and clarifications regarding the integrity, universal outstanding value, exact perimeter and authenticity of the heritage. So, one more time, Vietnamese scholars and their international expert advisers returned to the work of examining, assessing and agreeing on the explanatory content to be presented, in compliance with the ICOMOS requests. This was a period of intense hard work for the Vietnamese scholars, because time was very short—many had to work through the night. Then the race against time ended and Vietnam's explanations were submitted to the World Heritage Committee by the deadline.

In advance of the World Heritage Committee's 34th Session, Vietnamese delegates had already made informal presentations of the site's heritage value to members of the Committee. At the Committee's meeting on the evening of 31 July 2010, the Vietnamese delegation presented a summary of the application in the form of a meticulously produced documentary film. This emphasised that the outstanding universal value of the heritage corresponded to three criteria: the cultural heritage had developed over a continuous period of nearly one thousand years throughout different historical eras, including the Lý, Trần, Lê, Mạc, Nguyễn and Ho Chi Minh periods; the Imperial Citadel of Thăng Long was a place of assimilation and transformation for cultural values from China, India and other civilisations elsewhere in the world; and the Central Sector of the Imperial Citadel of Thăng Long demonstrates the site's political, economic and cultural centrality for Vietnam over a period of one thousand years.

After a spirited debate, the experts and delegates from the Committee's member countries reached agreement.[1] At 6 am on 1 August 2010 (Vietnam time), or 8 pm on 31 July 2010 (the time in Brazil, where the meeting was held), the World Heritage Committee voted by a large majority to inscribe the Imperial Citadel of Thăng Long as the nine hundredth site on the World Heritage List. The site's universal outstanding value was recognised under criteria (ii), (iii) and (vi). The Imperial Citadel of Thăng Long thus met three of the six cultural criteria, only one of which is sufficient to be eligible for world heritage status.

With the inscription of the Central Sector of the Imperial Citadel of Thăng Long–Hanoi on the World Heritage List, research and excavation continued at an increased pace. The management plan included archaeological investigation, heritage conservation, and research into the restoration of traditional festivals and of the Kính Thiên Palace space (including a masterplan drawn to a 1:500 scale). Plans for the conservation and exhibition of artefacts and for publicising the heritage were approved. After a journey of eight years from the discovery of the archaeological site at 18 Hoàng Diệu Street—and thanks to the research efforts of Vietnamese archaeologists, historians, geographers, anthropologists, and so on, and the assistance offered by scholars from Japan, Australia, France and other countries, as well as the UNESCO experts—the Imperial Citadel of Thăng Long was inscribed on the World Heritage List in time for Vietnam's celebration of the Millennial Anniversary of Thăng Long–Hanoi (1010–2010).

Before the Thăng Long–Hanoi millennial celebrations, the Institute of Archaeology and the Thăng Long–Hanoi Heritage Conservation Centre completed a number of tasks focused on the site's development. Some areas were handed over by the Ministry of Defence. Buildings built during the war were destroyed. Planning was conducted for joint access to the

Fig. 33. The citadel's central axis remained military land into the twenty-first century. Here, soon-to-be-decommissioned barrack buildings are viewed from the parapet of the Gate of Commencement (Đoan Môn), looking south (Photo: EFEO 2004).

Fig. 34. By 2010 the barracks had been cleared and the nearby football field repurposed into a civic space in front of the Gate of Commencement, the main gate to the Forbidden City, here viewed from the south (Photo: EFEO 2015).

central axis and excavation area (18 Hoàng Diệu Street). In the remaining buildings (built during the French period), exhibitions were organised, including 'One Thousand Years from Under the Ground' (Institute of Archaeology, working with the EFEO [École française d'Extrême-Orient] and French experts), 'Exhibition of Artefacts from Thăng Long Imperial Citadel' (Thăng Long–Hanoi Heritage Conservation Centre), and 'D67 House and Bunker' (Thăng Long–Hanoi Heritage Conservation Centre). The army's old football ground (in front of the Gate of Commencement) was turned into an open space for cultural events; to the rear, the pomelo orchard became a green space for visitors to walk in the shade. In recent years, buildings at 19c Hoàng Diệu Street have been used for ticket sales, presentation of the site, and a coffee shop. After the construction of the new National Assembly Building, the entire excavated areas of Sections A, B, C and D at 18 Hoàng Diệu Street were joined up to become an archaeological park.

In terms of research, after the millennial celebrations the Thăng Long–Hanoi Heritage Conservation Centre continued to coordinate research into the heritage with scholars and institutes in Vietnam and overseas. Since 2011, the centre has worked with the Institute of Archaeology to excavate the Rose Garden, an area of more than 10,000 m² beside Section C, and the 'Altar' site, which some scholars suggest was a site for worship of heaven and earth in the early years of the Lý dynasty (before the Lý built the Xã Tắc and Nam Giao altars). Excavations have continued on the citadel's central axis (in the area from the foundations of the Kính Thiên Palace to the Gate of Commencement). These revealed the very large scale of the drains built by the Lý dynasty in this central area: the main drain measures more than 2 m across, 2 m deep, and is oriented north–south in the Lê-dynasty Đan Trì courtyard. The excavations also revealed the perimeter of the Đan Trì (Long Trì) courtyard during the Lê period, measuring 87 m wide, 122 m long, with the Kính Thiên Palace Dragon Terrace to the north, the Gate of Commencement to the south, and the foundations of the Trường Lang gallery to the east and west. The vestiges of these Lý, Trần and Early Lê structures, the large Lý dynasty drain and other drains dating from the Trần dynasty all provide confirmation that the main axis of the Thăng Long Imperial Citadel remained unchanged through the Lý, Trần and Lê periods. Plans for research into the restoration of the Kính Thiên Palace space are underway. In the not too distant future, we will have sufficient evidence to identify the position of the main palace—named Càn Nguyên, Thiên An and Kính Thiên— through the Lý, Trần and Lê periods.

Fig. 35. Looking south from the parapet of the Gate of Commencement: once a football field within the military zone, now a green space open to the public. In the distance, the Imperial Citadel of Thăng Long visitor centre (right) and the Nguyễn-dynasty Flag Tower (centre) (Photo: Institute of Archaeology 2016).

Fig. 36. Trenches from the 2002–04 excavation were properly roofed and equipped with walkways for visitor access (Photo: EFEO 2015).

The management plan for the Thăng Long Heritage Area, providing for investment and conservation for the entire site, was approved and published in 2015. This includes the Archaeological Area at 18 Hoàng Diệu Street and the central area linking the Flag Tower, the Gate of Commencement and the Kính Thiên Palace; there are also plans for the restoration of the Lê-dynasty Kính Thiên Palace and Đan Trì courtyard. At 1 Hoàng Diệu, an L-shaped building built in 1907 during the French period, preparations are underway for the creation of the Thăng Long Imperial Citadel Museum, devoted to the display of artefacts unearthed during excavations at the site. In the future, further excavations will shed greater light on the Forbidden City and Imperial Citadel. This research and conservation work at the heritage site is serving the long-term goal of creating a 'historical and cultural park' in the heart of the ancient capital.

Note

1. See https://whc.unesco.org/en/criteria/ (consulted 5 December 2022).

PART II

Research into the History of the Citadel

CHAPTER 7

Thăng Long Imperial Citadel in Vietnamese Memory

Đào Hùng

Vietnamese memories of Thăng Long Imperial Citadel are surprisingly vague. The 'splendid and sumptuous palaces' mentioned in ancient texts are no more than ornate and formulaic words of praise: they give no indication of the old buildings' size and appearance. In the Vietnamese mind, however, Thăng Long Imperial Citadel conjures up the image of a golden age of prosperous dynasties building an enduring civilisation. The great events of the nation's history are all closely linked to the royal capital at Thăng Long and the citadel was the capital's heart, a place of assembly for dignitaries and men of note from throughout the northern region.

Until recently, our knowledge of the citadel and the surviving vestiges neither allowed us to form a complete picture of the site's architectural scale nor of the palace life of the nation's leaders over a period of nearly one thousand years. Ancient texts record only the monuments' names, without further description. The oldest set of historical books in Vietnam, normally considered to be the *Việt sử lược* (Summary History of Vietnam), was compiled under the Trần dynasty. Here we may read the following description of the citadel, just after it was built in 1010.

> Triều Nguyên Palace was built in Thăng Long Imperial Citadel. Tập Hiền Palace was built on its left, Giang Vũ Palace on its right, Phi Long Gate opened to its left, Đan Phượng Gate opened to its right, Cao Điện gate opened to the north… (*Việt sử lược* 1960: 70).

Later historical chronicles all contain such records. They provide no details, except such comments as 'on three sides of the communal house, fragrant flowers and exotic grasses grow; pond water runs into the river; there are skilfully executed sculptures, decorations and fine wooden works, the like of which has never been seen' (*Việt sử lược* 1960: 166). In 1782, Dr Lê Hữu Trác (1720–92), who was summoned from Nghệ An to the capital by Trịnh Sâm, wrote a few paragraphs describing the Trịnh lord's complex of palaces in his *Chronicle of a Journey to the Capital*:

> It was about one league [= ~720 m] in circumference. There were palaces everywhere, as well as towers, communal houses, bead curtains, jade doors, water reflecting the clouds; the whole way, there were extraordinary flowers, exotic grasses and beautiful animals as well as valuable birds, hopping and singing; a high mountain emerged from the middle of a piece of flat ground; huge trees gave cool shade; a painted bridge with stone banisters crossed a winding rivulet. I walked and looked as if in a land of dreams. (Lê Hữu Trác 1959: 41–2)

He had seen these things with his own eyes, but this great doctor still described them in clichés: he mentioned no specific examples. Words like 'bead curtains', 'jade doors' and 'a painted bridge' are merely the conventions people used when talking about powerful aristocratic families.

In the late eighteenth century, Phạm Đình Hổ (1768–1839), an eminent Confucian scholar who lived in Thăng Long for many years, left a more coherent description of the Trịnh lord's pleasure gardens in 1774–75:

> Lord Trịnh [viz Trịnh Sâm] watched the torchlight procession; he often strolled around the forbidden palaces on the West Lake and at Tứ Trầm and Dũng Thúy mountains; construction of temples and palaces never ceased. The Lord took his walk at Thụy Liên Palace by the West Lake about three or four times a month; guardsmen stood around the four sides of the lake; court officials all wore female veils and costumes; kiosks were erected around the lake to sell goods. (Phạm Đình Hổ 1960: 14)

The author described the scene with great care, yet provided no information about the architecture around the lake, apart from some memorable names.

From the seventeenth century, Westerners visiting Thăng Long left some paragraphs of description in their travel writings. Their descriptions are more specific, but they unfortunately provided few illustrations, so our knowledge remains very general. A British merchant, Samuel Baron, saw the monuments in Thăng Long Imperial Citadel in late seventeenth century. After more than a hundred years of civil war between the Lê and Mạc dynasties, the citadel had been scaled down. But Baron still expressed his astonishment at the ruins of one of the ancient palaces, which showed that it had been well built, with doors decorated with a type of marble (Baron 2006: 231).

Giovanni Filippo de Marini, an Italian priest, also visited Thăng Long around this time. He wrote that the king's palace was made of no more than wood, but added that it was raised on numerous strong pillars and its beams and rafters were of incomparable sophistication and beauty (Marini 1666: 117). Jean-Baptiste Tavernier's younger brother Daniel came to Thăng Long around 1643. He did not describe the citadel's structure but made many drawings, which Tavernier later printed in his *Relation nouvelle et singulière du Royaume de Tunquin* (1679). Unfortunately, the drawings were executed casually and reflected little of the scenery of Asia: they more closely resembled drawings of Europe during this period. These records do, however, allow later generations to feel a certain pride at the grandeur and splendour of the ancient Imperial Citadel.

All these buildings were destroyed in the warfare of the late eighteenth century. In 1786, the Tây Sơn leader, Nguyễn Huệ, led troops north from Phú Xuân (Huế) to eliminate the Trịnh lord and restore the Lê dynasty. After Nguyễn Huệ's army withdrew to the south, the newly enthroned king, Lê Chiêu Thống, venged himself on the Trịnh lord by burning his palaces. Then, when Lê Chiêu Thống sought reinforcements from the Chinese Qing dynasty to fight the Tây Sơn army, Thăng Long became a battlefield and houses and palaces were again destroyed.

In 1802, the Nguyễn dynasty united the country and established the capital at Phú Xuân. Thus ended Thăng Long's eight-hundred-year history as Vietnam's capital. The city became the seat of the northern region's military governor and was later renamed Hanoi. The citadel walls were rebuilt on a smaller scale. Inside, apart from the Kính Thiên Audience Hall, a royal residence was built for the monarch's visits to the north; other buildings included palaces and residences for the court officials responsible for northern citadel's defence—the viceroy of Tonkin, the provincial governor, the judges, the provincial army commander—and storehouses for keeping rice and coin. The new buildings were by no means as graceful as those of the former Imperial Citadel. The scenery was indeed so desolate that Nguyễn Du (1765–1820), a poet born in the former capital, lamented the changes on his return from refuge. He recorded his feelings in the melancholy lines of his poem *Thăng Long*, as follows:

> ... Tản Mountain, Lô River forever the same,
> I return to Thăng Long but my hair is white,
> Thousand-year mansions are now become roads,
> A brand-new citadel, an old palace gone from sight.

Even Nguyễn Công Trứ (1777–1849), a poet of talent who contributed much to government and the people's life under the Nguyễn dynasty, felt something had been lost when he viewed the barren scenery of the old Imperial Citadel:

Thăng Long Citadel
Grass and flowers, their endless cycle of blossom and decay,
Hills and rivers, their silent laughter at prosperity and decline,
Nature itself, a picture that constantly mutates.
Travellers saw the scene and asked,
How often do stars move, how often do things change?
Princely palaces, royal temples, where did they go?
In irony, gibbons sing, orioles call hello.

Bà Huyện Thanh Quan (Nguyễn Thị Hinh, 1805–48) was born in Thăng Long. A woman of great talent, she had been called to the court where she taught the royal palace maids. Memories of the Lê period remained in her mind as she witnessed the early nineteenth-century changes to the Imperial Citadel and grieved over the ruined scenery of the former capital:

Nostalgia for Thăng Long Citadel
The Creator made this senseless life a stage,
Time swiftly passes: in the morning dew, an age.
An ancient road with horse carts, bearing autumn grass,
The old palace foundations, the sun's declining rays.
Stone unshaken through the months and years,
Water glowers at Time's unceasing change.
Nature's thousand-year mirror reflects all things present and past,
The sight engulfs me with the unbearable anguish of loss.

In the late nineteenth century, Dr Hocquard may have been the last person to describe the citadel before it was levelled by the French. He arrived in Hanoi in 1884 and recorded what he saw in an illustrated book, providing considerable detail on the citadel area:

To obtain an accurate picture of this citadel in the period before our arrival, one must imagine a great flat area of land, rectangular in shape, measuring at least three kilometres along its longest side. This land is entirely enclosed by a high thick wall made of bricks. Outside, a broad moat filled with stagnant water runs parallel to the wall.

The wall is pierced by six monumental gates each giving access to the exterior over a brick bridge thrown across the moat. Each gate is topped by a small watchtower accessed by means of staircases set inside the wall. The soldiers on guard duty at the gate stand in this watchtower.

At the very centre of the land bounded by the great wall I have just described there is a second enclosure, similarly enclosed on all sides with a brick wall: this is the royal enclosure containing the king's pagoda.

The king's pagoda is a large building, wider than it is long; it is built on a square terrace, consolidated on its four sides by a wall. A monumental staircase gives access to the terrace; the staircase is bounded on each side by a banister made of granite admirably carved to figure those clusters of volutes that for the Vietnamese represent clouds. The staircase is divided into three sections, one central and two lateral, by two superb chimeras measuring at least two metres long, each carved from a single block of grey granite.

The architect has placed three gates, one beside the other, in the wall around the royal enclosure that faces this staircase. For those who understand Vietnamese customs, this arrangement alone is enough to mark the place out, without any doubt, as a king's residence. The mandarins and personalities of the court must never pass through the central gate, which is reserved for the sovereign alone, but always go through the side entries to the right and left. [...]

On a large cube of masonry in front of the royal enclosure, there stands a tower also built of brick, measuring six or seven metres high. This tower has six sides; inside, a spiral staircase has been built and is lit through small windows set at different heights. The staircase leads to a platform at the top of the tower, from where the surrounding countryside may be explored.

Nearby, there are some large brick buildings with tiled roofs; these are the rice storehouses. This is where the provincial governor locks away the annual tax revenues, which among the Vietnamese are mostly paid in kind by means of a levy made in advance of the harvest. Next to the rice storehouses live the high-ranking bureaucrats of the province, the *tông đôc* ('governor') and the two mandarins in charge of finance and justice (*quan bô* and *quan an*). Only the *quan bô*'s house still stands. [...]

> The immense area of land bounded by the Royal Pagoda in the centre and by the enclosure of outer walls on the periphery is almost entirely uncultivated and unoccupied. It is a vast desert, giving the citadel its abandoned, forlorn appearance.
>
> In the past, numerous straw huts stood here, serving as barracks for the Vietnamese soldiers. The old Hanoi garrison has been estimated at three thousand men, all of whom lived within the citadel. If one thinks that each of these soldiers lived with their family, one may picture the extraordinary animation which reigned at that time within this vast fortified camp, today abandoned and destroyed.
>
> The soldiers' straw huts have all been burnt or demolished but, from time to time, one still comes across the nice brick houses where the military mandarins lived. (Hocquard 1999: 101–6).

If an outsider like Hocquard was touched by the citadel's 'abandoned, forlorn appearance', the impression on insiders with many years of association with the palace must have been greater still. Yet for the people of Hanoi, a worse loss came with the French authorities' demolition of the Hanoi Citadel in 1894. An expansion of the French army camp was planned, along with the creation of French-style streets and the colonial authorities' palaces and offices. As a result, the entire citadel was razed except the North Gate, where traces remained of French soldiers' cannonades during their earlier attacks on the citadel, and a number of smaller buildings, including the Flag Tower. Kính Thiên Audience Hall was demolished, apart from the terrace decorated with dragon banisters described by Hocquard. The citadel was demolished between 1894–97 by Auguste Bazin, the engineer in charge, according to the book *Le Vieux Tonkin* (Bourrin 1941: 305; see Olivier Tessier's chapter for full details of this episode).

Vietnamese people have another memory of this event: the participation of a woman who started out as a prostitute and became rich from her association with a French soldier. She and her husband won a contract related to the demolition work. Her name was Tư Hồng and her story has entered the folklore of Hanoi. She made her fortune selling bricks collected from the demolished citadel to those building houses on the new streets of Hanoi. Association with the hand of this *me Tây*[1] and her collusion with a French boss defiled the story of the citadel's destruction, leaving a great wound in the people's mind.

The act of vandalism led a later governor-general, Paul Doumer, to make the following statement:

I arrived here too late to save considerable parts of the citadel. In particular, the Gates should have been maintained. They bore typical features and memories with historical values worthy of respect. They would have embellished the streets in the future. (Masson 1929: 85)

Since those days, memories of Thăng Long Imperial Citadel have blurred: there was nothing left to recall the splendid appearance of the past. When a detailed image of the old citadel was required, it could only be found through association with the image of Huế, where unique royal palaces survived the vicissitudes of time. But Huế could never replace Thăng Long. Huế Citadel is smaller and its architecture is gentle and elegant. Its dainty pillars and the shallow slope of its roofs contrast with the gigantic scale of the steeply curved roof-ends typical of northern monuments. People's memories thus became vague, and images lacked clear foundations. And as the memories blurred, people started to remember Thăng Long or old Hanoi through its thirty-six ancient streets, places where ordinary folk lived but never a king, queen or official of the court.

In this too, Hanoi differs from Huế. In its turn, the Nguyễn dynasty declined and its kings were abased, taking orders from the French *résident supérieur*. Yet the people of Huế remain proud of a dynasty that led Vietnam's expansion to the south: the royal lifestyle remains deeply engrained in Huế's modern lifestyle, in its art and culture and in the eating and drinking habits of its people. What features of the royal lifestyle have the people of Hanoi maintained? They have almost entirely disappeared. The only surviving vestiges of old Hanoi are the old pagodas, temples and shrines with their vernacular features. Such buildings may be found throughout northern Vietnam and often on a much grander scale. Or perhaps we may point to the old streets dating from the pre-colonial period, with their narrow houses, their rough and variegated architecture. These have been protected by the people of Hanoi; they stand out today as an untidy, squalid contrast to the city's modern architecture.

However, memories are still memories. Thăng Long–Hanoi remains closely linked to the glories of the nation's past, the wars of resistance against foreign aggressors, and the prosperous dynasties that gave rise to such Confucian talents as Chu Văn An, Nguyễn Trãi, Nguyễn Bỉnh Khiêm and Lê Quý Đôn. The city has always been the centre where Vietnam's greatest scientists and intellectuals congregate. And even the forces of French colonial rule chose Hanoi: when they invaded in the late nineteenth century, they first conquered the south and Saigon. A short time after occupying the whole country, they chose Hanoi as the capital of their Indochinese Union, headed by the French governor-general. Thăng Long–Hanoi has always played a significant role in the country's life. In 1945, Hanoi was where the August Revolution led to the establishment of an independent state headed by the late President Ho Chi Minh. It was in Hanoi that Ho Chi Minh pronounced the Declaration of Independence, ushering in a new era for the nation.

People in the south have always experienced feelings of great closeness towards their northern origins. Huỳnh Văn Nghệ—a poet and leader of the southern region's resistance against the French in 1945—expressed these feelings in two lines of verse that have now become immortal.

> Since we took sword to open the borders of our realm,
> The southern sky has yearned for the land of Thăng Long.

For these reasons, Vietnamese people all over the country, especially in Hanoi, greeted news of the 2003 discovery of underground archaeological vestiges of Thăng Long Imperial Citadel with great excitement. The event's significance was summed up in a speech delivered by General Võ Nguyên Giáp:

> I would particularly like to emphasise the historical depth of the site, which can be traced back to the pre-Thăng Long period. [Vestiges have been found from] Đại La citadel (seventh to ninth centuries), the Đinh and Early Lê periods (tenth century), and especially Thăng Long Imperial City of the Lý and Trần periods through the Later Lê, Mạc and Lê Restoration periods (eleventh to eighteenth centuries), as well as Hanoi Citadel of the Nguyễn period (nineteenth century). The underground site is closely associated with the vestiges of the Ho Chi Minh period revolution and resistance war, including Ho Chi Minh's house-on-stilts and Mausoleum, Ba Đình Square, the Vietnamese People's Army Headquarters during the resistance war against the USA and the Ba Đình National Assembly Building. Together, these form a priceless ensemble of national cultural heritage located in the capital city of Hanoi, dating from the seventh to the twentieth centuries. Compared to the capitals of other countries around the world, these features are rare and outstanding: they represent the great values of Hanoi's history. Over a period of history lasting thirteen centuries, this land has almost continuously served as the country's capital; since the eleventh century there have only been short gaps, during Tây Sơn and Nguyễn periods. (*Hoàng thành Thăng Long* 2003: 122)

A southerner, Professor Trần Văn Giàu, aged 90, also spoke with great emotion:

It is surprising even to me. I am moved because I am a historian. In Vietnam's history, no place has stood longer as the government's centre than Thăng Long–Hanoi Citadel [...] Hanoi may not possess architecture as grand and monumental as the temples and palaces in other countries. This, however, does not make us feel inferior. We have many other things to be proud of. The celebration of Thăng Long's millennium [in 2010] will show what our forebears left for their descendants during those 1000 years. In my view, this is a great lesson in national consciousness and patriotism. With it, no other lesson can compare. (*Hoàng thành Thăng Long* 2003: 124).

The sacred spirit of Thăng Long's landscape over a period of one thousand years was thus awakened and expressed in the emotions of many people across the country. After visiting the artefacts found at the Imperial Citadel, one person in Hồ Chí Minh City wrote:

It is as though the artefacts have a soul. It is as though the soul of our Ancestors, the soul of our mountains and rivers, are speaking to us from back in the distant past. I now feel prouder of our national culture and civilisation. I now better understand the strength marshalled and mobilised for our country's construction and defence! (*Hoàng thành Thăng Long* 2003: 130)

The artefacts seem to express something that allows those who see them to recall the great and sorrowful history of the Vietnamese:

It is as though the running steps of the Sát Thát fighters are still somewhere here. The brick foundations seem to have absorbed the teardrops of Princess Huyền Trân, shed before she left for her mission to the south. There remains a sad and majestic drop of Nguyễn Trãi's blood, shed on the day the verdict was announced, ordering the extermination of three generations of his descendants. Everything seems to be here, in the busy life of the people of Lạc Hồng blood, who honour the nation with every passing day. (*Hoàng thành Thăng Long* 2003: 130)

There are people who let their emotions go further still and reach conclusions bordering on the mysterious and even the fantastic. The historian Dương Trung Quốc made the following judgment after quoting some of the lessons of history:

History contains lessons for our contemplation. One of these is that, since the days of King Lý Thái Tổ, any individual or dynasty who moved the capital from the sacred land of Thăng Long would suffer a premature death. (*Hoàng thành Thăng Long* 2003: 128)

This sort of reasoning was advanced by Phạm Lưu Vũ (2005) through the theory of *long mạch*, the dragon vein in the land, a geomantic theory imbued with many of the mysterious characteristics of oriental cosmology: how can we measure it if it is, by its very nature, an inexact science? According to this authority, a place can become the country's capital if it lies on the 'great dragon celestial stem' (*đại can long*). This was the case for Thăng Long.

Many people from around the country have now visited the site. The archaeological finds at the Thăng Long Imperial Citadel site are interpreted in many ways. But however we interpret them, we may be in no doubt that they have given the Vietnamese proud visual images of their nation's past, in the form of the ancient royal architecture of palaces that successively stood on the land chosen as capital for almost a millennium.

Note

1.   *me Tây*, lit. 'Western mother' (from the French *mère*), pejorative term for a Vietnamese woman married to a Frenchman.

CHAPTER 8

Gao Pian (高騈), the Last Protector General of Annan

Franciscus Verellen[1]

Gao Pian (821–87), the architect of the medieval citadel of Hanoi and of large-scale defensive and communication works in several frontier regions of China and Vietnam, was a larger-than-life figure in the military and political history of both countries. A charismatic governor and commander, inclined to the occult arts of strategy, he was a man of wide learning and curiosity with a strong attraction to Daoism, as well as a gifted poet.[2] As will be seen in the pages that follow, his surviving poetry is also of autobiographical interest, expressing the thoughts and emotions of a man of action at key moments in an eventful career.[3] Reviled and revered for his pivotal roles in hastening the agony of the Tang dynasty (618–906) and the birth of Vietnam,[4] Gao Pian the benefactor became an object of local cults in his own lifetime, especially in Vietnam and in Sichuan, where his spectacular engineering works and contributions to peace and prosperity were attributed to divine inspiration. The presence of talented literati and communicators on Gao Pian's staff, especially Pei Xing (裴鉶) (825?–880?), author of the well-known collection of imaginative tales *Chuanqi* (傳奇), and the eminent scholar-poet Ch'oe Ch'iwŏn (崔致遠) (855–949) from the Korean kingdom of Silla, significantly contributed to this popular appeal.

1. THE POLITICS OF SECESSION

Gao was a native of Youzhou, the territory straddling northern Hebei and Liaoning, near modern Beijing, an important military and commercial crossroads under the Tang dynasty. More distantly, he hailed from a military family in Bohai in the extreme northeast, home to the Mohe people and the Parhae state (698–926) in the Manchurian borderland between China and Korea. His grandfather, Gao Chongwen (高崇文), prince of Bohai commandery and a celebrated general and military official, had distinguished himself by winning a decisive battle against the Turfan in 789.[5]

During the reigns of the late Tang emperors Yizong (r. 859–73) and Xizong (r. 873–88), Gao Pian in his turn served as military commissioner or governor in a succession of strategic border regions. As the most experienced and successful general at a critical juncture in history he assumed, with the rank of grand councillor from the year 873, an important role in the imperial campaign to contain the Huang Chao rebellion (875–84), the most serious threat to the survival of the Tang dynasty in the ninth century. Gao was not only a key figure on the frontiers of the empire but also at the heart of court politics. His appointment as supreme commander of the Tang forces provoked an acrimonious controversy that, in 879, led to the simultaneous dismissal of two senior chief ministers. At the turn of 880 to 881, Gao was serving as commander-in-chief in the lower Yangzi region when his failure to prevent Huang Chao and his followers from crossing the Yangzi precipitated the fall of the two Tang capitals, Luoyang and Chang'an (modern Xi'an), and the flight of the emperor into exile at Chengdu.

Gao Pian's surprising inaction at this point prepared the stage for his own establishment as a quasi-autonomous ruler of the Huainan region (between the Huai and Yangzi rivers, in modern Jiangsu and Anhui provinces), where he held the post of military governor and prefect of Yangzhou from late 879. The new stance adopted by the dynasty's hitherto staunchest defender earned Gao the condemnation of official historians as a secessionist.[6] What really moved Gao Pian to make his fateful decision may never be known unequivocally, but his motivations were more complex and more intricately tied to the underlying causes of the Tang's breakup than the verdict of China's official historiography suggests.[7] Suffice it here to observe that, willingly or unwillingly, the general stood aside, allowing the disintegration of the Tang to run its course. The eventual fall of the empire twenty-seven years later had far-reaching geopolitical repercussions, including the emergence of a multi-polar configuration of power in tenth-century China (Wang Gungwu 2007) and the independence or increased autonomy of other regions in Asia previously under Chinese control. The end of the Chinese Protectorate General of Annan (Annam) and the consolidation of an independent kingdom in northern Vietnam were part of this process.

2. THE BACKGROUND TO GAO PIAN'S MISSION IN ANNAN

Linking the main episodes of Gao Pian's military career prior to the Huang Chao rebellion was the protracted war to repel encroachments on China's southwestern frontiers by the Nanzhao kingdom during the second half of the ninth century (Backus 1981: 135–58; Wang Zhenping 2011: 135–228).

Several first-hand accounts by Chinese military and administrative personnel offer glimpses of how the deep south was perceived by the embattled garrisons far from home. The gazetteer *Illustrated Record of Marvels* (*Luyi tuji* 錄異圖記) by Wu Jiang (吳降), for example, was written when the latter served as a retainer under Gao Pian on the staff of the Annan expeditionary army *Rouyuan jun* (柔遠軍).[8] Wu Jiang's work was edited and supplemented in 883 by Ch'oe Ch'iwŏn, a native of the Korean kingdom of Silla who served as Gao Pian's secretary from 879–884 after obtaining the Chinese 'presented scholar' in 874 (Hamada 2013: 4–9). Citing other gazetteers of the territory of Jiaozhi (modern Hanoi), the administrative seat of the Protectorate, Wu Jiang reviewed the geography and administrative divisions of the territory, with special attention to the ethnic topography of the mountain range south of Jiaozhi. Here, various indigenous peoples reportedly dwelt in caves, six groups of Man (蠻) and Dan (蜑) occupied scattered settlements, and twenty-one districts were reserved for as many Shengliao (生獠) tribes, a derogatory term for Annan's ethnic minorities. Wu then offered examples of the strangeness of Annan and its customs in terms that resonated with ancient Chinese stereotypes for various peoples inhabiting the borderlands and regions beyond. They were described as devious and benighted, their hair dishevelled, and their bodies tattooed.[9] Their speech was a noisy babble of weird cadences. They were also noted for drinking through their noses[10] and covering their bodies with skins, shells and rudimentary fabrics. In caring for the young, husband and wife took turns, while grown sons vied with their fathers for supremacy. In matters of clothing and diet, mourning and matrimonial etiquette, warfare and medicine, Wu Jiang found local society sorely wanting.[11] To situate Annan in the wider world, the *Record of Marvels* places the Protectorate to the north-east across the sea from the kingdoms of Java and Arabia, and to the southeast, overland, from the Kingdom of Women (a mythical land in the Central Asian Pamir Mountains) and the adjoining territory of the Black Man (Nanzhao).

A systematic description of the different Man peoples in the ninth century, titled *Book of Man* (*Man shu* 蠻書), has come down to us from the brush of Fan Chuo (樊綽) (fl. 860–73), a personal adviser to Cai Xi (蔡襲) (d. 863), military commissioner of the Chinese Protectorate of Annan. The *Book of Man* was lost during the Ming dynasty (1368–1644), but modern editions have largely reconstituted it from citations in the *Great Compendium of the Yongle Period* (*Yongle dadian* 永樂大典) (1408).[12] A more objective observer than Wu Jiang, with a field ethnographer's keen eye for customs, clothing, headdress, gender roles, habitat, and food culture, Fan Chuo provided intelligence to the Chinese military on the identity of the cross-border minority groups that entered into alliances with the Nanzhao invaders.

3. NANZHAO, TIBET AND THE TANG FRONTIER

The Nanzhao kingdom in the region of the modern Chinese province of Yunnan, home to the ancient bronze culture of Dian (滇), had come under the Chinese sphere of influence during the Sui Dynasty (581–618). The region was placed under direct Chinese rule only as a result of the redrawing of borders by the Mongol empire in the wake of its Asian conquests in the thirteenth century. The inhabitants of Nanzhao, meanwhile, were minority peoples pejoratively referred to in Chinese accounts as 'Southern Barbarians' (Nan Man 南蠻), including the Hmong and other ethnic groups collectively designated as Miao (苗), as well as Tibeto-Burman peoples such as the Bai (白). Tang sources distinguish in particular between the White Man (白蠻) and the Black Man (烏蠻), the latter identified in the *Record of Marvels* as the inhabitants of the region adjoining Annan to the northwest. Although their respective ethnic identities cannot be reliably correlated with population groups in modern Yunnan, we know that the Black Man inhabited Dong Cuan (東爨), the eastern part of today's Yunnan, while the White Man lived in Xi Cuan (西爨), western Yunnan, the word *cuan* deriving from the name of the dominant local clan.[13] Linguistic and cultural criteria suggest that the White Man had undergone relatively extensive Sinicisation—probably since Han times—whereas the Black Man seem to descend from a later immigration wave of Tibeto-Burman origin (Zhang Zengqi (張增祺) 2010: 1–51; Blackmore 1961: 60–8).

Sandwiched between Tang China (618–906) and the Tibetan empire (608–866), Nanzhao originated in 740 as a modest principality established by the tribal chief Piluoge (皮羅閣) in the area of Lake Dali. Under Piluoge's son, Geluofeng (閣羅鳳), the Nanzhao began expanding their regional power base from 750 onwards, taking advantage of both the rise of Tibet as a Central Asian power and of China's weakened frontier defences during the An Lushan rebellion (755–63).[14] The southwestward thrust of this expansion reached the Gulf of Bengal, via Burma, in the early 760s (Stott 1963; Twitchett 2000). In 766 Nanzhao erected in its capital Taihe a 'Stele of Virtuous Suasion' (*Taihe Dehua bei* 太和德化碑) with an inscription that bears witness to the diplomatic balancing act pursued by the kingdom following a fresh breach with China.[15] In 794, the rulers of Nanzhao officially switched their allegiance back from Tibet to China (Beckwith 1987: 156) and started sending regular tribute missions to the Tang court. Intermittent conflict with China nevertheless continued during 785–805, a period when the Tang general and one-time ally of Nanzhao, Wei Gao (韋皋) (d. 805), led several successful campaigns from his base in Sichuan against the kingdom and their current Tibetan allies (Twitchett 2000: 161–3).[16] In turn, during the winter of 829–30, a brief but devastating incursion by the Nanzhao into the wealthy Sichuan plain left wide deprivation in its wake.

The sporadic fighting spread to Vietnam in 854 when discontented tribal chiefs in the highlands of the Protectorate prefecture Fengzhou (Vietnamese: Phong Châu) went over to the Nanzhao. The Nanzhao kingdom was in essence a federation of ethnic minorities. Crossing into the Tang territories of Annan and Guangxi, they now recruited local chiefs of trans-border minorities disaffected by Chinese rule.[17] This strategy was helped by growing discontent among the Annan minorities over heavy taxes imposed by the colonial administration and the treacherous actions of the protector general Li Zhuo (李琢). Rivalries among the Chinese garrison commanders that went unchecked by a distant and faltering Tang administration further undermined relations with the indigenous population and exposed critical Chinese positions to attack.[18] The Fengzhou prefecture bordered on northwestern Jiaozhou, the heart of the Protectorate General of Annan. It comprised the towns of Sơn Tây, Vĩnh Yên, and Việt Trì in the upper Red River Delta and extended into the valleys leading towards the frontier with the Nanzhao kingdom.[19] Strategically, it fell to Fengzhou prefecture to control the highland valleys and the frontier population.

4. THE NANZHAO INVASION OF ANNAN

Coming in the context of sporadic but violent border skirmishes—first in Sichuan and then, from 857–58, in Fengzhou—the full-scale invasion of the Protectorate General of Annan by a Nanzhao army of some 30,000 in 859–60 threatened the fertile Red River Valley and its trade routes connecting China with Southeast Asia.[20] In 860, reports were received at the Tang court in Chang'an that Jiaozhi had been attacked and sacked.[21] Following a fresh raid in the second month of 862, an even bigger alliance of Man tribes numbering some 50,000 men invaded Annan in the eleventh month of the same year.[22]

It was in the interval between these two events that the Tang military commissioner in Jiaozhou, Cai Xi, entrusted his secretary Fan Chuo with a delicate diplomatic and intelligence-gathering mission behind Nanzhao lines. By his own account, Fan received a secret commission in the third month of 862 to ride deeply into the 'bandit leader's' cantonment, accompanied only by a small guard. Arriving at the enemy's fortified camp four days later, Fan entered the inner lair through a series of stockades. He was received by three of the Man generals, all surnamed Yang—Yang Bingzhong (楊秉忠), Yang Achu (楊阿觸) ('of the Great Qiang' (大羌), an ancient Tibeto-Burman people), and Yang Qiusheng (楊酋盛)—whom Fan identified as members of the Black Man ethnic group. The negotiation quickly broke down in mutual distrust and Fan Chuo returned to the Chinese side with forebodings as to Nanzhao's intentions. He presented a report to Cai Xi's superior, the protector general Wang Kuan (王寬)—apparently to little avail, for Fan Chuo would subsequently place the blame for the rout of the Tang garrison squarely on Wang Kuan's poor grasp of the situation and lack of foresight.[23]

Confirming Fan Chuo's apprehensions, hostilities resumed the following year. On the seventh day of the second month of 863, after a siege lasting two weeks, the Jiaozhou prefectural city was sacked a second time in a ferocious attack that cost Cai Xi his life. Fan Chuo himself was wounded in the wrist by an arrow. He managed to escape, salvaging the commissioner's seal and presumably his own manuscript, by swimming across the Red River.[24] The remaining Chinese troops retreated to the riverbank, but finding that the last boats had withdrawn, decided to return to die fighting on the city ramparts sooner than perish in the water.

An undated poem titled 'Sighing for the Enlisted Man', in which Gao Pian adopts the voice of a common soldier in the Chinese army, gives empathetic expression to a recruit's dread of the 'red pennant' that signalled a unit to ready for battle:

Steadfast and valorous, arrows flying close—	心堅膽壯箭頭親
Ten years of hardship suffered on the battlefield.	十載沙場受苦辛
Exhausted by the roadside, unable to advance—	力盡路傍行不得
Spreading red pennant, whose is it to be?[25]	廣張紅旆是何人

The consequences of the war in Annan, and of the sack of Jiaozhi in particular, were keenly felt in China too, especially in the home villages of the soldiers who died defending the citadel in 863. Two years later, the poet and scholar Pi Rixiu (皮日休) (ca. 834–ca. 883)[26] visited Xuchang (許昌) in Xuzhou prefecture (許州) (Henan) on his way to sit the presented scholar examination at the capital. He entered Xuchang to the wailing of the relatives of two thousand men drafted there in 862 for a unit fielded in Jiaozhi.[27] The news that they had all lost their lives in the 863 battle had only just reached Xuchang. Moved by the scene he happened upon, Pi Rixiu composed a poignant poem mourning the soldiers' deaths and the empire's disgrace.[28] According to Sun Guangxian (孫光憲) (895?–968), the examination candidate's career suffered as a result of 'stirring up trouble for the state'.[29]

Following the sack of 863, the citadel was occupied by Nanzhao troops, and the surrounding countryside was extensively plundered by the invading mountain tribes. The Vietnamese population of Muong-Viet extraction, who had formed alliances with the invaders, now found themselves driven from their dwellings and reduced to seeking the protection of the retreating Chinese. In the summer of 863, the imperial government abolished the Protectorate General of Annan. A provisional prefectural seat, named 'itinerant Jiaozhou', was set up in the commandery of Haimen (海門) under the palace guards commander Song Rong (宋戎) as acting prefect.[30]

Haimen commandery was the nearest port on the Chinese mainland, situated on the northern shore of the Gulf of Tonkin, northwest of the Leizhou Peninsula and Hainan Island. It was located in modern Hepu county on the lower course of the Nanliu river, the artery that traverses the southeastern part of today's Guangxi Zhuang Autonomous Region and connects Yulin and Bobai with Hepu before spreading through the Nanliu delta into the Gulf. In Tang times, this was a malaria-infested land of exile. The dangerous journey on 'Miasma River', as the dreaded stream was called,[31] connected Annan to supplies from inland China via the ancient Lingqu canal.[32] An important link in the Han maritime silk road, Hepu had already served as an embarkation point for Ma Yuan (Chinese: 馬援, Vietnamese: Mã Viên), sent in AD 41–2 to suppress the anti-Chinese revolt of the Two Sisters Trung (Hai Bà Trưng) (Maspero 1918: 14). The strategic position of the port for trans-shipping supplies from China to Vietnam and its relative safety from Nanzhao attack made Haimen a refuge for retreating troops and fleeing civilians.

As a result of the decision to relocate the provisional seat of the Protectorate General there, Haimen became the logistical base for a gathering counter-offensive. After a series of inconclusive diplomatic and military reprisals by local garrisons, the Tang court's response to the Nanzhao firmed up. At the beginning of 864, Zhang Yin (張茵) was given command of 25,000 troops and was made acting governor of the provisional Protectorate General in Haimen. Massive shipments of grain began arriving by river and by sea, with large vessels making the journey from Fujian to Guangzhou in under a month.[33] The Salt and Iron Commission that oversaw transportation in the south also chartered ships to carry grain that had been collected from the Huainan and lower Yangzi provinces, as well as from Honan via the Grand Canal (Somers 1979: 696). Finally, an expeditionary army was raised to recover Jiaozhou and restore Tang control over the south. This force was placed under the command of General Gao Pian.

5. THE SOUTHERN CAMPAIGN

Gao had been serving as defence commissioner of the northwestern frontier prefecture of Qinzhou (near present Qin'an in Gansu province), a senior post to which he was appointed in 860 after distinguishing himself at the head of 10,000 palace troops in the suppression of a Tangut uprising in Changwu (modern Jingchuan, Gansu).[34] In late Tang times, imperial commissioners, in particular those in strategic border regions, became the increasingly important military counterpart to prefects, the chief civilian administrators. In the fourth month of 864, following an additional invasion of Yongguan by the Southern Man, Gao Pian was ordered to proceed there from Qinzhou at the head of 5,000 palace guards, reinforced by troops from several provinces along the way.[35]

Passing his home in transit through the capital, Gao Pian expressed the turmoil of successive campaigns in the discretely distraught, yet proud voice of his consort in a quatrain titled 'Sorrows of the Women's Quarters':[36]

| Inscrutable, the joys and sorrows of this world! | 人世悲歡不可知 |
| My lord, no sooner returned from routing Heishan, | 夫君初破黑山歸 |

> Now offers his strategy for waging war in the South—   如今又獻征南策
> Morning and evening, we rush to sew his belts   早晚催縫帶號衣
> and uniforms.

Gao Pian was first dispatched to Yongguan, a military commandery with administrative seat in Yongzhou prefecture (modern Nanning), the garrison controlling the minority areas in Guangxi and the Nanzhao–Guizhou border region. Situated on the banks of the Yong River, and linked to Guangzhou through a system of navigable waterways, it was a staging post for dispatching Chinese troops and their provisions to Annan. In the fall of 861, following the first sack of Hanoi, Nanzhao troops had captured and plundered this area (Backus 1981: 136). By 864, having depleted Yongzhou's resources, the Nanzhao ceased their raids on the prefecture. Yet the acting governor Zhang Yin, under orders to recover Jiaozhou with reinforcements provided by the imperial government, held back from launching the Chinese counterattack. Gao Pian was ordered to replace Zhang Yin, with the title of protector general of Annan,[37] thus setting the stage for his invasion of Vietnam.

The *Old History of the Tang* relates that, on arriving in Yongguan in the fifth month of 865, Gao secured his first victory of the campaign, allegedly against Man tribesmen from Champa (林邑蠻).[38] Two months later, at the height of summer, the small expeditionary force arrived in Haimen, where Gao Pian assumed his command and prepared for the Southern Expedition. Poised on the threshold of the new campaign, we find him setting into verse the sentiments of a soldier who has travelled 2,000 km in response to the emergencies buffeting the empire's frontiers from north to south. This poem is titled 'En Route to Annan, Sent to a High Official'. While looking south with new foreboding, it revives recent memories of war in the northwest. Gao Pian evokes two sites that were emblematic in the garrison poetry from outposts along that Tang frontier:[39] the Celestial Mountains (Tianshan 天山) in Xinjiang, and the Phoenix Grove Pass (Fenglin guan 鳳林關), situated in the heavily contested Sino-Tibetan borderland of Gansu and Qinghai:

> In the past we drove ten thousand horses up Tianshan,   曾驅萬馬上天山
> Coming and going in an instant like the wind and   風去雲回頃刻間
> clouds.
> Today at Haimen, we face troubles in the South—   今日海門南面事
> let them not become another Phoenix Grove Pass![40]   莫教還似鳳林關

Phoenix Grove Pass was on the south bank of the Yellow River, some 70 km southwest of Lanzhou. One of Gao Pian's feats as prefect of Qinzhou had been the heavily resisted recovery of this pass for the Tang in 861, together with the two nearby prefectures of Hezhou and Weizhou, from the Tibetan general Shang Yanxin (尚延心).[41] In Haimen, Gao Pian quickly became acquainted with the lack of collaboration among local Chinese officials there and the operational obstacles erected by their rivalries. The General Protectorate's army supervisor Li Weizhou (李維周), a palace eunuch official who feared competition from the new arrival, urged Gao to spearhead the attack with his small contingent. Li himself would then bring up reinforcements from the Haimen garrison of 25,000 under his command.[42] With misgivings, Gao Pian set sail.

Tang seafarers dreaded the Gulf of Tonkin, regularly buffeted by typhoons during the summer months, for its treacherous coastal waters, submerged rocks and reefs, powerful winds, waves, and aquatic creatures. Before taking to the sea, Gao confided his expeditionary force to divine protection. In the poem 'To the Shrine of the God of the South Sea' he offered a glimpse of his emotion on launching of the campaign to recover Jiaozhou:

Green ocean—eight thousand *li*.	滄溟八千里
Today as in the past we dread its swelling rollers.	今古畏波濤
May this day the commander of the Southern Expedition.	此日征南將
Calmly set his myriad hulls across!	安然渡萬艘

In person or by proxy, princes and officials of the Tang sought the patronage of the God of the South Sea for important seafaring ventures. The god's most prominent temple was established in the sixth century on the Pearl River estuary. It stood in full view of sea vessels approaching and departing from Guangzhou.[44] The deity worshipped there was Zhurong (祝融), the god of fire and the South (Kaltenmark 1948: 13–4), also known as Prince of Wealth Circulation (廣利王) in honour of the lucrative South China Sea trade. Sanctuaries to this and similar deities were scattered all along the South China Sea coast.

It seems, however, that Gao Pian had more than a conventional dedication of his expedition in mind. The specific God of the Sea who held sway in the strait separating the island of Hainan from Leizhou was the Wave-Subduing General Fubo jiangjun (伏波將軍). Fubo was a deified manifestation of two Han generals who had distinguished themselves in the conquest of Hainan and Vietnam, Lu Bode (路博德) (fl. 119–09 BC) and Ma Yuan (14 BC–AD 49), both of whom held a particular significance in the history, mythology, and religious life of the Hainan and Leizhou straits. According to local tradition, mariners sacrificed to Zhurong when going to sea out of Guangzhou and to Fubo when departing from Leizhou (Sutton 1989: 98–9, 109). The symbolic subtext of Gao Pian's act of worship, associating the Tang general with his deified Han predecessors, will not have been lost on either his embarking troops or the local population.

Nothing is recorded about the crossing. We know that a century after Gao Pian, in the autumn of 990, the Song official Song Hao (宋鎬) made the same perilous journey in 15 days.[45] Ma Yuan pursued his campaign aboard 'two thousand tower ships' transporting some 20,000 warriors.[46] Under the Tang, vessels of that denomination would have been large warships with triple decks,[47] but the number of Ma's boats suggests that they carried on average only ten soldiers. Two archaeological specimens from the Han period, excavated in Changsha and Guangzhou respectively, are just such modest craft, equipped with small cabins or deckhouses.[48] Too small to navigate the open seas, they hugged the coastline dotted with countless islands, reefs, and other obstacles. Even allowing for poetic licence, the 'myriad hulls' that Gao employed to transport 5,000 men suggests that they, too, were of small dimensions and limited seaworthiness.

Having disembarked near the modern port of Haiphong, Gao Pian and his advance party proceeded to Nanding in the Red River Delta.[49] Li Weizhou, hoping to rid himself of Gao Pian for good, withheld the agreed reinforcement troops. Arriving at Nanding in the ninth month of 865, Gao's troop of 5,000 ran into 50,000 tribesmen from Fengzhou in the upper Red River Delta. The highlanders were surprised in the act of raiding the rice paddies of the Nanding plain. Gao Pian charged with his small force and trounced their far superior number, confiscating the harvest they had gathered to feed his own troops.[50]

This incident illustrates how the plunder of the fertile delta by invading mountain peoples continued two and a half years after the sack of the La Thành citadel in 863. At this point, the historical narrative of Gao's campaign falls quiet until 866. What were his moves in the intervening period? It seems that the precariously small contingent, lacking supplies and reinforcements from Haimen, spent the winter months patiently intercepting Nanzhao communications and preparing for the assault to recover Jiaozhi (Wang Jilin 2011: 213; Maspero 1910: 568–9, n. 4).

In the sixth month of 866, the king of Nanzhao, Shilong (世隆) (r. 59–77), dispatched Yang Jizhu (楊緝助), military governor (節度使) of Shan Chan (善闡) in Nanzhao, and Duan Qiuqian (段酋遷), the Nanzhao-appointed military governor of Annan, to defend Jiaozhi. At the same time, the Tang military envoy Wei Zhongzai (韋仲宰) arrived in Fengzhou, commanding a force of 7,000 soldiers. With this reinforcement, Gao Pian resumed attacking the Nanzhao armies and achieved several victories. When reports of his victories were sent to the capital via Haimen, however, Li Weizhou intercepted and concealed them.[51] The emperor, astonished to have received no news in several months, sent an enquiry to the same Li Weizhou, who replied that Gao Pian was tarrying in Fengzhou, reluctant to engage the enemy. Incensed, the emperor relieved Gao Pian of his command and ordered the general Wang Yanquan (王晏權) to replace him as territorial commander of Annan. Gao Pian was summoned to court to be reprimanded.

In the meantime, Gao Pian had won another victory over the enemy entrenched at Jiaozhi, many of whom were killed or captured, and commenced to lay siege to the walled city.[52] In the tenth month of 866, after a siege of only ten days, the Man were hard-pressed and the city about to fall. At that moment, Gao received a dispatch that Wang Yanquan was on his way from Haimen with Li Weizhou. Gao Pian entrusted his command to Wei Zhongzai and returned north with a company of a hundred men. Wei Zhongzai had already sent his adjutant Wang Huizan (王惠贊) and aide-de-camp Zeng Gun (曾袞) ahead to report the victory at Jiaozhi directly to the court. When they arrived in Hạ Long Bay, they made out flags and pennants flying on the horizon. Upon learning from a passing boat that the new military commissioner and army supervisor were approaching, they hid among the islands to avoid being discovered and arrested. The flotilla of Li Weizhou passed by, and they hastened on towards the capital. Hearing the news of Gao Pian's successes, the emperor reinstated him as territorial commander of Annan, with a promotion to the rank of acting minister of works. As soon as Gao Pian reached Haimen and received the news, he returned to the battle scene.

Wang Yanquan is described as a man of weak character who deferred to Li Weizhou. Li, on the other hand, was of a violent and avaricious disposition. Gao's officers refused to carry out his orders, relaxed the siege and allowed more than half the Man inside the city to escape. When Gao Pian arrived back on the scene, he resumed the attack, captured the citadel, and killed the Man leaders Duan Qiuqian and Zhu Daogu (朱道古) in the tenth month of 866. In a gruesome act sealing the Chinese triumph over the Nanzhao invaders and local rebellion in Annan, Gao beheaded thirty thousand of the captured enemy. He also defeated the Tu Man (土蠻), the Gelao (仡佬) tribe in the Sino-Vietnamese border lands, killing their chieftain, but let 17,000 of the tribesmen return to their highlands.

The same month, Gao Pian sent a memorial to the throne reporting that the pacification of the Man invaders was complete. In the words of the Song historian Sima Guang (司馬光) (1019–86), peace had been restored at the end of ten years of troubles endured by the region since the time when Li Zhuo began harassing Annan in 854–5.[53]

Gao's poem 'Feelings on the Southern Campaign' appears to have been written at this time, marking the moment's conflicting feelings of triumph and regret: the general had decisively restored the military balance in favour of the Chinese Protectorate—thus repaying the emperor's trust—but the ferocious bloodshed remained a fresh memory and the eagerly anticipated return to China after the hardships of campaigning was suspended indefinitely:

Ten thousand *li* we urged the troops through Haimen.	萬裏驅兵過海門
In this life, it is today that we repay the Lord's kindness.	此生今日報君恩
Our return is adjourned till the beacons of war subside—	回期直待烽烟靜
Let not your tunics be stained with tears![54]	不遣征衣有泪痕

In the eleventh month of 866 the emperor proclaimed an amnesty in celebration of this victory, decreeing that the commanderies of Annan, Yongzhou, and Xichuan were each to secure their own borders and refrain from further offensives against the Nanzhao. In Annan, the Sea-Pacifying Army (Jinghai jun 靜海軍) was established under the command of Gao Pian as regional military governor.[55] The name of the army and Gao Pian's new function distinctly echo the title Wave-Subduing General of Lu Bode and Ma Yuan, the words 'sea' and 'waves' evoking, beside the maritime dimension of the southern campaigns, the 'barbarians of the four seas'. Their subjugation demanded pacification of both the elements and the waves of southern indigenous peoples assimilated with *jiao*-dragons and watery creatures (Kaltenmark 1948: 1).

6. A CAPITAL FIT FOR PRINCES

Consistent with the imperial edict, Gao Pian's first act as the new governor was to rebuild the city of Jiaozhi and improve its defences. To localise the citadel that Gao Pian built, the legend and history of Hanoi employ a wide variety of toponyms (Maspero 1910: 551–9; Taylor 1983: 233–9). This is partly due to the Vietnamese custom of making Chinese architectural and geomantic terms, as well as units of local administration, into place names. The name Jiaozhi, which originally designated the regional administrative seat established under the Former Han Emperor Wudi in 111 BC,[56] referred simultaneously to the capital of the Tang Protectorate General of Jiaozhou founded in 622, and to the Jiaozhi county seat located in the same place. The site further coincided with Songping (宋平, Vietnamese: Tống Bình), the seat of another of the eight counties that together constituted Jiaozhou prefecture (Maspero 1910: 551 ff).

The name 'Dragon Belly' (Chinese: *longdu* 龍肚, Vietnamese: Long Đô) applied to the township near the mound Nùng, the elevation on which the royal palaces were eventually built, and referred to the geomantic heart of the city on the southern bank of a meander in the Red River. The ninth-century citadel was deployed around this mound. According to the Record of Jiaozhou,[57] Long Đô was renamed Tô Lịch (Chinese: Su Li 蘇歷) in honour of the meritorious Jin dynasty (265–420) official of that name. In the eighth century, this deified benefactor lent his name to a minor branch of the Red River that encircled the city to the west. Finally, in the ninth century, the great meander to the north was transformed into Hanoi's current West Lake (Papin 2001: 25–30).

In architectural terms, the name Tử Thành (Chinese: *zicheng* 子城, 'inner walled city') referred to a fortress built there by Qiu He (丘和) in 621. Sacked repeatedly in the seventh century, it was replaced in 767 by Zhang Boyi's (張伯儀) La Thành (Chinese: *luocheng* 羅城, 'outer city wall'), a low, extended earth wall built on the north bank of the Tô Lịch. Thus the names Tử Thành and La Thành originally designated separate fortifications on both sides of the river undertaken in the course of several centuries to secure the Chinese headquarters (Tong Zhenzao 1937: 11–5; Nguyen Phuc Long 1975: 24; Papin 2001: 41–3).

In 808, a notable protector general, Zhang Zhou (張舟), raised a new outer enclosure 22 ft high, with a main gate to the south and two lateral gates on the east and west sides, respectively, each provided with watchtowers, drums, and horns to sound the alarm. A garrison comprising left and right guard units was housed in ten encampments inside.[58] This citadel was named Đại La Thành (Chinese: *da luocheng* 大羅城, 'great enclosure').[59] In 825, the protector general Li Yuanxi (李元喜), under attack from local rebels, temporarily abandoned Đại La Thành for a new site across the river Tô Lịch; he appears to have returned the headquarters to the south bank before the year was out.[60] This episode contributed to the aura that would soon surround Gao Pian's construction: although Li Yuanxi already used geomantic principles to establish his base, elevating the river deity Tô Lịch to the position of city god, a soothsayer declared his temporary installation to be the precursor of a larger city that would be built by 'one named Gao' fifty years later.[61]

Despite further improvements by the protector general Wang Shi (王式), who added high palisades and moats to the Đại La fortifications on the south bank in 858,[62] this citadel was overrun in the Nanzhao uprising of 863. Following the recovery of the site in 866 and 867, Gao built his new city there. The remains of this citadel, overlaid by a millennium of subsequent development of the Imperial Citadel of Thăng Long, were discovered in 2003 at the Ba Đình site of the National Assembly, in the political heart of modern Hanoi. In the following decade, archaeological excavation revealed numerous artefacts and architectural elements—remains distributed over several locations—that document the Tang occupation of the site during the different phases leading up to Gao Pian's final construction.

Taking advantage of the Red River as a natural moat, the general used divination to identify an emplacement later recognised as 'fit for a prince,' that is, apt to serve as capital for a future sovereign (Papin 2000: 621–2). In closely similar terms, also involving prophecy and geomancy, the ground was laid for the emergence in post-Tang China of the tenth-century independent kingdom of Shu in nearby Sichuan (Verellen 1998: 213–54). Clearly, the city Gao Pian built was to occupy a central part in the politico-religious foundation myth of modern Vietnam, in which he is credited as having introduced the Chinese practices of spell incantations and *fengshui* divination (Pham Le Huy 2014: 315–25; Niu Junkai 2011: 80–5). Many manuscript manuals on administrative geography and geomancy compiled and transmitted in Vietnam were apocryphally attributed to Gao Pian.[63]

What did Gao's city look like? Its outer wall measured, according to Sima Guang's short entry under the eleventh month of 866, 3,000 paces (步), that is, 15,000 ft (尺) or 5 km in circumference.[64] The more elaborate record preserved in the *Concise History of Viet*[65] makes this enclosure somewhat larger—19,805 ft or 6,601 m in circumference—as well as adding further figures, dimensions, and architectural features: the outer wall was 26 ft or 8.66 m high and 26 ft wide at the base; it had parapets 5.5 ft high on four sides, six outer city gates, five gate towers, 55 watchtowers, and 34 flights of stairs. Three water conduits were provided. Beyond the outer wall, a dike measuring 21,258 ft or 7,086 m in circumference constituted a further enclosure. It was 15 ft (5 m) high, 30 ft (10 m) wide at the base and was intended to protect the city and its thousands of new habitations from flooding.[66]

Gao Pian's citadel resumed the appellation of Đại La. At the same time, Gao conferred new honours on the city god Tô Lịch, already installed by Li Yuanxi as tutelary deity of the Protectorate headquarters

(Pham Le Huy 2014: 316). The cult of Tô Lịch eventually settled in the White Horse Temple (Đền Bạch Mã) in Hanoi's merchant quarter, where it is still found today. Gao Pian's geomantic siting and construction works essentially fixed the aquatic topography of modern Hanoi, 'within the river' (the city's nineteenth-century name), bounded as it still is today by the Red River to the east, by the West Lake to the north, and by the remains of the Tô Lịch river to the west and south (Papin 2001: 27–30; Taylor 1983: 250).

In the midst of these works, and perhaps spurned by his own desire to return to China, Gao Pian discovered the forgotten resting place of a banished Tang official while inspecting the north-central coastal region of Vietnam. Chu Suiliang (褚遂良) (596–658) was an early Tang statesman and a distinguished calligrapher. After serving two emperors as chancellor he was demoted in 655 for opposing the rise of the usurper Wu Zetian (武則天) (624–705) and banished to increasingly remote outposts. He died in 658 on the southern fringes of the empire, as prefect of Aizhou (愛州), between today's Thanh Hóa and Vinh.[67] On the fifth day of the lunar year 868, Gao Pian memorialised the throne:

> Five *li* north of Rinan commandery in Ai prefecture, there is the old tomb of the Secretariat director and duke of Henan Chu Suiliang. In 852, the former governor-general, Cui Geng (崔耿),[68] having visited the grave, erected a stele with an inscription: '[Chu] died at sea in the year 658 and was entombed in this place. Two of his sons and a grandson are buried with him there'.[69]

The *Essential Statutes of the Tang* report that Gao requested permission to carry out a search for the descendants and escort the Chu family remains from the tomb back for burial in their homeland. The emperor granted this. Moreover, he decreed that the Lingnan region appoint special agents to conduct the enquiry into any traces of the Chu clan on compassionate grounds.

By this time, Gao Pian was eagerly anticipating his own return to the Tang homeland. In a poem titled 'In Annan, sent to a Parting Official on his Return to Court' (安南送曹別勅歸), he wrote:

Clouds and water blur the setting sun	雲水蒼茫日欲收
In the fields, deep in mist, a partridge sounds despondent	野煙深處鷓鴣愁
Knowing that you, Sir, shall travel ten thousand *li* to court	知君萬裏朝天去
Speak for me—five autumns have I waged war in the south![70]	爲說征南已五秋

7. PATH OF HEAVENLY MIGHT

Like other commanders of southern expeditions and governors of Annan before him, Gao Pian was confronted with a pressing logistical difficulty of provisioning the Protectorate garrison and maintaining communications with the mainland administration. Moreover, after years of plunder and deprivation, improving the economic prospects of the local population was urgent. In the third month of 867, with the rebuilding of the Đại La citadel and other construction works still underway, Gao Pian petitioned the emperor with a request to improve Jiaozhou's communications by sea. The initiative proved to have far-reaching consequences, as documented in official and private sources. According to the account in the *Old History of the Tang*, Gao wrote:

> 'To reach Yongguan from the South, the journey by water is perilous, obstructed by large rocks and sand. I beg permission to have work-men open a canal and remove all obstacles to transportation by boat.'
> A decree was issued commending this.[71]

The coastal maritime corridor linking the Bạch Đằng river mouth with Haimen across the Gulf of Tonkin was the only practicable route for transporting grain and levies: the land route from Yongzhou, passing through mountainous terrain via the border crossing at Pingxiang, was slow and unsuited to bulk shipping. The even longer itinerary via Chengdu and Yunnan was blocked by the war with Nanzhao. Transportation by sea, moreover, permitted the trans-shipment of goods via Haimen, using either the river network and Lingqu canal connections with Yongzhou, Guangzhou and Yangzhou, or maritime shipping to the great seaports of Guangzhou and Fuzhou and their respective trade networks.

A close reading of the terse account in the *Old History* reveals that it conflates two distinct dimensions to Gao's project: one maritime, involving the clearing of sea lanes, the other land-based, involving the digging of a canal. The tenth-century collection of anecdotes, *Trivia from Beimeng*, quotes a different part of the petition memorial that explains the stakes of Gao's undertaking:

> Gao Pian reported from Annan concerning the opening of a sea route in said prefecture: along the northern sea route between Jiaozhou and the South Sea, large vessels frequently capsized. When Gao Pian went to inspect this, he found that obstructing rocks lay hidden in the water. Thus he requested authorisation to create an opening to benefit communications with the South Sea. The gist of his memorial read: 'Whether towed by men or rowed by oars, as soon as one

embarks upon a parting vessel, stony reefs and obstructing sand-banks do the netherworld's work...' In due course a decree was issued and executed.[72]

The Northern Song historical encyclopaedia *Antecedents from the Palace of Archives* preserves the same citation, but continues with the following phrase:

A small enlargement of the channel would accommodate the traffic. Then trade would naturally prosper with the movement of goods, bringing together China with the outlying regions.[73]

The main obstacle to maritime traffic between Jiaozhi and Haimen lay along the northern shore of the Gulf of Tonkin. Part of today's Guangxi Autonomous Region near the Chinese mainland border with Vietnam, in Tang times this area came under the administration of Jiaozhou prefecture. Halfway between Hạ Long Bay and Haimen, near today's cities of Fangchenggang and Qinzhou, the Jiangshan peninsula (江山半島) juts out far into the Gulf. From the tip of this peninsula a string of large rocks and banks of reefs called White Dragon Tail stretches into the sea, forming a wide arc of treacherous obstacles to navigation. Strong tides and currents, as well as violent winds and waves, created conditions dreaded by Tang navigators, as vividly recorded in the literature of the period (Wang Chengwen 2010: 611–27). The inland area to the north of the peninsula is difficult mountainous terrain that posed difficulties to overland transportation. To avoid these as well as the dangers of circum-navigating Jiangshan, attempts had been made since Han times to build a canal across the peninsula, thus connecting the two bays to the east and the west and shortening the sea voyage by more than 40 km.

This installation, baptised Path of Heavenly Might (Tianwei jing 天威徑), was a unique feat of hydraulic engineering, whose remains are known today as Tanpeng canal (潭蓬運河), after the modern Tanpeng village situated on its banks. The canal finally became operational under the Tang (Huang Quancai & Xu Bianyun 2008: 14–7). A commentary in the *New History of the Tang* identifies the place where Gao Pian had 'dangerous rocks levelled to permit the passage of boats' as North Garrison Beach (Beishu tan 北戍灘), 100 *li* southwest of Bobai county.[74]

Gao ensured that his labours—which were pathbreaking in more than one way—would be known to posterity. The text of the 'Stele Inscription on the Newly Breached Sea Channel Path of Heavenly Might' ('Tianwei jing xinzao haipai bei' 天威徑新鑿海派碑) was written by Gao's secretary, Pei Xing, a Daoist practitioner and writer of *Chuanqi* mirabilia.[75] Pei probably began his career as a retainer on Gao's staff as early as 860 in Gansu. Circumstantial evidence suggests that he served Gao continuously up to the time of the latter's posting in Chengdu (875–8), where he reached the senior rank of deputy military governor of Xichuan (Chen Junmou 1982: 17; Wang Chengwen 2010: 602). We know from the 'Path of Heavenly Might' inscription that Pei Xing redacted this text in his capacity as secretary to the Sea-Pacifying Army of which, as we have seen, Gao was the military governor since 866. The stele was erected in the year 870 on the site of the canal, where its presence was still attested at the end of the thirteenth century.[76] The original inscription was subsequently lost, and so was the copy—probably a rubbing—that the eleventh-century governor of Yongzhou prefecture Huo Zhongjin (霍中謹) used for a new engraving on a stele erected beside his prefectural hall. The text of the latter version, however, is preserved along with its colophon, dated 1098, in the *Outline history of Annan*.[77] A copy in the possession of the scholar Zeng Guo (曾果) from nearby Qinzhou was cited in 1178 by the Song official Zhou Qufei (周去非), who served in Guangnan and Guangxi in the 1170s.

Pei Xing's text opens, like Gao Pian's poem 'To the Shrine of the God of the South', with a description of the terrors of braving the Gulf of Tonkin, here with particular reference to the reefs of the Jiangshan peninsula:

> Flood without limit, blurred expanse touching the sky. Hurricanes reel and surge; breakers rise towering and race ten thousand *li* in a dazzling white flash like cascading mounds [of jades] or avalanches of snow. Even the divine power of Tianwu could not tame their power. The great whale struggles warily, the giant sea turtle fretfully rolls and sways. Where the sturdiest aquatic creatures cannot be tranquil, how much less can a ship's passage be smooth? Mast broken, sails rent, in no time it flounders and sinks, with no hope of rescue—How can this be!

巨浸無涯接天茫茫. 狂颶捲麼駭浪屹起. 若流[玉]堆而(起)[走]雪岫瞬息萬里 皚皚然. 縱天吳之神威亦不能抑遏其勢. 長鯨憂其蹭蹬巨繁(因)[困]其攏(圍) [闔]. 水族之偉者尚尒能安况橫越之舳艦焉能利涉(聊)[耶]. 即(滇櫂楄巾兀) [摧檣裂帆]覆溺而不可(極)[拯]有之乎.

Tang writers spoke of gale-force winds and huge waves in this area, while whales and 'lodestone mountains' (headland formations constituted of quartz and volcanic rock with large magnetite content) added further hazards to shipping (Wang Chengwen 2010: 612–5). Zhou Qufei adds that these dangerous conditions obliged grain transports to brave the open sea.[80]

Gao's biography in the *New History of the Tang* tells us that even the hero Ma Yuan failed to accomplish Gao Pian's feat.[81] Gao the inspired strategist is pictured here as an engineer of superhuman prowess with a magic knack. In an ironic reversal, Pei Xing's inscription claims that Ma, despite great sacrifices, had been forced to abandon the undertaking when his work was engulfed by boulders hurtled from the mountain top by thunderbolts. By contrast, Gao Pian succeeded thanks precisely to a thunder bolt that smashed the rock blocking his path, hence the canal's name: 'Path of Heavenly Might'.[82] In Pei Xing's words, 'the Wave-Subduer [Ma Yuan] lacked the wherewithal; unable to prevail, he could but desist.' The Tianwei canal inscription next mentions three unsuccessful attempts by Tang governors-general of Annan to complete the ill-fated Han project, referring especially to the labours of Zhang Zhou, who made a significant contribution to the Hanoi Citadel. Both of these constructions were undertaken in 808. The characters 元和三年 (AD 808), which are found roughly chiselled into the southwest wall of the midsection of the Tanpeng canal, commemorate the work of Zhang Zhou's expeditionary force here (Verellen 2019: 238–9 and fig. 4). Again, we note that Liu Zongyuan, in his funerary inscription eulogy, declared Zhang's attempt successful, already laying claim to the idea that 'demon laborers came to the aid [of Zhang], sparing the men's strength'.[83] According to Pei Xing, however, success came only 60 years later, as Gao Pian's culminating achievement of his Southern Campaign in 868.

In the late spring of that year, assisted by the chief executive Lin Feng (林諷) and the Hunan Army superintendent Xu Cungu (余存古), Gao mobilised more than a thousand soldiers and seamen to carry out the work. The Hunan Army appears indeed to have provided the main contingent of manpower: engraved also on the southwest wall of the Tanpeng canal are the characters for 'New Hunan Army' (新湖南軍), with the date 'Seventh day of the third month of the year Xiantong 9 (3 April 868)' (Verellen 2019: 240–1 and fig. 6). In the words of the Tianwei jing inscription:

> They started work on the fifth day of the fourth month of Xiantong 9 (1 May 868), wielding shovels and spades, equipped with ample provisions, axes sharpened and chisels hardened, to breach the mountain and cut through the rocks.[84]

8. EXPLOSIVE DEVOTIONS

From the outset, Pei Xing let it be known that Gao Pian 'summoned magic, enlisting a stratagem'. A similarly oblique remark in Gao's biography in the *Old History of the Tang* lent currency to the rumour that Gao's engineering relied on supernatural means:

> When Gao Pian had recovered the districts and townships of Jiaozhou, noting that the provisioning of victuals was obstructed, he inspected the sea route from Jiaozhou to Guangzhou. There were many large boulders blocking the path. Thereupon he recruited workers and performed a ritual [or: 'resorted to magic'] to remove them. From then on, boats plied their trade unimpeded and Annan laid up plentiful reserves. To this day they rely upon it.[85]

The narrative in *Trivia from Beimeng*—quoted partially above—adds a slightly more specific hint, but again leaves the reader in suspense as to how the breakthrough was achieved:

> [Gao Pian] then called up workmen, enticing them with big rewards. Eventually, they cut through the rocks. To this day, the people rely on the benefit that accrued to Jiaozhou and Guangzhou through that crossing. It is rumoured that Pian resorted to magic to avail himself of thunder and lightning to open it. The details are not known [...][86]

The suggestion that Gao Pian mobilised the forces of nature is just what the author of the Tianwei inscription wanted to convey. Another account emanating from Gao Pian's inner circle, Wu Jiang's *Record of Marvels*, offers an explanation along these lines:

> Then he caused the Mother of Lightning [電母] and the Lord of Thunder [雷公] to open a highway between the outlying regions and the court. The mountain spirits and water deities calmed the ocean's sun-dousing waves.[87]

Gao Pian was reputed to be given to ritual performances and spirit worship. In the various geographical and cultural settings of his far-flung campaigns, he was attentive to local tutelary deities and cultivated the cooperation of their devotees. In the Haimen and Qinzhou area this would concern especially the God of Thunder (雷神), also known as Lord of Thunder, whose cult in Tang China produced a particularly explosive amalgam on the shores of the Gulf of Tonkin through assimilation of the native practices of Vietnamese highland minorities. Their characteristic body tattoos served the worship of wind and rain-producing dragons. Their magnificent bronze drums were ritual instruments for rainmaking. The Thunder cult had its focus in Leizhou (literally, 'Thunder Prefecture'), the peninsula facing Hainan Island, where thunder rolled incessantly during spring and summer. During the autumn and winter, the thunder lords were said to retreat into the ground in the shape of pigs. The local southern Li (黎) people claimed their descent from a snake egg gathered by the Lord of Thunder. A story in the eighth-century *Guangyi ji* (廣異記) pits the Lord of Thunder in battle against a whale in the Leizhou straits.[88] Temples dedicated to Thunder featured 'linked drums' and 'thunder chariots' that represented the roll of spreading thunder.[89]

It was unusual for northern officials to show an interest in popular cult activities and local ritual. Indeed, many Tang administrators of outlying regions actively employed themselves in their repression. Gao Pian's approach was different. His eclectic and even eccentric religious interests were widely known and, in some circles, criticised. His spokesman, Pei Xing, was himself a Daoist practitioner deeply interested in local cults. Pei's book of marvels, *Chuanqi*, includes a narrative concerning the thunder cult of Leizhou, with a very peculiar twist. The story is set in the first half of the ninth century in the village Haikang in the midst of 'thunder country'. A villager named Chen Luanfeng (陳鸞鳳), described as upright and unafraid of demons or spirits, harangues an ineffectual local thunder god for failing to produce rain for his village during a drought. Chen then sets fire to the thunder god's temple and challenges the spirit, attacking it with a blade in an open field which causes it to transform into its alter ego, a swine. The hapless creature is then coerced to make rain for years to come.[90]

Was Pei suggesting in his 'Path of Heavenly Might' inscription that Gao Pian had also somehow harnessed the power of the god of thunder? Returning to that narrative, where we left the men with tools poised to begin work on 1 May 868, we learn that they encountered an intractable obstacle:

> In the space of one month, they were close to succeeding when in two places they encountered large boulders jutting forth, extending several tens of feet around. Tough as iron, no force could reduce them: chisel into them and the point would bend, apply an axe and the handle would break. The laborers stared at each other, dejected and feeble handed, utterly unable to devise a solution. Then, suddenly, on the twenty-sixth day of the fifth month (20 June 868) in broad

daylight, impetuous clouds gathered, and an angry wind arose. They could not make out the trees in the darkness nor see the palms of their hands. Shortly afterwards, there was a loud thunderclap and phosphorescent lightning. From the place of the boulder a shock spread several hundreds of li around. The laborers, trembling and shaking, blocked their ears and covered their eyes. At length they looked up and then rushed to inspect the scene: the boulder that impeded their progress had abruptly shattered. Piles of rocks were scattered about while those that could not be lifted by men had been flung up to the two crests.[91]

The inscription goes on to recount how the workers' progress was frustrated two more times by indestructible banks of rock. Each time a thunderstorm broke, and lightning pulverised the remaining two obstacles, one after the other. Where the boulders had disintegrated, a spring welled forth tasting like sweet wine. Zhou Qufei, based on additional sources available to him in the twelfth century, added that after the removal of the first monolith the water in the canal rose by ten feet. The remaining boulder, however, continued to prevent the passage of ships. After Gao Pian again prayed reverently, a new thunderstorm broke out and shattered the boulder, with the waterway now forming a vast stream. Henceforth, transport by boat passed unobstructed.[92]

Significantly, Pei Xing mentions that the method employed in previous unsuccessful attempts to breach the Tianwei impasse under the Tang involved the 'aspersion of vinegar on rocks heated in a pyre' (叠燎沃醯). Splitting rocks by applying heat and then drenching them with water or vinegar was widely practiced in Tang China, as well as the ancient Mediterranean world. It was the technological precursor to rock-blasting with explosives (Golas 1982: 453–8; Needham et al. 1986: 534–5). Pei Xing remarks that where Gao Pian's predecessors wasted their efforts by applying the methods of the past, Gao succeeded thanks to the effects of thunder and lightning. This raises the question whether Gao Pian may have used gunpowder explosives to such startling effect (Verellen 2019).

The phosphorescent flash, loud report, fractured rock, and workers' dumbfounded reaction could certainly be read in that light. The historian of Chinese science and technology, Joseph Needham, argued that the first formula theoretically capable of producing a chemical explosion dated to around 850 (Needham 1986: 85, 112). Gunpowder-propelled projectiles came into military use at the end of the Tang and early Five Dynasties, the first documented application dating to 919. With regard to mining and civil engineering, Needham listed Tang examples of the removal of rocks as obstacles to navigation and observed, with specific reference to the Tianwei breach, though unaware of Pei Xing's inscription, that Gao Pian's staff included Daoist alchemists who may have been in the lead of gunpowder experimentation at the time (Needham 1986: 539–42).[93]

The ingredients saltpetre (potassium nitrate), sulphur and charcoal (carbon) were long known. Not known was that reaching a threshold proportion of nitrate would raise the intensity of the reaction from a deflagration to a detonation. The discovery of this threshold was a matter of experimentation. The roughly contemporary alchemical *Synopsis of Essentials of the Mysterious Dao of True Origin* famously alerted experimenters to the dangers of this work: 'When sulphur [硫黃] and realgar [雄黃] are mixed with saltpetre [硝石] and honey and set alight, a blaze occurs that will burn your hands and face and reduce the house to cinders.'[94]

Ten years after the mysterious Path of Heavenly Might incident, when Gao was prefect of Yangzhou in 878–79, he would save the life of a technician condemned to death under the city's stringent fire regulations for causing a conflagration in a heavily populated area with just such a blaze that came from his house. Gao not only pardoned the man but retained him as a senior member of his staff.[95] The bibliography of the *Song History* attributes an alchemical 'hymn' (頌) to Gao Pian's authorship, an indication of the extent of his personal interest in this science.[96] A leader of exceptional ability and intellectual curiosity, Gao was active at the very intersection of the different areas of expertise that drove the development of gunpowder at that moment in time: mining, warfare, alchemy, and Daoist 'magic.'

The connection between gunpowder and Daoist thunder magic in late Tang times is an additional reason for suspecting Gao's use of explosives. Given the importance of the cult of the Lord of Thunder in the Gulf of Tonkin region, 'thunder' was employed in military campaigns to awe and subdue the local natives. Gao Pian's younger contemporary, Du Guangting (杜光庭) (850–933), tells the following story:

> The military governor of Yongzhou, Li Dan [李耽] [fl. 866], and the chief minister Li Wei [李蔚] [d. 879] revered the Daoist Zou Tingxi [鄒聽希] as their master. When Li Dan held a commission with special powers in Yongnan, indigenous Man tribes [溪洞蠻] slipped through security and ransacked the region, burning fields and hamlets and mounting an armed incursion. Li Dan ordered troops out to oppose them and shore up the defences. The population was terrified. Despite

sounding the alarm for reinforcements, no relief arrived. They were at the end of their tether. Zou Tingxi requested permission to hold a Divine Incantation of the Abyssal Caverns [洞淵神呪] ritual and hired thirty Daoist priests to officiate. On the night of the second day, with incense and candles burning in profusion and the moon and stars bright in the sky, the Man ramparts were suddenly shrouded in a cloud, while rolling thunder and lightning succeeding one another. A single thunderbolt crashed, lighting up the sky. When daylight arrived, watchmen galloped up to report that the host of Man had bolted. The following day, Li Dan interrogated a captured Man chieftain: 'You came from afar to violate our borders and then ran away without a fight—why?' The Man chieftain said: 'That day, after the shock of the thunderbolt, a spy announced the arrival of a vast relief army from the north. We dropped our weapons and fled.'[97]

The story concludes: 'For several years [the Man] continued to harass Annan until the chief minister Gao Pian put them down. If in the end they dared not attack Yongnan, this was due to the merit of Li Dan and of Zou Tingxi's Divine Incantation ritual.' Li Dan is mentioned beside Gao Pian in Emperor Yizong's amnesty decree of 866 in celebration of the recovery of Jiaozhi.[98] It is likely that the events recounted above took place during the Man incursions into Yongzhou in 861–4, one of the threats precipitating Gao Pian's arrival in the region. As the historian of Daoist thunder magic and related practices Judith Boltz aptly asked, with reference to this and similar accounts: 'Is it possible that stories told by Du Guangting and Hong Mai about thunderbolts quelling the menace of Southern Man also have the smell of explosive compounds behind them?' (Boltz 1993: 286, 301 n. 169). The strategic importance of the new technology and the secrecy necessarily surrounding its use, especially in the context of the Southern Campaign, could explain why hints of magic were propagated in accounts of the Tianwei breach, possibly fanned by deliberate mystification on the part of Gao Pian's adjutants.

Gao raised considerable controversy as a patron of alchemists and assorted Daoist practitioners. Both supporters and critics made much of his interest in occult methods—always a part of China's military tradition—the former seeing divine inspiration behind his technological feats, the latter declaring him susceptible to quackery. Gunpowder, 'fire powder' (火藥) in Chinese, was discovered by alchemists in whose mindsets ritual and laboratory practices merged seamlessly. Zhou Qufei and others reported—not improbably—that Gao Pian performed rituals and offered prayers to the gods of thunder and lightning prior to the momentous breach, Pei Xing intimating that Gao Pian summoned these deities 'by special means'. Thanks to his powers, 'Heaven and Earth came to the rescue of his men and Nature lent them support to overcome insuperable obstacles in a twinkling of the eye.'[99] Significantly, Pei also mentions that Gao constructed shrines for the worship of these gods and halls for the officiating clergy.

Even before the works were completed on 4 October 868, Gao Pian's wish to return to the capital had been granted. In the eighth month, a decree was promulgated naming him general of the Imperial Insignia Guard of the Right in Chang'an. The emperor also acceded to Gao Pian's request to be replaced in the Jiaozhi command by his grandnephew and protégé, Gao Xun (高潯) (d. 881), of whom it was said that when Pian went to battle, 'Xun was always in the vanguard, braving arrows and stones and urging the men forward.'[100]

Gao Pian returned to the capital via the new Tianwei canal, occasioning another farewell poem. The quatrain below is titled 'Passing Through the Path of Heavenly Might'. Having concluded his mission in Annan with the complete extirpation of the 'jackal-and-wolf' perpetrators of rebellion, Gao likens the canal to a broad and smooth highway, terms echoed by Zhou Qufei's 'vast stream' and Wu Jiang's 'highway between the outlying regions and the court.' Travelling officials and supply convoys would henceforth use it in place of the tortuous overland journey:

Jackals and wolves exterminated, we withdraw to court.	豺狼坑盡却朝天
Our war horses no longer neigh in swamp and mountain mist.	戰馬休嘶瘴嶺烟
For the road of return, once hazardous, is level now and broad:	歸路嶮巇今坦蕩
A single stretch of a thousand *li*, as straight as a bowstring.	一條千里直如弦

9. A PARTING OF THE WAY: GAO'S IMAGE IN CHINA AND IN VIETNAM

Soon after the end of the southern campaign and Gao Pian's return to the Tang court, representations of the man and his place in history began to evolve along separate paths in China and Vietnam. Inevitably, the personal destiny and quasi-mythical aura of Gao as a statesmen and warlord became embroiled in the controversies about loyalty, legitimacy, and regional autonomy characteristic of this period of dynastic decline and contention for power. Just as inescapably, Gao Pian's patronage of Daoism, the imperial cult of the Tang dynastic house that was also adopted by breakaway regimes to legitimise their secession (Verellen 1989b), fanned the polemic surrounding his status as traitor/hero.

For more than a decade, Gao Pian continued his distinguished career defending the embattled dynasty in far-flung posts across the empire. Having served six months in the capital as general of the palace guard, he was appointed military governor of the Tianping Army (天平軍) and prefect of Yunzhou in the northeastern province of Shandong in 869. At the end of 874, having successfully contained rebel activity in that region, he was redeployed to Sichuan to resume the war against the Nanzhao, who had renewed their attacks on China's southwestern border with deep raids into Xichuan province and a siege of its capital Chengdu. Appointed prefect of Chengdu and military governor of Xichuan in the first month of the following year, Gao Pian drove the Nanzhao back over the border and engaged in massive fortifications. Like Jiaozhi, the ancient city of Chengdu was provided with a new outer wall. His offensive-defensive strategy again proved highly effective.

By 878–79, the imperial court relied on Gao Pian to contain the now growing menace from the Huang Chao rebellion, first as military governor of the middle Yangzi province of Jingnan (Hubei), and then of the Zhenhai Army (鎮海軍) in Jiangsu. As military governor of Huainan (modern Jiangxi) and prefect of Yangzhou beginning in 879, he was in charge of the defence of the crucial lower Yangzi region against Huang Chao, whose army was now threatening to return to the central plains after sacking and plundering Guangzhou. During 880–82 Gao was appointed commander-in-chief of the Joint Expeditionary Forces, with overall responsibility for the war effort against Huang Chao. In addition, he held the key post of commissioner for salt, iron, and transport, with financial authority over southern and central China. He continued to rule with increasing autonomy in Yangzhou until his death in 887.

Gao's innovative civil and economic administration of Huainan prepared the foundation of the Five Dynasties kingdom of Wu (902–37) by Yang Xingmi (楊行密) (852–905), a former follower of Huang Chao who, in 883, switched allegiance and served as prefect under Gao Pian.[102] This outcome, after Gao's ambiguous military posture towards Huang Chao in 880–81, led to the charges of insubordination against him. Gao's deepening involvement with Daoist advisers was cited as the reason for his assassination in a power struggle to succeed him (Miyakawa 1974:

75–99). The rich documentary record for the Huainan period of Gao's career, including court and personal archives, official historiography, informal and polemical writings, poetry, and the testimony of literati retainers, reflects the widely diverging judgements that were, not surprisingly, brought to bear on an exceptionally gifted, powerful, and controversial actor on centre stage at a fateful juncture in history.

On the Vietnamese side, the transition to independence has been the subject of detailed studies.[103] Zeng Gun (曾袞), the junior staff officer under Gao Pian and former aide to Wei Zhongzai, succeeded Gao's grand-nephew, Gao Xun, in 877, becoming the last nominal governor-general of the Chinese Protectorate.[104] The year after Huang Chao's devastation of Lingnan of 879, the remaining Tang military presence in Annan succumbed to mutiny, obliging Zeng Gun to abandon his post. No serious attempt was made to re-establish Tang rule over Annan in the years up to the fall of the dynasty in 907 (Somers 1979: 739–40; Gardiner 1981: 70–7; Taylor 1983: 256–61).

The clan of Khuc Thue Du, representing the local elite empowered by Gao Pian, assumed control of the former Protectorate from Zeng Gun's departure until 930. That year, Gao Pian's citadel, Đại La, was briefly recaptured by the Southern Han (909–71) kingdom that had established itself in Guangdong and Guangxi after the fall of the Tang (Clark 2009: 153–5; Gardiner 1983: 38–43). The Southern Han held the Red River Delta, but little else, for one year. Their next and final attempt to control Annan was spectacularly defeated by Ngô Quyền (d. 944) in the naval battle of Bạch Đằng River of 938. The following year, Ngô Quyền proclaimed himself sovereign, thus formalising the de facto autonomy of tenth-century Vietnam and paving the way for the independent kingdom founded by the Lý dynasty in the eleventh century (Kawahara 1975: 5–28). Henceforth, the Song dynasty contented itself with managing the Sino-Vietnamese frontier as a tributary relationship (Anderson 2007: 39–67).

In the process of Vietnamese independence, the aura of Gao Pian's tenure in Annan played a vital role. The historical Gao Pian, once departed, disappeared from the official Vietnamese record—for some, into the mist of insanity, with Gao described as keeping to himself, 'riding astride a wooden eagle' (Papin 2001: 52). The contraption in fact represented a crane, the mount of immortals. It is not clear to what extent the rising political elite in Vietnam were aware of or interested in the historical vicissitudes of Gao's later career. However, their acquaintance of this lampoon concerning Gao's alleged dotage shows that they knew the late Tang satire *Bewitched in Guangling* (廣陵妖亂志) by the poet-essayist and self-avowed slanderer Luo Yin (羅隱) (833–910). Whatever their reading of late Tang internal politics, the rising Vietnamese leaders seized the opportunity offered by the weakened reach of the imperial court. In this regard, they were no different from their Chinese counterparts in neighbouring Lingnan and other regions of the continental mainland, including Sichuan and Huainan, both governed by Gao Pian after Annan. The shifting balance of power favoured the rise of regional autonomy not only in China proper and Đại Việt, but also in other Southeast Asian borderlands, such as Pagan, Sukhotai, and Angkor. Not unlike the independent regimes to the north, Annan was in search of an identity providing legitimacy for its secession—in other words, a foundation myth. Gao Pian's eclipse from Vietnamese historiography opened the door for mythology to enter. The character thus created, known locally as Prince Cao (高王), simultaneously played the parts of the last foreign occupier and the precursor of the sovereigns of the Viet kingdom.

10. PRINCE CAO

This apparent paradox had its roots in three overlapping sets of political ambiguities surrounding the emergence of independent Vietnam. The first arose from the brief restoration of Tang colonial rule, paradoxically seen in a favourable light as a liberation from the disastrous occupation by neighbouring Nanzhao. This turn of events set the stage for a Tang exit in the role of benign protector. The second ambiguity arose from the circumstances of Gao Pian's withdrawal from his role as defender of the Tang imperial house. The third stems from the strategy of the new Viet sovereigns to bolster their secessionist legitimacy in terms of the former occupiers' own dynastic ideology. Our concluding section will focus on this last aspect, that is, the portrayal of Gao Pian in Vietnam as a local dynastic founder in the Chinese mould, casting him in turn in the traditional roles of culture hero, benefactor, diviner, and tutelary spirit.

Keith Taylor, an historian of Vietnamese independence, astutely observed that the legacy of Gao Pian in Vietnam, alive for a millennium after his time, served to elaborate a new ideology by framing the narrative of Gao's Southern Campaign in the overall history of Vietnam's relations with China, with the parallel interventions of Ma Yuan and Gao Pian symmetrically providing a beginning and a closure (1999).[105] In Chinese founding myths, the removal of natural barriers, control of waterways, and opening of routes of communication were the traditional feats of the culture hero. The prototype was the legendary dynastic founder and controller of flood waters Yu the Great (大禹), who breached the Huashan mountain range in Shanxi with the help of the Yellow River god, unblocking the mighty stream through the breach of the Dragon Gate (Longmen 龍門). The heroic act stands for the civilising effect of local government, favouring the circulation of goods and development of prosperity. The theme of breaching the 'horse gate' and the Tianwei canal, essential features of the campaigns of Ma Yuan and of Gao Pian, respectively, portrays Vietnam's period *within* the Chinese realm as a state of fluid communications with the north. Vietnamese tradition placed Gao on a higher pedestal even than Ma (Papin 2001: 35–6; Taylor 1999: 244). The fifteenth-century Vietnamese historian Ngô Sĩ Liên went so far as to compare Gao Pian's act with that of 'Yu controlling the waters',[106] an idea already suggested in contemporary eulogies beginning with Ch'oe Ch'iwŏn's poetic comparison of Tianwei with Longmen.[107] The recasting of the last Chinese protector as local dynastic founder suggests perhaps that 'within' need not become 'without' under independence and that the figure of Gao Pian was there to stay. As the historian Philippe Papin pointed out, in the space of a few short years Gao Pian became a pillar of Vietnamese political culture, a reference for the first Vietnamese dynasties, and a central character of Vietnamese historical legend, offering the Sino-Vietnamese elite a focal point for developing a national ideology. Papin goes on to cite examples of new crystallisations of traditional Vietnamese founding myths around the figure of Gao Pian (Papin 2000: 621–4).

Not only mythology but also the official record depict Gao Pian as a benefactor: restorer of peace after a decade of turmoil, builder of Hanoi's defences and habitations, remover of obstacles to shipping, and creator of wealth through trade. We have noted the propaganda emanating from Gao's own camp and its role in shaping this image. Gao Pian surrounded himself with gifted and popular writers, seemingly aware of the importance of skilled communications for swaying public and official opinion.[108] Among such 'inner circle' writings, the 'Path of Heavenly Might' inscription, the *Record of Marvels*, and several among the 'Thirty Quatrains Commemorating Virtue' celebrate the general's benefactions to Annan.[109]

Gao Pian the diviner made use of natural features, such as the mound Nùng, to shape the site of the capital, and the Red River and Tô Lịch to serve as its moats. The apocryphal *Record of Gao Pian Miracles*, cited in a nineteenth-century collection preserved at the Hán-Nôm Institute in Hanoi, states that Nùng constituted the precise heart of the Đại La citadel. When the king, Lý Thái Tổ (Lý Công Uẩn), established the Lý dynasty there in 1010, he did so with express reference to Prince Cao's former capital 'situated between Heaven and Earth, where the Dragon coils and the Tiger crouches [i.e., embracing the antithetical categories of Chinese cosmology], where floods are no longer feared [thanks to Gao's dike] and the soil is fertile, the geomantic heart of the Viet territory.'[110]

Lý Công Uẩn renamed 'Prince Cao's old metropolis' Thăng Long. In local mythology, Prince Cao became associated with the Later Han governor Shi Xie (士燮) (137–226), also known as Sĩ Nhiếp or Prince Sĩ, who had served as grand protector (太守) of Annan for forty years. Both of these figures communicated with the early kings of the Lý dynasty in the eleventh century through dreams, apparitions, and miracles as recorded in the fourteenth and fifteenth century collections *Việt điện u linh* (越甸幽靈) and *Lĩnh Nam chích quái* (嶺南摭怪).

It is instructive to compare how at that time emerging separatist kingdoms in China were formulating their ideologies of legitimation with respect to the Tang dynasty. In the early tenth century, Du Guangting, the Daoist court divine who reported the thunder miracle deployed against the Southern Man in Yongzhou, served the king of independent Shu (蜀) in nearby Sichuan.[111] This is how he linked the sovereigns of that land with the culture heroes who had fashioned *its* early development:

> The mountains and rivers of Shu constitute a land of great blessings. It has long been fit to serve emperors and princes as capital. Many are the sages and worthies of preceding generations who for the sake of posterity established control over its hills and waters and breached its impasses with arteries of communications (cited in Verellen 1989b: 74–5).

Among the region's founding heroes were diviners, notably the founder of organised Daoism, Zhang Daoling (張道陵), who established the twenty-four dioceses of the nascent Heavenly Master church in Sichuan, using geomancy:

> The Perfected then pointed towards the mountains in the northwest and said: 'In this place a city shall be built.' And again he pointed south beneath the city and said: 'In this place the stream and mountains face each other; a place of blessing shall be established here.' In gratitude, later generations erected a shrine for him at that place. To this day their veneration and supplications continue unbroken (cited in Verellen 1997: 249–65).

According to Vietnamese legend, Gao Pian's geomantic insight had revealed the 'royal aura' of the nearby future birthplace of Lý Công Uẩn. However, Gao is said to have tried to obliterate that locality (Taylor 1999: 245). The implication is that the governor sought to prevent the rise of a Viet sovereign, adding an interesting dimension to the image of Gao as a transitory figure. The same ambivalent reticence resonates through many narratives relating his unsuccessful attempts to subdue local tutelary divinities: having tried in vain to neutralise Mount Tan-Vien, birthplace of the Hundred Tribes of Viet, Gao decided to integrate that feature into his capital; in a dream encounter with Cao-Lo, the mythical founder Cao Thong (皋通), Gao Pian confided in the spirit the difficulty of being a stranger in one's land of adoption; and the spirit of the Long Đô construction site for Gao's new capital appeared to him in a dream. The deity approved the building project but protested being relegated to the role of a tutelary god. Gao Pian acknowledged this complaint, addressing the spirit as king and city god, adding that Gao, for his part, was destined to return north and not dwell in this land. According to another version, Gao Pian withdrew from Vietnam because the presence of a dragon in the Tô Lịch river made it impossible for him to establish his sway there (Yamamoto 1970: 89–92; Papin 2001: 50–2).[112]

Like the God of the South Sea and the God of Thunder, however, the military deity Lý Phục Man (李服蠻), who was still worshipped in many villages of the Red River Delta in the twentieth century, came to Gao's aid and that of earlier Chinese generals battling local natives (Nguyen Van Huyen 1938: 17–8). Reducing a local deity to submission while claiming his territory is an act of exorcism. In Chinese feudal mythology, taking possession of a territorial conquest involved the subduing of the locality's tutelary spirit. Daoist ritual is heir to this tradition. The shadow government of the spiritual realm being the mirror image of civil administration in this world, the authority of the lord of a locality was founded on the fealty of the local Earth God (土地神) (Verellen 1997: 263). The inconclusive outcome of Gao Pian's conquest of the local gods of the South accounts for his ambivalent status as a founder of sorts who subsequently withdrew from his 'adopted' land.

This peculiar role did not prevent Gao Pian from becoming himself the object of local cults in several places. The construction of the Chengdu city walls, like the Tianwei canal, was considered to have been accomplished by divine intervention.[113] Gao's reputation as a miracle worker spread as far as Fujian, where his posthumous intervention thirty years later was held responsible for the opening of the Gantang Harbour (甘

棠港) situated—like the Path of Heavenly Might—on a jagged coastline, near the Huangqi (黃岐) peninsula north of Fuzhou. The opening of this harbour was accomplished by a strange apparition and thunder, presumed to have been harnessed by Gao Pian. The local king surnamed the site Road of Heavenly Might (天威路).[114]

Gao Pian's deification in Vietnam began in his own lifetime. Wu Jiang put it thus in his *Record of Marvels*, describing the southern minority peoples in characteristically denigrating language while evoking the magnificence of the lords of Chinese antiquity in the idiom of the *Book of Poetry*:

> The cave-dwelling savages and the Man-barbarians by the sea, every one of them inebriated with [Gao Pian's] bounty and sated by his benevolence [醉恩飽義],[115] submitted a petition to the distant imperial palace requesting that a shrine to him be erected in his lifetime.[116]

In a similar vein, one of Ch'oe Ch'iwŏn's *Thirty Quatrains* titled 'Living Shrine' underlined the singular veneration in which Gao Pian's memory was held in Vietnam in his own day:

Since ancient times, Man and Yi have been hardest to govern.	古來難化是蠻夷
In Jiaozhi who ever won their fond remembrance?	交趾何人得去思
The annals of the myriad generations of our sagely dynasty	萬代聖朝青史上
Solely record that the natives erected a Living Shrine to him.	獨傳溪洞立生祠

Notes

1. This chapter originated as part of a biographical project on Gao Pian, carried out with the generous support of the Chiang Ching-kuo Foundation for International Scholarly Exchange.
2. His collected poetry is listed as '*Gao Pian shi* (one scroll)' (高駢詩一卷) in the official Tang bibliography, *Xin Tang shu*, 60.1613. The collection subsequently disappears as an integral work from circulation. Fifty individual poems survive and are collected in ch. 598 of Complete Tang Poetry, *Quan Tang shi*.
3. For an overview of the main themes of Gao's poetry, see Xu Haibing (徐海冰) (2014).
4. To use the expression coined by Taylor (1983). On Gao Pian's role in the emergence of Vietnam as an independent kingdom, see especially pp. 254–6.

5. Gao Chongwen has biographies in both official histories of the Tang dynasty. See *Jiu Tang shu*, 151.4051, and *Xin Tang shu* 170.5161.

6. His biography in the *New History of the Tang* classifies Gao among 'insubordinate officials'. See *Xin Tang shu* 224B.6391–404.

7. See my forthcoming biography, provisionally titled *Trials of Allegiance: Gao Pian and the Fall of the Tang*.

8. This army had been established under the Annan Protectorate General in 791. See Wang Pu (2006: 73.1565).

9. The fourth century BC *Book of Mountains and Seas* (*Shanhai jing* 山海經) reports that their appearance assimilated the southerners with the *jiao*-dragon (蛟龍) that gave its name to Jiaozhi. See Kaltenmark (1948: 2).

10. This way of imbibing water (or perhaps liquor) using a straw regularly caught the attention of travellers. See Zhou Qufei (1999: 10.420–1).

11. 'Bu Annan luyi tuji' (補安南錄異圖記) (883), in *Guiyuan bigeng ji jiaozhu*, 16.553–61. The unflattering descriptions include standard ethnic slurs. See the annotations in 16.558–9. *Shengliao*, cf. *Xin Tang shu* 43B.1151.

12. See Fan Chuo, *Man shu jiaozhu.*

13. Fan Chuo, *Man shu jiaozhu* 4.81; Fujisawa 1969: 75–127.

14. See Wang Zhenping (2013: 97–137), and the chronology of Man insurrections against the Tang in Schafer (1967: 61–9).

15. See the text and translation in Chavannes (1900).

16. A truce between Tibet and Nanzhao seems to have been concluded in 822 (Beckwith 1987: 167).

17. See Fan Chuo, *Man shu jiaozhu* 4.87–8, 92–108, 10.238. Cf. Backus (1981: 138–9) and Taylor (1983: 240–1).

18. Chinese official historians dwell on such dysfunctions in the Protectorate administration. Taylor (1983: 239–49) develops the point persuasively.

19. On the administrative organisation of the prefecture, see Maspero (1910: 665–8).

20. In the eighth and ninth centuries, Jiaozhou rivalled and periodically eclipsed Guangzhou as the main conduit for trade between China and Southeast Asia. See Wang Gungwu (1958: 82–5).

21. See Sima Guang (1956: 250.8092). A variant source cited in the commentary suggests that the fall of the city had already occurred during an earlier raid. See also Taylor (1983: 243) on the fall of the La Thành citadel in 860.

22. Sima Guang (1956: 250.8101).

23. Fan Chuo, *Man shu jiaozhu* 4.87. Wang Kuan had been appointed protector general in 860, following the defeat of Annan by the Man that year. See *Xin Tang shu* 222.6282. According to Sima Guang (1956: 250.8094, 8096), Wang Kuan was military commissioner (經略使) of Annan from 861 until his replacement by Cai Xi in the second month of 862.

24. Fan Chuo, *Man shu jiaozhu* 4.101.
25. 'Tan zheng ren' (嘆征人), by Gao Pian, in *Quan Tang shi* 598.6919.
26. On the life and works of Pi Rixiu, see Nienhauser (1979).
27. On the multi-province enlistment following the 862 raid, see *Xin Tang shu* 19A.652 and Wang Pu (2006: 87.1895).
28. See *Quan Tang shi* 608.7015, with a note explaining the circumstances of the poem's composition.
29. Sun Guangxian (1999: 2.8–9); see also Appendix N, 'P'I Jih-hsiu and the Nan-chao War' in Taylor (1983: 344–8).
30. *Jiu Tang shu* 19A.654; Sima Guang (1956: 250.8101–6); Taylor 1983: 245–6.
31. *Jiu Tang shu* 41.1759.
32. Built by the first emperor Qin shi huang (秦始皇) (r. 220–10 BC) to link the Xiang and the Li rivers in Guangxi, a hydraulic engineering feat important for the history of China's relations with Southeast Asia.
33. *Jiu Tang shu* 19A.652; Wang Pu 2006: 87.1596; Backus, *Nan-chao kingdom*, 140.
34. Sima Guang (1956: 250.8110); *Jiu Tang shu* 182.4703.
35. *Jiu Tang shu* 19A.656.
36. 'Gui yuan' (閨怨), in *Quan Tang shi* 598.6919. Cf. the commentary in Xu Haibing, 'Gao Pian de xintai mingyun yu shige chuangzuo', 77.
37. *Xin Tang shu* 222B.6284, Sima Guang (1956: 250.8109–10).
38. *Jiu Tang shu* 19A.659. This curious information, suggesting the presence of Cham warriors from Central Vietnam in the Chinese mainland province of Guangxi, could be construed as illustrating the breadth of the alliance of minorities rallied in opposition to the Tang. But *Zizhi tongjian*, in his critical notes *Zizhi tongjian kaoyi* (資治通鑒考异) dismisses it as a confusion of ethnic identities. See Sima Guang (1956: 250.8112), attributing the error to Liu Xu (劉昫) (887–946), chief editor of *Jiu Tang shu*, and Sima Guang (1956: 249.8070), citing the *Man shu* with reference to an earlier attack of Annam in 858 that was also attributed to the Cham in *Jiu Tang shu* 19A.654-5 (cf. the annotations in *Man shu jiaozhu* 4.110). It is clear from Sima's notes that ethnic distinctions with respect to Champa were already blurred in the annalistic archives 'Veritable Records' (實錄) that underlay Tang official historiography.
39. Cf. no. 19 of Du Fu's (杜甫) (712–70) Qinzhou cycle (秦州雜詩二十首), which evokes Fenglin as a battle ground, as do the first of Gao Pian's 'Saishang qu ershou' (塞上曲二首) and 'Yuhuai' (寓懷) (cf. below).
40. 'Fu Annan que ji taisi' (赴安南却寄台司), by Gao Pian, in *Quan Tang shi* 598.6919.
41. See *Xin Tang shu* 216B.6108.
42. Sima Guang (1956: 250.8112).
43. 'Nanhai shen ci' (南海神祠), in *Quan Tang shi* 598.6918. Translation adapted from Schafer (1967: 105).

44. See the gazetteer *Da Qing yitong zhi*, 442.13a–b, and Wang Yuanlin (2006: 22–8).

45. *Song shi* 488.14061; Maspero, 'Protectorat général (II)', 699–670.

46. *Hou Han shu*, 24.839. For a detailed study of Ma Yuan's expedition, see Maspero (1918: 11–28).

47. See the Tang military manual *Taibo yinjing quanjie* (太白陰經全解), by Li Quan (李筌) (8th c.), ed. Zhang Wencai (張文才) and Wang Long (王隴) (Changsha: Yuelu, 2004), 4.226, tr. Joseph Needham et al., 1971: 685.

48. Bao Zunpeng (包遵彭), *Handai louchuan kao* (漢代樓船考) (Taipei: Zhonghua congshu, 1967), 103–4. While referring technically to war boats with multiple decks or 'castles', the Han term *louchuan* also designated naval forces generically.

49. The probable place of landing was Hải-khẩu (海口) at the mouth of the Bạch Đằng river (白藤江) in Thủy Nguyên district between Hạ Long Bay and Haiphong. Nanding was one of the eight counties into which the Tang administration divided Jiaozhou prefecture. See Maspero (1910: 566–9, 670). The demarcations of Nanding shifted over time, rendering any geographical correlation hazardous between the protectorate county in 865 and the modern Vietnamese province of the same name (Nam Định).

50. Sima Guang 1956: 250.8112.

51. Sima Guang 1956: 250.8114–5; *Xin Tang shu* 216B.6092.

52. Sima Guang 1956: 250.8112–6; Taylor 1983: 247.

53. Sima Guang 1956: 250.8115–6. See also *Jiu Tang shu* 19A.660 and Taylor (1983: 248).

54. 'Nanzheng xuhuai' (南征敘懷), in *Quan Tang shi* 598.6923.

55. Sima Guang 1956: 250.8116–7. The amnesty decree is preserved in *Tang da zhaoling ji*, 86.488–91.

56. *Han shu* 95.3859; 28B.1628–9; Yu Ying-shih 1987: 451–3.

57. *Jiaozhou ji* (交州記), quoted in *Việt điện u linh tập lục*, 27–8.

58. Wang Pu 2006: 73.1565; Lê Tắc 1995: 9.218–21.

59. *Đại Việt sử ký toàn thư, Ngoai Ky* (外紀) (Tokyo 1884 ed.), 5.161.

60. *Jiu Tang shu* 17A.515; Taylor 1983: 233–4; Maspero 1910: 553–5. For the transfer to Songping, see *Xin Tang shu* 43A.1112.

61. Lý Tế Xuyên, *Việt điện u linh tập* 87–9; *Đại Việt sử ký toàn thư, Ngoai Ky* (外紀) (Tokyo 1884 ed.), 5.162; *Việt sử lược* (Shanghai 1922 ed.), A.10b. Cf. Maspero 1910: 554.

62. Sima Guang 1956: 249.8066; Lê Tắc 1995: 9.226–7.

63. E.g. *Cao Biền di cảo* (高駢遺稿), Hanoi Han-Nom Institute ms A.2898, *Gao Pian di gao ji* (高駢地稿集), Paris Société asiatique ms B23, and *An-Nam địa lý cảo* (安南地理稿), Hanoi Vietnam National Library ms R1921. I am indebted to Pierre Marsone and Olivier Tessier for providing me with samples of the Paris and Hanoi manuscripts, respectively.

64. Sima Guang 1956: 250.8117.

65. *Việt sử lược* (Shanghai 1922 ed.), A.12b. *Đại Việt sử ký toàn thư, Ngoai Ky* (外紀) (Tokyo 1884 ed.), 5.167 essentially reproduces the following items, with small numerical variants.

66. *Zizhi tongjian*, followed by *Đại Việt sử ký toàn thư*, has 'more than 400,000 units of habitation,' *Việt sử lược* 'more than 5,000.' The wide disparity may be due to differing uses of the measure word *jian* (間) for units of construction. On the risks of flooding in that period, see Tong Zhenzao (1937: 12).

67. See his biographies in *Jiu Tang Shu* 80.2729-39 and *Xin Tang shu* 105.4024-30.

68. See Taylor (1983: 239).

69. Wang Pu 2006: 45.951. Cf. *Xin Tang shu* 105.4029.

70. In *Quan Tang shi* 598.6922. Translation adapted from Schafer (1967: 241).

71. *Jiu Tang shu* 19A.661. In another version (Wang Pu 2006: 87.1895), Gao Pian reports having already given the order for his men to dig an opening and remove the boulders, the initiative again earning the emperor's praise. See also 'Yongguan tongcao chuan zou' (邕管通漕船奏), in *Quan Tang wen bubian*, 87.1070, and Sima Guang 1956: 250.8118.

72. Sun Guangxian (1999: 2.9).

73. *Cefu yuangui*, 678.8103. Cf. Sima Guang 1956: 250.8118.

74. *Xin Tang shu* 43A.1109.

75. See the collection *Pei Xing chuanqi*.

76. See *Yuan yitong zhi*, 10.741. This location had already been the site of Ma Yuan's canal; see the commentary in *Xin Tang shu* 43A.1109.

77. Lê Tắc 1995: 9.232–43, collated with *Quan Tang wen*, 805.8463–4. References below are to the edition in Verellen (2019: 250–3). On the Song recension and colophon, see Wang Chengwen (2010: 604).

78. An aquatic deity from the fourth-century BC mythical geography *Book of Mountains and Seas* (*Shanhai jing* 山海經).

79. 'Tianwei jing xinzao haipai bei', Verellen 2019: 252, ll. 1–4.

80. Zhou Qufei 1999: 1.33–5.

81. *Xin Tang shu* 224B.6392.

82. According to the evidence examined by Wang Chengwen (2010: 606–11), the original name was Tianwei yao (天威遙). A southwestern dialect word, *yao*, meaning 'canal' in Tang and Song times, was met with incomprehension from northerners, giving rise to diverging appellations in the literature. Locally, the place is also known as Immortals' Ridge, alluding to the divine assistance afforded the works. The name Tanpeng dates to the 1982 declaration of the structure as a Guangxi Autonomous Region heritage site. See Huang Quancai and Xu Bianyun (2008: 16–7).

83. *Liu Zongyuan ji* 10.241. Huang Quancai & Xu Bianyun (2008: 15) speculate plausibly that sixty years after Zhang Zhou, Gao Pian dredged and widened the existing channel to admit larger boats with deeper draft.

84. 'Tianwei jing xinzao haipai bei', ed. Verellen 2019: 253, ll. 14–5; see also *Đại Việt sử ký toàn thư, Ngoai Ky* (外紀) (Tokyo 1884 ed.), 5.167–8.

85. *Jiu Tang shu* 182.4703.

86. Sun Guangxian (1999: 2.9).

87. 'Bu Annan luyi tuji' in *Guiyuan bigeng ji jiaozhu* 16.554–5.

88. Quoted in *Taiping guangji*, 464.3818. On the *Guangyi ji* and its compiler Dai Fu (戴孚) (*jinshi* 757), see Dudbridge (1995).

89. On Gao Pian and the thunder cult in Leizhou, see Kaltenmark (1948: 22–36), Schafer (1967: 105–6), and Wang Chengwen (2010: 636–8).

90. 'Chen Luanfeng' (陳鸞鳳) in *Pei Xing chuanqi*, 48–50.

91. 'Tianwei jing xinzao haipai bei', Verellen 2019: 253, ll. 16–21.

92. Zhou Qufei 1999: 1.33.

93. Cf. Wang Chengwen's speculations in favour of the use of gunpowder in the present context (2010: 640, 643).

94. *Zhenyuan miaodao yaolüe* (真元妙道要略) (tenth century?), attrib. Zheng Yin (鄭隱) (Western Jin dynasty, 265–316), *Daozang* 924, 3a. Needham (1986: 112) dates this passage to ca. 850, explaining that dry honey provided the necessary carbon.

95. *Yutang xianhua* (玉堂閒話), by Wang Renyu (王仁裕) (880–956), quoted in *Taiping guangji* 219.1679. On this work and its author, see Dudbridge (2013).

96. The entry reads '*Xingzhen jinyi song*, by Gao Pian, in one scroll' (高駢性 篋金液頌一卷). *Song shi* 205.5192.

97. Synopsis of 'Li Dan Shenzhou zhai yan' (李耽神呪齋驗), *Daojiao lingyan ji*, 15.299–300. On this work, see Verellen (1992).

98. *Tang da zhaoling ji* 86.489.

99. See the annotation on this passage in Wang Chengwen (2010: 631, n. 137).

100. See Sima Guang 1956: 251.8121 and *Xin Tang shu* 224B.6392.

101. 'Guo Tianwei jing' (過天威徑) in *Quan Tang shi* 598.6921. Cf. Shizunaga (2008: 67).

102. Sudō Yoshiyuki, 'Tō-matsu Wainan Kō Ben,' 191–9. On the state of Wu (902–37), precursor of the Southern Tang, see Kurz (2011: 1–22).

103. See especially Yamamoto (1943) and Taylor (1983: 250–301).

104. Lê Tắc 1995: 9.244-45 and Zeng's biographical notice in *Việt sử lược* (Shanghai 1922 ed.), A.13a.

105. Taylor (1999: 241–58) argues that this remembrance was revived in the nineteenth century to recommend to the Huế court a policy of relying on Qing China in the face of French invasion.

106. *Đại Việt sử ký toàn thư, Ngoai Ky* (外紀) (Tokyo 1884 ed.), 5.168.

107. 'Tianwei jing' (天威徑), *Qiyan Jide shi sanshi shou* (七言記德詩三十首) (880), in *Guiyuan bigeng ji jiaozhu* 17.595–6.

108. Modern as this attitude may seem, it was already widely current with respect, at least, to posthumous commemoration (Ditter 2014: 21–46).

109. 'Sheng ci' (生祠), 'She bian' (射鞭), 'Annan' (安南), 'Tianwei jing' (天威徑), 'Zuokou jing' (岧口徑), and 'Shoucheng bei' (收城碑), in *Qiyan Jide shi sanshi shou* (七言記德詩三十首), by Ch'oe Ch'iwŏn, in *Guiyuan bigeng ji jiaozhu* 17.593–7; see also Shizunaga (2008: 63–4).

110. *Cao Biền Linh ký*; see Papin 2001: 46, 350 n. 6.

111. For this author's testimony on Gao Pian's magico-religious leanings, see Verellen (1989a: 53–5).

112. See also Phan Văn Các & Salmon (1998: 28) and the Vietnamese sources cited there.

113. *Cefu yuangui* 447.5304; 'Xichuan luocheng tuji' (西川羅城圖記), in *Guiyuan bigeng ji jiaozhu* 16. 541–4.

114. See Sun Guangxian (1999: 2.9), where Sun Guangxian reports that the king of Min (Fujian), Wang Shenzhi (王審知) (r. 909–25), concerned about the sea shore's danger to navigation, dreamt that the god Wu Zixu (伍子胥) offered help clearing a harbour. The story is a sequel to the account of the Tianwei opening cited above. In the sequel, Gao Pian is named Bohai, a reference to his enfeoffment as prince of Bohai commandery (see *Xin Tang shu* 224B.6395).

115. Cf. the phrase (醉酒飽德) from the *Book of Poetry* signifying an age of Great Peace under the rule of a benevolent Lord. See *Mao shi zhushu* (毛詩注疏), in *Shisan jing zhushu* (十三經注疏), 17.603.

116. 'Bu Annan luyi tuji', in *Guiyuan bigeng ji jiaozhu* 16.555 and 560n15.

117. 'Sheng ci (生祠)', *Qiyan Jide shi sanshi shou* (七言記德詩三十首), in *Guiyuan bigeng ji jiaozhu* 17.593–4.

CHAPTER 9

The Scale and Location of the Forbidden City Within the Structure of Thăng Long–Hanoi Citadel Through History

Phan Huy Lê

1. THE STRUCTURE OF THĂNG LONG CITADEL

My earlier research into the structure of the Thăng Long–Hanoi Citadel contributed to locating the archaeological site uncovered at 18 Hoàng Diệu Street, with its vestiges of Thăng Long Imperial Citadel. I have published some of the results of that research elsewhere (Phan Huy Lê 2006; 2007). In this chapter, I pursue my examination of the citadel's structure with a focus on the Forbidden City and its evolution through history. I discuss some of the buildings inside the Forbidden City, but do not focus closely on the planning and architecture of the royal palaces or the political, social and architectural relations between the Forbidden City and the area outside its wall. My aim here is to provide further evidence to show that the site of the archaeological excavation at 18 Hoàng Diệu Street and the Nguyễn-dynasty Hanoi Citadel were indeed located in the central area of the Forbidden City of the Thăng Long Citadel as it existed through different periods of history.

After establishing Thăng Long as its capital, the Lý dynasty (1009–1226) built palaces and pavilions there, as well as citadel walls around them. During this period, the structure of Thăng Long Citadel consisted of three circles of walls. This structure recalls that of the citadel at Cổ Loa built by An Dương Vương in the second and third centuries BC, which had three circles of walls, locally known as the Inner Rampart, Middle Rampart and Outer Rampart. At Thăng Long Citadel, this structure existed from the Lý dynasty through to the Lê Restoration period (1593–1789), although it was modified on several occasions. The outer wall was named Đại La or La Citadel; the middle wall was named Long Phượng (Dragon Phoenix) Citadel under the Lý and Trần dynasties, and Imperial Citadel under the Lê dynasty; and the inner wall enclosed the Forbidden City.

The Outer Wall (Đại La Citadel or La Citadel)

There is a broad consensus among scholars on this wall: it enclosed the entire capital, the outer rampart that protected the court and population living there. In 1014, the Lý dynasty is recorded as building 'an earth rampart around the four sides of the capital's citadel'.[1] This was the beginning of the wall's construction. It was subsequently repaired and rebuilt many times. In 1078, it was repaired and named Đại La Citadel.

The wall followed the bank of the Nhị River (or Red River, 珥, Nhĩ and pronounced Nhị) to the east, the Tô Lịch River to the north and the west, and the Kim Ngưu River to the south. These rivers enclosed the citadel like a 'river quadrangle' and were used as waterways and a natural ditch and drainage system. The wall was a rampart, but also a dike to prevent flooding.

According to the laws of nature, however, rivers change course; their banks build up here and break down there. The Nhị River changed its course over time, and this led to changes in the position of the wall, which shifted gradually eastwards. From the Lý dynasty to the Early Lê, the east section of Đại La Citadel was located well to the west of the modern dike, possibly in the vicinity of Hoàn Kiếm Lake, which was then a branch of the Nhị River. Two of Thăng Long's important landings until the eighteenth century—Đông landing (*bến* Đông, or Đông Bộ Đầu, below Hoè Nhai rise, up from Long Biên Bridge) and Giang Khẩu landing (near today's Chợ Gạo and Nguyễn Siêu Streets)—were by the Đại La wall. Their locations also shifted over time.

To the north, the Tô Lịch River connected with the West Lake at Hồ Khẩu and flowed into the Nhị River at Giang Khẩu. The Tô Lịch is clearly marked on the Hồng Đức map of the Lê and Nguyễn dynasties. In the early nineteenth century, when the Nguyễn rebuilt the citadel in the Vauban style and named the city Hanoi, this river connected with the moat on the northwest side of Hanoi Citadel and flowed into the Nhị

River at Giang Khẩu. From 1894–97, the French government destroyed
Hanoi Citadel and filled in the moat and the section of the Tô Lịch from
Thụy Khuê to Giang Khẩu. As for the section from Bưởi past Hồ Khẩu
to Tam Đa rise, today it is a small ditch. To the west, it took water from
the Thiên Phù and Nhị Rivers at the Bưởi confluence and was a strong
stream with a considerable flow of water, but has been gradually filled in;
in recent times, its banks have been concreted and its weak flow means
it is heavily polluted. To the south, the Kim Ngưu was filled in during the
construction of Yên Sở drainage system.

The Đại La Citadel of the Lý and Trần periods had the following
gates: Triều Đông or Đông Bộ Đầu Gate (below Hòe Nhai rise), Tây
Dương Gate (at Cầu Giấy), Trường Quảng Gate (at Chợ Dừa), South Gate
(near Dền Bridge) and Vạn Xuân Gate (near Ông Mạc or Đồng Mác). The
Đại La Citadel of the Mạc period (1527–92) and the early years of the Lê
Restoration period (1593–1789) underwent several structural changes.
In the course of the war between the Lê and the Mạc, the Mạc consoli-
dated the citadel's defences (1588) and

> ordered troops from four commanderies to build three further em-
> bankments around the Đại La Citadel, from Nhật Chiêu ward past the
> West Lake, Dừa Bridge and Dền Bridge to Thanh Trì. These ramparts
> were ten poles taller than the Thăng Long ramparts and measured 25
> poles across. There were three ditches, each planted with bamboo and
> more than ten miles long, so as to surround the citadel completely
> on the outside.[2]

Đại La Citadel was thus protected by three further ramparts, the innermost of which was close to the Đại La rampart itself, and the West Lake
was now included in the protected area. But in 1592, during the battle
for the city, the Trịnh army 'ordered the army to level the Đại La earth
rampart for many thousands of poles of its length, to cut down the trees,
bushes and thorns, to fill in the ditches; and in a few days, the work
was done'.[3] At that point, the Đại La Citadel had all but disappeared
and Thăng Long had only two ramparts, the Imperial Citadel and the
Forbidden City. This was a major modification to the citadel's structure.

The Lê Restoration period was also characterised by political change,
with the emergence, parallel to the Lê royal court, of the palace of the
Trịnh lords. This led to further modifications to the citadel's structure.
The Lê royal court continued to serve as a figurehead for the country as
a whole, with relevance in rituals and foreign relations; it remained in the
Forbidden City. Real power was located in the hands of the Trịnh lords,
who built a complex of new palace buildings at a site by the Hoàn Kiếm

Lake, outside the Imperial Citadel, in the area where the townspeople lived and worked. The Trịnh lords' palace was surrounded by a wall but remained closely connected to the bustling socio-economic space of the capital's urban quarter. During the Lê–Trịnh period, the royal court and lords' palace engendered a new structure of power that impacted on the structure of the capital and its citadel.

Then, in the mid-eighteenth century, facing the threat of peasant rebellion, Trịnh Doanh gave the following orders: 'Thăng Long has been our country's capital since the Lý dynasty, which built the Đại La Citadel; now I want to repair the old rampart, to protect the capital from revolt' (1749). He had workers from nine nearby districts embank the rampart, which was named Đại Đô, according to the chronicle *Đại Việt sử ký tục biên* (1991: 217). This source states that the citadel had five gates, named An Hoa, Vạn Bảo, Vạn Xuân, Thịnh Quang and Thọ Khang, each built with a left door and a right door; meanwhile, the chronicle *Khâm định Việt sử thông giám cương mục, chính biên* (q. XL-33a; 1998: t. II, 601) records the existence of eight gates, each with a left and right door.[4] The Đại Đô rampart is clearly marked on the map *Hoài Đức phủ toàn đồ*, drawn by Lê Đức Lộc and Nguyễn Công Tiến in 1831.[5] On this map, the Đại Đô rampart runs from Yên Phụ, along Thanh Niên Avenue, across Hoàng Hoa Thám Street and along Ngọc Hà round the west side of the Botanic Garden to Kim Mã coach station, then along Giảng Võ Street, La Thành Street, Đại Cồ Việt and Trần Khát Chân Streets as far as Đống Mác Gate. Bounded by the Nhị River, its eastern section starts at Yên Phụ Street and follows Nguyễn Hữu Huân, Lý Thái Tổ, Lê Thánh Tông, Hàng Chuối Streets and then to Đống Mác Gate. According to this source, the citadel had sixteen gates, named Kim Hoa, Yên Thọ, Thanh Lãng, Nhân Hòa, Tây Long, Đông Yên, Mỹ Lộc, Trừng Thanh, Đông Hà, Phúc Lâm, Thạch Khối, Yên Tĩnh, Yên Hoa, Tây Hồ, Vạn Bảo, and Thịnh Quang.[6]

The sixteen gates also appear on Phạm Đình Bách's 1873 map of Hanoi, printed by the Indochina Geology Department in 1916, although some names had changed by that time. We can locate these gates on today's map of Hanoi, but the only standing vestige is Đông Hà Gate— also known as Quan Chưởng Gate—at the end of Hàng Chiếu Street. The West Lake and the west side of Thăng Long Citadel was now outside the wall: the Đại Đô wall enclosed the Forbidden City, part of the Imperial Citadel, the Trịnh lords' palace and a smaller inhabited urban area. The citadel's scale and structure had changed again, becoming smaller.

Đại La Citadel protected the entire area of the capital. Access was controlled at the gates, but the area was open to economic, social and cultural exchange with the surrounding territory, including crafts and farming villages.

The Middle Wall (Dragon Citadel, Phoenix Citadel or Imperial Citadel)

The middle wall was named Dragon Citadel and Phoenix Citadel under the Lý and Trần, and Imperial Citadel from the Early Lê period.

In autumn 1010, King Lý Thái Tổ moved the capital from Hoa Lư to Đại La and renamed it Thăng Long. There, he built a series of palaces and 'embanked ramparts and dug ditches on all four sides, with one gate on each side: Tường Phù Gate to the east, Quảng Phúc Gate to the west, Đại Hưng Gate to the south and Diệu Đức Gate to the north.'[7] In the past, this record led me and other historians to conclude that this wall, built in 1010 around the palaces, was the Forbidden City. But careful analysis of the information in the record shows that one of the four gates was Đại Hưng Gate, which all the sources identify as the south gate of the Imperial Citadel, not the Forbidden City. On this basis, I identify the rampart built in 1010 as the middle wall in the structure of Thăng Long Imperial Citadel. Under the Lý and Trần, this wall was named Dragon Citadel (Long thành), Phoenix Citadel (Phượng thành), or Dragon Phoenix Citadel (Long Phượng thành). It was known as the Imperial Citadel (Hoàng thành) under the Early Lê.

In their descriptions of palace construction in 1029–30, the chronicles *Đại Việt sử lược* and *Đại Việt sử ký toàn thư* record the existence of a rampart called Dragon Citadel. Many scholars, myself included, used to think that this was the wall around the Forbidden City. But before that date, during the Three Princes' Rebellion of 1028, *Đại Việt sử ký toàn thư* notes that, after hearing of King Lý Thái Tổ's death in Long An Palace, 'the three princes Đông Chinh, Dực Thánh and Vũ Đức sent their troops to lie in ambush in the Forbidden City, with Đông Chinh's troops lying in ambush in the Dragon Citadel' (q. II-10b). This indicates that at that time a distinction was already made between the Forbidden City and Dragon Citadel; the Dragon Citadel already existed. Later, recording the power struggle of the last years of the Lý dynasty, *Đại Việt sử lược* notes that in 1212 'Tự Khánh, who was furious, sent troops to the Dragon Citadel and ordered his commander Nguyễn Ngạch to lead the courtiers into the Forbidden City' (q. III-24b). Here I identify the Dragon Citadel as the middle enclosing wall, first built in 1010.

This wall was also called Thăng Long Citadel at this time, as it would be under the Early Lê. Thus, in 1024, one chronicle referred to 'repairs to Thăng Long Citadel' (*Đại Việt sử ký toàn thư* q. II-9b) while another recorded this as the 'construction of Thăng Long Citadel' (*Đại Việt sử lược* q. II-4a). A third, *Khâm định Việt sử thông giám cương mục*, described the same event more clearly: 'Repairs were made to Thăng Long Citadel, construction of which started in 1010' (q. II). My view is that Dragon Citadel was a short form of the name Thăng Long Citadel, with the wall built in 1010 and repaired many times, including in 1024 and 1029. In the historical texts, the name 'Capital citadel' (Kinh thành) or 'Thăng Long capital citadel' was usually used to refer to the entire area enclosed by the wall called Đại La Citadel. The names 'Thăng Long Citadel', 'Dragon Citadel' and 'Phoenix Citadel' referred to the middle wall, while 'Forbidden City' or 'Palace Citadel' (Cấm thành, Cấm trung or Cung thành) referred to the inner enclosure that protected the court and royal palace.

The first occurrence of the name Phoenix Citadel dates from 1049, when *Đại Việt sử lược* refers to the 'digging of a moat outside the Phoenix Citadel' (q. II-8b, 1960: 89). No location is given. The name existed through the Trần period into the Early Lê. Under the Trần, it appears in records for the years 1230, 1243 and 1304. In the latter record, 44 candidates were awarded doctorates in the second-degree examination, three of whom were placed first: Mạc Đĩnh Chi, Bùi Mộ and Trương Phóng. The three men were 'taken out through Dragon Gate in Phoenix Citadel to enjoy themselves in the city for three days'.[8] This gate, that led out to the city, must be the second wall and could not be the Forbidden City.

Phoenix Citadel was another name for Dragon Citadel.[9] In one document, Phoenix Citadel had a gate named Dragon Gate (Long Môn). According to the Trần dynasty's laws, one category of criminals sentenced to banishment was sent to 'clear the grass at Thăng Long and Phoenix Citadel, and placed under the orders of the Tứ Sương Army'. The Tứ Sương Army's only duty was to guard the gates and ramparts of the Dragon Citadel (or Phoenix Citadel, or Thăng Long Citadel, or Dragon Phoenix Citadel).[10] The Forbidden City, meanwhile, was guarded by the Forbidden City Guards (Cấm vệ). In 1490, when King Lê Thánh Tông enlarged the Imperial Citadel,[11] we read that 'the Phoenix Citadel was extended according to specifications dating from the Lý and Trần periods.' Under the Early Lê, the Imperial Citadel was the usual name but there are occurrences of the name Phoenix Citadel. All the above data have led me to conclude that this middle wall had many names, including Thăng Long Citadel, Dragon Citadel, Phoenix Citadel, Dragon Phoenix Citadel and Imperial Citadel.

The Dragon Citadel of the Lý dynasty, built in 1010, had four gates. On the east side, Tường Phù Gate was later named Đông Hoa Gate or

East Gate (Đông Môn). It opened in the direction of the Bạch Mã Temple and the mouth of the Tô Lịch River (Giang Khẩu). Vestiges survive in the form of Cầu Đông Pagoda (Đông Kiều Pagoda) or Cửa Đông Pagoda (Đông Môn Pagoda) at 38B Hàng Đường Street, Đông Môn Temple at 8 Hàng Cân Street, Hậu Đông Hoa Temple at 2 Chả Cá Street, and a stele dating from the sixteenth year of Gia Long's reign (1817) in the Fujian Congregation Hall at 40 Lãn Ông Street. Certain place names dating from the Nguyễn period also contain a memory of the East Gate. From Gia Long's reign, these include villages named Đông Hoa Môn and Hậu Đông Hoa Môn (Hữu Túc canton), and Hữu Đông Môn and Đông Thành (Tiền Túc canton) (Dương Thị The & Phạm Thị Thoa 1981: 256, 299, 330; Nguyễn Văn Siêu 1960: 106).[12] From Minh Mạng's reign, they include place names in land registers, such as Hữu Đông Môn and Đông Thành Thị villages (Thuận Mỹ canton) (Phan Huy Lê 2010b: 397, 408). These names also appear in the late nineteenth-century gazetteer *Đồng Khánh địa dư chí* (2003: 11, 52).

This eastern section of the Imperial Citadel was located in the vicinity of today's Thuốc Bắc Street. Here, Phạm Đình Hổ (1768–1839) saw the sign bearing the words 'Đông Hoa Môn' and commented: 'the sign inscribed with the word "Đông Hoa Môn" [Đông Hoa Gate] was really written by a king of the Lý dynasty; the calligraphy is strong and natural, quite unlike that of an ordinary person, with strokes that show an early development of the Vietnamese style of writing' (Phạm Đình Hổ, 1960: 30).

On the south side of the citadel, Đại Hưng Gate or South Gate was in the vicinity of the modern market at Cửa Nam; this section of the rampart roughly followed the line of today's Trần Phú Street. To the north, Diệu Đức Gate collapsed into the Tô Lịch River, according to the gazetteer *Đại Nam nhất thống chí* (1971: vol. III, 165). In 1427, during an attack on Đông Quan Citadel, King Lê Lợi ordered 'the construction of a wall from Yên Hoa to the citadel's north gate'.[13] In the seventeenth century, it was consolidated by the people of Yên Phụ village to separate Trúc Bạch Lake from the West Lake. Today, the wall has become Thanh Niên Avenue. It was protected to the north by Trấn Vũ Temple, so we may assume that Diệu Đức Gate, or North Gate, was situated on the south bank of the Tô Lịch in the area between today's Phan Đình Phùng and Hoàng Hoa Thám Streets.

The location of Quảng Phúc Gate remains unknown. One view is that it was in the vicinity of the One Pillar Pagoda, near Hùng Vương Avenue (Trần Quốc Vượng & Vũ Tuân Sán 1975: 151). Another is that it was beside the Tô Lịch River further west, on modern Bưởi Road (Trần

Huy Liệu 2000: 38–9). I have thought very hard about this gate's location and its connection to the Imperial Citadel's western area, and have investigated a site at Đoài Môn (lit. west gate) at Cống Vị on Bưởi Road, Ba Đình district (a place known to locals as Đầu Đong or Đầu Đong Quân). In October 2003, the National Museum of History and the Hanoi Department of Culture and Information excavated this site and found the vestiges of a small rampart in the shape of a square measuring 54 m × 52 m, dating from the mid-eighteenth century. Underneath, there was a cultural layer dating from the late Lý to Early Lê periods. In 2013, the Institute of Archaeology excavated several sites near Cầu Giấy, Đào Tấn and Đội Cấn Streets. On Bưởi Road, they discovered layers of embanked soil from the Lý and Trần periods, but these contained no evidence to prove the site was a vestige of Dragon Citadel or Đại La Citadel, or a dike of the Tô Lịch River. Moreover, the Institute of Archaeology has only made a brief announcement of the results of this research and has not yet had time to analyse the materials and publish a full report.

If Quảng Phúc Gate is indeed located somewhere along Bưởi Road (at a considerable distance from the Forbidden City), it is hard to explain how, in 1028 when Lê Phụng Hiểu was guarding the crown prince at Càn Nguyên Palace, he 'ran like the wind to Quảng Phúc Gate' to wipe out Prince Vũ Đức's troops, whom he 'ambushed at Quảng Phúc Gate, Dragon Citadel'.[14] My most recent opinion is that the Dragon Citadel's west section under the Lý and Trần must have extended from Hoàng Hoa Thám Street along Ngọc Hà Street as far as Kim Mã and Nguyễn Thái Học Streets. This corresponds to the west section of the Đại Đô Citadel, built in 1749 by Trịnh Doanh. This of course is only a hypothesis that needs to be verified through archaeological survey and excavation.

Under the Early Lê, the Imperial Citadel is clearly marked on the Hồng Đức map of Đông Kinh citadel. The name Imperial Citadel (Hoàng thành) first appeared at this time, in the *Đại Việt sử ký toàn thư* entry for 1463 and then for 1514 and 1516. The chapter on the Forbidden City Guards in the Lê dynasty's penal code *Quốc triều hình luật* contains many articles that lay down measures for the Imperial Citadel's protection and punishments for acts of trespass.[15] Under the Early Lê, the Imperial Citadel was also called Thăng Long Citadel, Dragon Citadel and Phoenix Citadel.

In 1467, King Lê Thánh Tông found that 'the wall was low and narrow' and mobilised the troops of five districts for further construction work.[16] However, we do not know if this work was done on the basis of the old Dragon Citadel of the Lý and Trần, or whether the wall was now

extended to cover new areas. If it was extended, it was probably to the
west, to bring the area covered by Hoàng Hoa Thám Street to the north,
Bưởi Road to the west, Kim Mã Street to the south into the Imperial
Citadel. The Hồng Đức maps (see Map 8 and Map 9 below) show a section
of wall running east from Linh Lang (Voi Phục Temple) and connecting

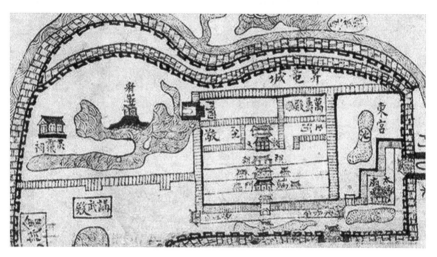

Map 8. Hồng Đức Map of Đông Kinh, detail (Institute of Hán-Nôm Studies,
ref. A.2499).

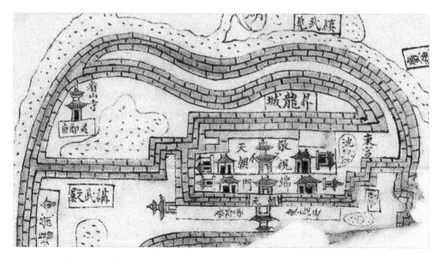

Map 9. Hồng Đức Map of Đông Kinh, detail (Institute of Hán-Nôm Studies,
ref. A.3034).

with the Forbidden City near today's Kim Mã Street.[17] Was this one of the sections built in 1467? Before Kim Mã Street was widened and other streets in this area were built, there remained vestiges of a series of mounds here, named Gò Dài, Gò Giữa, Gò Đất and Gò Miếu Ông, which follow a line from Voi Phục to Núi Bò approximately parallel to Kim Mã Street. Were these the vestiges of a section of this part of the rampart? Questions such as these need to be raised to verify the hypothesis of the Imperial Citadel's extension in 1467.

Under the Early Lê, there is no doubt that the Imperial Citadel underwent major extensions on at least two occasions, in 1490 during the reign of King Lê Thánh Tông (the twenty-first year of Hồng Đức era) and in 1516 during the reign of King Tương Dực (the eighth year of the Hồng Thuận era).

In 1490,

> the Phoenix Citadel was enlarged according to specifications laid down during the Lý and Trần dynasties. Fearing that Nhân Tông might be harmed, the king was vigilant, so he ordered his army to reinforce the rampart. At the same time, the area outside the martial arts arena was extended more than eight miles: the work took eight months.[18]

The arena had been a place for exercise in the martial arts since the Lý and Trần periods. It had been used for martial arts performances during the Ming occupation and corresponds to the modern area of Giảng Võ and Ngọc Khánh Streets, Ba Đình district. After its 1490 enlargement, the Imperial Citadel included a large area to the north, reached the bank of the Tô Lịch River to the west, and embraced the Giảng Võ–Ngọc Khánh area to the southwest. The wall followed Hoàng Hoa Thám Street to the north as far as Bưởi to the west, then to Cầu Giấy, La Thành Road, Giảng Võ Street and Nguyễn Thái Học Street. Excavations conducted by the Institute of Archaeology at Hoàng Hoa Thám Street in the vicinity of Văn Cao Street (2012) and at Cầu Giấy, Đào Tấn and Đội Cấn (2013) revealed vestiges of the Imperial Citadel of the Early Lê. Most of it was built with rammed earth, while the section that ran along the bank of the Tô Lịch was built with a series of layers of bricks and of broken bricks and tiles. Under the Lê, the walls of the Imperial Citadel were built of earth, with the outer wall built of bricks, as the Hồng Đức maps show.

In 1516, King Tương Dực

> extended the citadel to cover an area of many thousands of poles, encompassing Tường Quang Palace, Chân Vũ, Thiên Hoa Pagoda in

Kim Cổ village; it ran east to northwest, cutting off the Tô Lịch River; the wall was built above; gates and drains were built below; broken tiles, earth and bricks were rammed down; stone slabs and square bricks were built up; metal sections were placed across.[19]

Scholars have keenly debated this extension of the citadel. Some doubted the Lê's capacity to implement such a large construction project at a time the dynasty was weakening; King Tương Dực was assassinated by Trịnh Duy Sản in April 1516, only months after the extension plan was issued. But if the plan was indeed carried out, might Thụy Khuê Street be a vestige of the enlarged Imperial Citadel that now encompassed part of the Tô Lịch River? Several of the Hồng Đức maps of Đông Kinh represent the Imperial Citadel as having two ramparts. Was the northern one the section enlarged by King Tương Dực, corresponding to modern Thụy Khuê Street? To verify this, we must await the results of archaeological investigation in that street. But clearly, after the expansions of 1490 and 1516, Thăng Long Imperial Citadel occupied the largest area in its history.

On the Hồng Đức map, the Lê-dynasty Imperial Citadel could be entered through Đại Hưng Gate (South Gate), Đông Môn (East Gate), and Bảo Khánh Gate. Bảo Khánh Gate was on modern La Thành Street, near its junction with Giảng Võ Street. A vestige of the gate remained into the Nguyễn period in the form of the name of Bảo Khánh village.[20] The locations of Đông Môn and Đại Hưng Gate were unchanged. Outside Đại Hưng Gate, King Lê Thánh Tông ordered the construction of Quảng Văn Temple (1491), where court edicts were posted. According to Phan Huy Chú's *Lịch triều hiến chương loại chí* (1960: vol. II, 114), there were four gates in the Imperial Citadel under the Lê: Đông Hoa, Đại Hưng, Bắc Thần and Thiên Hựu. But this source does not distinguish between the Lê dynasty's early and later periods. Meanwhile, the annals indicate that in 1516 Bảo Khánh Gate still existed and Bắc Thần Gate had already been built.[21]

The whole area to the west covered by the enlarged Imperial Citadel after 1490 was excluded from the citadel area when the Đại Đô wall was built in 1749. The area became farmland; it was at this time that people from Lệ Mật village (Gia Lâm, Hanoi) and other parts came to work the land here and established the Thirteen Villages (Thập tam trại) (Nguyễn Quang Ngọc 1986). One section of the old Imperial Citadel's rampart was retained in the Đại Đô wall: the section with Đại Hưng Gate. Under the Tây Sơn dynasty, King Quang Trung had the section from Đông Hoa Gate to Đại Hưng Gate repaired.

Clearly, within the structure of the capital as a whole, the middle wall—named Dragon Citadel, Phoenix Citadel, Dragon Phoenix Citadel or Imperial Citadel—played a key role in its defence. The rampart was built of solid earth with its outer side, at least from the Early Lê period, faced with brick. The Imperial Citadel's scale changed many times over the period from the Lý to the later Lê, although the east section was almost completely unchanged. The Forbidden City was on this eastern side of the Imperial Citadel.

2. THE SCALE AND LOCATION OF THE FORBIDDEN CITY

Lý Period (1009–1226)

Different names for the inner wall are used by the chronicles *Đại Việt sử lược* and *Đại Việt sử ký toàn thư*. The former calls it the Forbidden Centre (Cấm trung 禁中) in entries for the years 1209, 1212, 1213 and 1214.[22] In a passage on the Three Princes' Rebellion (1028), the latter calls it Forbidden City (Cấm thành 禁城).[23] Other later annals—like the Tây Sơn dynasty's *Đại Việt sử ký tiền biên* (1997: 206) or the Nguyễn dynasty's *Khâm định Việt sử thông giám cương mục, chính biên* (q. 2–27a, 1998: vol. 1, 300)—call it the Forbidden City (Cấm thành), probably following *Đại Việt sử ký toàn thư*. On the stele at Sùng Thiện Diên Linh Tower (written by Nguyễn Công Bật, inscribed in 1121), the name Forbidden West (Tây Cấm 西禁) is used (Phan Văn Các & Salmon 1998: 136).[24]

Under the Lý, large-scale construction of palaces took place in 1010, 1029–30 and 1203. Regarding the work done in 1010, the chronicle *Đại Việt sử lược* notes that

> at the capital Thăng Long, the royal palace Triều Nguyên was built with Tập Hiền Palace on its left and Giảng Võ Palace on its right. Phi Long Gate was on the left, Đan Phượng Gate was on the right, with Cao Palace to the south. The terrace was named Long Trì and was built with a gallery surrounding it on all four sides. Behind Càn Nguyên Palace, two palaces—Long An Palace and Long Thụy Palace—were built, with Nhật Quang Palace on the left and Nguyệt Minh Palace on the right.[25]

In the same year, the chronicle *Đại Việt sử ký toàn thư* (Complete Annals of Đại Việt) records that

> palaces were built in Thăng Long citadel: Càn Nguyên Palace was built in front, for royal audiences, with Tập Hiền Palace on its left and

Giảng Võ Palace on its right. Long An and Long Thụy Palaces, where the King took his rest, were built behind Càn Nguyên Palace, with Nhật Quang Palace on the left and Nguyệt Minh Palace on the right. Phi Long Gate connected with Nghênh Xuân Palace, while Đan Phượng Gate connected with Uy Viễn Gate. Cao Minh Palace was built to the south. All were built with dragon terraces (Long Trì) surrounded by galleries on four sides. Behind Càn Nguyên Palace, the two palaces named Long An and Long Thụy were built as a place for the king to rest. Nhật Quang was built on the left, Nguyệt Minh was built on the right, with the two palaces named Thúy Hoa and Long Thụy behind, where the palace women lived.[26]

Based on these records, it is possible to draw a hypothetical plan of the palaces in the Forbidden City in 1010 (Map 10).

In 1010, while building these palaces, the Lý also raised the first rampart around the capital. It opened through four gates, including Đại Hưng Gate to the south that I have shown to belong to the middle rampart, later named Dragon Citadel, Phoenix Citadel and (from the Early Lê) Imperial Citadel. But was there a wall around the palaces of the Forbidden City? My view is that in the early years, after moving the capital to Đại La, the Lý dynasty borrowed the existing Đại La wall, built by Gao Pian. Indeed, some of the buildings in the enclosure might also have been inherited from earlier times. Evidence supporting this idea came to light in Section B of the archaeological site at 18 Hoàng Diệu Street, where a Đại La-period well was discovered with several layers of Lý-period bricks at its mouth. Vestiges of the Đại La wall were found in all the areas excavated at 18 Hoàng Diệu Street, including Section E (by the old Ba Đình National Assembly Building). They were particularly abundant in the Rose Garden (Vườn Hồng, where an underground car park was built for the National Assembly, south of Bắc Sơn Road), where the remains of a long section of the Đại La wall was found in the lowest layer. Making initial use of existing Đại La buildings, the Lý dynasty started building new palaces. These were used as royal audience halls, courtiers' working areas and the royal family's living quarters. At the Rose Garden, vestiges of a Lý-dynasty building were found above the remains of a section of the Đại La wall, proving that this section of the wall was destroyed by the Lý to build a new palace. This suggests that the Lý dynasty may have made early use of the Đại La wall to protect its palaces, but did not keep the entire citadel. Some of the sections of wall were improved or demolished, as we find on the south side.

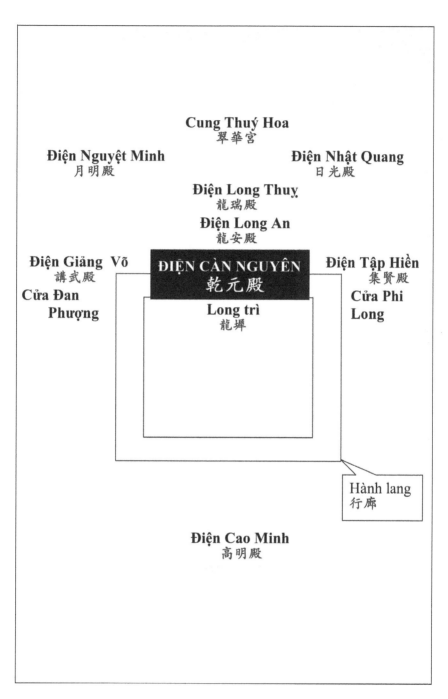

Map 10. Layout of palaces built in 1010 (Phan Huy Lê).

After the Three Princes' Rebellion of 1028 and Lý Thái Tông's accession to the throne in 1029, palaces were renewed, renamed and rebuilt, as recorded in *Đại Việt sử lược*:

> Càn Nguyên Palace was renamed Thiên An Palace; Tuyên Đức Palace was built on its left; Diên Phúc Palace was built on its right; the area in front was named Long Trì; Văn Minh Palace was built to the east; Quảng Võ Palace was built to the west. Facing each other to the left and right of Long Trì were the Chung Lâu bell towers, where hearings regarding unjust punishments were registered. A year later, in 1030, Thiên Khánh Palace was built, with Phượng Hoàng Palace behind it. (q. II-5b, 1960: 79)

The chronicle *Đại Việt sử ký toàn thư* adds the following information:

> Facing each other on the left and right sides of the dragon terrace were bell towers where the people could strike the bell to complain about injustice. Around the four sides of the dragon terrace, a gallery was built as a place where mandarins and six troops of guards assembled. Phụng Thiên Palace was built in front, with the Chính Dương Tower built on top of it, for observation of the hours. Trường Xuân Palace was built behind, with the Long Đồ Tower on top of it, as a place for looking at the view and relaxing. These palaces were surrounded by a wall named Dragon Citadel. [One year later,] Thiên Khánh Palace was built in front of Trường Xuân Palace; the palace was octagonal and served as a place for meetings of state.[27]

Based on these records, it is possible to draw a hypothetical plan of the palaces in the Forbidden City in 1029–30 (Map 11).

These two concentrated periods of construction took place during the Lý dynasty's period of prosperity. Even in the period of its decline, King Lý Cao Tông (1175–1210) had a large complex of palaces built to the west of a mausoleum. This work was done in 1203, as described in *Đại Việt sử lược*:

> The New Palace [complex] was built west of the mausoleum: Thiên Thụy Palace was in the middle, with Thiềm Quang Palace on its right and Dương Minh Palace on its left; Chính Nghi Palace was in front, Kính Thiên Palace above. One terrace was named Lệ Giao, with a gate in the middle named Vĩnh Nghiêm and another on the right named Việt Thành. Another terrace was named Ngân Hồng. Thắng Thọ Palace was built behind, with two towers, Nhật Kim Tower on the left and Nguyệt Bảo Tower on the right; a gallery was built all around it.

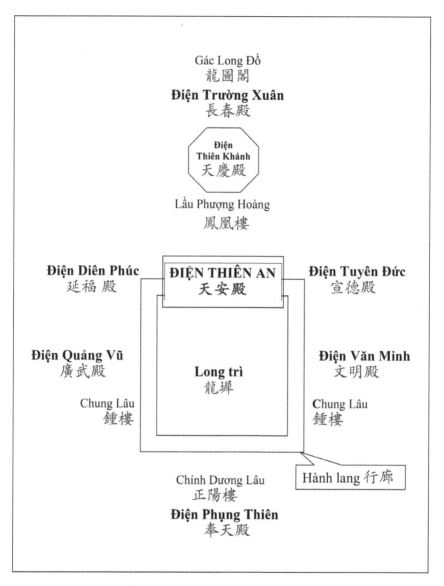

Map 11. Layout of palaces built in 1029–30 (Phan Huy Lê).

Another terrace was named Kim Tinh; Lương Thạch was built to the
right of Nguyệt Bảo Tower, with Dục Đường (a bath-house) to the
tower's west; Phú Quốc Tower was built behind, with its terrace named
Phượng Tiêu; behind that was Thấu Viên Gate and Dưỡng Ngư Pond
(a fish pond), with Ngoạn Y Temple on the pond; on three sides of

the temple, they planted fragrant flowers and unusual grasses; the pond was connected to the river; the carvings and decorations were skilfully executed, with fine work in wood the like of which had never been seen before. (q. III-14a, 14b, 1960: 165–6)[28]

This text mentions directions such as left and right, in front and behind, above and middle. I see these directions as viewed by someone looking from the north southwards. Right is west, left is east, in front is south, behind is north. Furthermore, Kính Thiên Palace was built 'on' the existing Chính Nghi Palace: this not easy to understand, as it apparently means that a new palace was built on an existing palace. However, the chronicle *Đại Việt sử lược* from 1206 noted that 'the king was sitting in Kính Thiên Tower' (q. III-16b). This allows me to offer a better interpretation of the earlier text: Kính Thiên Tower was built on Chính Nghi Palace in the same way that Thánh Thọ Tower was built on Thắng Thọ Palace. In another case, that of Việt Thành Gate, the texts record that the gate was located to the right of—in other words west of—Chính Nghi Palace; but other descriptions in *Đại Việt sử lược* show that Việt Thành gate was to the east: 'Việt Thành Gate opens out onto Triều Đông landing (East landing or Đông Bộ Đầu landing)' (q. III-19a). This description is not completely clear, making it difficult to picture many of these places. For this reason, the plan of the New Palace built in 1203 (Map 12) is very hypothetical and other scholars may have different views.

The New Palace complex was built in the Lý dynasty's period of decadence, when King Lý Cao Tông devoted himself to his pleasures and ordered costly construction works while, according to *Đại Việt sử lược* (q. III-16b, 1960: 170), 'bandits rose up like bees' and factions fought each other fiercely. We do not know how well built the New Palace was, or indeed whether it was completed. The same text reports that Thiên Thủy Palace was finished in 1205 and 'to celebrate the palace's completion, the king gave his courtiers a three-day banquet'. Some of the New Palace's buildings—including Việt Thành Gate, Kính Thiên Palace, Thiên Thụy Palace and Thắng Thọ Palace—were also mentioned in connection with historical events of the last years of the Lý dynasty. The relationship between the New Palace and the old palaces of the Forbidden City is not clear, but we can see that in these last years of the dynasty many of the old structures—including Long Trì and Thiên An Palace—remained in use. In the disorder of these years the king sometimes had to leave the Forbidden City. In 1215, he moved to a 'palace of grass built at the house of Đỗ An' (*Đại Việt sử lược* q. III-29b), a house in Chỉ Tác Alley

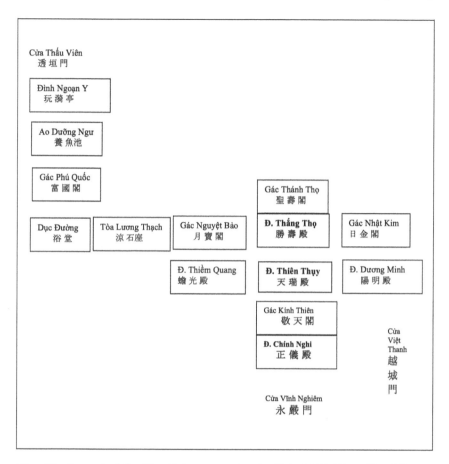

Cửa Thấu Viên
透 垣 門

Đình Ngoạn Y
玩 漪 亭

Ao Dưỡng Ngư
養 魚 池

Gác Phú Quốc
富 國 閣

Gác Thánh Thọ
聖 壽 閣

Dục Đường
浴 堂

Tòa Lương Thạch
涼 石 座

Gác Nguyệt Bảo
月 寶 閣

Đ. Thắng Thọ
勝 壽 殿

Gác Nhật Kim
日 金 閣

Đ. Thiềm Quang
蟾 光 殿

Đ. Thiên Thụy
天 瑞 殿

Đ. Dương Minh
陽 明 殿

Gác Kính Thiên
敬 天 閣

Cửa
Việt
Thanh
越
城
門

Đ. Chính Nghi
正 儀 殿

Cửa Vĩnh Nghiêm
永 嚴 門

Map 12.   Layout of the New Palace complex, built in 1203 (Phan Huy Lê).

near Tây Dương Bridge (modern Cầu Giấy). Again in 1216, 'a grass palace modelled on the Forbidden City was built at Tây Phù Liệt (Thanh Oai)' (*Đại Việt sử lược* q. III-30a).

In the Forbidden City, Càn Nguyên/Thiên An Palace and Sân Rồng (Long Trì)—the Dragon Terrace in front of Càn Nguyên/Thiên An Palace— played a key role in the court's activities and ceremonies. Càn Nguyên Palace was the main hall for audiences and ceremonies of national importance. It was built in 1010, when the capital was first established there. In 1017, the palace was struck by lightning, so (according to the commentary in *Khâm định Việt sử thông giám cương mục*) the king gave audience in a palace to the east named Tập Hiền. In 1020, the palace to the east was also struck by lightning, so the king gave audience in a palace to the west. This (according to the commentary in *Khâm định Việt sử thông giám cương mục*) was Giảng Võ Palace. He then undertook the construction of three new palaces: a palace in front for audiences and the two rear palaces for the discussion of state affairs. Although Càn Nguyên Palace had been struck by lightning and collapsed, the king regarded its foundations as the 'land of the victorious dragon' (*Đại Việt sử lược* q. II-5b) and 'a place located between heaven and earth' (*Đại Việt sử ký toàn thư* q. II-19B). That is why, in 1029, the palace was rebuilt on the same foundations and renamed Thiên An.

The Dragon Terrace (Long Trì) in front of Càn Nguyên/Thiên An Palace was surrounded by galleries 'where mandarins and six troops of guards assembled'. Here, in 1029, King Lý Thái Tông had bell towers built to the left and right, for people to 'strike the bell to complain about injustice' (*Đại Việt sử lược* q. II-5b). In 1033, the king ordered the casting of a bell of great weight (10,000 *cân*) to be placed there. The people were permitted to enter and strike the bell to complain of injustice, a rare phenomenon for a monarchy. Meanwhile, the crown prince lived at Long Đức Palace, outside Trường Quảng Gate, one of the Đại La Citadel's gates.

Many national religious festivals took place at the Dragon Terrace in front of Càn Nguyên/Thiên An Palace. These included La Hán festival (to amnesty prisoners) in 1040, Nhân Vương festival in 1077 and again in 1126, and others. In 1044, after defeating Champa, King Lý Thái Tông organised a ceremonial announcement of the victory at Thái Tổ Temple and a celebratory banquet at Thiên An Palace. In 1225, it was at Thiên An Palace that King Lý Chiêu Hoàng organised a festival on the occasion of his abdication of the throne in favour of Trần Cảnh. It was also at the Dragon Terrace that the Lý dynasty held entertainments, including shuttle cock games played by the king and princes (in 1126 and 1130) and elephant capture spectacles (1149).

Many Lý-dynasty vestiges were unearthed at 18 Hoàng Diệu Street, including 53 foundations of buildings, 7 foundations of enclosing walls, 6 wells, and 13 drains. The Lý palaces left traces of foundations, foundation borders, stone pillar bases and courtyards. Foundations were built of packed clay overlaid with bricks. Courtyards were paved with yellow bricks fired at high temperatures. Theirs was a timber architecture, with the building's entire weight concentrated on wooden pillars set on stone plinths. Each plinth held the pillar's foot in place, and was supported by its own solid foundation. Pillar foundations were square, measured 1 m–2 m on each side and 1.5 m–3 m deep, and were made of multiple compacted layers of brick, tile and terracotta, with gravel to prevent subsidence. Vestiges of these foundations allow us to work out the size of the palaces. Most were rectangular, with rafter assemblages ranging from two to eight rows. Architectural types varied and included long galleries with multiple bays as well as large buildings with 10–13 bays. The timbered structures collapsed long ago but building materials remain in abundance, including bricks, yin-yang tiles, tube-tiles, tiles decorated with leaf and dragon images, terracotta statues of dragon heads, phoenixes and loving ducks used for roof decoration (Tống Trung Tín & Bùi Minh Trí 2010: 20–4).

Some of the buildings were 'octagonal' and 'hexagonal'. Historical sources provide some information of relevance. The construction of three octagonal palaces in the Forbidden City is recorded in the chronicles *Đại Việt sử lược* and *Đại Việt sử ký toàn thư*. These were Thiên Khánh Palace (1030),[29] Hồ Thiên Palace (1058),[30] and a building used for storing scriptures (1021).[31] The octagonal palace named Hồ Thiên was built beside Kim Minh Pond, which had been dug in 1049, while a mountain with three peaks and the Ngũ Phượng Bridge were built above the pond. These historical data help us identify the octagonal buildings unearthed at the site. Hexagonal buildings also appear: a bell tower (1058) built in the shape of a lotus flower was recorded as a 'single pillar hexagonal lotus flower bell tower' (*Đại Việt sử lược* q. 2-11a). It was this type of bell tower that was built in 1029 on either side of the Dragon Terrace. Archaeologists discovered several hexagonal buildings at 18 Hoàng Diệu Street, eleven in the eastern sector and three in the western sector distributed symmetrically along an axis: these were not bell towers, but they do assist our analysis of this architectural style.

The text *Lĩnh ngoại đại đáp* (嶺外代答) by Song-dynasty author Zhou Qufei (周去非) contains an interesting piece of information: in addition to Thủy Tinh and Thiên Nguyên Palaces, the palaces of the Lý included one 'with a sign identifying it as the palace of the viceroy of Annam'.[32] Thiên Nguyên Palace here is likely to be Thiên An Palace, rebuilt in 1029 by the Lý king on the foundations of Càn Nguyên Palace, which had collapsed. As for the 'palace of the viceroy of Annam', this may have been a Đại La building that the Lý dynasty continued to use.

At this point, I would like to discuss three questions that have been raised by historians and archaeologists.

(1) What was the Forbidden City's Name?

In the chronicle *Đại Việt sử lược*, the name Forbidden Centre (Cấm trung) was consistently used, but the authors of *Đại Việt sử ký toàn thư* called it Forbidden Citadel or Forbidden City (Cấm thành). *Đại Việt sử lược* is our earliest surviving historical text; its authorship is debated, but compilation was completed during the late Trần dynasty, around 1377. Meanwhile, the part of *Đại Việt sử ký toàn thư* compiled by Ngô Sĩ Liên in 1479, draws from historical data in the chronicle *Đại Việt sử ký*, compiled by Lê Văn Hưu in 1272, and a text by Phan Phu Tiên covering the late Trần and Ming occupation periods. In his preface to *Đại Việt sử ký toàn thư*, Ngô Sĩ Liên stated clearly that 'this book is based on two sources, which are *Đại Việt sử ký* by Lê Văn Hưu and *Đại Việt sử ký tục biên* by Phan Phu Tiên.'[33] *Đại Việt sử lược* was compiled closer in time to the Lý dynasty, earlier than *Đại Việt sử ký toàn thư*, and is thus of greater value. But some events recorded in *Đại Việt sử ký toàn thư* are not mentioned in *Đại Việt sử lược*. For example, *Đại Việt sử lược* only records three events in connection with the transfer of the capital from Hoa Lư to Đại La: (1) the capital's name changed, (2) the capital was moved, and (3) palaces and a wall were built. *Đại Việt sử ký toàn thư* has more information: (1) a springtime visit to Cổ Pháp district, (2) the full text of the edict on the transfer of the capital, (3) the date the capital moved, in the autumn during the seventh lunar month, and (4) the announcement of certain policies, including a general amnesty and an administrative reform, with ten *đạo* (counties) renamed as ten *lộ* (circuits). The same historical event was recorded differently in the two texts. So which is the right name for the Forbidden City? Cấm trung in *Đại Việt sử lược* or Cấm thành in *Đại Việt sử ký toàn thư*?

The name Cấm trung appears in Chinese texts going right back to the Qin period and was used until the Ming. The name Cấm thành appeared during the Jin period and was used until the Song. There was thus a period during which the two names were used in parallel. This was under the Song dynasty, contemporary with the Lý in Vietnam. Was the innermost wall of the Thăng Long capital citadel named both Cấm trung and Cấm thành, with both names used in parallel? In this case, the records in *Đại Việt sử lược* and *Đại Việt sử ký toàn thư* would be different but not wrong.

The Forbidden City was also named Đại Nội,[34] Cấm Đình,[35] and Cấm Nội,[36] although the name Đại Nội at times appears in contexts where it is not easy to identify and may not refer to the Forbidden City.

(2)   Was There a Wall Around the Forbidden City?

All the palaces and other buildings marked on the above plans (Maps 10–12) were in the Forbidden City, but was this area enclosed by a wall under the Lý? This is not easy to determine. The inscription on the stele at Sùng Thiện Diên Linh Tower (written by Nguyễn Công Bật in 1121) states that 'a rostrum was built for Quảng Chiếu, facing the courtyard in front of the Gate of Commencement (Đoan Môn)' (Viện Văn học 1977: vol. I, 404, 390). This means that the Gate of Commencement already existed at the time the Quảng Chiếu lantern festival was held. The Lý kings celebrated the Buddhist festival of Quảng Chiếu, or Universal Illumination, four times: in the years 1116, 1120 and twice in 1126, during the first and ninth lunar months. The sources indicate that the first of these was held outside Đại Hưng Gate, while the fourth was held at Long Trì.[37] The lantern festival recorded on the Sùng Thiện Diên Linh stele was held before 1121—in 1116 or 1120—so we may say that the latest date of construction of the Gate of Commencement is 1120.

The Gate of Commencement that stands today in Hanoi is a Lê reconstruction of a gate that had stood, according to some scholars' interpretation of the historical and archaeological evidence, on the same site since the Lý. During the archaeological investigation carried out in 1999, Lý and Trần materials were unearthed under its foundations. A section of road foundation was discovered leading towards Kính Thiên Palace bordered on both sides with bricks arranged in lemon flower patterns characteristic of the Trần. This section of the road was 15.8 m long; the roadway itself was 1.3 m wide. This finding led archaeologists to conclude that the Gate of Commencement was built by the Lý using bricks and tiles decorated with lotus flowers in the Lý style, and that it was then rebuilt by the Trần using Trần materials as well as re-used Lý materials (Tống Trung Tín et al. 2000).

However, although the research yielded data demonstrating the presence of Lý and Trần architectural vestiges under the gate's base, whether those vestiges belonged to a Gate of Commencement of the Lý or Trần period remained an open question for which broader archaeological investigation would be necessary. In the fifteenth century, the Lê razed the old building that stood there and built a new Gate of Commencement, the remains of which—repaired many times since—still stands.

In my view, at the time the citadel gate named Gate of Commencement was built, there was already an enclosing wall. One detail worth raising here is King Lý Thái Tổ's construction in 1010 of the Five Phoenix Pavilion (Ngũ Phượng tinh lâu). I have already mentioned the Lý dynasty's reuse of buildings from the Đại La Citadel, as well as their reuse of that citadel's rampart, or at least part of it. According to research by Phạm Lê Huy, the Five Phoenix Pavilion was the south gate of the Forbidden City, following the model in use in China from the Tang to the Northern Song (Phạm Lê Huy 2012b: 40–3). My view is that the great importance of this gate as the entrance to the Forbidden City explains why Lý Thái Tổ had the Five Phoenix Pavilion built here. Later, in 1120 at the latest, it took the name Gate of Commencement (Đoan Môn).

Indeed, the gazetteer *Hà Nội địa dư* compiled by Dương Bá Cung in 1851 records the existence of Ngũ Môn: 'a Five Gates Pavilion' at Vọng Palace, in the middle of which the two characters 'Đoan Môn' were inscribed: this was the Lý dynasty's Five Phoenix Pavilion' (Dương Bá Cung 2007: 244). Dương Bá Cung and other authors of his time thought that the Lê-period Đoan Môn was in the same position as the Lý-period Đoan Môn and that the word 'Đoan Môn' (端 門) had existed since the Lý dynasty. This subject needs further research, but one point that we may draw from this discussion is the link established between the Five Phoenix Pavilion and the Gate of Commencement under the Lý.[38]

The circumference of Đại La Citadel was nearly 6 km, making it larger than the Hanoi Citadel of the Nguyễn, which was approximately 4 km. In 1803, the Lê-dynasty Forbidden City was destroyed. A new wall was built by King Gia Long, who observed that 'the current rampart is too restricted' and wanted to enlarge it.[39] This indicates that Nguyễn-dynasty Hanoi Citadel was bigger than the Lê-dynasty Forbidden City. As for the Đại La Citadel, it consisted of a Forbidden City inside surrounded by a defensive outer wall with three gates to the east, west and south (Phạm Lê Huy 2012a: 34–51).[40] We do not know how the Đại La wall was re-used during the Lý period. It is unlikely they used its whole 6 km length; they probably repaired and rebuilt specific sections within a new plan.

In the excavation of the Rose Garden, a section of wooden wall bearing traces of holes for placing pillars was discovered. It was oriented east–west and was located to the south of Đại La Citadel. One of the archaeologists present at the excavation, Phạm Văn Triệu, suggested that this wooden wall was part of the Forbidden City's south wall. If it was indeed part of the Lý-dynasty wall around the Forbidden City, it indicates that the Lý destroyed the Đại La Citadel's south wall and built a new wall further to the south. If this is the case, although the name Đoan Môn lasted from the Lý to the end of the Lê in the late eighteenth century, the gate's location changed between Lý and Lê dynasties.

Vestiges of the foundation of a Lý-dynasty wall were discovered inside the Forbidden City area at the archaeological site at 18 Hoàng Diệu Street. The foundation was oriented east–west and measured 170 m long and 1.9 m wide. Archaeologists suppose that it was a wall that divided the Forbidden City in two, with an outer court to the south where the king and court worked and an inner court to the north where the royal family lived (Tống Trung Tín & Bùi Minh Trí 2010: 23). In Section E (in the area of the old Ba Đình National Assembly Building), archaeologists revealed the foundations of a smaller wall that surrounded an area of palaces; they also identified vestiges of a gate. These traces of walls combined with historical evidence allow us to make a deeper study of the spatial organisation of the area inside the Forbidden City. If walls surrounded specific areas inside the Forbidden City, then we may be sure that a wall surrounded the Forbidden City itself.

It was possible to go into the Forbidden City by boat from the Tô Lịch River, as we see from a record for the year 1174, when Prince Long Xưởng was stopped at Ngân Hà Gate as he tried to enter (*Đại Việt sử lược* q. 3-9a). This gate was built in 1063 (*Đại Việt sử lược* q. 2-12a). Was Ngân Hà Gate—like the Ngọc Hà Gate of the Lê period—an entrance into the Forbidden City on a waterway from the Tô Lịch?

From the Lý period onwards, the need for heavily guarded defences meant that in addition to the walls around palaces, the entire Forbidden City had its own rampart and gates, consisting at the very least of the Gate of Commencement in the south and one water entrance allowing access from the Tô Lịch River.

(3) Where was the Forbidden City's Central Axis in the Lý Period?

Vietnamese and Japanese archaeologists studied the Lý architectural remains in Sections A, B, C and D and produced an outline plan of the vestiges. This shows a set of buildings arranged symmetrically along a north–south axis that inclines slightly to the east (Inoue 2010: 45). Among the buildings along that axis there is a large octagonal building: its foundations cover an area of 682 m² (Bùi Minh Trí & Tống Trung Tín 2010: 33). Further out, to the southwest, there are the remains of a foundation bordered with bricks lying on their sides, in which two layers—Lý and Trần—may be identified from the respective periods' distinctive motifs on the bricks. In the excavated area at the Rose Garden, south of the archaeological site at 18 Hoàng Diệu Street, archaeologists found large Lý pillar bases also lying on the same axis. South of that area, they discovered a section of the Đại La wall, with foundations that held thick stakes to contain mud and prevent subsidence. South of the Đại La wall, the discovery of an unusual structure continues to perplex scholars: until research into its function bears fruit, this structure is known as the Altar (Đàn tế). This site dates from the Lý dynasty and lies on the central axis, also at a slight inclination to the east.[41]

These discoveries raise important questions. Did these buildings make up the central axis of the Forbidden City during the Lý period? What was their relationship with the other buildings within the Forbidden City? If this was indeed the central axis of the Forbidden City under the Lý, the octagonal building must have been Thiên Khánh Palace, indicated on the sketch of the palaces built in 1029–30 (see Map 11), with the main Thiên An Palace to its south. But archaeological excavation has not yet yielded sufficient evidence to prove this hypothesis. The central axis of the Forbidden City has been identified as the Doan Môn-Kính Thien axis. It was constructed during the Le period and continues to exist today. Did the central axis shift eastward during the period between the Lý and Early Lê?

Here we must consider a further point raised by our historical sources. These state that Càn Nguyên/Thiên An Palace during the Lý and Trần periods and Kính Thiên Palace during the Lê were both built on Mount Nùng or Mount Long Đỗ (lit. dragon's navel), a place where geomancers held that the sacred energies of the region's mountains and rivers converged.[42] If these sources are correct and if the geomancers' prescriptions were respected, the main palace was always built on Mount Nùng—and that means that there was no change in its location over the Lý, Trần and Lê periods.

The area from the Gate of Commencement to Kính Thiên Palace, excavated from 2011–14, was found to contain many architectural vestiges of the Lý and Trần. These include the remains of a large Lý channel (2 m wide, 2 m high) with a tiled bed and brick sides buttressed with wooden props. The channel was in the area north of the Gate of Commencement, oriented east–west. Alongside it there were a number of Lý buildings with gravel foundations for pillars and floors paved with bricks. Architectural vestiges of the Trần period were also found here. But to prove that the central axis of the Forbidden City did not change over the Lý, Trần and Lê periods, we must await results of excavation in the area of the central axis under the Lê.

In the light of these archaeological discoveries, no one can deny the existence of an ensemble of buildings symmetrically disposed along a central axis that crosses the octagonal building in Section C. The Altar, discovered in 2014 at the Rose Garden, is only 1.7 m off this axis, although it is outside the Đại La Citadel. The Lý built other structures in this outer area: the Xã Tắc Altar (1148) outside Trường Quảng Gate and the Viên Khâu Altar (1154) at the Đại La Citadel's south gate. Both were in the south, both were outside the Forbidden City, both were even outside the Imperial Citadel. My view is that this was a complex of religious structures that brought together strands of Buddhism and popular religion.

In the light of this, we may ask: Was that octagonal building built to house the scriptures? In 1021, King Lý Thái Tổ ordered the construction of an octagonal building to keep the scriptures. Before that, in 1018, he sent envoys to China to request Buddhist scriptures, which arrived in 1020. Did the need to develop Buddhism and receive the Buddhist scriptures incite the Lý to build a prestigious building for the scriptures here? At present, this idea is no more than a hypothesis for research.

Trần Period (1226–1400)

In the last years of the Lý period, conflict at court caused damage and destruction to the palaces. Many had to be rebuilt after the Trần took power. Then, during the thirteenth century, Thăng Long was occupied by three Mongol invading armies, with devastating consequences for the citadel. Returning there after his 1288 victory, 'the king had to place his throne in the guards' gallery, as all the palaces had been burnt down by the enemy'.[43] In the aftermath of war, it was natural that the Trần dynasty repair and rebuild many palaces.

The building at the centre of the Forbidden City remained Thiên An Palace under the Trần, with the Dragon Terrace (Long Trì) in front. In 1351, the king is recorded as seated on his throne in Thiên An Palace for an inspection of Forbidden City Guards at the Dragon Terrace. The palaces were named Tập Hiền, Thọ Quang, Bát Giác, Diên Hồng, Đại Minh and Diên Hiền. In 1236, Lệ Thiên Palace—where the royal concubines lived—was renamed Thưởng Xuân. The two most important palaces were Thánh Từ Palace (or Vạn Thọ or Phụ Thiên), where the king's father lived, and Quan Triều Palace, where the king lived. Under the king-senior emperor regime of the Trần, the king abdicated the throne in favour of his son and became the senior emperor (*thượng hoàng*), but continued to wield great power, follow state affairs and make important decisions. He could even dethrone the king. The senior emperor usually moved to Thiên Trường Palace (Nam Định) but continued to use Thánh Từ Palace at the capital. At the palace, he had a secretariat run by a member of the aristocracy or a mandarin. In 1236, Prince Trần Liễu was appointed head of Thánh Từ Palace secretariat, while in the following century Nguyễn Trung Ngạn held this position before his posting to Thanh Hóa province in 1326. In short, the organisation of Thánh Từ Palace resembled that of the king's palace, Quan Triều.

A long gallery was built in 1368 from Nguyên Huyền Palace to Đại Triều Gate in the west to shelter the mandarins from the sun and rain as they came to attend court. The book *Tam tổ thực lục* records that a pagoda named Tư Phúc was located in the central palace area. This pagoda may have been situated among the palaces of the Forbidden City, as we know King Trần Nhân Tông used to take his midday rest there.[44] In *Lịch triều hiến chương loại chí*, Phan Huy Chú (1960: 189) noted that Thiên Phúc Pagoda was located near the palace where King Trần Anh Tông once got drunk and slept in a stupor through a visit to the palaces by Senior Emperor Trần Nhân Tông.

After his stay in Thăng Long (1293), the imperial envoy Trần Phu wrote the following description in his text *An Nam tức sự*:

> At the chief's residence, there is a gate named Dương Minh Gate; a tower named Triều Thiên Tower is built on top; the small gate to the left is named Nhật Tân; the small gate to the right is named Vân Hội; its skylight named Thiên Tỉnh measures more than 6 m across.[45] From the terrace steps, we can see a sign placed under the pavilion inscribed with the words 'Tập Hiền Palace'; on top of it there is a large tower named Minh Linh; to the right, a path leads to a large palace named Đức Huy; the gate on the left is called Đồng Lạc, the gate on the right is called Kiều Ứng; all the signs were written in characters of gold.[46]

There is also a description of the Trần royal palace in the book *An Nam truyện*:

> The gate to the palace called Ngũ Môn has a sign inscribed with the words Đại Hưng Gate; there are side gates on its left and right; the main palace called Thiên An has nine compartments and is inscribed with the words Thiên An Throne Hall; Chính Nam Gate is inscribed with the words Triều Thiên Tower.[47]

Đại Hưng Gate was the south gate of the second enclosing wall known as Phoenix Citadel or Dragon Phoenix Citadel under the Trần. It had five archways (Ngũ Môn): a main archway as well as two secondary and two side archways. Dương Minh Gate was the Forbidden City's entrance. Triều Thiên Tower was on top of the gate, and there were two smaller gates named Nhật Tân and Vân Hội on either side. Inside, there was Tập Hiền Palace with its tower named Minh Linh, then Đức Huy Palace, Đồng Lạc Gate and Kiều Ứng Gate. Thiên An Palace was thus known as Thiên An Throne Hall, had nine compartments, and was regarded as the main palace, occupying the central position in the architectural layout of the Forbidden City.

There is no mention here of the Gate of Commencement's existence since the Lý dynasty. But this description states that Dương Minh Gate (with its tower named Triều Thiên) was also named Chính Nam Gate, and Chính Nam was the name used by the Trần for the Gate of Commencement. This fits with a description in the chronicle entry for 1281: Sài Xuân, an ambassador of the Yuan, rode his horse straight through Dương Minh Gate and dismounted from the horse only when he reached Tập Hiền Palace.[48] It fits too with a record from 1292, when another Yuan ambassador, Trương Lập Đạo, entered Thăng Long after crossing Ngoạn Nguyệt Bridge and passing Trường Minh Palace. He then arrived at Chính Dương Gate, where he dismounted and carried the imperial edict through Minh Dương Gate; his aides-de-camp entered through Vân Hội Gate while the Vietnamese mandarins entered through Nhật Tân Gate (Lê Tắc 2009: 93). Chính Dương Gate was the south gate, the citadel's main gate, and was also named Dương Minh (wrongly recorded here as Minh Dương). It had two side gates named Vân Hội and Nhật Tân.

At 18 Hoàng Diệu Street, archaeologists unearthed the remains of seven foundations, two wells, two drains and nine enclosing walls from this period. A distinctive feature of Trần architecture, found both at Thăng Long Imperial Citadel and Thiên Trường Palace (Nam Định), is that walls were bordered with bricks and tiles arranged in lemon flower patterns. The Thăng Long vestiges show how Lý buildings were borrowed in the early years of the Trần dynasty, and how the area was then gradually restructured, with some Lý buildings destroyed and new buildings raised on the foundations of the old. The decorative details on bricks, tiles and terracotta figures used to decorate roofs show that the architectural arts of the Trần were robust and frank in their expression. Large quantities of palace ceramics were discovered alongside the architectural remains, including white glazed, celadon, brown glazed and blue and white pieces, with many brown-glazed pieces of great size. The vestiges show that the Thăng Long pottery kilns were founded during the Lý period and continued to develop during the Trần, producing high-quality products for the court and for export (Tống Trung Tín & Bùi Minh Trí 2010: 26–7).

Early Lê (1428–1527), Mạc (1527–92), and Lê Restoration (1593–1789) Periods

After overthrowing the Ming in 1428, Lê Lợi ascended the throne at Kính Thiên Palace, founding the dynasty known as the Early Lê (1428–1527). This was the first occurrence of the name Kính Thiên. The citadel of Đại Việt's capital, known to the Trần and Ming as Đông Đô or Đông Quan, was renamed Đông Kinh. Kính Thiên Palace was rebuilt as early as 1428, along with Vạn Thọ Palace, the left and right palaces, and Cần Chánh Palace, as part of a major redevelopment of the Forbidden City. Under the Early Lê, the Forbidden City was also called the City of Palaces (Cung thành) (1467).

A major event of the Early Lê took place in 1459. One night in the tenth lunar month, Prince Lê Nghi Dân and his accomplices used ladders to scale the Imperial Citadel at the East Gate, entered the Forbidden City, assassinated King Lê Nhân Tông and the Queen Mother, and seized the throne. The following year, Lê loyalists killed the usurpers and established Lê Tư Thành on the throne: this was King Lê Thánh Tông. In the light of the events of 1459, the new king was highly vigilant and planned a new building programme for the walls around the Imperial Citadel and Forbidden City. Work was due to start in 1467, but that year's bad harvest and high price of rice meant it was postponed.

The Forbidden City of the Early Lê appears on the map of Đông Kinh in the *Hồng Đức bản đồ* map collection. Commissioned by King Lê Thánh Tông and prepared on the basis of meticulous research, this was the country's first national collection of maps. In 1466, the king divided the country into twelve administrative territories called *thừa tuyên* (one of which was equivalent to two or three modern provinces), adding a further one—Quảng Nam—in 1471. In 1467, he ordered the gathering of topographical, historical and economic information in each territory for the purpose of compiling a set of annotated maps of the whole country. In 1469, he asked the Ministry of Finance to collate data, documents and maps for each territory. The maps were completed in 1490, the twenty-first year of the Hồng Đức reign era. The original Hồng Đức collection is no longer extant, but copies made under the late Lê and early Nguyễn dynasties have survived, albeit with the addition of place names and architectural constructions dating from later periods.

The extant Hồng Đức collection consists of fifteen maps: one of the whole country, one of the Đông Kinh citadel (Thăng Long citadel), and thirteen of the *thừa tuyên* territories. The maps were drawn using

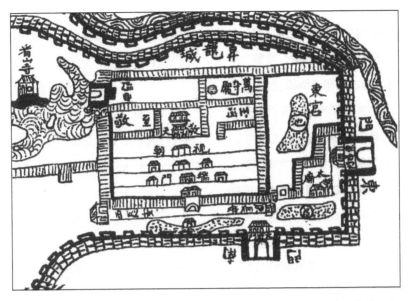

Map 13. Hồng Đức Map of Đông Kinh, the Forbidden City, detail (Institute of Hán-Nôm Studies, ref. A.2499).

the charting methods of the time: field survey with accurate data. Scales and orientation were not used. Each map shows the area's topography— mountains, rivers, coast, and islands—administrative units and important buildings (see Map 13 for a representation of the Forbidden City on the Hồng Đức map of Đông Kinh).

This plan locates Kính Thiên Palace in the centre of the Forbidden City, with Chí Kính Palace to its west, Ngọc Hà to its east, and Vạn Thọ Palace above Ngọc Hà. In front of Kính Thiên Palace was Thị Triều Palace, and then the Gate of Commencement. The Forbidden City was sur-rounded by a wall that formed a rough square. The West Gate stood to the northwest. There was a large gate to the south, protected by two outer gates named Đông Tràng An and Tây Tràng An. Several walls divided up the space inside the Forbidden City. To the east, the East Palace was located by a large lake and surrounded by a wall; southeast of the East Palace area was the Thái Miếu ancestral temple. The Forbidden City was located on the eastern side of the Imperial Citadel, which was named Thăng Long Citadel and had two gates, to the east and south.

The map only shows a few of the Forbidden City's palaces, among which the main palace, Kính Thiên, has a prominent central position and is surrounded by a wall to the north, east and west. The Early Lê chronicles relate the construction of many palaces that do not appear on the Hồng Đức map. These include: Cần Chánh Palace and two other palaces, one on each side (1428); Càn Đức Palace and Hội Anh Palace (1434); Khánh Phương Temple (1440); Thừa Thiên Tower (1448); Nghị Sự Road and Tường Quang Palace (1460); Cẩn Đức Palace (1465); Phụng Nghi Road (1467); Đồ Trị Palace, Thượng Dương Palace, Giám Trị Palace, Trường Sinh Palace, Lưu Bôi Palace, Hoàng Cực Palace, Hưng Minh Palace (1504); Trường Lạc Palace (1505); Kim Quang Palace, Đoan Khang Palace (1509); Trùng Hoa Palace (1510); and Quang Trị Palace (1513).

The Forbidden City of the Lê period was described by Nguyễn Văn Siêu (1799–1872) in *Phương Đình dư địa chí*:

> As it appears on the Hồng Đức map of Thăng Long Citadel, the Forbidden City is shaped like a carpenter's ruler. Its three sides to the east, south and north form a regular square, while its west side is long. Outside the East Gate, there is Đức Môn village (formerly Đông Môn village) in Đồng Xuân canton; if one goes north from here, one reaches the Tô Lịch River; if one follows the left bank of this river to the west one reaches the North Gate, which is opposite Nhật Chiêu ward; if one goes south, one reaches Bảo Khánh Gate, with Văn Miếu in front on the right and Cửa Nam behind on the left. Here, there are the vestiges of old Thăng Long Citadel, with the Forbidden City in the middle, and the Forbidden City's gate the Gate of Commencement (Đoan Môn). After passing the Gate of Commencement, one reaches Thị Triều Palace, then Kính Thiên Palace. Chí Kính Palace is to the right of Kính Thiên Palace; Vạn Thọ Palace is to the left. Tây Tràng An is to the right of the Gate of Commencement; Đông Tràng An is to the left. Ngọc stream is inside. Outside the Forbidden City is Thăng Long Citadel. To the east are Thái Miếu Temple and the East Palace. (Nguyễn Văn Siêu 2010: 533)

Nguyễn Văn Siêu's description informs us that the Imperial Citadel was named Thăng Long Citadel, that as shown on the Hồng Đức map the Forbidden City and its palaces were located inside the Imperial Citadel, and that the Thái Miếu Temple and East Palace area was located outside the Forbidden City.

The rules on protocol for those attending audience during the Hồng Đức period contain additional information about the gates that opened into the Dragon Terrace (named Đan Trì at this time). According to a 1472 rule, before entering the royal presence, military officers had to line up outside the Gate of Commencement, on its east and west sides. On the first day of the new moon, they had to wait at Văn Minh Gate and Sùng Vũ Gate; after hearing three drum rolls, they entered the courtyard or terrace named Đan Trì to parade their guard of honour. The officers' route to Đan Trì thus informs us that after entering the Gate of Commencement, one reached Văn Minh Gate and Sùng Vũ Gate.

A 1485 rule laid down that courtiers and mandarins entering for audience had to dismount at the Gate of Commencement; dukes and other aristocrats could be accompanied by two attendants while first grade mandarins could be accompanied by one attendant, who were allowed to proceed as far as Ngoạn Thiềm Gate. The attendants' route thus informs us that after entering the Gate of Commencement, one reached Ngoạn Thiềm Gate. Another 1485 rule laid down the protocol for entering the king's presence:

> From now on, on the day of the audience, after the first drum roll, mandarin of the guards will enter Đan Trì in order of rank; after the second drum roll, all mandarins will enter Đan Trì in order of rank, but only those invited, and without jostling or disorderly conduct. Mandarins who remain outside of Chu Tước Gate after the third drum roll, or who remain to the right or left of the Gate of Commencement after the fiftieth stroke of the bell will refused entry by the gatekeepers; the guards will report the matter to the throne for punishment.[49]

Đan Trì was the ceremonial space located in front of Kính Thiên Palace. Mandarins who went in for audience at Đan Trì had to pass through Chu Tước Gate and then the Gate of Commencement before they arrived at Đan Trì.

As they entered, mandarins dismounted at Đại Hưng Gate in the Imperial Citadel and went from there on foot through to Đan Trì. Outside this gate, King Lê Thánh Tông had a pavilion built for mandarins to use during their wait for the time appointed for their royal audience. Soon after ascending the throne in 1497, King Lê Hiến Tông (r. 1497–1504) added two further buildings to Đãi Lậu Pavilion (lit. waiting for the appointed hour), each consisting of three compartments and two wings.[50]

The gates in the Imperial Citadel were named Đông Hoa, Thiên Hựu, Đại Hưng and Bắc Thần, according to the articles on Forbidden City Guards in the criminal code (*Hình luật chí*) section of Phan Huy Chú's *Lịch triều hiến chương loại chí* (1960). This source notes that the Forbidden City had several layers of walls. Indeed, the wall around the Forbidden City was called 'forbidden wall' (*tường cấm*) and its gates were 'forbidden gates' (*cửa cấm*); the walls around palaces were called 'palace wall' (*tường điện*) and their gates were palace gates (*cửa điện, cửa cung*). The forbidden wall had many layers of many forbidden gates, named Đoan Minh (Đoan Môn?), Tả Dực, Hữu Dực, Tường Huy, Đại Định, Trường Lạc, Đại Khánh, Kiến Bình and Huyền Vũ. Palaces could be entered through palace gate one, palace gate two and other palace gates (Phan Huy Chú 1960: 114). The Hồng Đức map of Đông Kinh clearly shows the walls that divided the space inside the Forbidden City. Kính Thiên Palace was surrounded by a wall on its north, east and west sides, with its gate to the south. History records that during heavy rain in 1491, the water rose to a height of 4 m, causing the Kính Thiên Palace wall to collapse. The *Hình luật chí* section of Phan Huy Chú's work notes that climbing over the forbidden wall was punishable by garrotting and climbing over a palace wall was punishable by beheading. The chapter on the Forbidden City Guards in the Lê dynasty's penal code *Quốc triều hình luật* contains different articles distinguishing the forbidden wall from the forbidden gates, and different types of palace walls and palace gates, and laying down severe punishments for trespassing in the Forbidden City.[51]

Historical sources, such as those cited above, inform us of the names of the palaces and gates of the Forbidden City, but it remains difficult to determine their precise locations or represent them on a comprehensive plan.

* * *

Kính Thiên Palace and Đan Trì Terrace formed the country's most important architectural space, which was used for ceremonial occasions involving the king's presence, including the reception of ambassadors. Kính Thiên Palace was built in 1428 and rebuilt in 1465. In 1467, a flight of nine steps was built up to the terrace with four stone balustrades that divided the staircase into three separate flights of stairs. The middle flight was reserved for the king's use, while the other two were used by mandarins. At some point under the Early Lê (the exact date is unknown), two large bells—named Càn Nguyên bells—were hung at Kính Thiên Palace. In 1509, they crashed to the ground when their supports broke.

When giving audience, the king took his seat on the throne in Kính Thiên Palace; in hierarchical order, the courtiers came into the royal presence on Đan Trì Terrace. In 1473, at the gates and on Đan Trì Terrace, mandarins entering for audience were prohibited from spitting or throwing chewed betel on the ground (in those days, betel was chewed by men, women, commoners, aristocrats and mandarins alike). It was on his throne in Kính Thiên Palace that the king received the ambassadors of the Ming dynasty when they presented their credentials, while audiences with ambassadors were held in Cần Chánh Palace.

Under the Early Lê, the king and court placed strong emphasis on Confucian education and examinations. In 1442, for the first time, the second-degree examination was organised inside Thăng Long Citadel. After the examination, successful candidates were admitted to Đan Trì Terrace to sit a further examination with questions set by the king. The king handed down the questions from his throne in Kính Thiên Palace, and after assessing the exam papers, returned to his throne there for the ceremonial announcement of the new doctors' names and the congratulations of the mandarins in court dress. A roll of honour listing their names was posted outside Đông Hoa Gate and, from 1502, at the door of royal academy. In ways such as these, by comparison with the Lý and Trần, the Early Lê dynasty's centralisation of the monarchy and embrace of Confucianism brought changes to the ceremonial use of Kính Thiên Palace and Đan Trì Terrace.

Under the Mạc dynasty (1527–92), there was no new construction in the Forbidden City. However, the ramparts of the Đại La and Imperial Citadels were rebuilt and new embankments were raised outside the Đại La Citadel against attacks by the Trịnh army. In 1584, Mạc Mậu Hợp ordered large-scale repairs to the citadel, establishing new factories for the production of bricks and tiles, ordering An Bang and Ninh Sóc districts to send bamboo and timber to the capital. The work lasted a year and was completed in 1585,[52] but no text records the construction of any specific building or of any palace in the Forbidden City.

During the Lê Restoration period (1593–1789) the Trịnh lords established their residence outside the Imperial Citadel. As a result, the Forbidden City was poorly maintained and gradually lost its former magnificence. Parts were damaged, other parts collapsed. The chronicles record some construction and repair work—the renovation of Thái Miếu Temple in 1596 and the construction of an inner palace and ten galleries in 1630—as well as the collapse and burning down of some palaces— the destruction by a meteorite of part of Kính Thiên Palace in 1599 and the burning of the Gate of Commencement in 1619.

In 1749, with the construction of Đại Đô Citadel, the outer walls protecting the Forbidden City were reduced in extent. The Lê king's activities were limited to certain national ceremonies: the Thái Miếu and Nam Giao ceremonies, the royal audience and accession to the throne ceremonies, the investiture of the Trịnh lords as grand marshals, the reception of ambassadors, and so on. To the end of the Lê period, the chronicles continue to record the existence of many palaces, including Kính Thiên, Thị Triều, Vạn Thọ and Cần Chánh.

The Forbidden City of Thăng Long of the seventeenth and eighteenth centuries may be studied using texts written by priests and merchants from Western countries. For Samuel Baron, in the late seventeenth century,

> Stupendous, indeed, are the triple walls of the old city and palace; for by the ruins they appear to have been strong fabricks with noble large gates, paved with a kind of marble; the palace seems to have been about six or seven miles in circumference; its gates, courts, apartments, etc. testify amply its former pomp and glory. (Baron 2006: 203–4)

In foreign eyes, the Forbidden City and its palaces were in ruins, but the ruins reflected a glorious past.

In 1786, after leading an army north and overthrowing the Trịnh lord's regime, the Tây Sơn general, Nguyễn Huệ, visited King Lê Hiển Tông. At that time, the king was lying sick in Vạn Thọ Palace. On the seventh day of the seventh lunar month a royal audience was held. Nguyễn Huệ paid ceremonial respects to the Lê king, explained his killing of the Trịnh lord and support for the Lê, and submitted the accounts and lists of the military and civilian population that symbolised the Lê king's sovereignty. The ceremony was held in Kính Thiên Palace, which his delegation of Tây Sơn generals reached after passing the Gate of Commencement and Đan Trì Terrace. On the seventeenth of the same month, guards of honour presented arms and ceremonial music was played on the east and west sides of Đan Trì Terrace, King Lê Hiển Tông issued a royal edict of unification and ordered it to be posted outside Đại Hưng Gate (Ngô Cao Lãng 1995: 576, 579). This was an important ceremony of royal audience held by a Lê-dynasty king inside the Forbidden City of Thăng Long.

In 1788, Nguyễn Huệ acceded to the throne at Bân Sơn (Huế), established the Tây Sơn dynasty, took the reign name Quang Trung and named Phú Xuân as his capital. The following spring, he routed a Qing invading army and liberated the Imperial Citadel and the country as a whole. Thăng Long now became capital of the north, with seven inner provinces (Thanh Hoa Ngoại, Sơn Nam Thượng, Sơn Nam Hạ, Sơn Tây, Kinh Bắc, Hải Dương, Phụng Thiên) and six outer provinces (Lạng Sơn, Cao Bằng, Tuyên Quang, Hưng Hóa, Thái Nguyên, Yên Quảng).

King Quang Trung rapidly established diplomatic relations with the Qing and, in the summer, a Tây Sơn embassy headed by Nguyễn Quang Hiển was solemnly received in Beijing. By the end of the year, a Qing delegation travelled to Thăng Long to confer Quang Trung with the kingship and royal seals of Annam. On the morning of the fifteenth day of the tenth month (1st December 1789), the Qing diplomats left their residence at Kiên Nghĩa Temple (vestiges of which remain at 2A Nguyễn Hữu Huân Street), passed Quảng Văn Temple, went through the Gate of Commencement and reached Tiếp Thụ Palace before arriving at Kính Thiên Palace for the ceremony. Phạm Công Trị accepted the ritual offerings on Quang Trung's behalf and then received the embassy at Cần Chánh Palace (*Đại Việt quốc thư* 1972: 219).

The Nguyễn dynasty (1802–1945) took Phú Xuân–Huế as its capital, establishing Thăng Long as the capital of the north and, from 1831, of the province of Hanoi. In 1805, the Nguyễn demolished the Forbidden City, built new ramparts in the Vauban style and, in 1831, renamed them Hanoi Citadel. Hanoi Citadel's central axis closely corresponded to the central axis of Thăng Long Forbidden City. The Nguyễn rebuilt some of the Forbidden City's palaces and redeveloped them into a citadel that served as a royal visit palace where the Nguyễn kings could stay when in the north. In 1816, the timbers of Kính Thiên Palace were found to be rotten; the palace was dismantled and a new one built. Repairs and rebuilding continued through the reigns of Gia Long (1802–20) and Minh Mạng (1820–41), such that by Thiệu Trị's reign (1841–47) the royal visit palace in Hanoi consisted of a great palace, rear palace, Coi Châu Palace and Cần Chính Palace, as well as Kính Thiên Palace, renamed Long Thiên Palace in 1841 (*Khâm định Đại Nam hội điện sự lệ* 1993: vol. 23, 442).

The French attacked and occupied Hanoi in the late nineteenth century, garrisoning troops in the citadel. In 1886 they destroyed Long Thiên Palace and built the headquarters of their artillery where it once stood. Then, in 1894–97, they destroyed the whole citadel (see Olivier Tessier's chapter). All that remained from the old Forbidden City was the Gate of Commencement, the foundation of Kính Thiên Palace, and the staircase to the terrace with its dragon balustrades. From the old Hanoi Citadel, there remained the North Gate and the Flag Tower.

The Scale and Location of the Forbidden City

Standing monuments and the results of archaeological excavation reveal the position of several architectural features of the Forbidden City during the Early Lê and Lê Restoration periods, as follows.

The Gate of Commencement (Đoan Môn) was the inner south gate of the Forbidden City. The Gate of Commencement of the Early Lê dynasty remains standing today, in the form of five U-shaped archways built of stone and brick. The central archway is the largest of the five (4 m high, 2.7 m wide) and bears the characters 'Đoan Môn' carved onto a piece of stone above its arch. Only the king could enter through this gate. Two smaller side archways (3.8 m high, 2.5 m wide) were used by mandarins and members of royal family, while the two smallest auxiliary archways to their left and right were for soldiers and servants. These five archways gave Đoan Môn its other name: Ngũ Môn, meaning five gates.

The Gate of Commencement is a large structure (46.5 m wide, 26.5 m long, 6 m high). Examination shows that it has been repaired many times. The gate tower was destroyed at some point; the current tower was built in the temple style by the Nguyễn and restored in 1998. Archaeological investigation in 1999 revealed architectural remains from the Lý and Trần under the gate's foundations. Excavation of the Rose Garden revealed vestiges of a section of the Forbidden City's wall directly to the west of the Gate of Commencement. This wall was built of earth, with a brick façade on both sides.

Kính Thiên Palace was the Forbidden City's main palace, built on Mount Nùng. This was where the geomancers' 'dragon's navel' was located, where the energies of mountains and rivers converged, and where heaven and earth joined. Kính Thiên Palace was demolished in 1816. Long Thiên Palace—the royal visit palace of the Nguyễn kings—was demolished in 1886. Today all that remains is the palace foundation and the staircase to the terrace, with its nine steps and four stone balustrades (dated 1467). The two middle balustrades were carved with five-clawed dragons and other motifs characteristic of Early Lê art. Behind the palace there was also a terrace with a sculpted pair of dragons in Lê Restoration style (seventeenth century). Trial excavations in four trenches at the front and rear terraces show that Kính Thiên Palace was built in two stages: in the fifteenth and seventeenth centuries.

Đan Trì court—or Dragon Terrace—was located between Kính Thiên Palace and the Gate of Commencement. In a photograph taken by Hocquard in 1886, vestiges of the court were still visible in front of Long Thiên Palace, but its terracotta paving tiles had already been removed and all that remained was the royal road between the main palace to the Gate of Commencement (Hocquard 1999: 103, 105). Excavation of an area of nearly 1,000 m² (in 2011–13 and 2014) revealed vestiges of Đan Trì court and the royal road in two layers dating from the Early Lê and

Lê Restoration (seventeenth century). The court had been built with great care, its tiles paved on a foundation of yellow clay, while the foundations of the royal road were bordered on both sides. A wall surrounded the court in the Lê period: excavation (in 2013–14) revealed part of its foundations, its western section, which was 1.7 m wide and 57 m long in the excavated area, and its eastern section, which was 1.5 m wide. The wall was built of earth with a brick façade. Some of its bricks were inscribed with the characters *Thu Vật hương Thu Vật huyện* (收 物 縣 收 物 鄉), like others discovered at a Lê-period site at 18 Hoàng Diệu Street. The wall was about 120 m long, including both east and west sections. Among the vestiges found in the Đan Trì court were some Lê Restoration pillar foundations of a very large size.[53] On the Hồng Đức map, some buildings, including Thị Triều Palace, do indeed appear in the area between Kính Thiên Palace and the Gate of Commencement.

The historical and archaeological research presented above allows us to locate these monuments within the Forbidden City. At the centre of the Forbidden City was Kính Thiên Palace. Today vestiges remain of its foundation and stone staircase. The western side of the Forbidden City was the area of the One Pillar Pagoda and Khán Sơn Mountain. The One Pillar Pagoda was the Diên Hựu Pagoda of the Lý; an 1121 inscription on Sùng Thiện Diên Linh Tower locates it west of Tây Cấm Garden, west of the Forbidden City. According to the Hồng Đức map and other sources, Khán Sơn Mountain was outside the Forbidden City to the northwest. But when the Nguyễn built their new citadel at Thăng Long (named Hanoi Citadel after 1831), Khán Sơn was inside its northwest corner,[54] near the modern crossroads of Phan Đình Phùng and Hùng Vương Streets.

The Forbidden City's northern edge was south of Tam Sơn Mountain. This originally consisted of two natural knolls about 80 m apart and was later banked up into a single mound with a circumference of about 120 m. Tam Sơn was north of the adjoining mound of Mount Nùng, where the main palace of the Forbidden City was built: geomancers saw it as a 'pillow' for Mount Nùng. When the Nguyễn built their citadel here, Tam Sơn was inside its wall, near today's North Gate on Phan Đình Phùng Street.[55] The northern side of the Forbidden City was thus located in the area south of the North Gate, between the gate and the Rear Palace.

The southern edge of the Forbidden City was the Gate of Commencement. The Hồng Đức map and other sources show that entering the Forbidden City by its southern entrance required passing through a series of gates, with the Gate of Commencement the innermost. According to the Hồng Đức map, when going south out of the citadel from the Gate of Commencement, one came first to a large gate, then to the two gates named Đông Tràng An and Tây Tràng An, then once outside there was a further smaller gate beside a large lake. The map was not drawn to scale and does not mark all the names, making some of the sites difficult to identify. But historical sources give the names of gates outside the Gate of Commencement: Văn Minh, Sùng Vũ, Ngọc Thiềm, Chu Tước. They allow us to identify the outermost gate as Tam Sơn Gate, or Chu Tước Gate.

The Flag Tower, known as Kỳ Đài or Cột Cờ, was built by the Nguyễn in 1805–12. According to the text *Long Biên bách nhị vịnh* by eighteenth-to-nineteenth-century author Bùi Quang Cơ, the tower was built on the foundations of Tam Môn gate, which had once stood in front of Ngũ Môn gate (i.e., the Gate of Commencement).[56] According to Dương Bá Cung's nineteenth-century text *Hà Nội địa dư*, 'it is said that Kỳ Đài used to be Chu Tước Gate or Tam Phượng Tower' (Dương Bá Cung 2007: 52).[57] This gate had three archways, so was called Tam Môn or Tam Phượng, just as the Gate of Commencement had five archways and was called Ngũ Môn Lâu or Ngũ Phượng Lâu. The Flag Tower still stands; it marks the site of the outermost gate on the southern side of the Forbidden City.

On the eastern side of the Forbidden City, there is no such landmark. However, on the Hồng Đức map, it is clear that the Forbidden City was roughly square (leaving out the East Palace and Thái Miếu Temple area). Once we see the Forbidden City as square, we can use several known landmarks to help us locate key points, as follows:

- The foundations of Kính Thiên Palace were centrally located.
- The Forbidden City was bounded to the north by Tam Sơn, which was just south of today's North Gate.
- To the south, the Forbidden City's innermost and main gate was the Gate of Commencement, while its outermost gate was Tam Môn or Chu Tước Gate, where the Flag Tower is today.
- The One Pillar Pagoda was west of the Forbidden City. Khán Sơn—at the crossroads of modern Phan Đình Phùng and Hùng Vương Streets—was also outside the Forbidden City, to the northwest.

That was the area covered by the Forbidden City under the Lê. According to my previous calculations using digital maps of Hanoi, the distance from the Flag Tower (Tam Môn/Chu Tước) to a point south of Tam Sơn was 700 m, allowing me to estimate that each side of the Forbidden City was about 700 m long (Phan Huy Lê 2006).[58] Field survey data gathered by the Center for Thăng Long Heritage Conservation now yields measurements of greater precision. Let us look first at the north–south line. No vestige of Tam Sơn remains to help us determine its location, only that it was north of the Forbidden City and inside Hanoi Citadel, just south of Hanoi Citadel's North Gate. My hypothesis is that Tam Sơn was at the Rear Palace, where archaeologists have unearthed vestiges of a Lý palace (regarded as located in the northern area of the Forbidden City). Based on this hypothesis, the distance between Tam Sơn and the Flag Tower was 771 m. Thus, the distance from Tam Môn/Chu Tước to a point just south of Tam Sơn—corresponding to the north–south length of the Forbidden City—was approximatively 770 m. Under the Lê, that was the entire area of the Forbidden City of Thăng Long.

However, the Hồng Đức map shows that the Forbidden City's wall did not extend as far south as the outermost gate—Chu Tước Gate—but was aligned with the main south gate, the Gate of Commencement. The wall is not drawn clearly on the map. But excavation at the Rose Garden revealed a section of the Forbidden City's wall that is exactly aligned with the Gate of Commencement. This archaeological data suggests that the east–west wall on the south side of the Forbidden City was linked to the Gate of Commencement. This gate marked the Forbidden City's southern edge, while its northern edge was just south of Tam Sơn. The distance between Tam Sơn and the Gate of Commencement was 462 m. This was the central area of the Forbidden City, where the palaces of the court and the royal family were concentrated, including the main palace and the Dragon Terrace. This area was smaller than the Forbidden City as a whole, and was rectangular in shape, its east–west sides measuring 770 m and north–south sides 462 m.

From this identification of the Forbidden City's scale and location we may conclude that the whole archaeological site at 18 Hoàng Diệu Street is on land that was in the Forbidden City. Moreover, the site is only about 100 m from the foundations of Kính Thiên Palace—very close to the Forbidden City's centre. At 18 Hoàng Diệu Street, archaeologists discovered vestiges of four buildings dating from the Early Lê period, as well as nine wells, three drains and many objects (Bùi Minh Trí & Tống Trung Tín 2010). Building materials found there include tiles decorated with dragon and chrysanthemum motifs, especially those fired with the distinctive yellow and green glazes that only existed under the Early Lê. High-quality ceramics were unearthed, including pieces bearing images of five-clawed dragons, indicating their exclusive use by the king, or inscribed with the words 'Mandarin' (*quan* 官, 'Trường Lạc Palace' [Trường Lạc Cung 長樂宮], or 'Trường Lạc Guards' [Trường Lạc khố 長樂庫]).

Fewer vestiges and objects date from the Mạc and Lê Restoration periods. This is due to the Lê–Mạc war, the Forbidden City's decline under the Lê kings and Trịnh lords, and the destruction of cultural layers caused by new construction under the Nguyễn. However, archaeologists still found some royal ceramics decorated with dragons, as well as bricks and tiles with dragon motifs or fine enamel. Archaeological excavation has clearly shown that this area was inside Forbidden City. A key point that emerges from this research is that the Forbidden City of the Early Lê was on almost exactly the same land as the Forbidden City of the Lý and Trần. That was why archaeologists working at 18 Hoàng Diệu Street and across the road in the old Hanoi Citadel area have discovered so many examples of palace architecture and such large quantities of objects for use at court dating from a continuous period of Thăng Long's history that extended from 1010 to 1788. This also answers the question of why a site that is not very large contains so many cultural layers, overlapping and intermingled, that tell the whole history of the citadel at the capital Thăng Long.

Notes

1. *Đại Việt sử ký toàn thư* (q. II-7a; 1998: vol. I, 244).
2. *Đại Việt sử ký toàn thư* (q. XVII-18b; 1998: vol. III, 164).
3. *Đại Việt sử ký toàn thư* (q. XVII-29b–30a; 1998: vol. III, 173).
4. *Khâm định Việt sử thông giám cương mục, Chính biên* (q. XL-33a; 1998: t. II, 601).
5. The original map is kept at the Institute of Social Science Information in Hanoi, ref. A.2.3.32. It was redrawn in 1956 by Trần Huy Bá with notes in Vietnamese, and made public in 2010 on the occasion of the Thăng Long-Hanoi Millennium.
6. The map *Hoài Đức phủ toàn đồ* further mentions Hàm Long city gate: 'from Thịnh Quang city gate (ô) to Hàm Long city gate is 3 miles...' This point needs further research.
7. *Đại Việt sử ký toàn thư* (q. II-3a–3b; 1998: vol. I, 241); *Đại Việt sử lược* (1960: 70).
8. *Đại Việt sử ký toàn thư* (q. VI-19a; 1998: vol. II, 88).
9. *Đại Việt sử ký tiền biên* (1997: 329).
10. *Đại Việt sử ký toàn thư* (q. V-6a; 1998: vol. II, 12).
11. *Đại Việt sử ký toàn thư,* (q. XIII-65a; 1998: vol. II, 508).
12. See also *Bắc Thành địa dư chí lược, Đại Việt địa dư toàn biên.*
13. *Đại Việt sử ký toàn thư* (q. X-43a; 1998: vol. II, 278).
14. *Đại Việt sử ký toàn thư* (q. II-12a; 1998: vol. I, 248).

15. *Quốc triều hình luật* (Penal Code of the Royal Court, or Hồng Đức Code), articles 51, 52, 53, 56, 62, 80, 81, 82, 91, 92, 94 and 96.
16. *Đại Việt sử ký toàn thư* (q. XII-44a; 1998: vol. II, 430).
17. See Institute of Hán-Nôm Studies, ref. A.2499, A.2716, A.1362, A.73, A.3034, A.1081.
18. *Đại Việt sử ký toàn thư* (q. XIII-65a; 1998: vol. II, 508).
19. *Đại Việt sử ký toàn thư* (q. XV-26b; 1998: vol. III, 74).
20. Bảo Khánh village (*thôn*) belonged to Giảng Võ hamlet (*trại*), Nội canton (*tổng*), Vĩnh Thuận district (*huyện*). See 'Địa bạ thôn Bảo Khánh năm Gia Long thứ 4-1805' [The land register of Bảo Khánh village for the fourth year of Gia Long's reign, 1805] in Phan Huy Lê (2010b: 582–3).
21. *Đại Việt sử ký toàn thư* (q. XV-27b; 1998: vol. III, 75).
22. Regarding *Đại Việt sử lược*, the edition printed in 1936 under the name *Việt sử lược* should be compared with the Trần Kinh Hòa edition, published in Tokyo in 1987 under the name *Đại Việt sử lược* (translated by Trần Quốc Vượng and published in Hanoi in 1960). See entries for the years 1209 (q. 3-19b), 1212 (q. 3-24b), 1213 (q. 3-25a), 1214 (q. 3-26a).
23. *Đại Việt sử ký toàn thư* (q. 2-11a; 2010: 153).
24. The passage 'quảng Diên Hựu chi danh tự' is blurred on the inscription; some read 'quảng', others read 'xưởng' (Viện Văn học 1977: vol. 1, 397).
25. This source starts by referring to Triều Nguyên Palace, then a few lines later it uses the name Càn Nguyên, as in *Đại Việt sử ký toàn thư*. The source notes that Cao Palace was built in the south, using the term *chính dương*, which means south, not north as translated. According to *Đại Việt sử ký toàn thư*, Cao Palace was Cao Minh Palace.
26. *Đại Việt sử ký toàn thư* (q. II-3a; 1998: vol. I, 241). The source notes that Thúy Hoa and Long Thụy Palaces were built behind Nhật Quang and Nguyệt Minh Palaces. But *Đại Việt sử lược* mentions only Thúy Hoa Palace, because Long Thụy Palace had already been built behind Càn Nguyên Palace.
27. *Đại Việt sử ký toàn thư* (q. II-19b-20a; 1998: vol. I, 254).
28. The comment on this point in *Đại Việt sử ký toàn thư* is vague: 'much woodwork went into the construction of the palaces' (q. IV-23a: 1998, vol. I, 331).
29. *Đại Việt sử ký toàn thư* (q. II-20a; 1998: vol. I, 254).
30. *Đại Việt sử lược* (q. 2-11a).
31. *Đại Việt sử ký toàn thư* (q. II-9a; 1998: vol. I, 246).
32. Zhou Qufei [周去非], *Lĩnh ngoại đại đáp* [嶺外代 答 Description of the land beyond the southern passes], 1178, q. 2.
33. *Đại Việt sử ký toàn thư* (q. Thủ-1a; 1998: vol. I, 93).
34. *Đại Việt sử lược* entries for 1045 (q. 2-8a), 1055 (q. 2-10a), 1063 (q. 2-12a), 1180 (q. 3-10a); *Đại Việt sử ký toàn thư* entries for 1045 (q. II-36b; 2010:

165), 1055 (q. III-1a; 2010: 168); *Thiền uyển tập anh: truyện thiền sư Chân Không* (q. hạ, 65a).

35. *Đại Việt sử lược* entries for 1074 (q. 2-15b), 1148 (q.3-4b); *Đại Việt sử ký toàn thư* entries for 1041 (q. 2-19b; 2010: 156), 1074 (q. 3-8a; 2010: 170).

36. *Đại Việt sử lược* entry for 1137 (q. 3-2b); *Thiền uyển tập anh*, truyện thiền sư Đại Xả (q. thượng, 29b).

37. *Đại Việt sử lược* entry for 1116 (q. 2-22a); *Đại Việt sử ký toàn thư* entries for 1120 (q. 3-20b), 1126 (q. 3-24a, 24b).

38. Đặng Xuân Khanh (2007: 408) notes that Ngũ Lâu Gate was built by the Lý dynasty in front of Mount Nùng palace and inscribed 'Đoan Môn'. Đoan Môn had five doors, hence its other name Ngũ Lâu Môn (Five Gate Tower).

39. *Đại Nam Thực Lục tiền biên, chính biên* (q. 20; 2007: vol. 1, 543).

40. *Đại Việt sử lược* describes Đại La Citadel as having a perimeter of 5.94 km, with the Forbidden City inside. It was thus bigger than the Nguyễn dynasty's Hanoi Citadel (perimeter 4 km). The rampart built by Trương Chu had three gates (east, west and south), as did the rampart built by Trương Bá Nghi. There is no description of the Forbidden City. The excavation of Sections A, B, C, D and E (old Ba Đình National Assembly Building) and north of the Rose Garden revealed many Đại La vestiges, including a section of the Đại La rampart.

41. Bùi Văn Liêm, '*Báo cáo tổng hợp di tích kiến trúc tâm linh đặc biệt thời Lý phát hiện tại lô E*' [General report on Lý-period unusual religious buildings discovered in Section E], Institute of Archaeology report.

42. See the following texts: *Hoàng Việt địa dư chí, Đại Nam nhất thống chí, Đại Việt địa dư, Thăng Long cổ tích khảo, Bắc thành địa dư chí lược, Hà Nội địa dư*.

43. *Đại Việt sử ký toàn thư* (q. V-55a; 2010: 246).

44. The text *Tam tổ thực lục* (in the section on the Zen Buddhist king Trần Nhân Tông) notes that 'the King usually rested at noon in Tư Phúc Pagoda in the Forbidden City' (p. 2a); it also notes several times (in the section on Zen Buddhist Pháp Loa) the location of 'Tư Phúc Pagoda in the Forbidden City'.

45. This is calculated according to measurements in *Chung-kuo tu-liang-heng shih* (1984: 66), which states that one 'thước' measured 30.72 cm in the Nguyên period.

46. Trần Phu, *An Nam tức sự* [Contemplating landscapes of Annam] in *Trần Cương Trung thi tập* [Trần Cương Trung's collected poems], q. 2.

47. *Nguyên sử, An Nam truyện* [Story of Annam], q. 209, Tứ khố toàn thư (四庫全書), digital edition.

48. *Đại Việt sử ký toàn thư* (q. V-40b, 41a; 1998: vol. II, 46–7).

49. *Đại Việt sử ký toàn thư* (q. XII-74a; 2010: 476) and (q. XIII-46a, 46b; 1998: vol. II, 495)

50. *Đại Việt sử ký toàn thư* (q. XIII-85a; 1998: vol. II, 525).
51. *Quốc triều hình luật*, articles 51, 52, 53, 54, 55, 56, 58, 59.
52. Lê Quý Đôn 1978: 344; *Đại Việt sử ký toàn thư* (q. XVII-14b; 1998: vol. III, 161); *Khâm định Việt sử thông giám cương mục* (q. XIX-15b, 1998: II, 177).
53. Institute of Archaeology, 'Preliminary report on the excavation results at Kính Thiên main palace in 2014', Thăng Long–Hanoi Heritage Conservation Centre report.
54. See the following texts: *Đại Nam nhất thống chí, Hoàng Việt địa dư chí, Thăng Long cổ tích khảo, La Thành cổ tích khảo, Tây Hồ chí.*
55. See the following texts: *Đại Nam nhất thống chí, Đại Việt địa dư, Hoàng Việt địa dư chí, Thăng Long cổ tích khảo, Bắc Thành địa dư chí lược.*
56. Bùi Quang Cơ, *Long Biên bách nhị vịnh*, Institute of Hán Nôm Studies document, ref. A.1310.
57. Under the Nguyễn, Chu Tước gate still stood to the south of Hanoi Citadel. Descriptions in *Đại Nam thực lục, chính biên* entries for 1804, 1820, 1841 and 1842 note that Chu Tước Gate was south of the citadel, outside the Gate of Commencement; from there, one reached the Nhị River landing. The Nguyễn destroyed Tam Môn/Chu Tước Gate to build the Flag Tower. After 1805, they probably rebuilt Chu Tước Gate to the royal visit palace.
58. I consulted other authors in my effort to locate the Forbidden City. Trần Quốc Vương and Vũ Tuân Sán (1975: 152) estimated the Forbidden City's circumference at 4,700 m, larger than the circumference of Hanoi Citadel under the Nguyễn. Phạm Hân (2003: 95) calculated that each side of the square measured about 700 m, similar to my earlier estimate. Nguyễn Quang Ngọc (2012: 15) used Baron's observation (2006: 204) that the palace was 'about six or seven miles in circumference' (about 3,330 m or 3,885 m) as the basis for a hypothesis that each side of the square citadel measured about 900 m. But these are English miles, one of which is equivalent to 1.6 km; 6 miles is thus equivalent to 9.6 km and 8 miles is equivalent to 12.8 km. This was probably an observation about the size of the Imperial Citadel, not the Forbidden City.

CHAPTER 10

Đại Việt and Champa, Viewed from the Excavation Trenches at 18 Hoàng Diệu Street

Nguyễn Tiến Đông

1. A MOMENT OF DISCOVERY

During the last days of the year 2002, the weather had just turned wintery and almost all the researchers at the Institute of Archaeology started work at 18 Hoàng Diệu Street, where they were planning to build a new National Convention Centre and National Assembly. Vietnam's heritage law stipulated that before major construction work anywhere in the country could proceed, an archaeological excavation had to be conducted. This was the job we now had to do in the heart of the capital. For me and many colleagues, this excavation was a pleasure and a great opportunity, as we hoped we might discover traces of Vietnam's ancient capital, Thăng Long. At the time, I only thought we might, nothing more.

When I arrived at the archaeological site on the first day, I was surprised: this residential area—or more correctly this area inhabited by military families—had been evacuated. I knew the place well, as many of my friends lived there, but now most of the families were gone, and there remained only one or two who were making the most of their final days there selling cake, noodle soup and tea.

All that was left were the abandoned houses. Then the houses were destroyed and the excavation started. The smallest trenches covered an area of several hundred square metres. We started digging and went down about 1 m. Then we encountered groundwater. It flowed in abundance, turning the earth to mud; with dirty water everywhere and the weather cold, I became fed up. This was the first time in my life I found myself fed up with the work of excavation. But having agreed to this job, I had to continue. I will never forget the image of archaeologists and workers in their endeavour to find traces of ancient buildings splashing about in mud and water.

A number of artefacts dating from the Lý–Trần period (eleventh to fourteenth centuries) had been uncovered previously, including bricks and tiles. But they were isolated objects, not found in the context of architectural vestiges: it was not possible to prove the existence of an architectural site. The archaeologist in charge of the dig, Tống Trung Tín, knew this, and now ran from one trench to another with a single question: 'Have you found traces of buildings yet?' As an archaeologist with some years' experience of research on architecture, I understood and shared his anxiety. I knew that the excavation of an architectural site, especially a royal citadel, that does not reveal ruins of foundations, steps, courtyards, pillar bases, and so on, has basically failed.

Like other archaeologists there, I hoped that my hand would uncover traces of the ancient capital at Thăng Long. I am sure that Tống Trung Tín was even keener than I, as his research focused on the Lý and Trần dynasties, the period of Việt culture's most dazzling development. When he came to the trench I was responsible for, he said: 'Do try and find architectural vestiges: the merest trace of bricks used to pave a courtyard, build a wall, or whatever is of great value. And from time to time, can you help me by visiting other trenches to see if they have found any architecture?' At that moment, I was pleased to enjoy the boss's confidence, especially in my professional ability.

We discovered countless artefacts large and small dating from the Lý, Trần and Lê periods, including bricks, tiles, stone dragons, and loving ducks. Then came a day I shall never forget, the day I first found a brick used in construction.

That day the weather was very cold, Tết was approaching, and the trench was full of water. With my hand I could feel a dozen or so bricks attached to each other. Instinct and experience told me that I had just found the remains of a building. I immediately called for the pump to be turned on full. Once the trench was empty of water, I cleaned the area to reveal a surface of around 6 m^2 that was evenly paved with bright red bricks, beside a gutter built with bricks of the same type. I recognised these bricks as characteristic of the Trần period. I said nothing and just stood there staring. The people working nearby wondered what had happened to me. I realised that I had just discovered a Trần-period building in the area that historical texts call the capital city of Thăng Long. And the unrelated objects we had previously found scattered around the site suddenly appeared linked to one another, with all of them calling out in unison: 'There's a Trần-dynasty building here.'

2. THE FIRST VISITORS

After that, architectural remains were found in nearly every trench, with brick foundations, steps and courtyards as well as countless other objects, including architectural materials and ceramics. The ruins of the citadel of Vietnam's capital at Thăng Long had now been discovered and identified. For me, the winter of that year turned out mild and beautiful.

By mid-2003, most of the trenches had been extended to join up with each other and formed a vast excavated area covering nearly 10,000 m². The sites and material were evidence of the presence of the capital city and its citadel, and at that time we even thought we were looking at the Imperial Citadel's central area. There was a vast quantity of architectural remains, including building verandas, courtyards and especially the piers made of gravel mixed with brick and tile rubble, which had served as the foundations for pillars, and the stone bases that had supported those pillars and which now still lay intact on their foundations. Besides these, there were many millions of artefacts, including beautiful materials used to decorate the buildings, such as dragons, phoenixes, lotus flowers, and chrysanthemums, as well as countless pieces of ceramic that were of such high quality they could only have been used in the royal court. All these were unearthed and subject to preliminary analysis. The archaeological material taken together with other historical records were sufficient for scholars to conclude: the Imperial Citadel of Thăng Long had been discovered under the archaeologists' hands.

At this point, I and my colleagues were saddened by the thought that this site would be removed to allow the construction of new buildings. Until that time, the only knowledge the Vietnamese possessed of Thăng Long was gleaned from historical texts, legends and folklore, and a small number of isolated archaeological artefacts. In particular, no evidence of the architecture of the Imperial Citadel during the Lý–Trần period had ever been found. We had now discovered and identified an important part of that citadel and brought to light its key central area. We possessed the basis for unequivocal identification of Thăng Long over a period of one thousand years. So why remove it?

We thought we should do everything possible to preserve the site. There was a debate at that time, with one side supporting the removal of the archaeology and the construction of the National Assembly and National Convention Centre buildings on the site, and the other maintaining that this national heritage should at all costs be preserved for future generations. The conservationists of course included the archaeologists working on the excavation.

When the excavation started, no one was allowed to reveal anything about our work. This was the rule and we abided by it. But then there came a fine day when, for reasons I did not understand, we started receiving visitors. They were surprised and amazed at the excavation's results. I still recall an autumn day in 2003: the National Assembly was holding its end-of-year session, meeting in its old building on Ba Đình Square (now demolished), and I was working in my trench. My boss called me to his office. I thought the visitors were from the Institute of Archaeology's parent institution, the Academy of Social Sciences. I went into the office and saw some men there talking. I did not know them. My boss introduced them: one turned out to be General Phạm Chuyên, director of the Hanoi police department and member of the National Assembly. He had heard there was an excavation here and wanted to see it.

I showed him and his colleagues around the excavated area and talked about the history of the capital at Thăng Long, explaining the different sites and materials that had been unearthed. Phạm Chuyên and his colleagues listened intently. At that time, I did not imagine that he and his friends would become determined supporters of the site's conservation, and would call for the new government buildings' construction on another site. I still recall Phạm Chuyên's face as he stood before the different sites and the dragons and phoenixes of ancient Thăng Long: it was a face full of emotion, especially when we came to a well first built at the time the Chinese ruled Vietnam (ninth century) and refurbished during the Lý period for continued use.

Then Phạm Chuyên astounded us by kneeling down, scooping some water out of the well and drinking it with an attitude of reverence. He apologised, saying that he had learned of the excavation too late, even though he was a member of the National Assembly and attended its meetings every day just a few feet from the excavated area. He immediately called the editor of the newspaper *An ninh Thủ đô* (*Capital Security*), an agency under his jurisdiction, and asked for a reporter to be sent to the site to take photographs and write an article on the discovery of the Thăng Long Imperial Citadel. He said that he would bring the matter up in the National Assembly. And he did. We were pleased, as we wanted the newspapers and people to know about the site, so that we could together call for the heritage to be conserved.

3. A SURPRISING QUESTION

Soon after, a series of newspapers asked to visit and report. People from countless government agencies came to the site and asked questions about the citadel, and groups of National Assembly members, government officials, top leaders and former heads of state also visited. At that time, despite our fatigue and the hard work excavating, we were all willing to explain the history of Thăng Long and the history of Vietnam. We took the opportunity to speak of the site's importance and the need to protect the heritage and turn this place into a museum to preserve it for posterity. Most of the National Assembly members, the country's leaders and the representatives of government agencies and the Hanoi municipal authorities, agreed with us and supported the site's conservation.

At that time, whenever you came to the excavation trenches, you could see archaeologists holding megaphones presenting the site to groups of visitors to the newly discovered Imperial Citadel. I am a big talker, so was often recruited to serve as guide. Each time I showed a group around, I looked up at the wall separating the archaeological site from Hoàng Diệu Street and saw lines of Hanoi residents standing on their mopeds, peering over the wall and straining to hear: an indescribably moving sight.

On one occasion, after visiting the site and listening to my commentary, a National Assembly member asked the following question: 'You speak of the Lý dynasty and the Trần dynasty, then the Lê dynasty, but I don't know which came first, were the Lý before the Trần or was it the other way round?' I was surprised, but after that I kicked off my commentary with a clearer explanation.

'Ladies and gentlemen, the history of our country after the end of Chinese rule is made up of successive royal dynasties. These were the Đinh and Early Lê (tenth century), Lý (1010–1226), Trần (1226–1400) and Hồ (1400–07). After twenty years under China's Ming dynasty (1407–27), the Lê dynasty (1427–1789) came to power, but the Lê period was interrupted by the Mạc dynasty (1527–92) and the country's division between the Trịnh and Nguyễn lords. Then came the Tây Sơn (1789–1802). The Nguyễn dynasty completed the unification of the country's territory and ruled from 1802 to 1945, when the August Revolution put an end to the monarchy. This Imperial Citadel of Thăng Long was the capital used by the kings of the Lý, Trần and Lê dynasties and you can see material evidence from each of those dynasties at this site. Our capital city, Thăng Long–Hanoi, will soon celebrate its 1000th anniversary.'

Another time, a student asked, 'How can you tell which site is Trần, which is Lý, which is Lê?' I explained that each brick, each stone pillar base, each roof tile was inscribed with different motifs and differed in its stylistic characteristics, technique of manufacture, colour, and so on. So, for example, the dragon of the Lý period is lithe and agile, while the phoenix of the Trần resembles that of the Lý but has a stronger shape and bears designs that are cruder, less meticulous, less dainty. Under the Lê dynasty, influence from China grew, introducing further differences in the motifs used to decorate the buildings' materials and architecture. These characteristics, the materials' location in cultural layers in the excavation trenches, and the use of dating technology allow us to distinguish between the different historical periods.

On the subject of foreign cultural influence on the citadel's architecture, I recall a question posed by a Czech woman of Vietnamese origin. She was silent throughout my entire two-hour presentation, then came up to me rather hesitatingly and asked: 'Excuse me, I liked your presentation of the Imperial Citadel's architecture and artefacts, and as a Vietnamese I am very proud of them, but I noticed that many motifs and decorative designs on the buildings here, especially from the Lý–Trần period, rather resemble those on the Cham towers and in the Cham Museum in Đà Nẵng. Isn't that so?' I was surprised and thanked her for her question, and actually thanked her twice, because it gave me the chance to talk about something that had long been on my mind: foreign cultural influence at the Imperial Citadel, especially from Champa.

4. CHAMPA AND ĐẠI VIỆT

My reply to her at the time was not short, and I have added some extra thoughts and details here. Before this excavation, material evidence of ancient Thăng Long was scarce, all the more so for the Lý–Trần period. It was certainly not enough to serve as the basis for ground-breaking, accurate conclusions, especially regarding the influence of Champa culture. But from the body of evidence we now had, it is possible to say that Champa culture left a strong mark on the citadel of Thăng Long.

In the following discussion, I will mention only the building materials and artistic features of the Lý–Trần period, first examining material found at sites outside the Thăng Long Imperial Citadel, mostly discovered before 2002, and then focusing on the results of the 2002–04 excavation at 18 Hoàng Diệu Street.

Evidence of Champa Culture Around Thăng Long

After attacking Champa, almost every king and general of Đại Việt brought home captive soldiers, artisans, dancing girls and musicians to contribute to the construction of new artistic and architectural traditions in Đại Việt. These Cham people were settled in areas around Thăng Long, to the north, south, east and west. Scholars know about sites such as Bà Già village beside the West Lake (today part of Phú Gia village, Phú Thượng ward, Tây Hồ district, Hanoi), where Cham prisoners were settled during the reign of Lý Thánh Tông (Nguyễn Vinh Phúc 1987: 280–1). One such site was on the Red River's north bank, at Võng La village, a site located beside the river. Here, in the building of a village pagoda, archaeologists found two authentic Champa statues, one a sandstone statue of Siva (Figure 37), the other a statue of Champa's indigenous goddess Thiên Y A Na (Figure 38). Unfortunately, a fake was substituted

Fig. 37. A sandstone figure of Siva, found at Võng La village on the Red River (Photo: Nguyễn Tiến Đông).

Fig. 38. The Champa goddess Thiên Y A Na at Võng La village, a modern copy (Photo: Nguyễn Tiến Đông).

for the goddess's statue during the 1960s. However, the original Siva remains, as well as a copy of the trafficked goddess. Looking at them, no one can say that they were not made by Cham people (Nguyễn Tiến Đông, Nguyễn Hữu Thiết 2005: 806–8).

Many documents suggest that Võng La village may have been one of many villages in the northern delta inhabited by Cham people in the past. Several pagodas built in the Lý dynasty contain evidence of the presence of Champa culture, including a stone pillar at Dạm Pagoda, a lotus pedestal at Phật Tích Pagoda and a statue of the bird god Garuda at Phật Tích Pagoda. We know that stone pedestals carved with lotus flowers have been found at many Vietnamese pagodas, with carvings of great delicacy that show, in my opinion, the participation of Cham artisans. Towers such as Chương Sơn and Bình Sơn, with their recognisable brick and terracotta features, and especially their decorative elements that closely resemble those of Champa culture, have long been known; Nguyễn Hồng Kiên and I have argued that these sites show the contribution of Champa artisans, whom Nguyễn Hồng Kiên does not hesitate to identify as captured in Champa (Nguyễn Hồng Kiên 2000: 744–5). The objects found at the Thăng Long Imperial Citadel include white-glazed ceramic pieces used to decorate buildings bearing dancing girl figures (Figure 39). These recall the Cham bas-reliefs of Apsara figures on the Mỹ Sơn E1 altar at the Đà Nẵng Museum of Cham Sculpture (Figure 40).

In the region of the Đáy River in Đan Phượng district (former Hà Tây province, on the outskirts of old Thăng Long), in addition to pagodas containing lotus pedestals influenced by the designs on Champa altars mentioned above, remains of human habitation were found. These included a well built with Champa construction technology at Song Phương commune. This suggests that Cham people who came to Đại Việt did not only bring works of art but also knowledge and technology, which they used to improve the daily life of their community (Nguyễn Tiến Đông & Ogawa Yoko, 2000: 717–8).

There is one type of statue that displays, in both tangible and intangible dimensions, a Cham origin that we cannot fail to mention in the context of Đại Việt: the Phỗng Chàm (lit. Cham guard) statues. Throughout the north, from the provinces of the northern mountains to the plains of the Red River and Thanh Hoá, pagodas, temples, and communal houses contain this type of statue. According to folklore:

> In the past, at Xuân Phả village, Xuân Trường commune, Thọ Xuân district, Thanh Hoá province, a game was still played at the village festival that was called Champa Game [*trò Chiêm Thành*], with fourteen

Fig. 39. From Thăng Long Imperial Citadel, white-glazed ceramic used for architectural decorations, with apsaras (Photo: Institute of Archaeology).

Fig. 40. Champa apsaras, from reliefs now in the Đà Nẵng Museum of Cham Sculpture (Photo: Nguyễn Tiến Đông).

> players, including one lord, one lady, two guards [*phỗng*], ten soldiers. The role of the two guards was to kneel and offer incense and the way of kneeling was very similar to the way of kneeling of the guards portrayed in the *phỗng Chàm* statues. (Nguyễn Xuân Diện 2000: 727)

I must add that intangible Champa culture used to be present in many parts of Đại Việt but is no longer easily discernible. For example, I have the sense that the melodies of the alternating *quan họ* love songs famous in Kinh Bắc are somehow the melodies of Cham music. The melody of the folk dance '*Con đĩ đánh bồng*', often performed at village festivals in the northern delta, especially in Kinh Bắc and Phú Thọ, resembles the melody of the dance '*Múa Bóng*' at Bóng village in Nha Trang city, which is a clear vestige of Champa dance music (Ngô Văn Doanh, 2006: 48–53).

Evidence of Champa Culture at Thăng Long Imperial Citadel

Such material is scarce and cannot serve as the basis for any definitive conclusion. But with the mass of evidence excavated in 2002–04, some conclusions are now possible.

Bricks

The bricks of the Đại La period (Tang dynasty, seventh to ninth centuries) are mostly grey, fired at high temperatures, hard and difficult to carve. But the bricks of the Lý–Trần period are mostly a fresh red colour, of fine quality, fired at low temperatures and easy to cut and sculpt. These technical characteristics indicate that between the two periods a change took place in the technology used to manufacture bricks, which were put to different construction and artistic uses in the later period. My view is that this technology was learned through study of Champa brick manufacture technology. The people of Champa were master producers of bricks and builders of brick buildings in the Southeast Asian region at that time.

This view was reinforced when we discovered a brick bearing Cham letters inscribed on both sides (Figure 41). Careful examination shows that the letters were written before the brick was fired, perhaps even when it was not yet dry. They were certainly not inscribed after firing. For research, the brick's presence is of great significance.

First, it shows that that Cham artisans did indeed work at the Thăng Long Imperial Citadel, as historical texts record. Second, and this for me is more important, it indicates that those Cham artisans manufactured bricks: it was they who brought the technology for the manufacture of bricks of fresh red colour and fine plasticity to Thăng Long. It was they, too, who introduced the red colour of the materials used in the construction of roofs of wondrous beauty, which were raised on the luxurious buildings of Thăng Long, and which marked a great contrast with the heavy grey Chinese-style bricks of the previous period.

Fig. 41. The inscription in Cham lettering, made when the brick was not yet dry, may be instructions for its placement. Cham artisans were at work in the Thăng Long Imperial Citadel (Photo: Institute of Archaeology).

In December 2014, at a conference on 'The EFEO [École française d'Extrême-Orient] and the Social Sciences and Humanities in Vietnam' held in Hanoi, Arlo Griffiths, an EFEO expert on the Sanskrit and ancient Cham languages, commented on the inscription in Cham script on a brick found at the Thăng Long Imperial Citadel site. One of the legible words was '*vok*', meaning 'place, put in a particular place'. From this we may understand that the brick was intended to provide technical guidance at the construction site.

This information is of great importance to anyone studying the influence of Champa culture on the capital at Thăng Long. It proves that Cham artisans did not only manufacture bricks but also participated as highly skilled workers, people the Vietnamese call 'foremen' who were in charge of technically difficult aspects of the construction, gave instructions to other workers, and even worked on project design, because they knew the requirements of the building they were about to build and where in the building those materials (brick, stone, etc.) should be placed. For this purpose they wrote instructions on the construction materials, such as the brick mentioned above. That brick gives us a key insight into the important role played by Cham workers in the construction of the Thăng Long Imperial Citadel.

Fig. 42. Architectural element in sandstone from Thăng Long Imperial Citadel (Photo: Institute of Archaeology).

Fig. 43. Architectural element in sandstone from Dương Long tower, Bình Định province (Photo: Nguyễn Tiến Đông).

Stone

At the Thăng Long Imperial Citadel, many building components are made of stone—mostly sandstone, a type of stone favoured by Champa artisans as it is grainless and easy to carve and shape. Almost all the bases for the pillars of the buildings at the citadel are made of stone. They are beautifully carved with lotus flower images, especially those dating from the Lý period. There were sculptures of dragons and, during the Lý period especially, staircases were ingeniously decorated with dragons, phoenixes, waves, clouds and creepers. It is likely that these wonderful works of art expressing Vietnamese ideas were created with the intervention of Champa stone masons (see Figures 42 and 43).

Art

First, regarding the bodhi tree leaf symbol at the Imperial Citadel, this was a material used to decorate architecture, yet it also gave expression to royal authority. Large sculptures of bodhi leaves, with dragons or phoenixes, were placed in the middle of the top ridge of roofs (where sun, moon, and wine gourd images were placed on Chinese or Chinese-influenced buildings). This was an invention of our ancestors, as this motif is not used in China. But why the bodhi leaf? My view is that the inspiration for this creation came from a type of leaf (*lá nhĩ*) often carved on the tympanum of Champa temples. In Champa, these leaves decorate deities and are placed over temple doors, while in Đại Việt bodhi leaves decorate sacred animals, like dragons and phoenixes, and are placed in the middle of roof ridges (see Figures 44 and 45). Neither Champa nor Chinese people would recognise this as theirs: it is characteristic of Đại Việt.

As for the slanting bodhi leaf (see Figure 48), looking at it we seem to see the floating shadow of the cornerpiece decorations found on Champa towers. In Champa they were placed on the corner of the tower or temple to give a gigantic mass of bricks and stone the impression of lightness and flight. Here in Thăng Long the leaves are placed along both sides of the roof ridge; they run down the ridge then follow the curve of the roof, soaring into the air and following the rows of tubular tiles—each with its head elaborately carved and a bodhi leaf ingeniously placed on its back—to create a roof of delicate beauty and lightness. As a result, no one can fail to recognise the roof of a Đại Việt palace.

Let us turn to other works of sculpture, like the dragon. Dragons from the Lý–Trần period (see the front cover) are easy to recognise, with their nose, teeth and tongue giving them an appearance similar to that of the makara of Champa (Hà Bích Liên 1998: 75–80). However, the Đại Việt dragon holds a piece of jade in its mouth and has a mane that flows lightly from the nape of its neck, something that could not be found in Champa. And the curling body of the Lý–Trần dragon, especially the Lý dragon, was a Đại Việt masterpiece (see Figure 48). Those rage-filled faces, too, seem inspired by the kala masks of Champa (compare Figures 46 and 47). The Garuda and Kinari of Champa also appear in significant numbers in Lý–Trần architecture (Kinari is easily recognised in a statue at Phật Tích pagoda, Bắc Ninh).

I told the Czech lady: 'The art and architecture of Champa was a boundless source of inspiration for Đại Việt art during the Lý–Trần period.

Figs. 44 & 45. The bodhi leaves standing on the roof ridges of palaces in the Thăng Long Imperial Citadel (terracotta, unearthed at 18 Hoàng Diệu Street) seem inspired by the use of the bodhi leaf shape in Champa sculpture, here containing a dancing Siva (stone bas-relief from Trà Kiệu, Quảng Nam province, courtesy the Đà Nẵng Museum of Cham Sculpture) (Fig. 44. Photo: Institute of Archaeology. Fig. 45. Photo: EFEO).

Figs. 46 & 47. From the kala at Mỹ Sơn G1 to the tiger at the Thăng Long Imperial Citadel. More comparisons of Champa art with the expressive terracottas of the Citadel (Fig. 46. Photo: Lerici Foundation. Fig. 47. Photo: Institute of Archaeology).

Fig. 48. Slanting bodhi leaf in terracotta decorated with a dragon, unearthed at 18 Hoàng Diệu Street (Photo: Institute of Archaelogy).

Cham culture enriched Đại Việt and contributed to the development of a unique Đại Việt identity at that time.'

5. CONCLUSION

A year after ascending the throne, Lý Công Uẩn issued the edict on the transfer of the capital to Đại La Citadel (1010). During the early years of the Lý dynasty this was followed by the construction of a new citadel for the capital, built on the basis of the achievements of the old Đại La Citadel. The construction project was undoubtedly pursued with great intensity, with new achievements—the achievements of a new regime—being made in architecture and sculpture, and with those achievements marking a clear difference with those associated with the previous regime. Lý Công Uẩn and his court realised that they needed a new architectural model for the citadel at the country's capital. For this and subsequent dynasties, especially the Trần, the assertion of a distinctive Đại Việt character with regard to its huge neighbour, of whom imitation was in many respects unavoidable, was deemed 'essential' (Trần Quốc Vượng 2000: 142).

The Lý–Trần period thus appears as a time of strong renaissance. However, the period's achievements were not an accident of chance. On the basis of a local culture containing the vestiges of Đông Sơn culture combined with cultural factors from abroad, the Vietnamese created architectural, sculptural and musical traditions—and a capital—that were Việt in character but also contained much of the essence of other civilisations. One source of inspiration was Champa, a neighbouring country that possessed a dazzling civilisation and an attractive artistic tradition. This southern source became one of the factors impacting the reduction of the imitation of China, or as the Trần Quốc Vượng called it, 'de-sinisation'.

A millennium of Chinese rule meant that the Chinese inputs to Việt culture were multiple and contributed, along with indigenous factors, to the country's unique southern identity. For Trần Quốc Vượng (2000: 142), 'imitation of China was inevitable' for the following reasons:

a.   Because of China's presence during a millennium of rule.
b.   Because of the implicit and explicit pressure exerted by China from the tenth century, impeding the country's development.
c.   Because 'whatever Vietnam does, it must keep one eye on its northern neighbour. China is large, Vietnam is small; imitation of China demonstrates that Vietnam is "not less" and "no different" from China, and as "cultured" as China, which means Vietnam has no need for Chinese rule'.

The tenth century saw the beginning of a period of restoration of national independence and renaissance of national culture. Long-standing influences from Indian culture (Buddhism and Hinduism), shown in the veneration of Đế Thích and Nhị Thiên Vương (Lý-dynasty divinities of the sun and moon), and new influences arriving from Champa and Chenla, two great non-Chinese civilisations, acted as counterweights for Vietnamese culture, serving to balance Chinese cultural influence and increase the uniqueness of Vietnamese identity.

These ideas led me to agree that it was entirely natural for Đại Việt to look south for inspiration, and that Champa served as a counterweight to China, giving new forms to Vietnamese efforts to escape from Chinese cultural constraints. The people in the past did not make straight copies of Champa cultural models, but learned from them, absorbed them, and used them to create unique cultural forms on the basis of an indigenous culture. What we see unearthed today at the Thăng Long Citadel is evidence of a political transformation and cultural renaissance in Đại Việt during the centuries after Lý Công Uẩn chose Gao Pian's town for his capital, justified this choice with Chinese geomantic ideology, and initiated a building programme strongly inspired by the art forms and construction technologies of Champa.

CHAPTER 11

Ancient Thăng Long Through Old Maps

Phạm Văn Triệu

In December 2002, staff of the Institute of Archaeology and several hundred workers opened the first trench in the most important excavation in the history of Vietnamese archaeology, the Thăng Long Imperial Citadel site at 18 Hoàng Diệu Street, Hanoi. By March 2004, after nearly a year and a half of intense, enthusiastic and unceasing labour conducted in a spirit of great responsibility towards the nation's history, a vast quantity of artefacts and the vestiges of several dozen palaces were brought to light. They were greeted with great passion by researchers in many disciplines. The discovery inspired today's generation of Vietnamese, filling them with national pride.

A whole series of questions was raised by the discovery. What was this place? How do the architectural vestiges and artefacts discovered here increase our knowledge of the nation's history?

A burden of responsibility was thus placed on the shoulders of our country's historians and archaeologists, as well as researchers in other disciplines. The creativity and experience of hundreds of scholars in many fields—history, geology, biology, muscum studies, anthropology, history of architecture—was called upon. The participation of ordinary people in all this was greeted by the archaeologists with particular emotion. Despite their advanced years, a number of elderly people who had managed to preserve old books handed down from previous generations that contained records of Thăng Long did not hesitate to travel great distances to entrust us with these images of Thăng Long, straight from their hearts.

Thus, in July 2004, on a hot and sultry summer's day, one of the site's guards opened the door and interrupted our siesta: 'There's someone here to meet you, he says he wants to discuss something.' I woke up, thinking, 'There's no meeting in the diary, why should someone be looking for me during the hot siesta hour and saying they want to discuss something?'

I went out to the site gate, where I saw an elderly man—perhaps seventy years old, with grey hair, bright eyes, and the manner of a Confucian scholar—standing there clutching a book. Hearing that I was a member of the Institute of Archaeology's staff working on the site, he told me that he was from Thanh Trì (on the outskirts of Hanoi) and had a book about Thăng Long he wanted to show us. Could it be useful for the study of Thăng Long?

I took the book from his hands.

It was a very old volume, its paper yellowed and black. A glance at the cover showed its title, *Historical Poems from the Period of Resistance Against Invasion*, and its author's name, Huỳnh Lý. Reading it that evening, I found two poems—'*Hà thành chính khí ca*' ('Song of the Heroes of Hanoi Citadel') and '*Hà thành thất thủ ca*' ('Poem on the Fall of Hanoi Citadel')—that praised heroes who sacrificed their lives for their country, such as Hoàng Diệu, and lambasted corrupt officials who showed weakness in the face of the enemy and in defending the citadel. The book's final section contained a critical commentary, some illustrations and a map with the title *Hanoi around 1873–1884*, written in Vietnamese Romanised script. The map showed the Hanoi Citadel, with its Vauban shape and place names that have imprinted themselves on the consciousness of anyone who has, even only once, ever visited Hanoi: Hoàn Kiếm Lake, the Flag Tower, the Temple of Literature, and so on.

This meeting—where no appointment was made, yet an appointment was kept—made a deep impression on me, marking the life of a young and inexperienced researcher less by the historical value of the book, which would require further study, than by the old man's good heart. That was something of immense value for a member of the younger generation like myself and meeting him was an early experience I shall never forget. I silently felt that the book's true content was precisely this heart, this emotion, these thoughts and this national pride, which the old man had passed down to my generation.

* * *

Research into questions raised by the excavation was done by seven teams, each headed by a professor and leading specialist. I was assigned to Sub-Committee 1—'General Research on Thăng Long Imperial Citadel'— headed by Phan Huy Lê. Our work involved the following research: study of Thăng Long through old records in Vietnam; study of Thăng Long through old maps; study of Thăng Long through old records in China; study of Thăng Long–Hanoi from the perspective of the West; comparison of Thăng Long with other capitals in the region, in countries such as China, Thailand, Laos and Cambodia; and study of Thăng Long through field research. The research questions were broad and very difficult.

Of the different subjects, I was most interested in the cartography. This was partly because of the impression the elderly man had left on me, filling me with curiosity to see the shape of our country's thousand-year-old heart and how, in the past, earlier generations had viewed it themselves. I wanted to make comparisons with the results of field research. I hoped to find in today's Hanoi—as it rushes urgently onward along the road to industrialisation—an image of Thăng Long: a profound, silent and majestic image which every Vietnamese child wants to admire at least once, so as to 'yearn for the land of Thăng Long'.[1] Although they live in Hanoi, today's inhabitants know the Thăng Long–Hanoi Citadel only through its remaining toponyms; its buildings have been restored and repaired many times. These include the Flag Tower, Gate of Commencement, Rear Palace and North Gate. More recently, people have been able to admire the nine stone steps and two royal dragons leading up to the Kính Thiên Palace in the Thăng Long Citadel. This further impelled me to learn about Thăng Long, concealed in the heart of Hanoi.

When I started work on the old maps, I got in touch with a specialist who had many years of experience in Hán-Nôm studies and owned many maps: Ngô Đức Thọ. I should also mention that in the 1980s, scholars had published the first maps of Thăng Long–Hanoi. Among them was Bùi Thiết, author of many cartographical studies, who worked for many years at the Institute of Information on Social Sciences. These scholars published almost ten maps and contributed many insights based on the data they contained. However, the maps were too few in number and they were published at different times; analysis and evaluation suffered from interruptions in the chronology.

Working with Ngô Đức Thọ and younger scholars at the Institute of Vietnamese Studies and Development Sciences, I visited the different libraries where we hoped the maps we needed were kept: the National

Library and the libraries of the Institute of History, the History Department at the University of Social Sciences and Humanities, and the Institute of Hán-Nôm Studies. After more than ten days' reading and recording map reference numbers, we agreed to record every map we saw that might yield information on Thăng Long. Then, after further discussion and with some help from Ngô Đức Thọ, we realised that cartographical information about Thăng Long before the Nguyễn period was all held at the library of the Institute of Hán-Nôm Studies, while maps of Hanoi should be sought at the Institute for Information on Social Sciences. We thus established our working method as we sought to collect the different source materials. In fact, I realised I wanted to make a deeper study of the maps produced by the generations of historical geographers during the Đại Việt period, that is, of maps drawn during the fifteenth to eighteenth centuries.

By 14 June 2004, we had verified all the referenced documents at the Institute of Hán-Nôm Studies and collected seventeen maps of Thăng Long. These were maps of the Thăng Long Citadel included in several geographical studies. They were all found in books, rather than as separate sheets, were drawn on Nepal [*dó*] paper, and showed the Thăng Long Citadel or networks of waterways in which the waterways of Thăng Long held a prominent position.

When we opened the maps, we were amazed to find that the different representations of Thăng Long's geographical features were highly consistent: they gave the place the shape of a revolver. River names and other toponyms that have survived to the present include the Tô Lịch River, Nhĩ River (Red River), Kim Ngưu River, Trấn Vũ Temple, and so on, while within the citadel, the name of each palace was also recorded.

The maps had one thing in common: none had a scale. Distances were all estimated. As a result, scholars had not yet agreed on the exact location of the Thăng Long Citadel's boundaries. Secondly, regarding dating, while dates are clearly indicated on some of the documents (e.g., map A.2531), some authorities suggest that they were redrawn by later generations on the basis of the map produced in the Hồng Đức era (late fifteenth century). Additional materials, combined with data from other research methodologies, are required to test these ideas before a clear picture comes to light. However, these maps—our oldest illustrated documents—do offer a portrait of the capital at Thăng Long drawn by Vietnamese and they remain essential for scholars studying the scale and location of Thăng Long.

Maps drawn to scale by French or by Vietnamese Confucian scholars influenced by French cartographical knowledge become available only in the nineteenth century (see Maps 2–4 in the opening pages). On these, clear and lively details appear and valuable data about Hanoi in the nineteenth and twentieth centuries is presented. At that time, Thăng Long had already changed: the citadel had been reduced in size and built in the Vauban style, a common model for citadel construction invented by a French military architect.

Maps are valuable for the study of historical geography, providing data on locations and distances, and the factors that shaped a specific area over a particular period of time. They assist our understanding of the evolution of the landscape. We should note that no cartographical documents on Thăng Long dating from before the Lê period have yet been found. This is despite the fact, as recorded in historical documents, that under the Lý dynasty attention was paid to the drawing of geographical configurations, rivers, and mountains, and this work was done by high-ranking mandarins. In 1075, for the convenience of the administration of three southern districts—Địa Lý, Ma Linh and Bố Chính (present-day Quảng Bình, Quảng Trị, Thừa Thiên)—the Lý dynasty king dispatched Lý Thường Kiệt with an army to survey and map those districts. But no historical record tells us whether any maps of Thăng Long were drawn.

No mention is made of mapping for several centuries. Then, in 1469, for the purposes of territorial administration, King Lê Thánh Tông 'ordered maps of the prefectures, districts, outer districts, communes, villages and hamlets of the 12 commanderies'. This cartographical representation was full, systematic and methodical, and followed a standardised, hierarchical system reaching from the prefecture down to the commune, village and hamlet. These maps give us our first picture of the Thăng Long Citadel. (See Map 1, at the beginning of the book.)

Of the seventeen maps we collected and studied, six indicate the mountains and rivers of the citadel area and its surroundings: they mark the location of Thăng Long without providing an image of it. As a result, these maps play no more than an auxiliary role in our research, which bears principally on the other eleven maps where Thăng Long appears along with clearly marked locations of its palaces and rivers.

Among the vestiges unearthed at the Thăng Long Imperial Citadel site at 18 Hoàng Diệu Street, the traces of lakes and rivers are of great interest. These are evidence of people's relationship with their natural environment, based on a spirit of interdependency. This was the capital's citadel, yet when our forebears built their palaces they did not fill in the lakes and rivers. They adapted their construction work to fit the existing geographical configuration, and even had new ponds dug to create places of recreation and relaxation.

When the excavation started, I was assigned responsibility for trench A7. Here, the first layers and objects discovered raised the question: Could these be the traces of a lake or pond? At that time I thought, surely there could not have been lakes or ponds within the citadel. If there were, would we discover similar vestiges here? Excavation of other parts of the site showed clear traces of the existence of lakes and ponds together with various biological matter, including lotuses, the branches and leaves of soft-stemmed plants, and so on. On the banks of the rivers and lakes, our forebears built hexagonal pavilions for recreational purposes. We can feel the place's beauty and charm, the harmonious combination of natural space and magnificent palaces. This beauty could only be seen at Thăng Long.

> Nhị Hà quanh bắc sang đông
> Kim Ngưu, Tô Lịch là sông bên này

> The Red River curls around from north to east,
> Kim Ngưu and Tô Lịch are the rivers on this side.

The folk poem names the three main rivers around which Thăng Long was based, and this is the way people in the past described and summarised them. But the couplet does not tell the whole story: other rivers and lakes are identifiable on the maps, indicated with clear lines that wind and curl and curve. Within the borders of these lines, water is represented with wavy fish-fin shaped lines or continuous dots; sometimes the space is left blank. The illustrations are relatively realistic. The fish-fins or waves on the surface of the lakes and rivers seem to wish to tell us something: that, over and above its 'gilded mansions' and 'purple residences', the Vietnamese built Thăng Long to become the capital where all things crystallised and converged, as the saying goes, 'with an ear to the soul of the hills and streams'.

Thăng Long, then, was a capital of many rivers and lakes—both inside the citadel and in the surrounding area—in addition to its three main rivers: the Red River, Tô Lịch and Kim Ngưu. To the north, outside the citadel, the West Lake is pictured on the maps. This lake lay west of the citadel and was connected to the Tô Lịch River. That linking channel was called Long Khê (or Dragon Stream) and may still be seen today on

Thuy Khuê Street. To the West Lake's east, there is Trúc Bạch Lake, and further to the north, Thiên Phù River. The eastern and western sides of Thăng Long Citadel are enclosed by the Red River and Tô Lịch River respectively.

There are many lakes to the south, stretching on in a continuous line: their streams emerge from a large lake called Đại Hồ (Great Lake). This lake and its streams stretch southward beyond Đại Hưng Gate to embrace the Temple of Literature, the Observatory (Thiên Giám), and Phúc Khánh, flowing down to the Nam Giao Shrine area. Today, this is where the Temple of Literature, Hàng Cỏ railway station, and Khâm Thiên Street are located. Over to the east, we find Hoàn Kiếm Lake, connected to the Red River. Beyond, there are other lakes that are not named.

Within the citadel, lakes are shown in many places. Between Đại Hưng Gate and the South Gate, a long lake stretches from Đông Trường An to Tây Trường An. There is another lake below Thái Điện. Neither of these lakes are named. To the east, inside the citadel and on the left as you enter, there is a place called 'Trì Pond' near the East Palace (Đông Cung). To the west, a long winding lake with many small streams extends from the West Gate and Khán Sơn Temple to the Linh Lang Temple; the lake is not named. Below, in the Giảng Võ area, there is another unnamed lake.

Within the Forbidden City—in other words, inside the citadel's innermost square rampart—there is the toponym Ngọc Hà (the word Hà means river, while Ngọc is jade), suggesting, in my opinion, that an important river flowed through the heart of the citadel. At 18 Hoàng Diệu Street, there are traces of an ancient river that flowed north–south: some scholars think this was the Jade River marked on the maps.[2]

Study of the rivers and lakes in the Thăng Long Citadel area offers a diverse and concrete perspective on the geography, geology and planning of ancient Thăng Long. This study has produced some results but differences of interpretation remain; these will need to converge before clear conclusions may be drawn.

Despite the countless upheavals of history, the central area of the Thăng Long Citadel did not change. After marching on Thăng Long, Nguyễn Huệ and his generals entered the citadel through the South Gate and were received by King Lê Hiển Tông at the Kính Thiên Palace.

The maps show the Thăng Long Citadel during the Lê period. In addition to historical data on ramparts and palaces, they contain information on the location of temples and shrines in the surrounding area. To the east: outside Đông Hoa Gate, a toponym on the map refers to

Bạch Mã Temple, on the line of access to the citadel from the east (today's Hàng Buồm Street). Bạch Mã Temple appears on the map as a building with a boat-shaped roof. Entering through Đông Hoa Gate, the East Palace was ahead, with Thái Miếu Temple on the left. To the north, the Tô Lịch River ran alongside the rampart, with Trấn Vũ Temple on the far side. To the west, Bảo Khánh Gate is marked as an archway surmounted by a two-storey watchtower with a boat-shaped roof.[3] Hội Thí Trường Temple lies beyond Bảo Khánh Gate, with Giảng Võ Palace further to the south. After passing a wall blocking the line of access, we come first to Linh Lang Temple, then Khán Sơn Temple. The West Gate appears at the top corner of the Forbidden Citadel.

South was the citadel's most important direction, always used by the king when he entered or exited. All important rituals, like the making of offerings and the appointment of officials, took place in the area of the South Gate and Đại Hưng Gate. Outside Đại Hưng Gate, a series of toponyms is marked: the southernmost is Nam Giao Shrine. Above this, on some maps, there is a square block: this is Vương Phủ (Prince's Palace), with gates to the east (Tuyên Vũ Gate) and south (Chính Môn, or Main Gate). Above Vương Phủ is Báo Thiên Tower, with six storeys and a boat-shaped roof. The next toponym is the Temple of Literature (Quốc Tử Giám, although some maps use the word đại học, university). Then one reaches Đại Hưng Gate, after which two toponyms are marked on some maps: Đông Trường An and Tây Trường An.

One finally arrives at the innermost square block (the Forbidden Citadel), accessed through its South Gate called Đoan Môn (some maps call it Ngũ Môn, or Five Gates). On the maps, the South Gate appears with three arches: a main entrance and two lateral passages. There are also two secondary gates (still visible today). Beyond the South Gate, one arrives at Thị Triều, where the king dealt with affairs of state and heard mandarins' reports (*thị* means oversee; *triều* is the court). Further on, Kính Thiên was the most important of Thăng Long's palaces—where the king lived and worked—built on Nùng Mount, the highest point in the citadel. To the left of Kính Thiên Palace there is Chí Kính Palace, with Vạn Thọ Palace on the right.

The maps recorded all these data about Thăng Long. They are simple and sparse in their details, inaccurate in their scale. But they do allow us an overview of Thăng Long, enough for anyone who wishes to see the attraction and harmony of this place, and recognise the distinction of Thăng Long.

Notes

1. The author cites a line from the poetry of southern writer Huỳnh Văn Nghệ: 'The southern sky yearns for the land of Thăng Long', cited in the chapter by Đào Hùng (editors' note).
2. See Institute of Hán-Nôm Studies map A.2499.
3. See Institute of Hán-Nôm Studies map A.3034.

CHAPTER 12

From Thăng Long to Hanoi: The Downgrading and Destruction of the Nineteenth-Century Citadel

Olivier Tessier

With Gia Long's ascension to the throne in 1802 and the transfer of the reunified country's capital to Phú Xuân-Huế, Thăng Long lost its status as political centre and could possess neither an Imperial Citadel nor a Forbidden City. A citadel inspired by Vauban principles of fortification was built in their place (see Map 14).[1] This first upheaval in the urban landscape is our point of departure as we retrace the main stages in the citadel's complete transformation during the nineteenth century. The first kings of the Nguyễn dynasty stripped Thăng Long of the physical features and celestial symbols of royal power; the colonial authorities then sought to turn Hanoi into a showcase of European supremacy.

1. THE NGUYỄN PERIOD: THE DECLINE OF THE FORMER ROYAL CAPITAL OF THĂNG LONG

On 1 June 1802, Nguyễn Ánh, after a solemn ceremony in the ancestors' temple at Huế, declared the Cảnh Hưng era ended and inaugurated the Gia Long era. Two months later, on the twenty-first day of the sixth lunar month (20 July), he entered Thăng Long, then known as the Citadel of the North (Bắc Thành 昇龍). Thus, fifteen years of civil war were brought to

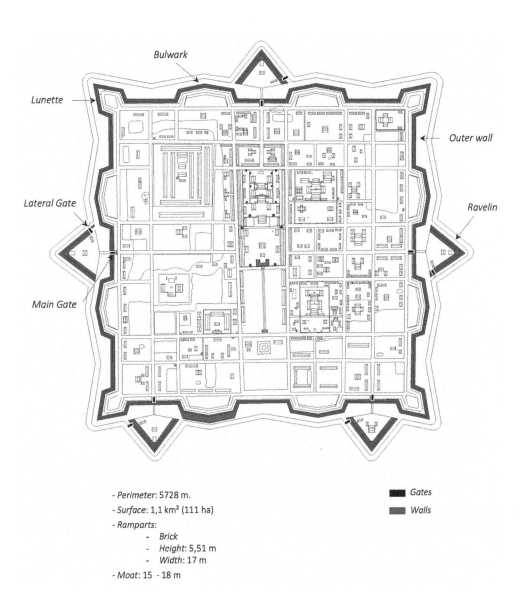

Bulwark

Lunette

Outer wall

Lateral Gate

Ravelin

Main Gate

- *Perimeter*: 5728 m.
- *Surface*: 1,1 km² (111 ha)
- *Ramparts*:
  - *Brick*
  - *Height*: 5,51 m
  - *Width*: 17 m
- *Moat*: 15 - 18 m

Gates

Walls

Map 14. The Nguyễn-dynasty Hanoi Citadel: the walls (Olivier Tessier, based on EFEO photo library, map VIE 23474).

a close: the Nguyễn, former rulers of the south, had finally reconquered the entire territory of Vietnam from the forces of the Tây Sơn. The chronicles record that: 'the enemy mandarins presented themselves before him in submission. All the bandits [Tây Sơn] were annihilated, a great victory was achieved'.[2]

The king's most urgent task was to set up a new civilian and military mandarinate to restore order and consolidate the unity of the recently reunified country. He divided Vietnam's territory into three large regions: the centre, with the new capital Huế at its heart (Quảng Đức province); the south, or *lưu trấn* Gia Định (which would become *tổng trấn* Gia Định in 1808); and the north, or *tổng trấn* Bắc Thành. The latter was divided into eleven inner and outer provinces (*trấn*), all placed under the authority of a governor-general, the *tổng trấn* Bắc Thành. Gia Long thus opted for an organisational form consisting of three regional blocs that resembled a federal structure more than a centralised monarchy. He strengthened his policy of peace and reconciliation by bringing in former mandarins of the Lê–Trịnh period, placing them at the head of the Bắc Thành authority and provinces in the Red River Delta (Maybon 1927: 106).

Thirty years later, Minh Mạng, a deeply Confucian and legalist ruler, felt that allowing these two regional authorities to persist ran the risk that openly secessionist movements would plunge the kingdom into a new civil war, leading to the country's partition. In the tenth lunar month of 1831, he launched a general administrative reform that resulted in major boundary changes: the government general of Bắc Thành was abolished, and the country was divided into 31 provinces governed directly from Huế.

The Construction of Fortifications in Nineteenth-century Vietnam

The construction of the citadel in Hanoi was part of a general programme of fortification that took place during the nineteenth century. All the fortifications were more or less inspired by so-called Vauban defensive principles, techniques that Pigneau de Béhaine had presented to Nguyễn Ánh (the future Gia Long) in translated French military treaties. The first was built in 1790 in Saigon, using designs made by a handful of young officers of the French marines. Vietnamese military engineers then built the citadels of Thăng Long (1803–05) and Huế (1804–19). It was during Minh Mạng's reign that the territory was covered in fortifications, including citadels at Sơn Tây and Quảng Trị (1822), Quảng Bình (1824) and Thanh Hóa (1828); crenellated ramparts around the provincial capitals at Nghệ An (1831); and citadels at Hưng Yên (1832), Nam Định and Hà Tĩnh (1833), Thái Nguyên and Đồng Hới (1837).

The function of these edifices was not, however, purely military. Each contained barracks for the officers, soldiers of the royal guard (vệ), and provincial regiments (cơ). But they also sheltered offices of the province and region's state administration, residences of the civilian and military mandarins in charge of the territory, the treasury, rice granaries and storehouses where the revenues of taxation were kept, a prison, and religious buildings (temples and pagodas). The vital organs necessary for the province or region's functioning were protected by the citadel's ramparts, which symbolised the presence and power of the state and served as the administration's last place of refuge in the event of peasant revolts. There were many of these: four revolts per year under Gia Long, eleven per year under Minh Mạng, eight per year under Thiệu Trị, three per year under Tự Đức, totalling more than 400 revolts throughout the kingdom in sixty years (Lê Thành Khôi 1992: 382).[3] In other words—and this is one of the major paradoxes of the period—while the first rulers of the Nguyễn dynasty established themselves as great builders through the construction of citadels, roads, bridges and ports, the strengthening of the network of dikes that protected the northern region from the violent floods of the two main river systems (Red and Thái Bình Rivers), and the digging of impressive canals in the Mekong Delta, they were unable to bring about a significant improvement in the living conditions of the majority of the population.

Among the nineteenth-century citadels, the one at Thăng Long had its own unique status, a logical consequence of its history. Formerly the heart of royal power and now relegated to the rank of regional capital, Thăng Long nonetheless still bore the signs, inscribed in its very body, of the geomantic and architectural organisation of a capital founded eight hundred years earlier. Moreover—and this element is essential—in the eyes of China, Vietnam's suzerain, Thăng Long remained the capital.[4] Thus, the royal investiture ceremonies were not held at Huế: it was at Thăng Long, and later Hanoi, that Gia Long, Minh Mạng and Thiệu Trị were consecrated as king by Chinese ambassadors,[5] who alone were authorised to bestow celestial legitimacy and the royal attributes (seals and patents) in the name of the emperor of the Middle Kingdom. Only in 1848 was the ambiguity about the city's status lifted, and the construction and destruction of buildings there from 1802 to 1848 can only be understood in the light of that ambiguity.

Gia Long's First Years: The Royal Investiture and the Citadel's Construction

The first reference to the construction of new buildings at Thăng Long was made in the context of preparations for Gia Long's investiture ceremony (*đại lễ bang giao* 邦交大禮), held in the first lunar month of 1804, for which the Chinese emperor sent the Grand Judge of Guangxi to bestow the vassal's seal on Gia Long in his name. In 1802 (eleventh lunar month), the king ordered the governor of Bắc Thành to renovate the ruler's royal visit palace (*Hành cung* 邦交大禮) and the Ambassadors' Residence (*Sứ quán* 使館), where the Chinese ambassador and his retinue would be received. According to the text of the decree:

> Seeing that diplomatic protocol is a matter of the greatest importance, the king orders the mandarins of Bắc Thành to seek inspiration from the ancient practices of the Lê dynasty and have new palaces (*điện vũ*) built. The Palace of Royal Audience (Cần Chánh 勤政殿) should be located within the Gate of Commencement (Đoan Môn 端門), in front of Kính Thiên Palace (敬天殿). A great tent should be raised outside Cần Chánh Palace, with Chu Tước Gate (朱雀門)[6] in front. The palace for the reception of the ambassadors should be located beside the river.[7]

The wording is confusing, but there is no doubt that the former royal palace, Kính Thiên, was now used as the king's residence during his visits to the city. This is evident from a decree issued four months after the investiture (on the first day of the fourth lunar month of 1804): 'Repair of the royal visit palace in Bắc Thành. In the past, the Lê dynasty's Kính Thiên Palace was chosen for use as the royal visit palace. Now, we order the construction behind that palace of a new building, to receive the king during his visits'.[8] The new building's size was specified by decree: it had five bays and two outbuildings, and it was located behind Kính Thiên Palace,[9] in the northern sector between that palace and the future Hậu Lâu (後楼), the Rear Palace built in 1821.

Regarding the construction of the ramparts around the citadel, a decree was issued in 1803 (first lunar month):

> Construction of Thăng Long Citadel. The king noted that the current rampart is too restricted and wanted to enlarge it. He ordered the governor-general [of Bắc Thành] to draw up a plan for execution by the soldiers and use the budget to pay for the materials. All those who force the inhabitants to pay will be punished and the inhabitants concerned will be reimbursed.[10]

The official geography *Đại Nam Nhất Thống Chí* notes that the existing wall, rebuilt by the Trịnh in 1749[11] on the ruins of the old fortifications of the Dragon Citadel (Long Thành 龍城) and badly damaged during the Tây Sơn Rebellion, did not comply with regulations. In other words, it did not comply with the new status of Bắc Thành. This was a policy to reduce the former Royal Citadel's perimeter, so that it should cover a smaller area than the Huế Citadel, then under construction.

But the initial plan made by the French officers in Gia Long's service drew strong objections from geomancers and literati, who regarded the proposed citadel as too European in design. After heated discussion, changes were made to the project, notably a reduction in the ramparts' height. The building work, interrupted in 1804, could thus resume and the new citadel was completed in 1805 (Madrolle 1925: 20–1). In 1805 (sixth lunar month), a decree was issued for the 'construction of the Thăng Long citadel gates (southeast, southwest, east, west and north gates). An inscription in stone is to be placed in front of each gate'.[12]

The citadel then covered an area within two districts: Thọ Xương and Quảng Đức (which became Vĩnh Thuận in 1805). Square in shape, with five monumental gates, the citadel's wall was 5,728 m long and enclosed an *intra-muros* area of around 1.1 km², or 110 ha.[13] This rampart, initially rising to a height of around 5 m (1 *trượng* 1 *thước* 2 *tấc*) was surrounded by a moat measuring 15–18 m across and 5 m deep, filled with water diverted from the Tô Lịch River. Each side had three curtain walls linking two central bastions and a lunette bastion at each corner. On the east, west and north sides, a gate was built in the middle section of the curtain; the south side had two gates, in the left and right sections of the curtain. Each gate was protected by a demilune (*dương mã thành*)[14] separate from the main wall. A brick bridge linked the gate in the main wall to the demilune. There was a second gate (*nhân môn*) in the right-hand flank of each demilune, linked to the outside across a second bridge, also built of brick. To enter the citadel, one thus crossed two bridges: one across the moat around the demilune, the other from the demilune to the main gate. The five gates were built of brick; on top of each, two large open-air staircases provided access to a watchtower (*thú lâu*) made of light material. The gate itself consisted of thick wooden doors set in an imposing arch measuring 23 m long. Its name was inscribed in characters sculpted in relief on a rectangular block of stone above the entranceway.

Building, Destroying and Transforming the Citadel: Erasing the Traces of Thăng Long's Royal Past

During the reigns of Gia Long and Minh Mạng, a series of transformations to pre-Nguyễn sites in Thăng Long was apparently intended to strip the former capital of its most conspicuous royal attributes and celestial pre-rogatives. As early as 1803, Gia Long had the Lê-dynasty Shrine (*đàn* Nam Giao) destroyed and its bricks used in the construction of the ramparts.[15] Clearly the factual argument about the need to reuse materials, a recurrent practice after changes of dynasty,[16] does not suffice to explain this act of destruction. The ceremony of 'sacrifice to Heaven and Earth', which took place at the winter solstice (first lunar month) on a circular mound south of the capital, was of immense importance as it legitimated the function of the king invested with the mandate of heaven (*thiên mệnh*) (Langlet 1970: 89).[17] By destroying the site, the ruler indicated to all—mandarins, literati and common people—that Thăng Long was no long the country's capital. Two other decisions would confirm this state of affairs.

The first was dated 1804 (third lunar month) and involved the removal of the Lê dynasty's temple to Thanh Hóa province. According to the chronicles:

> This temple is located in Thăng Long Citadel and the [descendants of the] Lê seek permission to move it to Bố Vệ commune [in Đông Sơn district, the Lê's former base]. The king said: 'the Lê cult is an important matter for the court'. For this reason, he instructed the governor of Thanh Hóa to have the temple renovated [built?] by the local population. He selected the head of Thiệu Thiên prefecture, Phan Tiến Quý, to manage the work. Then he recruited 100 inhabitants of Bố Vệ commune to work as servants in the temple.[18]

Gia Long thus demonstrated his intention to succeed to the Lê and his guarantee that their ancestors would be regularly honoured by the state, but in a temple located in Thanh Hóa province, close to the Nguyễn ancestors' temple, and not in Thăng Long. The cult's maintenance in Thăng Long might become a rallying point for political forces nostalgic for the former reigning dynasty and hostile to the new regime.

The second decision, certainly the most symbolic and mentioned by numerous authors, involved a change in the city's name. The chronicles note that in 1805 (first day of the seventh lunar month), 'the city of

Thăng Long (升龍) took the name of Thăng Long (昇隆), the prefecture of Phụng Thiên was renamed the district of Hoài Đức, and the district of Quảng Đức became the district of Vĩnh Thuận'.[19] The character *long* (龍, 'dragon'), was replaced by the character *long* (隆, meaning *thịnh*, 'prosperous, flourishing'); the characters 升 and 昇 are synonyms meaning 'rising'.[20] The city of the 'rising dragon' was now reduced to the city of 'rising prosperity', losing its royal character.[21] We note the calculated subtlety involved in this conservative semantic transformation: the use of a homophone rendered the change painless for the majority of the city's population, who were long accustomed to the name, while its political significance was discernible only to a narrow elite of literati and manda-rins who knew Sino-Vietnamese characters. The former royal prefecture Phụng Thiên (奉天府) was renamed Hoài Đức (懷德) for the same reason, to empty it of royal dignity. The name Phụng Thiên ('offering to heaven') implied that the king offered the heavenly powers this land with the capital that it sheltered, while its new administrative name was devoid of all connotations of royalty (Papin 2001: 198).

In 1806, Gia Long continued his recasting of the city's symbolic space, ordering that a shrine to the 'gods of the soil and harvests' (*xã tắc đàn*) be built near the West Gate. The land was levelled using fifteen tonnes of soil brought in from the eleven provinces of the northern region (*tổng trấn* Bắc Thành), the administrative unit born of the kingdom's reorganisation into three distinct politico-administrative regions (Langlet 1990: 83–4). In the same year, he ordered the construction of a 'house of steles' (*đình bia* 碑亭) dedicated to his military feats, as a reminder of the Nguyễn family's ascendancy over the kingdom's entire territory (Trần Hùng & Nguyễn Quốc Thông 1995: 37).

From that point until the end of the reign, almost no new building work took place in the citadel, with the significant exception of the construction in 1812 of the Kỳ Đài (旗臺), now named Cột Cờ, the Flag Tower, a structure found in all the citadels built during the nineteenth century. From a pole placed on top of this sixty-metre-high tower a great red standard flew during the king's visits to Thăng Long (昇隆). It was raised for important rituals and on the first and fifteenth days of the lunar month.[22]

The construction of the final great monument was decided three months before Minh Mạng's investiture, making its state of progress at the time of the ceremonies uncertain. This was the Palace of the Peaceful

North (*lầu* Tĩnh Bắc 靖北樓), also called Rear Palace (Hậu Lâu).[23] In 1821 (first day of the tenth lunar month), an order was given

> for the construction of a great pavilion in the northern inner part of the Royal Visit Palace of Bắc Thành to be named Palace of the Peaceful North. It was built of brick and covered with a tiled three-ridged roof. The storeys were connected with a spiral staircase. All the façades had large windows and balconies to allow light to enter. On the top floor, there was an altar to the Three Eminent Divinities [Thích-Ca 釋迦; Văn-Thù 文殊; Phổ-Hiền 普賢], represented by their statues, to whom prayers were addressed to bring well-being to the population. Below [the pavilion], lychees were planted, as well as other well-known trees.[24]

Then, in 1822, Minh Mạng had another monument built, 'a palace surrounded by its own wall, to shelter the funerary tablets of the former kings, dedicated to their memory' (Azambre 1958: 280). Unfortunately, the author did not cite the source of this information and it has not been confirmed elsewhere. During the rest of Minh Mạng's reign, the annals mention only two new building projects here, both of lesser importance. In 1825, he ordered the construction of holding cells (*nhà khám*) and a prison (*nhà ngục*) in all the country's citadels: both were built near the North Gate, and each consisted of three bays with two outbuildings.[25] Finally, in 1826, a council house (*nhà Nghiệp nghị* 協議堂) was built near the southeast gate, with six rooms in which all documents (books and letters) and official and administrative texts (*công văn*) were kept. On the twenty-seventh of each month, the population could go there to file complaints and claims.[26]

Other building work mentioned in the chronicles involved repairs, or reconstruction of structures deemed beyond repair. Some of this work was substantial, including the 1819 renovation and reinforcement of the citadel itself. This was a vast enterprise, involving the mobilisation of 5,300 soldiers from Bắc Thành's five armies (*ngũ quân* 五軍) and its elephant unit (*tượng quân* 象軍). Historical sources inform us that the troops drafted for this work were exempted from missions to the capital and received a donative of 35,000 ligatures and 35,000 bushels (*phương*) of rice.[27]

A number of other isolated improvements were of symbolic importance. In 1807 (first day of the seventh month), a decree was issued for the renovation of the Royal Ancestors' Temple (Thái miếu),[28] a sign that the city's royal past had not yet been completely erased. Then, in 1815, Kính Thiên Palace's dilapidated condition furnished the ruler with an opportunity to hasten the eradication of its history. According to the chronicles, the king

> issued an order. The wooden parts of Kính Thiên Palace at Bắc Thành are worm-eaten and cannot be replaced. The palace must be dis-mantled and [the materials] collected in one place. On the palace foundations thus laid bare, blocks of wood should be brought and prepared for the construction of a secondary residence [*nhà phan vọng*] consisting of three bays: this building should be suitable for the ceremonies of the first and fifteenth days [of the lunar month] and royal audiences. The secondary residence at Bắc Thành is named Royal Visit Palace [*hành cung*]. Its front building is inscribed with the four characters '*Hành cung tiền điện*' [行宮前殿, front royal visit palace]; its rear building is inscribed with the four characters '*Hành cung chính điện*' [行宮正殿, main royal visit palace].[29]

Built in 1428 by the liberator king Lê Thái Tổ, this palace incarnated the continuity and prestige of royal power. Named the Palace of Reverence for Heaven (Kính Thiên), it was located at the heart of the Forbidden City, on Nùng Mountain. This was the site of the former Càn Nguyên Palace, the Palace of Heaven, built in 1010. Kính Thiên Palace was in a state of advanced disrepair and now disappeared, four centuries after its construction and after multiple renovations. Its original function had already been deformed in 1802, when it was turned into a secular utilitarian building, the sovereign's royal visit palace (see above). Its final demolition marked a new stage in the downgrading of the former Impe-rial Citadel.

Yet Kính Thiên Palace possessed such power of historical evocation that its name continued to appear in the chronicles long after the actual building had disappeared, especially in the texts that laid down the pro-tocol of investiture ceremonies and reported on their proceedings (see below).[30] After 1815, in other words, the building referred to by writers of imperial historiography with the name *điện* Kính Thiên was no long the Palace of Reverence for Heaven, but the foundation upon which that palace had been built. This was Nùng Mountain, the mound that had received the spirit of a dragon raised to the rank of 'great princely high-ness, tutelary divinity of Thăng Long' at the beginning of the eleventh century (Papin 2001: 26).[31] This highly symbolic site was definitively deconsecrated in 1841, when the royal visit palace built on the site of the former Palace of Reverence for Heaven (*điện* Kính Thiên) was officially renamed the Palace of the Heavenly Dragon (*điện* Long Thiên). This signified that Nùng Mountain on which it was built was no longer the site of convergence for the terrestrial and celestial forces that conferred legitimacy on royal power.

Finally, as the seat of royal power, Huế Citadel had to impose itself as the kingdom's most impressive and sumptuous citadel. For this reason, in 1835 the height of the Hanoi Citadel's ramparts was reduced by 1 *thước* 8 *tấc* (0.72 m), making them lower than the citadel walls at Huế.

The City's Ambiguous Status: The Investitures of Minh Mạng and Thiệu Trị

Eleven days after the death of Gia Long, on 3 February 1820 (nineteenth day of the twelfth lunar month 1819), the deceased king's fourth son, Prince Đảm, ascended the throne and assumed the reign name Minh Mạng (first day of the first month 1820). As in the case of his father, Minh Mạng's investiture by the Grand Judge of Guangxi in his role as Chinese ambassador gave rise to new effervescence in the former capital.

The preparations for the investiture ceremonies went through several stages. In 1820, a royal decree announced that the king would travel north the following year. The Ministry of Public Works was ordered to examine the royal visit palaces along the road to Thăng Long and select those where the king could stop and rest.[32] In the seventh lunar month of the same year, orders were given for the construction of royal visit palaces at Bắc Thành and ambassadors' residences in the provinces of Kinh Bắc and Lạng Sơn.

> The royal visit palace at Bắc Thành, Thị Triều and Cần Chính Palaces were built in front of the Kính Thiên Palace at Bắc Thành, both of them roofed with tiles. A long gallery was built outside the Gate of Commencement [*Đoan Môn*], leading to Chu Tước Gate. The Ambassadors' Residence was built on the south bank of the Nhị River [Red River], roofed with tiles; on the river's north bank, relay stations were established along the route from the ambassadors' residence at Gia Quất to Lạng Sơn [...] The sum of 15,200 ligatures was set aside for the purchase of the materials necessary for the construction of the royal visit palaces and ambassadors' residences.[33]

This extract from the chronicles is very similar to the 1802 text on the preparations made for Gia Long's investiture. That is not in itself surprising, as rituals and protocol were precisely codified and admitted only minor modification. On the other hand, the order given to build royal visit palaces and the Cần Chính Palace is a source of surprise: these buildings already existed, as is evident from the royal decrees of 1802, 1804 and 1815 (see above). The confusion increases when we note that the order given in 1841 (fourth lunar month) for the preparations for the investiture of Thiệu Trị is identical to that of 1820.[34]

We cannot entirely dismiss the possibility that this successive rebuilding resulted from the irreversible deterioration of the wooden structure of certain palaces. But the hypothesis is unconvincing in view of the short lapse of time between the two investitures, just twenty years. A more plausible explanation is offered *a posteriori* by a series of reorganisations of the Hanoi palaces recorded in the official register of imperial institutions and regulations, *Khâm định Đại Nam hội điển sự lệ*. First, in 1835, the king ordered:

> Only in Hanoi does the royal visit palace (*hành cung*) consist of more than twenty buildings; it is twice the size of those in other provinces, much greater and more beautiful, and requires a budget for renovation that has been too high in the past five years. For the royal visit palace, a single building suffices, and it is always possible to build new structures when [the king] visits. [The state's resources] should not be wasted on too much construction. For this reason, it is ordered that the two main palaces (*chính điện*) be kept and the other buildings immediately dismantled. Of these, two may be transferred: one to Quảng Yên province, to serve as royal visit palace in that province; the other to Nam Định province, which may later modify it; the other buildings may be kept and used by Hanoi according to its needs.

In the same year, the rear palace (*hậu điện*) was dismantled and moved to Sơn Tây, to replace that province's dilapidated royal visit palace. The king also 'approved the governor of Nam Định's request to dismantle the remaining buildings and turn them into a treasury and prefectural administrative offices'.[35] The citadel's buildings were redistributed in this way: some of its palaces were dismantled after the investiture ceremony and rebuilt for administrative use in other provinces, while others were placed in storage. This mobility was possible because of the buildings' wooden structure. Their pillars and beams formed bays, which were single units that could be independently disassembled and reassembled.[36] A similar undertaking is described in 1842, after Thiệu Trị's investiture ceremony in Hanoi (third lunar month, Bính Tý day) when buildings erected for the occasion were moved to Nam Định. According to the chronicles:

> The royal visit palace in Hanoi: the Long Thiên Palace [former Kính Thiên], the main pavilion (*nhà chính*) and the secondary pavilion (*nhà phụ*) were joined to make a single building. The main palace (*chính điện*), rear palace (*hậu điện*), front palace (*tiền điện*), Trị Triệu Palace, left and right galleries (*tả vu hữu vu*) and tea pavilions (*nhà chè*) were dismantled and transported on military boats to Nam Định province. After reassembly, the buildings will be used as tax collection offices, granaries and travel palaces.[37]

During the first half of the nineteenth century, there were thus two types of buildings inside the citadel: (1) fixed architecture, consisting of masonry structures (ramparts, gates, the Gate of Commencement) and symbolic sites (the mounds, the foundations of the Kính Thiên Palace); and (2) mobile architecture that could be arranged like theatrical scenery according to the needs of pomp and protocol on the occasion of investiture ceremonies.

The Provincialisation of Hanoi: The 1831 Administrative Reform and the Recognition of Huế As Royal Capital

In 1831 (tenth lunar month), ambivalent relations between the Huế court and the two regions of Bắc Thành (11 provinces) and Gia Định (留鎮嘉定, five provinces) led Minh Mạng to launch a centralising reform of the whole country's administration, involving major boundary changes for its political and administrative units. The need for reform was underlined by worrying developments in Gia Định: Lê Văn Duyệt, governor since 1820 and unanimously respected by the population, had established himself as the region's strongman, openly challenging the king's legitimacy and jeopardising the construction of a lasting national unity (Trần Hùng & Nguyễn Quốc Thông 1995: 119). The government general of Bắc Thành was dissolved in 1831 and the country was divided into 31 provinces governed directly from Huế, although Minh Mạng had to await Lê Văn Duyệt's death in 1832 to implement his reform in the south. The reform was completed in 1832, with a change in the country's name: it was now rebaptised Đại Nam (Great South), a name which lasted until 1945.

With this dissolution, Thăng Long lost its status as the seat of government for the northern region and was renamed Hanoi, meaning 'inside the river', thus losing all reference to its past as royal capital. It was now no more than the administrative centre of the province of Hanoi, made up of four prefectures and fifteen districts. As a result, the area inside the citadel was reorganised and the number of buildings reduced. Some of the buildings previously occupied by the civilian and military mandarins in charge of the former region of Bắc Thành were redeployed for the use of the new authorities of Hanoi province. The residences of the military mandarins and the barracks of the four armies—*tiền, tả, hữu, hậu*—were dismantled and rebuilt in their province of origin, while the Royal Visit Palace, Temple of Literature and Temple of Assemblies (Hành cung, Văn miếu and Miếu Hội đồng) were moved to Hưng Yên.[38]

In 1839, Minh Mạng sent a further signal that Hanoi was now just a provincial capital when he renewed his criticisms of the splendour and excessive size of the royal visit palace there and ordered the dismantling of all its wooden buildings, including some sections that were worm-eaten, leaving only one building consisting of three bays and two outbuildings. According to the chronicles, the king issued an order:

> The royal visit palaces in the provinces are not like the royal palace at the capital and are not frequently visited. It suffices that they are big enough to receive the [provincial] mandarins when they present themselves to greet His Majesty. During my last visit to the north, Hanoi province built excessively large front and principal palaces (*tiền điện, chính điện*); this is wasteful. For this reason, it is ordered that all these parts be dismantled, and the model set in the thirteenth year of Minh Mạng's reign followed, that is, the structure built should consist of no more than three bays with two outbuildings, in compliance with regulations.[39]

With the accession of Tự Đức, the city's destitution was brought to its conclusion. In autumn 1847, the court of Huế dispatched the chief ambassador (*Chánh sứ*) to the court of Beijing in China with official notification of Thiệu Trị's death. At the same time, a request was made for a change in diplomatic protocol, to allow the organisation of Tự Đức's investiture at Phú Xuân–Huế, the Nguyễn dynasty's capital, and not at Hanoi. Two arguments were presented: (1) The situation had changed, Hanoi was no longer the country's capital;[40] (2) It was dangerous for the king to travel so far and for such a long period from the royal capital (*Kinh sư* 京師).[41]

There were two other reasons that are not explicitly stated in the annals. The first was political and could not be stated. The change of location freed the ruler and his successors from any form of dependence on Hanoi and possible claims of the mandarin elites and the literati. The second was of a factual nature. Organisation of the journey from

Phú Xuân–Huế to Hanoi represented a significant expense for the state and required the implementation of a large-scale logistical operation several months in advance in view of the size of the procession that accompanied the sovereign. Thus, for his investiture, Gia Long ordered as early as April–May 1802, eighteen months before the ceremony, the date of which he did not yet know:

> Following the imperial order, a military officer (*giám thành cai đội*) at the head of a group of twenty-five soldiers takes the mandarin road from the city of Thăng Long southwards to the province of Nghệ An at Mount Hoành Sơn [the present-day border between the provinces of Quảng Bình and Hà Tĩnh] to measure distances. Every 4,000 trượng [16.8 km], a royal visit palace must be built.[42]

To get a sense of the resources mobilised on an occasion of such fundamental importance as a royal investiture, we may note that the entourage accompanying Minh Mạng from Huế to Thăng Long in 1821 consisted of 1,782 civilian and military mandarins and 5,150 soldiers (Huỳnh 1917: 100). The journey from Huế to the old capital took place from 10 October to 12 November, that is, thirty-two days, during which it was necessary to feed this retinue of almost 7,000 men by drawing on local resources (peasants, district and provincial rice granaries, taxes) (Gaultier 1935: 26–7).

In 1848, China gave a favourable response to the request to modify the protocol despite the additional constraints it entailed: the delegation of the Grand Judge of Guangxi, consisting of about one hundred and forty people, took more than a month to get to Huế (Cadière 1916: 302).[43] This marked a turning point in Hanoi's fortunes: it signalled the end of the suspended sentence which the city had hitherto enjoyed. Even before his investiture at Huế (10 September 1849), Tự Đức, unconstrained by the diplomatic status which had protected Hanoi, ordered that the last royal palaces there be destroyed and that all finely carved and sculpted valuable wood and stone objects be sent to the capital (Trần Hùng & Nguyễn Quốc Thông 1995: 38).

1820–31: The Citadel's Appearance and Spatial Organisation

The École française d'Extrême-Orient's (EFEO) photograph library contains two photographs of two variants of the same plan for the citadel's development: in one, buildings are represented in black ink; in the other, they are not.[44] Although the plan is undated, we know it was drawn between 1821 and 1831. On the one hand, we note the presence of the

Rear Palace (Hậu Lâu), whose construction was ordered in 1821 (first day of the tenth lunar month). On the other hand, the titles of certain buildings were no longer in use after the 1831 administrative reform (palace of the governor-general of the North—*quan chánh tổng trấn*; palace of the ministry of justice—*dinh hình bộ*; etc.). Two of its features make the plan a unique and remarkable historical document:

- It was drawn in the Western style, either by French officers in Gia Long's service, who remained at the court of Huế until 1824, or by Vietnamese engineers.
- Captions in Sino-Vietnamese characters[45] indicate most of the places represented (buildings, space), with distances and building sizes expressed in *tầm* = 2.12 m (5 *thước*), *thước* = 0.424 m (10 *tấc*) and *tấc* = 0.0424 m. Not all the structures and sets of building are identified, however: examination shows that the plan was chiefly drawn to give details of the citadel's defensive organisation and was produced for military use.

Comparison of information on this plan with data from a map reproduced and translated by Trần Huy Bá from an original dated the fifteenth day of the fifth month (24 June) 1831, five months before the 1831 administrative reform, yields insights into the citadel's spatial organisation. Four groups of buildings were arranged according to two principles (see Map 15):

- A radial principle, extending outward from the centre, Nùng Mountain (濃山) (platform of the former Kính Thiên Palace), towards the ramparts. This principle established the diminishing importance of the citadel's buildings and of their occupants' status as one moved away from the royal visit palace (*hành cung*) where the king stayed, down to the barracks of the ordinary soldiers.
- An axial principle, established by the north–south orientation of the royal visit palace area (the former Forbidden City). This principle divided the citadel's space into two halves: east and west.

Superimposed onto this spatial organisation was a network of roads and paths that divided the citadel into a relatively regular grid. The first group of buildings consisted of camps and barrack buildings for some of the officers, the soldiers of the royal guard (*vệ*) and provincial regiments (*cơ*), and (in the southern sector) the elephants' quarters. These formed a military ring that extended across the entire area between the rampart and the four roads nearest to it. This peripheral strip, a hundred or so

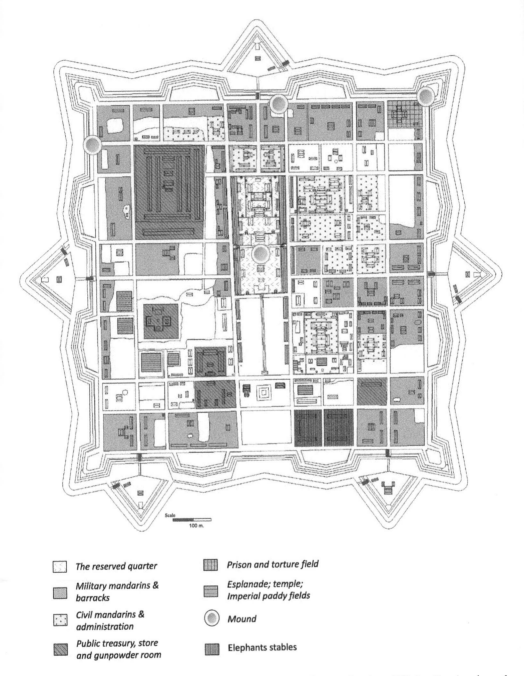

Scale
100 m.

The reserved quarter		Prison and torture field
Military mandarins & barracks		Esplanade; temple; Imperial paddy fields
Civil mandarins & administration		Mound
Public treasury, store and gunpowder room		Elephants stables

Map 15. The Nguyễn-dynasty Hanoi Citadel: internal organisation (Olivier Tessier, based on EFEO photo library, map VIE 23474).

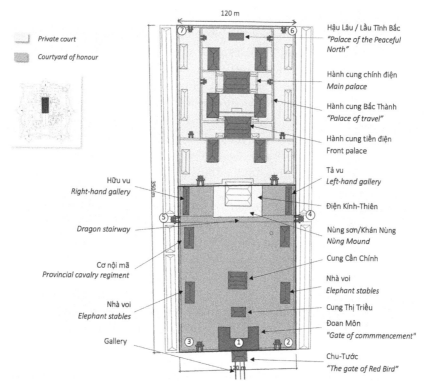

Map 16. The Nguyễn-dynasty Hanoi Citadel: the area reserved for the king, formerly the Forbidden City (Olivier Tessier, based on EFEO photo library, map VIE 23474 detail).

metres across, was a veritable buffer zone between the outside world, with its potential dangers, and the citadel's political, administrative and financial heart. The execution ground (*trường hình*) and prison compound (*sân nhà ngục*) were located in the northeastern corner.

The second group was in the eastern sector, the citadel's nobler half (see above). On the immediate right of the area reserved for the king were the residences of the governor-general (*Quan Chánh tổng trấn* 正總鎮) and his deputy (*Quan phó* 副總鎮, or *Hiệp tổng trấn* 協總鎮). Further out, in an area about 100 m wide located between the military zone and the residences of the governor and deputy governor, there was a concentration of mandarin residences, as well as the administrative buildings of two of the three regional departments (*tào*),[46] representing three of the six central ministries of the capital, the Departments of Military Affairs (*binh tào* 兵曹) and Justice (*hình tào* 刑曹). Two notable exceptions may be observed, however. First, the residence of the mandarin in charge of the regional department of the Ministry of Finance (*hộ bộ dinh* 戶部營) and the regional department of the Ministry of Finance (*hộ tào ty viên* 戶曹司員) were located near the north gate, in the vicinity of the treasury and royal storehouses, which he controlled. Second, the residence and services of the head of the provincial department of the Ministry of Public Works (*công phòng chủ sự* 工防主事; *công tào biện lý* 功曹辦理) were located in the central axis to the north of the restricted area, as was the regional service civil status (*hộ tịch* [*tào*] *sở* 戶籍[曹]所), which came under the jurisdiction of the mandarin in charge of finance.

The third group was located in the western sector, to the right of the former Forbidden City's central axis according to a north-to-south reading. It was here that one found the storehouses where tax revenues in money and in kind were kept, as well as the rice granaries and treasury (*công khố*). These storage facilities occupied a vast area in the citadel's northwest quarter, as well as a smaller area in the southwest quarter.

The fourth group of buildings was the reserved area (the former Forbidden City) (see Map 16). This group's strict north-to-south orientation, while the citadel as a whole is oriented slightly north-northeast to south-southeast, gives an off-centre and asymmetrical impression which may be noted on certain late nineteenth-century maps drawn by the French Department of Cartography. It is a rectangular area, measuring 350 m by 120 m (42,000 m²) divided into two courtyards of equal size: a private enclosure to the north and a ceremonial enclosure to the south, separated by a wall with two gates. This separating wall was aligned with a rear façade of the old Kính Thiên Palace. The terrace was accessed up sculpted staircases. The staircases on the east, north and west sides were decorated simply with dragon banisters. The staircase on the south side, the main façade, consisted of a triple flight of steps and their dragon banisters were masterpieces of fifteenth-century Vietnamese sculpture (Bezacier 1958: 93).

The reserved area was accessed through two gates on its north side that opened onto the private enclosure, two side gates that opened onto the ceremonial enclosure, and three gates to the south (see Map 16). The main south gate, the Đoan Môn or Gate of Commencement, was itself made up of five gateways. We may conclude with an extract from the description of the reserved area given in the 'Gazetteer of the Northern Provinces' (*Bắc Thành địa dư chí*) compiled by Lê Chất (1769–1826) when he was governor-general of Bắc Thành (1818–26):

Inside the citadel, on Nùng Mountain, five royal palaces and six houses have been built on the left and right sides; around [this area], an enclosing wall has been built with five gates, as well as a side gate giving access to the ceremonial enclosure where all the mandarins in court attire assemble for great ceremonies and the rituals of the first and fifteenth days of the lunar month. A staircase and a lane have been built; the Đoan Môn gate is located beyond the lane. (1969: 4)

This description corresponds to the representation of the buildings given in the 1821–31 plan, with one exception: the plan shows a succession of six palaces and not five, a difference that can probably be explained by the fact that the Palace of the Peaceful North (Hậu Lâu / *lầu* Tĩnh Bắc) had not yet been built (1821) when this treatise, drawn up between 1818 and 1821, was compiled. The other elements put forward are faithful to their rendition on the plan: six houses were located on either side of the Main Palace (*Hành cung chính điện* 行宮正殿) and the Front Palace (*Hành cung tiền điện* 行宮前殿) and six gates gave access to the reserved area (two to the north, two to the south and two to the side leading to the courtyard of honour at the level of the staircase on the south side of the Kính Thiên terrace). These gates with a purely functional purpose should be distinguished from the Gate of Commencement (Đoan Môn) with its sacred dimension and its location dictated by geomantic considerations established at the beginning of the eleventh century. Subdivided into five gateways, its use was governed by a strict hierarchical protocol: the central gateway, the most imposing, was exclusively reserved for the sovereign; the two side gateways of decreasing importance placed on each side of the central gateway were used by the mandarins according to their hierarchical status and function.

A final important observation: this plan makes no reference to the sacred, an absence which confirms its terrestrial and functional vocation. To fill this gap, we have recourse to later plans (1866, 1873, 1886), although less well documented and sometimes approximate, to identify and locate places of worship and sacrificial spaces within the citadel, a list which does not claim to be exhaustive (see Map 15). They were of three types. Firstly, they were buildings of worship in the narrow sense; four in number, they were dedicated, with the exception of the House of Steles (Đình Bia), to deities whose cult was widespread in the north of the country (deity of Military Arts: Vũ (võ) Miếu (武廟); Harvest deity: Chùa Tắc (稷庙); Earth deity: Chùa Xã (社庙)).[47] Secondly, three sacrificial spaces were dedicated to deities, two of which worked directly to secure and improve rice harvests, cereals vital for the survival of the peasantry and a major source of income for the state via taxation. The third space was devoted to two natural elements, the mountains and waters, the deities of which were worshipped at an Esplanade: *Sơn Xuyên đàn* (山川壇).[48] Finally, there were the mounds, which defined the geomantic geography of the city, in the forefront of which was the Nùng Mound (Khán Nùng), the receptacle of the dragon's spirit (see above).[49]

2. THE COLONIAL PERIOD: FROM THE CITADEL'S CAPTURE (1873) TO ITS DEMOLITION (1897): THE DESTRUCTION AND TRANSFORMATION OF URBAN SPACE

After Tự Đức's investiture (1849), historical sources mentioning Hanoi become increasingly scant. The Huế court's attention was focused on the French threat to the country's central region. Under pressure from missionary societies seeking to end the persecution of Christians and business interests dreaming of a powerful commercial base in Asia, the French government sent an expedition to Vietnam in 1858. After the bombardment of Tourane (Đà Nẵng) in September of that year, Saigon was captured on 17 February 1859. Treaties signed by China and France at Beijing (1860) and Saigon (1862) were successively revoked, leading to the French seizure of Cochinchina, which became a colony in 1865.

During the second half of the nineteenth century, the country's northern region became the theatre of devastating violence caused by the intrusion of Chinese armed bands (the Black Flags, Yellow Flags, and Red Flags). Spreading rapidly throughout Tonkin, after 1883 this source of instability was subsumed into the French war of conquest. Armed attacks, acts of plunder, alliances with the different Chinese bandit groups that were made and broken by the Huế court and the colonial forces, the threat of broader conflict with China, the Vietnamese resistance movement (*cần vương*, 'serving the king'): after 1850, Vietnam descended into a never-ending spiral of insurrections with dramatic consequences for the population and local economy. The disruptive effects of natural disasters and the frequency of movements of sedition against royal authority had forced the king to maintain the country in a permanent state of military repression, rendering it all the more vulnerable to foreign invasion.

The Citadel is Captured Twice: 1873 and 1882

We need not be concerned with the circumstances that led naval officers Lt. Francis Garnier and Capt. Henri Rivière to seize the citadel, respectively on 20 November 1873 and 25 April 1882. There are many more or less romanticised accounts of the two events,[50] and numerous archives of the Service Historique de la Défense (SHD) in Vincennes contain detailed descriptions.[51] Our aim here is to examine the changes made to the citadel by the French troops after they took possession. At the outset, we should recall that by 1873 the Rear Palace (Hậu Lâu, built in 1821) was in ruins; that the Kính Thiên Palace, long abandoned by the Trịnh lords, was demolished under Gia Long and a royal visit palace (later renamed Long Thiên) built in its stead; and that Tự Đức had several of the citadel's former buildings removed and sent to other provinces of the north.

A certain amount of damage was done to the citadel during Garnier's attack, mainly from artillery fire. To facilitate surveillance, Garnier had the gates closed and blocked up, with the exception of the East Gate, which gave access to the commercial town. In a letter to the admiral governor of Cochinchina on 3 December 1873, Garnier described some of the work he was doing or planning in the citadel. His aim was to assert and secure the French presence there:

> I am having the large Vietnamese building that was used as the king's quarters lit and divided up. [...] In a few days, barracks will be built to quarter the company of marines infantry. Apart from the provincial authorities' building, there are in fact no inhabitable buildings in the citadel; my troops are currently quartered there and the new officials remain without buildings. It is better to return the Vietnamese buildings to them and quarter our men in European lodgings. (Masson 1929: 71)

After Garnier's death on 21 December 1873 at Cầu Giấy, the Red River Delta saw a wave of anti-French and anti-Catholic uprisings. In an attempt to cope with the chaos, Lt. Paul Philastre signed an agreement with the Huế court's ambassador, Nguyễn Văn Tường, providing for the evacuation of the delta's four citadels and withdrawal of French troops into the French concessions in Hanoi and Haiphong.

> Finally on 12 February 1874, the Hanoi Citadel was evacuated in its turn, and our soldiers marched through the populace who spared them neither mocking laughter nor jibes. In the eyes of these Asian peoples who yield only when confronted with force, our prestige suffered a dreadful blow: the persecutions and massacres recommenced with increased violence. (SHD c10H1-d1)

The troops fell back on Haiphong. Under the terms of a treaty signed on 15 March 1874, the consul and a small force of 50 men temporarily occupied the examination ground in Hanoi to start work on the French concession in the former south fort, built under the Tây Sơn. The concession was initially 2.5 ha in area, but grew rapidly to 18 ha. The work was completed in autumn 1876 and the examination ground returned to the provincial authorities on 15 October, in time for the triennial examinations that November.

In the aftermath of the evacuation, what state was the citadel in? The precise description made by Capt. Chapotot on 16 November 1875 (reproduced *in extenso* by Masson 1929: 210–8) suggests that French troops changed little there during their short stay (20 November 1873–12 February 1874). The four gates bricked up by Garnier were opened, as Capt. Chapotot noted: 'Communication with the outside world took place through five gates set in the centre curtain walls, protected by demilunes. [...] These passages are obstructed by wooden doors which are currently in a state of disrepair'. (Masson 1929: 210–1). The provincial authorities and Vietnamese troops reoccupied the citadel: 'The provincial troops consist of [?] regiments of militia. [...] There are currently two regiments under the governor of Son Tây, a certain number of men posted in the Phu [prefectures] and the remainder, around 1,000 men, make up the town's garrison and live in the citadel' (Masson 1929: 212).

On the pretext that the mandarins had admitted the Black Flags into the citadel at the end of 1881, the French launched their second attack on 25 April 1882. As in 1873, it fell in a few hours, despite the resistance organised by provincial governor Hoàng Diệu, who committed suicide rather than face dishonour as his predecessor Nguyễn Tri Phương had ten years earlier.[52] The casualty list included four wounded on the French side, and around forty dead and twenty wounded among the Vietnamese (SHD c10H1-d1). As for material damage directly attributable to the attack, it was limited and concentrated on the outer edge of the North Gate, which still today bears the scars of artillery fire.

Unlike Garnier, Rivière did not wish to occupy the citadel:

> After resting for two hours, Rivière had the citadel put out of defensive service. The cannons and their carriages were thrown from the ramparts, as were the beams kept up there for rolling down on assailants. This work continued for several days, whereupon the dismantled citadel was returned to the mandarins, with the exception of its highest point, the Royal Pagoda [Long Thiên Palace], which is easy to defend. (SHD c10H1-d1)

Another document notes that Capt. Rivière did not wish to occupy the citadel definitively, given the small number of troops he had, and 'had breaches made in the rampart, with a view to future operations. Our troops withdrew into the Concession, where improvement work had been completed' (SHD c10H20-d9).

Three comments must be made on these two extracts. First, Rivière tried to disable the ramparts of the southeast side of the citadel by making breaches, but gave up the attempt: 'To the left and right of this gate [southeast], one may see breaches made to disable the citadel on the orders of Capt. Rivière, who had to abandon such a colossal enterprise. The breaches were summarily obstructed with beams and rafters' (Bonnal 1925: 92). Second, the citadel's return to the provincial authorities (to the Quan Án mandarin, named acting governor) was not motivated by respect for the site's symbolic and political value: Rivière's shortage of troops and inability to defend such a vast area obliged him to withdraw his forces to the concession barracks. Finally, to pursue the preceding point, the infantry captain who remained posted at the 'Royal Pagoda' transformed the Long Thiên Palace into a 'fortified redoubt', 'replaced its openwork bannister with a hideous crenelated wall and transported several cannons there' (Masson 1929: 81). This rough wall and its battlements completely deformed the structure's flowing outline, as France Mangin notes (2006: 59), but the transformation was only utilitarian and defensive; it did not cause irreversible destruction.

Repeated attacks by the Black Flags between March and May 1883 and Rivière's death at Cầu Giấy (19 May 1883) accelerated events. A state of siege was declared on Hanoi, Bắc Ninh and Haiphong, and the Harmand Treaty (23 August 1883) imposed a Protectorate on Tonkin.

1883–87: Destructions and Transformations Inside the Citadel

All changed with this new status for Tonkin and the arrival of reinforcements to restore order in Hanoi and launch France's decade-long war of conquest.

> Reinforcements were requested from the Metropole: in January 1883, a battalion of marines were embarked for Tonkin. To quarter them, we have a rice granary available in the citadel which we now control: this storehouse is made of masonry and is big enough to house the whole battalion in very suitable conditions. (SHD c10H20-d8)

This text makes the first explicit mention of a military use for the citadel's buildings (apart from the 'fortified redoubt'), a change that was not

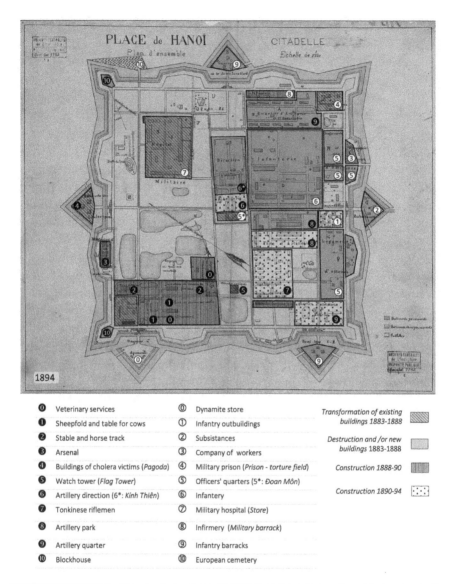

Map 17. The first phase of the destruction and transformation of the citadel, 1883–94 (Olivier Tessier, based on ANOM map 1PL/2022).

Legend:

⓿	Veterinary services	⓪	Dynamite store
❶	Sheepfold and table for cows	①	Infantry outbuildings
❷	Stable and horse track	②	Subsistances
❸	Arsenal	③	Company of workers
❹	Buildings of cholera victims (*Pagoda*)	④	Military prison (*Prison - torture field*)
❺	Watch tower (*Flag Tower*)	⑤	Officers' quarters (5*: Đoan Môn)
❻	Artillery direction (6*: *Kính Thiên*)	⑥	Infantry
❼	Tonkinese riflemen	⑦	Military hospital (*Store*)
❽	Artillery park	⑧	Infirmery (*Military barrack*)
❾	Artillery quarter	⑨	Infantry barracks
❿	Blockhouse	⑩	European cemetery

Transformation of existing buildings 1883-1888

Destruction and /or new buildings 1883-1888

Construction 1888-90

Construction 1890-94

accompanied by the demolition of any existing structure. This is confirmed by a plan dated 20 August 1883 in which the barracks and artillery were respectively positioned in the citadel's southwest and southeast sectors, zones during this period that only contained a few buildings of

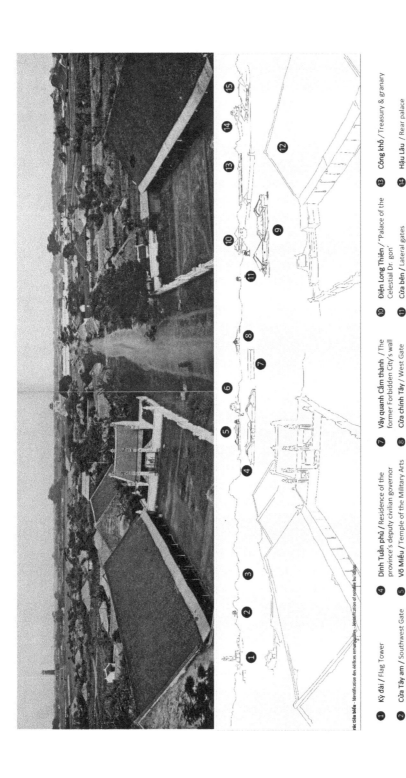

các tiêu biểu - Identification des édifices remarquables - Identification of notable buildings

① Kỳ đài / Flag Tower
② Cửa Tây am / Southwest Gate
③ Thành lũy / Rampar.

④ Dinh Tuần phủ / Residence of the province's deputy civilian governor
⑤ Võ Miếu / Temple of the Military Arts
⑥ Đoan Môn / The "Commencement Gate"

⑦ Vây quanh Cấm thành / The former Forbidden City's wall
⑧ Cửa chính Tây / West Gate
⑨ Dinh Đề Đốc / Residence of the province's military governor

⑩ Điện Long Thiên / "Palace of the Celestial Dr. gon"
⑪ Cửa bên / Lateral gates
⑫ Dinh Tổng Bình / Commander of the province's troops

⑬ Công khổ / Treasury & granary
⑭ Hậu Lâu / Rear palace
⑮ Dinh Tổng Đốc / Residence of the province's civilian governor

Fig. 49. This photograph by Gsell from 1875–77 reveals the former royal capital's decline, showing the 'ruralisation' of the area inside the citadel. (Guimet Museum 09-522961, AP 9381 detail.)

reduced and uncertain size. The troops were housed in thatched huts, temporary and vulnerable constructions not marked on the plan. Only two new structures appear: blockhouses built at the end of 1882 in the northwest and southeast bastions of the citadel.

In June 1883, the same author described how the situation was changing:

> Beyond the citadel and concession, Hanoi was a completely open town: pirates entered, spreading fire and massacre almost on a daily basis. We resolved to build a wall around it, taking advantage of the citadel and concession walls, as well as permanent intermediary structures; at the same time, a bridgehead was built on the Red River's left bank with a redoubt built of masonry. Reinforcements of 2,400 men and 200 horses were expected for the end of July, and barracks had to be prepared for them. (SHD c10H20-d8)

The strategic axis that linked the citadel and concession, then known as rue des Incrustateurs (today's Tràng Tiền and Trang Thi Streets), was thus fortified to protect circulation between these two crucial sites for the French presence. Above all, rapid preparations had to be made for the installation of the expected new troops. It was decided that one battalion should be posted at the examination ground and the other in the citadel. To this end, construction started in early 1884 of thirty-two barrack buildings (wood and brick) measuring 6 m by 20 m, eight measuring 6 m by 12 m and two measuring 11 m by 69 m. The contract for labour and materials was given to a Chinese entrepreneur, Yuen Tay (Masson 1929: 49). On an 1885 map, these first permanent structures appear in the northeast quarter of the citadel. They mark the start of a series of acts of deliberate destruction and spatial transformation that, in time, would grow to a *crescendo* (see Map 17).

During the same period, during his short stay in the citadel (late February to early March 1884), Dr Hocquard succinctly described the environment he found himself in: 'The high-ranking officials of the province live near the rice granaries, the *tông đôc* (governor) and the two mandarins in charge of finance and justice (*quan bô* and *quan an*). Only the *quan bô*'s house remains standing'[53] (Hocquard 1999: 105–6).

This description confirms that the palace of the provincial governor-general (*tổng đốc đường*), the assembly building (*nhà hội nghị*), and the residence of the mandarin of the provincial Justice Department (*án sát đường*) were destroyed in 1883. Thus, if we cross-reference the panoramic photograph taken by Gsell in 1876 (see Figure 49) with the plan of the same year and the plans of 1820–31 and 1888, we can see that the residence of the vice-governor of the province (*tuần phủ đường*), the residence of the military commander of the province (*dinh đề đốc*), the residence of the colonel of the provincial troops (*chánh lĩnh binh*), the central camp of the rear guard protection regiment (*hậu bảo trung dinh*), as well as the services office (*nhà thủ bộ*) were also razed between 1883 and 1888.

This is in fact what an 1897 report on the demolition of the citadel states: 'Since our occupation, the old buildings [in the citadel] have almost entirely disappeared; they were of no value.[54] We have replaced them with barracks.'[55] Hocquard continued:

> The immense area of land delimited in the centre by the Royal Pagoda and on the perimeter by the outer ramparts is almost entirely uncultivated and unoccupied. It is a vast desert and gives the citadel a sad and unoccupied appearance. In the past, numerous thatched huts here served as barracks for the Vietnamese troops. [...] The soldiers' huts have been burnt or demolished, but there remain, isolated from one another, some pleasant brick houses where the military mandarins lived. (Hocquard 1999: 106)

This description underlines a paradox that appears as soon as one examines the different plans of the citadels drawn between 1873 and 1890, and may best be expressed with a question: Why destroy the buildings in the citadel's northeast quarter while vast empty spaces remained available for building, even though several notable monuments remained (the temples Khánh Sơn, Vũ Miếu, Bà Liễu Hành)? No practical reason appears to justify this choice, not even the need to site the barracks near the East Gate for direct access to the commercial town, as the southeast quarter was almost entirely empty, and thus available. By default, one is inclined to conclude that this was the first deliberate act of destruction orchestrated by the new masters of Hanoi, who demonstrated their long-term presence to the population and the Huế court by making it materially impossible for the mandarins to return to the heart of the citadel.

In May 1884, the Tonkin Expeditionary Corps, numbering 6,096 men, was struck by an unprecedented epidemic of cholera. The concession's hospital was inundated with men suffering from fever and dysentery: 'we replaced it with the citadel's rice granary, where an entire battalion of infantry had earlier been barracked; this well-equipped though hardly luxurious building rendered great services' (SHD c10h20-d8). The new hospital received its first sick and wounded on 30 June 1884. But its creation in the heart of the citadel was an inadequate response to the situation, which continued to deteriorate. By General de Courcy's arrival in Hanoi on 17 August 1884, 4,500 cases of cholera had been recorded and 800 men were dying every month. Observing their deplorable conditions of housing and hygiene, the general drew up a plan for the troops' disposition:

> On his orders, and for the first time, a general plan was made for the repartition of the troops and the military establishments assigned to them. The projects drawn up on this basis for a total of 12,000 Europeans would cost 14,000,000 francs; in early October General de Courcy received a telegram promising these funds and permission to start the proposed work immediately. He immediately ordered the engineers to ensure that, by 1 April 1886, all the troops should be housed in barrack buildings made of iron and brick. (SHD c10H20-d8)

In a letter from the Minister of War to General de Courcy dated 10 September 1885, the former replied to the latter's request to set up a hospital in Quảng Yên and make improvements to the Hanoi Citadel:

> From the Navy Ministry, you must already have received Tollet and Moisant material consisting of 13 officer barrack buildings with a capacity of 65 officers, 53 troop barrack buildings with a capacity of 3,000 men, 41 ambulance buildings with a total of 756 beds. You should use this material for the quartering of the troops and the establishment of hospitals. (SHD c10H6-d9)

However, on 24 December 1885 the work was interrupted for lack of funding: of the 14,000,000 francs promised, only 4,000 were actually granted (SHD c10H20-d9).

None of the archives consulted contain a precise description of the buildings actually constructed at the end of 1885, but a photograph bearing the caption 'Hanoi: citadel barracks (1885–86)' confirms that the barrack buildings of the infantry and marines artillery in the northeast quarter of the citadel were completed, as well as the officers' quarters, some of them at least, along the east side of the citadel. This group of buildings is clearly visible on an 1888 plan.

The point of no return was reached at the beginning of 1887 with the destruction of Long Thiên Palace and the levelling of Nùng Mountain, and the construction on that site of a headquarters for the artillery. Since 1873, this structure had suffered some disgraceful transformations, but these had remained reversible in the sense that the building could still

Fig. 50. The Mirador (French name for the Flag Tower/Kỳ Đài). Albumen print in the collection of the Bibliothèque de l'ancien Musée des colonies (Paris), housed at the Université Côte d'Azur (Public domain).

have been restored to its initial appearance (Mangin 2006: 59). With this act of ostentatious demolition, the French military authorities destroyed the original site of Hanoi's foundation by King Lý Thái Tổ and replaced it with a secular building, removing all hope of the situation's reversal.

The dates of the razing of the other artificial mounds around which the geomantic geography of the former Royal Citadel were arranged are more difficult to determine. In the citadel's west section, Cung Mountain (Thái Hoà Palace) disappeared with the construction of the first barracks. Claude Madrolle noted in 1925:

> Tam Sơn located near the citadel's north gate is now just a low mound; in 1886, according to M. Dumoutier, it had the appearance of a long terrace, culminating at one end with a raised section in the shape of a bowl [...]. In 1890, to the west of the former royal residence, Khán Sơn was still a fairly high hillock with a round wooded summit, from which King Lê Thánh Thông (1460–97) watched military manoeuvres. (Madrolle 1925: 18–9)

The Albert Sarraut Lycée was built on this site. Today, its buildings house the Departments of Exterior Relations and Human Resources of the Party Central Committee.

From 1885, the Flag Tower, built in 1812 to fly the royal standard, was used as an optical telegraphy tower for communication by Morse code with the Bắc Ninh citadel, which was similarly equipped. Painted white for this purpose, it was renamed Mirador (see Figure 49). From 1887 it was put to a more peaceful use as a tribune for watching horse races: 'A 1,200-metre racing track was built on the land that separates it [the mirador] from the Royal Pagoda and which is used today as an exercise ground and sports field' (Masson 1929: 84). This secular use for a site on the historical axis of the Kính Thiên Palace symbolises the city's Europeanisation and underlines the growing power of the civilian authorities.

1888–97: The Citadel is Dismantled

King Đồng Khánh's royal order of 3 October 1888 accelerated this trend, with his declaration that 'the territories of the cities of Hanoi, Haiphong and Tourane [Đà Nẵng] are established as French concessions and ceded by the Vietnamese Government which renounces all its rights over the said territories' (ANOM GGI d20244). Strengthened by its status as a French town within the Protectorate, Hanoi's recently established (19 July 1888) municipal authority was now free to impose Western rationality on the organisation of urban space. Up to this point, the city had been arranged around three main centres: (1) the citadel, seat of military power; (2) the concession, where the civilian administration was located, and which was extended after 1886 into the area southwest of Hoàn Kiếm Lake, leading to the destruction of two important Buddhist buildings (the city hall was built on the site of Tàu Pagoda and the central post office on the site of the Báo Ân Pagoda); (3) the Catholic mission's quarter, where the mission secured its future ownership of expropriated land by destroying the Báo Thiên Monastery (1885) and building St Joseph's Cathedral in its stead (1885–87). The European quarter developed around Hoàn Kiếm Lake and on either side of the road between the citadel and the concession (the road's fortifications were destroyed in 1886). From 1888, the new municipal authority redesigned Hanoi as a colonial city; its growth would now be guided by a general development plan. This is not the place to discuss the changes of axis this implied, but we may note that it presaged the citadel's gradual dissolution as a coherent historical entity and unique architectural ensemble.

At this time, in June 1888, the French troops in Hanoi, most of whom were quartered in the citadel, were accommodated as follows:

BARRACK BUILDINGS (NUMBER OF PLACES)									HOSPITALS		
OFFICERS			TROOPS			HORSES					
A Permanent new buildings	**B** Requisitioned Vietnamese buildings	**C** Thatch huts	**A** *idem*	**B**	**C** *idem*	**A** *idem*	**B**	**C**	**A** *idem*	**B** *idem*	**C** *idem*
156	–	48	2,556	120	1,429	68	–	251	604	–	30

Note: Sourced from SHD c10H20-d8.

Examination of these figures highlights two points. First, few troops were quartered in 'requisitioned Vietnamese buildings' (B), suggesting that by 1888 the mandarins' residences and offices had been completely demolished, and almost completely demolished in the case of the former provincial storehouses transformed into a hospital. Second, more than half the troops were quartered in 'thatch huts' (C); these troops were mainly Vietnamese officers and riflemen.

This second point anticipates work that would be done in the citadel from 1888 to 1894. When plans dating from those two years are compared, striking changes may be observed. Part of the southeast quarter is divided into plots, there is a set of barrack buildings for the Vietnamese riflemen, and a new artillery area near the southeast gate. The 1894 plan is particularly interesting as it distinguishes between structures that were permanent, semi-permanent and thatched. The thatch huts were mainly concentrated in the two areas recently divided into plots (as well as the hospital sector, which at that time was being redeveloped). A pencilled line on the plan also indicates a project, proposed in 1893, for the citadel's decommissioning. What was this project?

On 28 July 1893, Hanoi's municipal authority published a proposal for the destruction of the citadel's ramparts and the decommissioning of its western half to make room for the creation of a new European quarter. This project was part of the city's general development plan, involving the construction of three boulevards parallel to the old rue des Incrustateurs extending westward from the old concession. This new network of streets was gradually built from 1890 to 1906, years in which it was connected to the Mandarin Road (today's Lê Duẩn Street), which passed the railway station.

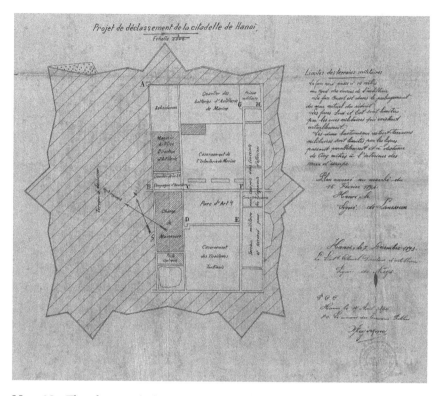

Map 18. The decommissioning project (7 December 1893) ratified on 14 February 1894 (ANOM 1PL 2022).

From 7 December 1893, a plan for the decommissioning of part of the citadel was drawn up by the military authority and presented to the municipal authority, which countersigned it. The plan appears as an appendix to the contract (7 February 1894) on the citadel's demolition (see Map 18). One cannot but be surprised, first by the rapidity with which this decommissioning plan was executed, and second by the docility of the military authority which did not flinch at the loss of more than half the territory it controlled, including the military hospital. One hypothesis is that the decree of 28 July 1893 merely formalised a project that had been prepared over a period of several years. This may be deduced from a map of the city dated December 1891, drawn by the municipal authority's department of roads, entitled 'Distribution of water in the city of Hanoi'. The decommissioning project was officially published two years later, yet the water pipes are routed very precisely around the territory that would remain military after decommissioning, carefully avoiding the

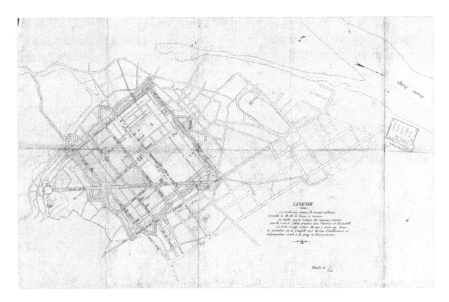

Map 19. Bazin's plan, in a map published by the city of Hanoi, 1894, Mairie de Hanoi. Service de Voirie (ANOM GGI 7753 098).

western half of the citadel and the military hospital, which one thinks might have benefitted from a supply of water. This hypothesis sheds new light on regrets expressed by Governor-General Paul Doumer on his arrival in Hanoi in early 1897: 'I arrived too late to save the interesting parts. The gates in particular were worth conserving. They had great character, in addition to the historical memories attached to them, which give them the right to our respect' (cited by Masson 1929: 85). There is no reason to doubt the sincerity of these sentiments. At the same time, there is no denying that the transformations—both symbolic and material— had become irreversible.

Hanoi Citadel's gates and ramparts were demolished from 1894–97 (in two stages: 1894–95, and 1895–97) under a contract signed between Governor-General Jean-Marie de Lanessan and Auguste Bazin, a civil engineer from Paris (7 February 1894). Under the terms of the contract, the latter agreed to '1. demolish the walls and parapets; 2. fill in the ditches and ponds with rubble from the parapets; 3. build streets in the decommissioned area, not including ballasting, steam-rolling and tree-planting which is the Protectorate's responsibility; build a wall around the preserved section of the citadel, with a raised walkway for infantry' (ANOM GGI d7751). In return, the concessionary received remuneration of 60,000 piasters and ownership of all the decommissioned land, excluding 5 ha which reverted to the Protectorate. This nonetheless represented a grant of 90 ha of building land. The concessionary was given three years to fulfil the contract. Two 1894 maps contain details of the new military zone's boundaries and the development plan for the decommissioned area.

One map was entitled 'Project for boulevards on the land in the citadel granted to Mr Bazin – general plan' (see Map 19). Dated 24 May 1894, it was published by the Hanoi municipal authority's department of streets. The map's key indicates the area of military land granted, the areas allocated within the citadel for streets and squares, and the streets to be built outside the citadel's perimeter at the government's expense (both of construction and expropriation). The military land between the new enclosing wall and the line of the ramparts was thus granted to private entrepreneurs for commercial use.

This complicity between the public sphere and private interests was at the origin of unusual protests sparked off by the demolition project. French public opinion in Tonkin unanimously favoured the complete disappearance of the citadel, or at least a reduction in the imposing size (130 ha: intramural space, moat, and buffer zone) of these military fortifications deemed indefensible and dangerous to public health, as the 1897 report on its demolition states:

> However, large spaces were left free; they contained ponds whose stagnant water constituted a source of pestilence. The miasmas that exhaled from them were joined by those coming from the ditches when the water level was low. This situation, so contrary to public health, had been the cause of complaints from the inhabitants of Hanoi for several years. The municipal council made itself the interpreter of the feelings of the population; it undertook, on July 28, 1893, a deliberation in which it asked for the demolition of the citadel. (ANOM BIB SOM d2637, p. 71)

As for the Vietnamese, they were obviously not consulted.

Criticisms were not levelled at the project itself—the decommissioning of the citadel—but at the terms of the contract signed with the engineer Bazin. Most of the protests were voiced by the newspaper *Indépendance Tonkinoise*, which launched a vitriolic press campaign against Governor-General de Lanessan, denouncing an act of cronyism by which the concessionary profited from exorbitant grants of free land, while a different company (E. Le Roy) was prepared to do the same work for 40,000 piasters with no grant of decommissioned land (Bourrin 1941: 306–9). The author of this editorial, Le Vasseur, described this contract as 'disgusting [...] because it was motivated by base reasons of land speculation and personal interests, to the detriment of the general interest [...] a contract by which the [European] cemetery was part of the land ceded [...] in such a way that M. de Lanessan has just tampered with our Hanoi cemetery, as he has with all the rest.'

Despite the campaign, the contract of 15 February 1894 was upheld (ANOM GGI d7752). Work started on 10 August 1894 with the demolition of the north and west demilunes and was completed in May 1897. For the historian Charles Fourniau: 'It was Lanessan who signed the contract for the demolition of the Hanoi Citadel, of which only a fragment was conserved. Lanessan took the opportunity to have numerous buildings constructed at no cost at all, as the entrepreneur was paid in vacant land —this was specifically prohibited under the rules of public accountancy' (Fourniau 1989: 219).

The mode of representation used in drawing the 24 May 1894 map, allowing the reader simultaneously to visualise the existing ramparts (those still standing after the demolition) and the development plan, offers unintentional evidence of this complicity. The demolition of the ramparts had scarcely begun, yet the street plan was already in place, with multiple plots of land traced and ready for subdivision and construction for wealthy customers. Indeed, the plan was executed without major modification and imposes its shape to the present day on the organisation of the Hanoi district that has become the political quarter of Ba Đình.

As an epilogue to the troubled episode of the destruction of the citadel, the conclusions of a report by the Ministry of Justice pointed out the irregularities and faults committed by Governor-General de Lanessan, within the framework of the contract with Bazin, but ruled out any sanction against him. One should not be overly surprised by the leniency he enjoyed despite the seriousness of the charges against him because, as the historian Charles Fourniau explains:

> It is appropriate here to place the case of the demolition of the citadel in the context of the time when the infrastructure and development projects in Indochina undertaken at the beginning of colonisation were bathed in an atmosphere of business, conflict of interest and corruption at all levels of the administration, where fortunes were built in a few years. From this point of view, the citadel affair is only an epiphenomenon in comparison with the scandals that shrouded

the implementation of other major works: the construction of the docks of Haiphong, the development of the port of Tourane, the awarding of the opium farm in Annam, etc. (Fourniau, 1989: 211)

* * *

From 1802 to 1848, the former Royal Citadel of Thăng Long underwent a series of acts of construction and destruction of its buildings, as well as transformations in the use and changes to the names of its symbolic and territorial spaces. At first glance, this long-term undertaking seems rather chaotic and confused, but it reflects the search by the first kings of the Nguyễn dynasty for a satisfactory compromise between their wish to erase the traces of the citadel's royal past and the need to keep up appearances vis-à-vis their Chinese overlords. This ambivalence in the city's status, stripped by the country's new masters of its rank as capital but conserving it in the eyes of the power that granted the legitimacy of investiture, is a key feature of Hanoi's history during the first half of the nineteenth century. After the diplomatic constraints were thrown off in 1848, the city was left to slumber until the French conquest.

In the space of fifteen years (1882–97), the colonial authorities overturned the entire structure of the city and, most particularly, the citadel. The citadel's transformation took place in three chronological stages. The first (1882–86) was dominated by ignorance of the cultural, religious and political significance of the former Royal Citadel of the Lý, Trần and Lê dynasties; its original vocation was utterly deformed through its utilitarian and secular use by the French army, yet the changes were not irreversible. The second stage (1887–93) was characterised by a series of deliberate acts of destruction of royal and mandarin buildings inside the citadel. The defining moment of this period was the demolition in 1886–87 of the Long Thiên (former Kính Thien) Palace, which marked the point of no return. The third stage (1894–97) was the logical outcome of this negation of the citadel's value in terms of history and identity. The systematic dismantling of its ramparts erased it from the landscape as a coherent architectural entity and the central organising principle of urban space, dissolving it into the colonial city's general development, as designed by the Hanoi municipal authority. This transformation reminded the whole population—Vietnamese and European—that power now lay 'definitively' in the hands of the civilian colonial authorities, who through a restructuring of the city sought to minimise the remaining traces of its history.

The dismantling of the citadel was important, yet was only one feature of the restructuring of urban space brought about by the colonial authorities from the 1880s. The Paul Doumer Bridge (1902) radically changed the city's configuration by opening it up to the river's opposite bank. The municipal theatre (1911), a poor replica of the Garnier Opera House in Paris, underlined the supremacy of European culture. The railway station (1902) was similarly designed to showcase European technological superiority. These grandiose structures were built to overwrite architectural references symbolising Vietnam's ancient history and culture and facilitate the penetration of the political, religious and cultural model of the new masters of Tonkin.

For Paul-Lévy and Sigaud, voluntarist spatial re-mouldings of this type are state-imposed manifestations of a new political order, which may also establish a new social order through the creation of new symbolic space (Paul-Lévy & Sigaud 1983: 248). What could be more symbolic than to rename places associated with geomantic spatial arrangements in use for several centuries, to destroy temples and pagodas and build Catholic and secular buildings on their ruins, to raze the former examination camp and replace it with an exhibition park, and so on?

It was only in the early years of the twentieth century that the notion of heritage, understood as a set of markers identifying a particular community and produced by a shared history, appeared in colonial Vietnam, mainly through the work of the EFEO, which was founded in Saigon in 1900 and moved to Hanoi in 1902. From 1905, the EFEO undertook to describe, document and restore the city's main pagodas, the Temple of Literature and the Thanh Hà Gate (Ô Quan Chưởng), intervention that saved the latter from the municipal authority's project for its destruction. On the basis of this work, a list was drawn up of seven major buildings that were given legal protection by the first decree classifying the 'Historical Monuments of Hanoi', issued on 14 November 1906 by the Résident Supérieur du Tonkin.[56] A second decree was issued on 25 May 1925.[57] This contained a list of nineteen protected monuments that included the last remaining vestiges of the old citadel: the North Gate, the Gate of Commencement, and the Flag Tower, which now became a symbol of the city.

Notes

1. It has become customary to say that the citadel was inspired by principles laid down by Vauban, Louis XIV's military engineer. In reality, it

drew more from the models developed by Bellamarto or Errard (Mangin 2006: 42).

2. *Đại Nam Thực Lục chính biên* (Đệ nhất kỷ quyển XVII; 2007: vol. 1, 504).

3. For example, from 1821–27, peasant leaders like Phan Bá Vành and mandarins haunted by nostalgia for the former Lê dynasty led thousands of poor peasants in a six-year resistance to the army, in the coastal region of Quảng Yên.

4. Gia Long did not want to recognise Chinese suzerainty, but as soon as he had possession of the Tây Sơn's seals and patents (on the capture of Huế on 13 June 1801), he sent an embassy to the Chinese emperor led by Trịnh Hoài Đức with instructions to: (1) return the seal and patents granted by the emperor to the Tây Sơn in 1793; and (2) make a declaration of fealty in the name of Gia Long, presenting him as the Lê dynasty's legitimate successor and asking the emperor to choose a new name for the country (Cadière 1916: 297–8). Referring to Vietnam's history, notably the conquest of the south, Gia Long suggested that the reunified territory be named Nam Việt, symbolising the return of peace and indicating the historical legitimacy of the new dynasty. But the emperor refused, considering that the characters Nam Việt (南越) were too close to those of Đông Tây Việt. He opted for Việt Nam, arguing: 'The first character Việt (越) shows that the country developed on the basis of heritage from previous generations. The second character Nam (南) underlined that the country had been enlarged through integration of the south. A new historical page thus opened. The new name is beautiful and legitimate. It is also clearly distinguished from the names Lưỡng Việt [two Việt countries inside China]'. *Đại Nam Thực Lục, chính biên* (Đệ nhất kỷ q. XXIII; 2007: vol. 1, 580–1). This first embassy was followed the same year by a second, requesting Gia Long's investiture (Boudet 1942: 14).

5. Note here that the rulers of the Nguyễn dynasty conferred on themselves the title of emperor (*Hoàng đế*) in contradiction to their status as vassals of China.

6. Châu (Chu) Tước Gate (lit. 'Red Bird') was one of the gates giving access to the inner enclosure of the Kính Thien Palace. Its name indicates that it was to the south: the red bird is the symbolic animal that presides over the south. This was undoubtedly the central gate of the three ornate gates in the façade of the inner wall (Huỳnh 1917: 101).

7. *Đại Nam Thực Lục, chính biên* (Đệ nhất kỷ q. XIX; 2007: vol. 1, 535).

8. *Đại Nam Thực Lục, chính biên* (Đệ nhất kỷ q. XXIV; 2007: vol. 1, 595).

9. *Khâm định Đại Nam hội điển sự lệ tục biên* (tập VII, quyển 206; 2005: 33).

10. *Đại Nam Thực Lục chính biên* (Đệ nhất kỷ q. XX; 2007: vol. 1, 543).

11. The original wall, Đại Đô thành, built in 1749 by the Trịnh lords to contain a revolt by Nguyễn Hữu Cầu, had eight gates. Their number was increased to 16 in 1831, nine of which opened onto the Red River. The only one remaining today is Ô Quan Chưởng (Thanh Hà), enlarged in

1817 to allow carts to pass. This gate was nearly destroyed in 1905, but was placed by the EFEO on the list of seven major (religious and secular) monuments designated as historical monuments in a decree issued on 14 November 1906 (Papin 2001: 154–6).

12. *Đại Nam Thực Lục chính biên* (Đệ nhất kỷ q. XXVI; 2007: vol. 1, 632).

13. Many descriptions of the citadel are available in the literature; here we summarise the main features indicated on the map.

14. These demilunes were also known to inhabitants as *giác thành* 'rampart angles' or *mang cá* 'fish gills' (Trần Hùng & Nguyễn Quốc Thông 1995: 37).

15. Đại Nam Nhất Thống Chí, t. III.

16. For example, the Tây Sơn built the city ramparts from Đông Hoa Gate to Đại Hưng Gate using bricks removed from Báo Thiên Monastery (Nguyễn Thừa Hỷ 1993: 59).

17. This ceremony's importance was such that it was one of the rare royal prerogatives that the Trịnh and Nguyễn lords did not dare transgress with the Lê. Thus, in 1724, Trịnh Cương refused to take the place of King Lê Dụ Tông, who was indisposed, and lead the rites himself, for fear of committing *lèse-majesté*. In the south, the Nguyễn were not encumbered by the king's presence, yet did not dare to adopt the honour for themselves, preferring to replace it with a substitute ceremony (Đặng Phương Nghi 1969: 44).

18. *Đại Nam Thực Lục, chính biên* (Đệ nhất kỷ q. XXIII; 2007: vol. 1, 590–1).

19. *Đại Nam Thực Lục chính biên* (Đệ nhất kỷ q. XXVII; 2007: vol. 1, 640).

20. *Bắc Thành địa dư chí* (1969: 4).

21. According to Vietnamese geomantic ideas that originated in China, the simultaneous presence of the Blue Dragon and White Tiger constitute two fundamental qualities of the earth: the presence of both is imperative to determine the site of a capital and its spatial organisation, with the royal place placed in the centre (Bezacier 1952: 191).

22. *Bắc Thành địa dư chí* (1969: 6).

23. The Rear Palace (Hậu Lâu), named the Ladies' Palace (Pagode des Dames) by the first French in Hanoi, was in a state of ruin by the end of the nineteenth century. It has been renovated several times and is today an emblematic vestige of the period.

24. *Đại Nam Thực Lục, chính biên* (Đệ nhị kỷ q. XI, 2007: vol. 2, 164).

25. *Khâm định Đại Nam hội điển sự lệ* (tập VII, 2005: 125).

26. *Bắc-Thành địa dư chí* ([1845]1969: 4)

27. *Đại Nam Thực Lục, chính biên* (Đệ nhất kỷ q. LIX; 2007: vol. 1, 981).

28. *Đại Nam Thực Lục, chính biên* (Đệ nhất kỷ q. XXXIII; 2007: vol. 1, 705).

29. The fourteenth year of Gia Long's reign (1815) is given in *Khâm định Đại Nam hội điển sự lệ tục biên* (2005: 34) without any mention of month, while the *Đại Nam Thực Lục, chính biên* (2007) includes a concise note dated 1816 (third lunar month, Canh Dần day): 'Repair of

the Royal Visit Palace at Bắc Thành. Report reached the king that, after so many years, the wood of the Kính Thiên Palace is in ruin. The king ordered the destruction of the old palace and the construction of a new one' (*Đệ nhất kỷ* q. LII; 2007: vol. 1, 922).

30. '1821 (Minh Mạng), winter, twelfth month. On the *Giáp ngọ* day, the enthronement ceremony ended. Very early that morning, the great royal carriage and the insignia of the cortege were prepared, from the courtyard of the Kính Thiên Palace to the Chu Tước Gate. Military elephants lined up from outside the Chu Tước to the jetty by Nhị River [Red River] making a very majestic scene.' *Đại Nam Thực Lục, chính biên* (*Đệ nhị kỷ* q. XII; 2007: vol. 2, 177).

31. This semantic shift has lasted to the present day, assisted by the preservation of the Kính Thiên's Palace's original foundation terrace, accessed on its southern side up the dragon staircase.

32. *Khâm định Đại Nam hội điển sự lệ tục biên* (tập VII, q. 206, 2005: 34).

33. *Đại Nam Thực Lục, chính biên* (*Đệ nhị kỷ* q. IV; 2007: vol. 2, 80–1).

34. Identical, with the exception of two place names changed in the 1831 administrative reform (Hanoi replaced Bắc Thành and Bắc Ninh replaced Kinh Bắc) and the suppression of the passage on the funding of construction work. *Đại Nam Thực Lục, chính biên* (*Đệ tam kỷ* q. VII; 2007: vol. 6, 141–2).

35. *Khâm định Đại Nam hội điển sự lệ tục biên* (tập VII, q. 206, 2005: 38).

36. The bay was the unit used to regulate the size of public and private buildings. This construction principle gave buildings considerable flexibility, as their size could easily be increased or reduced by the addition or removal of one or more bays.

37. *Khâm định Đại Nam hội điển sự lệ tục biên* (tập VII, q. 206, 2005: 43).

38. *Đại Nam Thực Lục, chính biên* (*Đệ nhị kỷ* q. LXXVI; 2007: vol. 3, 237–8).

39. *Khâm định Đại Nam hội điển sự lệ tục biên* (tập VII, q. 206, 2005: 39).

40. 'As soon as the country regained peace, we established diplomatic relaions (*thông hiếu*) with the Qing, to change the country's name to Việt Nam, and to inform the emperor that the royal capital was in Phú Xuân [Huế] and no longer in Thăng Long as under the Đinh, Lý, Trần, Lê dynasties.' *Đại Nam Thực Lục, chính biên* (Đệ tam kỷ q. LXXVI; vol. 6, 2007: 1069).

41. *Đại Nam Thực Lục, chính biên* (Đệ tam kỷ q. LXXVI; 2007: vol. 6, 1069).

42. *Khâm định Đại Nam hội điển sự lệ* (tập VII, 2005: 33).

43. On this subject, Mgr. Pellerin castigated the conduct of this procession in these terms: 'The Chinese profess great contempt for the Annamites: also, during the journey, they subjected them to a thousand vexations, wasting with impunity the provisions amassed for their use". Mgr. Pellerin, *Annales de la Propagation de la Foi*, (1850, tome 22) quoted by Cadière (1916: 302).

44. There is no notice for these two photographs (VIE 23474 and 23478). They are marked simply: 'Taken in Hué, December 1954'.

45. For the translation of the captions into Vietnamese, our thanks to Nguyễn Văn Nguyên of the Institute of Hán-Nôm Studies.

46. From north to south: the residence of the mandarin in charge of the regional department of justice (*hình tào quan*), the residence of the head of cabinet of the regional Department of Justice (*Hình tào lang trung chủ sự*), the regional Department of the Ministry of Justice (*Hình tào ty (tư) viên* – 刑曹司員), the regional Department of the Ministry of Military Affairs (*Binh tào ty (tư) viên* 兵曹司員, the residence of the mandarin in charge of the regional Department of Military Affairs (*Binh tào quan* 兵曹官), and the Department of the Military Rolls (*Binh tịch sở* 兵籍所).

47. The pagoda denomination '*chùa*' used on the 1873 plan seems inaccurate and should be replaced by temple '*miếu – đền*'.

48. Imperial rice fields reserved for the 'Opening of the Furrow' (Tịch Điền 籍田) ceremony; esplanade dedicated to the deities of 'Soil and Harvest' (*Xã Tắc đàn*).

49. Tam Sơn (三山): Three Summits Mount (mound) (also called 'the ear of the city'); Khán Sơn (看山): Khán Mount (mound); Thổ Sơn (土山): Earth Mount.

50. Among others: Bonnal (1925), Hocquard (1999), Madrolle (1925), and Masson (1929).

51. For example, the SHD dossier c10H1-d1 'Conquête du Tonkin—1ère partie—premières opérations militaires (1867–83)' contains chronological details of the events and circumstances of the first capture of the Hanoi citadel, its evacuation on 12 February 1874, and second capture in 1882. Specific details are also given of the military operations, forces mobilised by both sides and respective casualty numbers and material losses.

52. In a letter from the Minister of External Relations of the Court of Hué to the Governor of Cochinchina, Charles Antoine Francis Thomson, dated 28 March 1883, the Emperor protested against the second capture of the citadel of Hanoi in these terms: 'Lately Commandant Rivière bombarded the citadel, killed mandarins and soldiers, and settled in the Hành-cung; he also seized public funds and usurped the right to collect taxes; these are acts of flagrant violation of the peace treaty concluded between the two nations. What my government desires is the strict observance of the treaty for the freedom of trade; it hopes that the negotiations in Peking between Mr. Plenipotentiary Bửu and Mr. Lý Trung Dường, which can only be favourable [...] If the two countries did not agree to back down [and respect each other], complications, always very disgraceful and of no use whatsoever, would result, and this must be avoided at all costs. My government is always animated by its feelings of faith and friendship towards France.' ('Avis de la prise de la citadelle, 1882', ANOM Fonds

Amiraux GGI d13922). But this call for restraint and respect for past agreements went unheeded.

53. Hocquard makes a location error: only the residence of the mandarin in charge of finance (*Bố chánh đường*) is located on the left near the shops; the residences of the governor-general of the province (*dinh Tổng đốc đường*) and the provincial mandarin in charge of justice (*Án sát đường*) are in the northeast quarter.

54. However, this vision was not univocal, as shown by this reflection of Sergeant Frédéric Garcin, who expressed his disapproval of the disrespectful occupation of the Long Thiên Palace, known as the Pagoda of the King's Spirit: 'I am resuming my visit to the Citadel. We arrive at the Pagoda of the King's Spirit. It is a masterpiece of Annamite architecture. With what art these fantastic animals – large stone dragons – are sculpted! What a striking appearance they give to the pagoda! And we call the Annamites savage! Are we then the sons of a much higher civilisation, we who, in this beautiful monument…'. Frédéric Garcin, *Lettres d'un sergent* (1884–85, R. Chapelot éditeur) quoted by Mangin (1996: 101).

55. See p. 71 of the 1897 report by La Borde (Director of Civil Affairs and the Seal at the Ministry of Justice) entitled 'Demolition of the citadel' (ANOM BIB SOM d2637).

56. 'Documents administratifs', BEFEO 6, 1906, pp. 492–5.

57. 'Documents administratifs', BEFEO 26, 1926, pp. 546–7, 551–4.

List of Archives

Archives Nationales d'Outre-Mer (ANOM), Aix-en-Provence, France

GGI d13922	Avis de la prise de la citadelle, 1882
GGI d7751	Démolition de la citadelle de Hanoï (contrat Bazin) 1893–94
GGI d7752	Démolition de la citadelle de Hanoï, marché de gré à gré 1894–97
GGI d7753	Exploitation du contrat par la société générale d'Etudes industrielles et commerciales pour la Chine et l'Indo-Cine 1894–97
GGI d20244	Ordonnances du 3 octobre 1888: 1° érigeant en concessions françaises les terrains d'Hanoi, Haiphong et Tourane; 2° accordant aux citoyens français le droit de posséder en Annam et au Tonkin.
BIB SOM d2637	La Borde, 1897, (directeur du Affaires civiles et du Sceau au ministère de la Justice), 'Rapport – Démolition de la citadelle', in 'Rapport au Président de la République française présenté par les ministres des finances et des

colonies sur l'état de la liquidation financière de l'Annam et du Tonkin; [suivi des] Travaux de la Commission extraparlementaire chargée d'examiner les contrats et engagements du protectorat de l'Annam et du Tonkin', pp. 71–82.

Archives: Service Historique de la Défense (SHD), Vincennes, France

c10H1-d1	Conquête du Tonkin – 1ère partie – premières opérations militaires (1867–83)
c10H1-d6	Conquête du Tonkin – Annexes (1883–84)
c10H1-d2	Conquête du Tonkin – Historique (16/12/1883–28/8/1884)
c10H1-d1	Conquête du Tonkin – 1ère partie – premières opérations militaires (1867–83)
c10H6-d1	Rapport du commandant Berthe de Villiers sur la prise de la citadelle, avril 1882
c10H6-d9	Documents diplomatiques et opérations militaires (1885–86), Général de Courcy
c10H20-d1	Historique du 4ème Régiment d'artillerie coloniale, stationné au Tonkin (1882–1930)
c10H20-d8	Rôles du service du Génie au Tonkin (1875–88)
c10H20-d9	Rôle des officiers du génie dans la conquête, la pacification et l'équipement de l'Indochine (1884–1929)
c10H20-d11	Historique de la direction d'artillerie Annam-Tonkin (1888–1930)

Abbreviations

c	carton
d	dossier
GGI	Gouvernement Général de l'Indochine

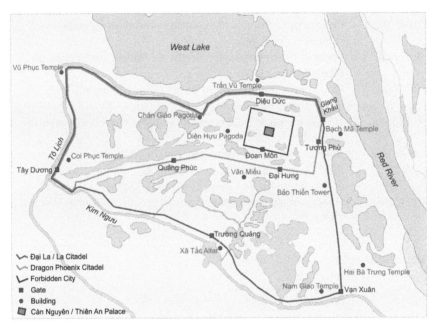

Map 20. Ramparts and monuments of the Imperial Citadel of Thăng Long: Lý and Trần dynasties (Federico Barocco for the EFEO).

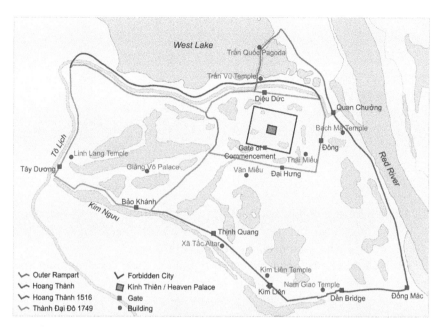

Map 21. Ramparts and monuments of the Imperial Citadel of Thăng Long: Lê dynasty (Federico Barocco for the EFEO).

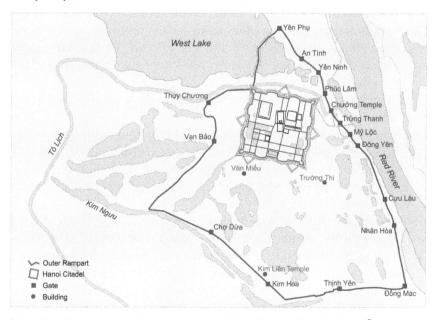

Map 22. Ramparts and monuments of the Hanoi Citadel: Nguyễn dynasty (Federico Barocco for the EFEO).

GLOSSARY

An Dương Vương: Reign name of Thục Phán, from 257 BC, legendary first king of Âu Lạc (formed from two previous realms, Âu Việt and Lạc Việt), who established his capital at Cổ Loa.

Ba Đình Club: The colonial *cercle sportif* built in 1930. Its swimming and tennis facilities were later used by Vietnam's party nomenclatura. The building on Ba Đình Square was demolished in 2008.

Ba Đình National Assembly Building: see National Assembly Building.

Bắc Thành (lit. Citadel of the North): Administrative region consisting of eleven northern provinces ruled by a governor-general (*tổng trấn*), established by Gia Long in 1802, abolished by Minh Mạng in 1831.

Càn Nguyên Palace: Lý Công Uẩn's name for the central palace of Thăng Long Imperial Citadel. His successor, Lý Thái Tông, renamed the rebuilt palace on this site Thiên An. Under the Lê the palace was named Kính Thiên.

Cảnh Hưng reign era: 1740–86, corresponding to the reign of Lê Hiển Tông.

Cao Biền: See Gao Pian.

Cẩu Mẫu and Cẩu Nhi: Dogs linked in several portents with the foundation of Thăng Long (in the Year of the Dog, 1010). King Lý Công Uẩn saw a bitch (Cẩu Mẫu) having eight puppies (Cẩu Nhi), prefiguring the eight kings of the Lý dynasty. A temple bearing the dogs' names was founded by Trúc Bạch Lake.

Chu Văn An (1292–1370): Mandarin and literatus of the Trần period, he taught at the Temple of Literature before retiring in scholarly seclusion after his memorial on corrupt officials displeased the king.

Cổ Loa: Site of the citadel (Đông Anh district, Hanoi) at An Dương Vương's capital (third century BC), used by the Early Lý (sixth century) and Ngô (tenth century) dynasties.

Cột Cờ: See Flag Tower.

Cửa Bắc: See North Gate.

D67: Name of the bunker built in 1967 under the former Kính Thiên Palace and used by the DRV's wartime military command.

Đại Hưng Gate: The Imperial Citadel's south gate (also known as Cửa Nam).

Đại La: See Gao Pian.

Đan Trì: The Lê dynasty's name for Long Trì.

Đình: Communal house, temple.

Đoan Môn: Gate of Commencement, the main gate to the Forbidden City at the heart of the Imperial Citadel, to its south. The gate visible today was built under the Lê and extended under the Nguyễn.

Đông Đô (lit. eastern capital): Name for Thăng Long under the Hồ dynasty.

Dragon King (Long Vương): According to a legend about Lê Lợi (King Lê Thái Tổ, r. 1428–33), this deity lived in Hoàn Kiếm Lake and gave the future king a sword he used to defeat the Ming dynasty army.

Dragon Phoenix (Long Phượng) Citadel: The middle rampart around the Imperial Citadel at Thăng Long of the Lý and Trần periods mentioned in historical sources. Also known as Dragon Citadel and Phoenix Citadel. See Imperial Citadel.

DRV: Democratic Republic of Vietnam (1945–76).

Đường Cao Tông: See Gaozong emperor.

Flag Tower (Cột Cờ, Kỳ Đài): Tower built under the Nguyễn dynasty (1812), known to the French as Mirador.

Gate of Commencement: See Đoan Môn.

Gao Pian (Cao Biền, Cao Vương): Governor of Vietnam under Chinese rule (from 865–8), he established his capital at Tống Bình (present-day Hanoi), building a double rampart from which the city took its name until 1010: Đại La Thành (lit. great external rampart).

Gia Định: Administrative region consisting of five southern provinces ruled by a governor-general, established by Gia Long in 1802, abolished by Minh Mạng in 1832.

Hành cung: See royal visit palace.

Hậu Lâu: See Rear Palace.

Hoa Lư: Site of the capital of the ninth-century Ngô and Đinh dynasties (Hoa Lư district, Ninh Bình).

Hoàng Diệu: Nineteenth-century governor of the north who committed suicide after the fall of Hanoi Citadel to French forces in 1882. After 1954, his name was given to the former Boulevard Victor Hugo in the citadel area of Hanoi.

Hoàng Thành: See Imperial Citadel.

Hồ dynasty: Short-lived dynasty (1400–07) founded by Hồ Quý Ly, with its capital in Thanh Hóa.

Hồng Đức: Reign era of King Lê Thánh Tông, 1470–97.

Imperial Citadel: The Lê dynasty's name for the middle of the three walls that surrounded Thăng Long. It was known as Dragon Citadel, Phoenix Citadel and Dragon Phoenix Citadel under the Lý and Trần. See Dragon Phoenix Citadel.

Kính Thiên Palace (lit. palace of reverence for heaven): Lê and Nguyễn dynasty name for the central palace of the Imperial Citadel, which served as the monarch's audience hall and later as the Nguyễn monarchs' residence during visits to Thăng Long. Destroyed in 1815, only its Lê-period staircase with dragon banisters still stands. The palace site, with a bunker dug underneath it in 1967, was used for the DRV's war command during the 1960s and 1970s.

Kyongju: Site of the Korean Silla dynasty's capital from the first to tenth centuries (Kyongsan province).

Long Đỗ (lit. the 'dragon's nombril'): The tutelary spirit of Thăng Long, worshipped at the temple of the White Horse (Bạch Mã) at 76 Hàng Buồm Street, Hanoi.

Long Trì: Dragon Terrace, the courtyard located in front of the royal audience hall (Lý and Trần dynasties).

Luy Lâu: Site of the third-century capital of Vietnam (Jiaozhi) under Chinese rule (Thanh Khương commune, Thuận Thành district, Bắc Ninh).

Nam Giao shrine (*đàn*): Shrine for the royal ceremony heralding the start of the year, a ritual ploughing of the first field.

Nara: Site of Japan's eighth-century capital (Nara prefecture).

National Assembly Building: The DRV's first major post-independence public architecture, built in 1959 in time for the Third Party Congress in September 1960, demolished in 2008 to make way for a new building completed in 2014.

Nguyễn lords: Rulers of the region south from today's Quảng Bình, sixteenth to eighteenth centuries.

Nguyễn Trãi (1380–1442): Mandarin and literatus, participant in Lê Lợi's uprising against the Chinese, suspected assassin of King Lê Thái Tông, executed with the members of his three families (his own, his wife's and his mother's).

North Gate (Cửa Bắc): The Hanoi Citadel's North Gate, built by the Nguyễn dynasty, accessed today from Phan Đình Phùng Street.

Nùng Mount: A mound of geomantic significance chosen as the site for the Imperial Citadel's central palace.

Quần Ngựa: See Racecourse.

Racecourse (Quần Ngựa): Site of French-era racecourse located to the west of the Hanoi Citadel (between today's Hoàng Hoa Thám and Đội Cấn Streets), excavated during the colonial period, where earlier scholars suspected the Imperial Citadel was located.

Rear Palace (Hậu Lâu): Also named the Palace of the Pacified North (Tĩnh Bắc), built in 1821.

Royal visit palace (*hành cung*): Palaces in the provinces for the king's use.

SRV: Socialist Republic of Vietnam (1976–).

Tây Đô (lit. western capital): Capital established by the Hồ dynasty (Tây Giai commune, Vĩnh Lộc district, Thanh Hóa).

Tây Sơn: Led by Nguyễn Nhạc and Nguyễn Huệ (Quang Trung), the Tây Sơn Rebellion started at Tây Sơn in the hills of modern An Khê town (Gia Lai province) in the 1770s, overthrew the Nguyễn and Trịnh lords and the Lê dynasty and captured Thăng Long in 1789; the Tây Sơn dynasty was overthrown in 1802 by Nguyễn Ánh (Gia Long), founder of the Nguyễn dynasty.

Temple of Literature (Văn Miếu Quốc Tử Giám): Founded by King Lý Thánh Tông as a Confucian temple (*văn miếu*) in 1070; site of Vietnam's royal academy (*quốc tử giám*) which functioned there from 1076 to 1779.

Thiên An Palace: See Càn Nguyên Palace.

Tống Bình: See Gao Pian.

Trấn: Administrative unit of territory corresponding to Vietnam's provinces, renamed *tỉnh* in Minh Mạng's 1831 administrative reform.

Trịnh lords: Rulers of the region north from today's Quảng Bình, sixteenth to eighteenth centuries.

Xi'an (Chang'an): Site of China's capital (Shanxi province) used by the Han, Sui and Tang dynasties, third to sixth centuries.

Xã Tắc: Altar (*đàn*) for the worship of the spirits of Heaven and Earth.

BIBLIOGRAPHY

Abbreviations

ANOM	Archives Nationales d'Outre-Mer
BAVH	*Bulletin des Amis du Vieux Huế*
BEFEO	*Bulletin de l'École française d'Extrême-Orient*
BSEI	*Bulletin de la Société des Études Indochinoises*
EFEO	École française d'Extrême-Orient
IDEO	Imprimerie d'Extrême-Orient
JA	*Journal Asiatique*
KHXH	Khoa học Xã hội
Nxb	Nhà xuất bản
SHD	Service Historique de la Défense

Maps

Institute of Hán-Nôm Studies, Vietnam Academy of Social Sciences, Hanoi, Vietnam

Reference	Document	Map
A.2499	Hồng Đức bản đồ	
A.2628	Thiên hạ bản đồ	
A.1106	Bản quốc dư đồ	
A.1603	Nam Việt bản đồ	Trung đô Thăng Long thành nhất phủ nhị huyện đồ
A.2300	Thiên Nam tứ chí lộ đồ	
A.3034	An Nam hình thắng đồ	Trung đô nhất phủ nhị huyện hình thắng chi đồ
A.2716	Thiên tải nhàn đàm	Thăng Long thành Phụng Thiên phủ nhất phủ nhị huyện
		Nam hành địa diện tự Thăng Long chí Cao Biền
A.2006	Thiên tải nhàn đàm	Trung đô nhất phủ nhị huyện chi hình
A.1081	Toàn tập thiên Nam lộ đồ	Trung đô sơn xuyên hình thắng chi đồ nhất phủ nhị huyện tam thấp lục phường
A.1174	Thiên tải nhàn đàm	
A.2531		An Nam quốc trung đô tính thập tam thừa tuyên hình thắng đồ hoạ

continued from previous page

Reference	Document	Map
A.1362	Thiên hạ bản đồ	Trung đô xứ nhất phủ nhị huyện tam thập lục phường nhất danh Phụng Thiên phủ
A.343	Địa chí	
A.30	Thiên tải nhàn đàm	Thăng Long thành Phụng Thiên phủ nhất phủ nhị huyện
A.414	Càn khôn nhất lãm	
VHt.41	Hồng Đức bản đồ	Trung đô nhất phủ nhị huyện hình thắng chi đồ
A.73	Thiên Nam tứ chí lộ đồ	Trung đô Thăng Long thành nhất phủ nhị huyện đồ

Imperial chronicles, histories and geographies

Bắc Thành địa dư chí [Gazetteer of the northern provinces] (books 1 & 2, written by Lê Chất 1818–21, revised and published by Nguyễn Văn Lý 1845). Hanoi: Nxb Văn Hóa, 1969.

Cefu yuangui 冊府元龜 [Antecedents from the Palace of Archives] (written 1013), ed. Wang Qinruo (王欽若) et al. Hong Kong: Zhonghua, 1960.

Ch'oe Ch'iwŏn (崔致遠), *Guiyuan bigeng ji jiaozhu* 桂苑筆耕集校注 [Tilling with my brush at Cassia Grove] (written 880–5), ed. Dang Yinping 党銀平. Beijing: Zhong-hua, 2007.

Da Qing yitong zhi 大清一統志 [Comprehensive geography of the Great Qing] (written 1743), *Jiaqing chongxiu yitong zhi* 嘉慶重修一統志 edn. Shanghai: Shanghai Commercial Press, 1966.

Đại Nam nhất thống chí [Encyclopedia of Đại Nam]. Hanoi: Nxb KHXH, 1971.

Đại Nam nhất thống chí [Encyclopedia of Đại Nam], tr. Phạm Trọng Điềm. Huế: Nxb Thuận Hóa, vol. III, 2006.

Đại Nam Thực Lục, chính biên [Veritable record of Đại Nam, main compilation]. Hanoi: Nxb Giáo Dục, 2007.

Đại Việt quốc thư [Diplomatic correspondence of Đại Việt]. Saigon: TT Học liệu (Bộ Giáo dục), 1972.

Đại Việt sử ký toàn thư [Complete annals of Đại Việt] (compiled 1479 by Ngô Sĩ Liên 吳士連, completed 1697). Hanoi: Nxb. KHXH, 1983–85, reprint 1998.

Đại Việt sử ký toàn thư 大越史記全書 [Complete annals of Đại Việt] (ed. Chen Jinghe 陳荊和). Tokyo: Tōkyō daigaku tōyō bunka kenkyūjo, 1984.

Đại Việt sử ký toàn thư [Complete annals of Đại Việt] (bản in Nội các quan bản). Hanoi: Nxb. KHXH, 1993.

Đại Việt sử ký toàn thư [Complete annals of Đại Việt] (bản in Nội các quan bản). Hanoi: Nxb. KHXH, reprint 2010.

Đại Việt sử ký tục biên [Annals of Đại Việt—supplement]. Hanoi: Nxb KHXH, 1991.

Đại Việt sử lược [Abridged annals of Đại Việt] (trans. Trần Quốc Vượng). Hanoi: Nxb Văn sử địa, 1960.

Daojiao lingyan ji 道教靈驗記 [Divine manifestations of Daoism], in *Du Guangting jizhuan shizhong jijiao* 杜光庭記傳十種輯校 [Collected edition of ten narrative works by Du Guangting (850–933)], (ed. Luo Zhengming 羅爭鳴), Beijing: Zhonghua, 2013.

Đồng Khánh địa dư chí [The descriptive geography of the Emperor Đồng Khánh/ La géographie descriptive de l'empereur Đồng Khánh] (compiled 1886–88), ed. Ngô Đức Thọ, Nguyễn Văn Nguyên & Philippe Papin. Hanoi: EFEO/ École Pratique des Hautes Études/Viện Nghiên cứu Hán Nôm, Nxb Thế giới, 2003.

Dương Bá Cung. 'Hà Nội địa dư' [Gazetteer of Hanoi] (compiled 1851, Viện Nghiên cứu Hán Nôm, ref. A.1154), in *Địa chí Thăng Long–Hà Nội trong thư tịch Hán Nôm* [Hanoi gazetteers in the bibliography of works in Hán-Nôm]. Hanoi: Nxb Thế giới, 2007.

Fan Chuo 樊綽 (fl. 860–73). *Man shu jiaozhu* 蠻書校注 [Book of Man], ed. Xiang Da 向達. Beijing: Zhonghua, 1962.

Han shu 漢書 [History of the Han] (written 1st century CE). Beijing: Zhonghua, 1962.

Hou Han shu 後漢書 [History of the Later Han] (written 5th century). Beijing: Zhonghua, 1965.

Jiu Tang shu 舊唐書 [Old history of the Tang] (written 945). Beijing: Zhonghua, 1975.

Khâm định Đại Nam hội điện sự lệ [Đại Nam imperial register of institutions and regulations]. Huế: Nxb Thuận Hóa, 1993.

Khâm định Đại Nam hội điển sự lệ, Tập VII Quyển 205–223 [Đại Nam imperial register of institutions and regulations, vol. VII, books 205–23]. Huế: Nxb Thuận Hóa, 2005.

Khâm định Việt sử thông giám cương mục, chính biên [Imperially ordered text and commentary of the complete mirror of Viet history, main text]. Hanoi: Nxb Giáo dục, 1998 (1855).

Lê Hữu Trác. *Thượng kinh ký sự* [Chronicle of a journey to the capital] (written 1783, first published 1885), tr. Phan Võ. Hanoi, Nxb Văn Hóa, 1959.

Lê Quý Đôn. *Đại Việt thông sử* [History of Đại Việt]. Hanoi: Nxb KHXH, 1978.

Lê Tắc 黎崱. *An Nam chí lược* 安南志略 [Concise history of Annam] (written early 14th century), ed. Wu Shangqing 武尚清. Beijing: Zhonghua, 1995.

Lê Tắc 黎崱. *An Nam chí lược* [Concise history of Annam] (written early 14th century). Hanoi: Nxb Lao động, 2009.

Liu Zongyuan ji 柳宗元集 [Collected works of Liu Zongyuan (773–819)], ed. Wu Wenzhi 吳文治 et al. Beijing: Zhonghua, 1979.

Lý Tế Xuyên 李濟川 (fl. 1329). *Việt điện u linh tập* 越甸幽靈集 [Departed spirits of the Viet Realm] (expanded critical recension 新訂較評 of 1774), in *Yuenan hanwen xiaoshuo congkan* 越南漢文小說叢刊, ser. 2, vol. 2, ed. Chen Qinghao 陳慶浩 et al. Taipei: EFEO/Taiwan xuesheng shuju, 1992.

Pei Xing chuanqi 裴鉶傳奇 [Transmitted singularities by Pei Xing (ca. 825–ca. 880)], ed. Zhou Lengqie 周楞伽. Shanghai: Shanghai guji, 1980.

Phạm Đình Hổ. *Vũ Trung tùy bút* [Notes taken on rainy days], tr. Nguyễn Hữu Tiến. Hanoi: Nxb Văn Hoá, 1960.

Phan Huy Chú. *Lịch Triều Hiến Chương Loại Chí* [Annals of the laws and institutions of successive dynasties] (written under Gia Long, 1802–20). Hanoi: Nxb Sử Học, 1960.

Quan Tang shi 全唐詩 [Complete Tang poetry] (originally published 1705). Beijing: Zhonghua, 1979.

Quan Tang wen 全唐文 [Complete Tang prose] (originally published 1814). Beijing: Zhonghua, 1983.

Quan Tang wen bubian 全唐文補編 [Supplement to complete Tang prose], ed. Chen Shangjun 陳尚君. Beijing: Zhonghua, 2005.

Sima Guang 司馬光. *Zizhi tongjian* 資治通鑑 [Comprehensive mirror in aid of government] (originally published 1084). Beijing: Zhonghua, 1956.

Song shi 宋史 [History of the Song] (originally published 1346), ed. Toghto 脫脫. Beijing: Zhonghua, 1977.

Sun Guangxian 孫光憲 (896–968). *Beimeng suoyan* 北夢瑣言 [Trivia from Beimeng], ed. Lin Aiyuan 林艾園. Shanghai: Shanghai guji, 1981.

Taiping guangji 太平廣記 [Extensive records for the Taiping era] (originally published 978), ed. Li Fang 李昉 et al. Beijing: Zhonghua, 1961.

Tang da zhaoling ji 唐大詔令集 [Grand edicts and statutory orders of the Tang] (originally published 1070). Beijing: Zhonghua, 2008.

Việt sử lược 越史略 [Summary history of Vietnam] (ca. 1377–88). *Shoushan ge congshu* 守山閣叢書, Shanghai: Bogu zhai, 1922 reprint.

Việt sử lược [Summary history of Vietnam], tr. Trần Quốc Vượng. Hanoi: Nxb Văn Sử Địa, 1960.

Wang Pu 王溥 (922–82). *Tang hui yao* 唐會要 [Essential statutes of the Tang]. Shanghai: Shanghai guji, 2006.

Xin Tang shu 新唐書 [New history of the Tang] (originally published 1060). Beijing: Zhonghua, 1975.

Yuan yitong zhi 元一統志 [Comprehensive geography of the Yuan] (originally published 1294), rev. Bo-lan-xi 孛蘭盻 et al. (1303), ed. Zhao Wanli 趙萬裏. Shanghai: Zhonghua, 1966.

Zhou Qufei 周去非. *Lingwai daida jiaozhu* 嶺外代答校注 [Representative answers from the Region beyond the mountains] (originally published 1178), ed. Yang Wuquan 楊武泉. Beijing: Zhonghua, 1999.

Colonial and secondary sources

Anderson, James. *The Rebel Den of Nùng Trí Cao: Loyalty and Identity along the Sino-Vietnamese Frontier*. Seattle: University of Washington Press & Singapore: NUS Press, 2007.

Azambre, George. 'Les origines de Hà-Nội', *BSEI* XXXIII, 3 (1958): 1–40.

Backus, Charles. *The Nan-chao Kingdom and T'ang China's Southwestern Frontier.* Cambridge: Cambridge University Press, 1981.

Bảo tàng lịch sử Việt Nam năm 1979 [Museum of Vietnamese History 1979], Hanoi.

Bảo tàng lịch sử Việt Nam. *Nội san Viện Bảo tàng lịch sử* [History Museum intramural bulletin]. 1 December 1979.

Baron, Samuel. 'A Description of the Kingdom of Tonqueen' (written 1680s, originally published 1732), in *Views of Seventeenth-Century Vietnam, Christoforo Borri on Cochinchina and Samuel Baron on Tonkin*, intr. Olga Dror & K.W. Taylor. Ithaca, N.Y.: Cornell University Press, 2006.

Beckwith, Christopher I. *The Tibetan Empire in Central Asia: A History of the Struggle for Great Power among Tibetans, Turks, Arabs, and Chinese during the Early Middle Ages.* Princeton: Princeton University Press, 1987.

Bezacier, Louis. 'Conception du plan des anciennes citadelles-capitales du Nord Viêt-Nam', *JA* CCXL, 2 (1952): 185–95.

———. *L'art vietnamien.* Paris: Éditions de l'Union Française, 1958.

Blackmore, Michael. 'The Ethnological Problems Connected with Nanchao', in *Symposium on Historical, Archaeological and Linguistic Studies on Southern China, South-East Asia and the Hong Kong region*, ed. Frederick Drake. Hong Kong: Hong Kong University Press, 1961, pp. 60–8.

Boltz, Judith M. 'Not by the Seal of Office Alone: New Weapons in Battles with the Supernatural', in *Religion and Society in T'ang and Sung China*, ed. Patricia Buckley Ebrey & Peter N. Gregory. Honolulu: University of Hawai'i Press, 1993.

Bonnal, Raymond. *Au Tonkin 1872–1881–1886 – Notes et souvenirs.* Hanoi: Éditions de la Revue Indochinoise, 1925.

Boudet, Paul. *Les archives des empereurs d'Annam et l'histoire annamite*, Hanoi: 39ᵉ Cahier de la Société de Géographie de Hanoi, IDEO, 1942.

Bourrin, Claude. *Le Vieux Tonkin 1890–1894.* Hanoi: IDEO, 1941.

Bùi Minh Trí & Tống Trung Tín. 'Giá trị nổi bật toàn cầu, tính chân thực và tính toàn vẹn khu trung tâm Hoàng thành Thăng Long–Hà Nội: Từ phân tích, đánh giá di tích khảo cổ học' [Global outstanding values, truthfulness and perfectibility of the central Thăng Long–Hanoi Imperial Citadel from the analysis and assessment of archaeological site], *Khảo cổ học* [Archaeology] 4 (2010): 27–42.

Bùi Tuyết Mai, ed. *1000 năm Thăng Long–Hà Nội* [1000 years of Thăng Long–Hanoi]. Hanoi: Nxb Văn hóa Thông tin, 2004.

Cadière, Léopold. 'Comment l'empereur de Chine conféra l'investiture à Tu-Duc', *BAVH* 3 (1916): 297–314.

Chavannes, Edouard. 'Une inscription du royaume de Nan-tchao', *JA* 19 (1900): 387–450.

Chen Junmou 陳君謀. 'Pei Xing ji qi *Chuanqi* 裴鉶及其《傳奇》' [Pei Xing and his *Chuanqi*], *Suzhou daxue xuebao* 蘇州大學學報 [Journal of Suzhou University] 1 (1982): 17–25.

Chung-kuo tu-liang-heng shih (History of weights and measures in China/ *Trung Quốc độ lượng hoành sử*). Shanghai: Shanghai Shu-tien (Nxb Thượng Hải thư điếm), 1984, reprint of 1937 ed.

Clark, Hugh R. 'The southern kingdoms between the T'ang and the Sung', in *The Cambridge History of China*, vol. 5, part 1, ed. D. Twitchett & P.J. Smith. Cambridge: Cambridge University Press, 2009, pp. 133–205.

Đặng Phương Nghi. *Les institutions publiques du Viet-Nam au XVIIIe siècle*. Paris: EFEO, 1969.

Đặng Xuân Khanh. 'Thăng Long cổ tích khảo' (compiled 1956, Viện Nghiên cứu Hán Nôm, ref. HVv.1271), in *Địa chí Thăng Long–Hà Nội trong thư tịch Hán Nôm* [Hanoi gazetteers in the bibliography of works in Hán-Nôm]. Hanoi: Nxb Thế giới, 2007.

Ditter, Alexei. 'The commerce of commemoration: commissioned *muzhiming* in the mid-to late Tang', *Tang Studies* 32 (2014): 21–46.

Đỗ Văn Ninh. *Thành cổ Việt Nam* [Vietnamese ancient citadels]. Hanoi: Nxb. KHXH, 1983.

_____. 'Tìm hiểu vài loại gạch cổ khai quật ở Ba Đình' [Research on ancient brick types excavated at Ba Đình], *Xưa Nay* 203 (2004): 49–50

Doumer, Paul. *Situation de l'Indochine (1897–1901)*. Hanoi: F.H. Schneider, 1902.

Dudbridge, Glen. *Religious Experience and Lay Society in T'ang China: A Reading of Tai Fu's Kuang-i chi*. Cambridge: Cambridge University Press, 1995.

_____. *A Portrait of Five Dynasties China: From the Memoirs of Wang Renyu (880–956)*. Oxford: Oxford University Press, 2013.

Dương Thị The & Phạm Thị Thoa, eds. *Tên làng xã Việt Nam đầu thế kỷ XIX, thuộc các tỉnh từ Nghệ Tĩnh trở ra (các tổng trấn xã danh bị lãm)* [Vietnamese village names of the early 19th century in the provinces north from Nghệ Tĩnh]. Hanoi: Nxb KHXH, 1981.

Feilden, Bernard M. & Jukka Jokilehto. *Management Guidelines for World Cultural Heritage Sites*. Rome: ICCROM, 1985.

Fourniau, Charles. *Annam-Tonkin 1885–1896 – Lettrés et paysans vietnamiens face à la conquête coloniale*. Paris: L'Harmattan, 1989.

Gardiner, Ken. 'Vietnam and Southern Han (I)', *Papers on Far Eastern History* 23 (1981): 64–110.

_____. 'Vietnam and Southern Han (II)', *Papers on Far Eastern History* 28 (1983): 23–48.

Gaultier, Marcel. *Gia-Long*. Saigon: S.I.L.I.C. Ardin, 1933.

_____. *Minh-Mang*. Paris: Larose, 1935.

Golas, Peter J. 'Chinese Mining: Where Was the Gunpowder?' in *Explorations in the History of Science and Technology in China*, ed. Li Guohao et al. Shanghai: Shanghai Chinese Classics Publishing House, 1982.

Hà Bích Liên. 'Nghệ thuật cổ Chămpa – Những dấu ấn của giao lưu văn hoá khu vực' [Art of ancient Champa—vestiges of regional cultural interactions]. *Nghiên cứu Đông Nam Á* 2 (1998): 75–80.

Hà Văn Tấn. 'Từ cột kinh Phật năm 973 vừa phát hiện ở Hoa Lư' [A Buddhist pillar dated 973 recently discovered at Hoa Lư], in *Theo dấu các văn hoá cổ* [Following the traces of ancient cultures], ed. Hà Văn Tấn. Hanoi: Nxb KHXH, pp. 786–815.

Hamada Kōsaku 濱田耕策, ed. *Kodai Higashi Ajia no chishikijin Sai Chien no hito to sakuhin* 古代東アジアの知識人崔致遠の人と作品 [The ancient East Asian intellectual Ch'oe Ch'iwŏn and his works]. Fukuoka: Kyūshū daigaku shuppankai, 2013.

Hoàng Đạo Thúy. *Phố phường Hà Nội Xưa* [Hanoi streets and quarters in the past]. Hanoi: Nxb Hà Nội, 1998.

Hoàng Thành Thăng Long [The Imperial Citadel of Thăng Long]. *Đặc san Xưa & Nay*. Hanoi: Hội Khoa học Lịch sử Việt Nam, 2003.

Hocquard, Charles-Edouard. *Une campagne au Tonkin* (first published 1892). Paris: Arléa, 1999.

Huang Lou 黃樓. 'Tubo Shan Yanxin yi He, Wei jiang Tang shiji kaolüe: jian lun Tangmo Gao Pian yu huanguan jituan zhi guanxi 吐蕃尚延心以河、渭降唐事迹考略—兼論唐末高駢與宦官集團之關系' [The Tibetan Shan Yanxin's surrender of He and Wei prefectures to the Tang and the late Tang Gao Pian's relations with the eunuch faction], *Wei Jin Nanbei chao Sui Tang shi ziliao* 魏晉南北朝隋唐史資料 [Historical materials on the Wei, Jin, Northern and Southern Dynasties, Sui, and Tang] 28 (2012): 202–13.

Huang Quancai 黃權才 & Xu Bianyun 徐變雲. 'Tanpeng yunhe: Tangdai Tianwei jing tanxi 潭蓬運河—唐代天威徑探析' [The Tanpeng canal: An investigation into the Tang period Path of Heavenly Might]. *Guangxi shifan xueyuan xuebao* 廣西師範學院學報 [Journal of Guangxi Normal University] 29, no. 4 (2008): 14–7.

Huỳnh…, Ministre des Rites. 'Minh-Mang va recevoir l'investiture à Hanoi', tr. Hoàng-Yên, *BAVH* 2 (1917): 9–109.

Inoue, Kazuto. 'Di tích cung điện Hoàng thành Thăng Long: phân tích về các vết tích khai quật chủ yếu ở khu A. B, D4, D5 và D6' [Palace remains of Thăng Long Imperial Citadel: Analysis of main excavated findings in the Sections A, B, D4, D5, and D6], *Khảo cổ học* [Archaeology] 4 (2010): 43–72.

Institute of Archaeology. *Những phát hiện mới về khảo cổ học 1978* [New Archaeological Discoveries in 1978]. Hanoi: Nxb KHXH, 1979.

Kaltenmark, Max. 'Le dompteur des flots', *Han Hiue/Bulletin du Centre d'études sinologiques de Pékin* 3, 1–2(1948): 1–113.

Kawahara Masahiro 河原正博. 'Betonamu dokuritsu ōchō no seiritsu to hatten ベトナム独立王朝の成立と発展' [The establishment and development of Vietnam as an independent kingdom], in *Betonamu Chūgoku kankeishi: Kyoku-shi no taitō kara Shin-Futsu Sensō made* ベトナム中国関係史—曲氏の抬頭から清仏戦争まで [The history of relations between Vietnam and China: From the rise of the Khúc clan to the Sino-French War], ed. Yamamoto Tatsurō 山本達郎. Tokyo: Yamakawa Shuppansha, 1975, pp. 5–28.

Kurz, Johannes L. *China's Southern Tang Dynasty, 937–976*. London: Routledge, 2011.

Langlet, Philippe. 'La tradition vietnamienne, un État national au sein de la civilisation chinoise', *BSEI* XLV, 2–3 (1970): 1–395.

_____. *L'ancienne historiographie d'État du Vietnam – Raisons d'être, condition d'élaboration et caractères au siècle des Nguyễn*. Paris: EFEO, vol. I, 1990.

Lê Thành Khôi. *Histoire du Viet Nam des origines à 1858*. Paris: Sudestasie, 1992.

Lieberman, Victor. *Strange Parallels: Southeast Asia in Global Context, c. 800–1830*. Cambridge: Cambridge University Press, 2 vols., 2003, 2009.

Logan, William S. *Hanoi: Biography of a City*. Sydney: University of South Wales Press, 2000.

Madrolle, Claude. *Indochine du Nord – Tonkin, Annam, Laos*. Paris, Hachette, 1925.

Mangin, France. 'Une lecture historique des plans de Hanoï: 1873–1951' in *Hanoï, Le cycle dé métamorphoses. Formes architecturales et urbaines*, ed. Pierre Clément & Nathalie Lancret. Paris: Éditions Recherches/Ipraus, 2001, pp. 97–115.

_____. *Le patrimoine Indochinois – Hanoi et autres sites*. Paris: Recherches/Ipraus, 2006.

Marini, Giovanni Filippo de. *Histoire nouvelle et curieuse des Royaumes de Tunquin et de Lao*. Paris: Gervais Clouzier, 1666.

Maspero, Henri. 'Le Protectorat général d'Annam sous les T'ang: Essai de géographie historique', part I in *BEFEO* 10, 1 (1910): 539–51; part II in *BEFEO* 10, 4 (1910): 665–82.

_____. 'Etudes d'histoire d'Annam', *BEFEO* 18, 1 (1918): 1–36.

Masson, André. *Hanoi pendant la période héroïque (1873–1888)*. Paris: Librairie orientaliste Paul Geuthner, 1929.

Maybon, Charles. *Lecture sur l'histoire moderne et contemporaine du pays d'Annam de 1428 à 1926*. Hanoi: IDEO, 1927.

Miyakawa Hisayuki. 'Legate Kao P'ien and a Taoist magician Lü Yung-chih in the time of Huang Ch'ao's rebellion', *Acta Asiatica* 27 (1974): 75–99.

Needham, Joseph, et al. 'Nautical Technology' in *Science and Civilization in China*, vol. 4, part 3. Cambridge: Cambridge University Press, 1971.

Needham, Joseph, et al. 'Military Technology: The Gunpowder Epic' in *Science and Civilisation in China*, vol. 5, part 7. Cambridge: Cambridge University Press, 1986.

Ngô Cao Lãng. *Lịch triều tạp kỷ* [Miscellaneous records of the successive dynasties]. Hanoi: Nxb Khoa học xã hội, 1995.

Ngô Văn Doanh. 'Lễ vía Bà Thiên Yana với tục thờ Mẫu của người Chăm và người Việt' [Veneration of the goddess Thiên Yana and worship of goddesses among the Cham and Việt], *Nghiên cứu Đông Nam Á*, 2 (2006): 48–53.

Nguyễn Hồng Kiên. 'Có hay không nghệ nhân – tù binh Chămpa trong việc xây dựng tháp Then – Bình Sơn' [Were Champa prisoner-artisans involved in the construction of Then tower – Bình Sơn'], in *Những phát hiện mới về khảo cổ học năm 1999* [New archaeological discoveries 1999]. 2000, pp. 744–5.

Nguyễn Minh Tường. *Cải cách hành chính dưới triều Minh Mệnh* [The administrative reforms of Minh Mệnh's reign]. Hanoi: Nxb KHXH, 1996.

Nguyen Phuc Long. 'Les nouvelles recherches archéologiques au Vietnam (Complément au *Việtnam* de Louis Bezacier)' *Arts Asiatiques* 31 (1975): 3–151.

Nguyễn Quang Ngọc. 'Góp thêm ý kiến về Hoàng thành Thăng Long thời Lý, Trần và lịch sử Thập tam trại' [Further thoughts on the Imperial Citadel of Thăng Long in the Lý and Trần periods and the history of the Thirteen Villages], *Nghiên cứu lịch sử* 1 (1986): 25–33.

Nguyễn Thừa Hỷ. *Thăng Long–Hà Nội, thế kỷ XVII-XVIII-XIX* [Thăng Long–Hanoi in the 17th–19th centuries]. Hanoi: Hội Sử học Việt Nam, 1993.

Nguyễn Tiến Đông & Nguyễn Hữu Thiết. 'Hai bức tượng Chăm tại chùa Bạch Sam (Hà Nội)' [Two Cham statues at Bạch Sam pagoda (Hanoi)' in *Những phát hiện mới về khảo cổ học năm 2004* [New archaeological discoveries 2004]. 2005, pp. 806–8.

Nguyễn Tiến Đông & Ogawa Yoko. 'Hai giếng nước có kỹ thuật Chămpa ở xã Song Phương (Đan Phượng, Hà Tây)' [Two wells built with Champa technology at Son Phương commune (Đan Phượng, Hà Tây)], in *Những phát hiện mới về khảo cổ học năm 1999* [New archaeological discoveries 1999]. 2000, pp. 717–8.

Nguyen Van Huyen. 'Contribution à l'étude d'un génie tutélaire Annamite, Li Phuc Man', *BEFEO* 38 (1938): 1–110.

Nguyễn Văn Siêu. *Phương Đình dư địa chí* [Phương Đình Gazetteer]. Saigon: Cơ sở Báo chí và Xuất bản Tự do, 1960. Republished in 2010 as *Thành Thăng Long, Địa chí loại* [Thăng Long Citadel, Monograph], quyển II in *Tuyển tập địa chí* [Anthology of gazetteers]. Hanoi: Nxb Hà Nội, vol. III.

Nguyễn Vinh Phúc. 'Tìm ra thôn Bà Già Hà Nội' [Discovery of Bà Già village, Hanoi], in *Những phát hiện mới về khảo cổ học năm 1986* [New archaeological discoveries 1986]. 1987, pp. 280–1.

Nguyễn Xuân Diện. 'Những phát hiện mới về loại các tượng phỗng Chàm trong các di tích' [Discovery of new types of Cham phỗng statue at different sites], in *Những phát hiện mới về khảo cổ học năm 1999* [New archaeological discoveries 1999]. 2000, pp. 727–8.

Nhật Minh. *Di sản vô giá của Kinh thành Thăng Long/Priceless Heritage of Thăng Long Imperial Citadel*. Hanoi: Nxb Thông tin và Truyền thông, 2015.

Nienhauser, William H. *P'i Jih-hsiu*. Boston: Twayne, 1979.

Niu Junkai 牛軍凱. 'Shilun fengshui wenhua zai Yuenan de chuanbo yu fengshui shu de Yuenan hua 試論風水文化在越南的傳播與風水術的越南化', *Dongnan ya nanya yanjiu* 東南亞南亞研究, 1 (2011): 80–5.

Papin, Philippe. 'Des « villages dans la ville » aux « villages urbains »: l'espace et les formes de pouvoir à Hà-Nội de 1805 à 1940', PhD thesis, University of Paris 7, 1997.

_____. 'Géographie et politique dans le Viêt-Nam ancien', *BEFEO* 87, 2 (2000): 609–28.

_____. 2001, *Histoire de Hanoi*, Paris: Fayard, 2001. Tr. Mạc Thu Hương: *Lịch sử Hà Nội*. Hanoi: Nhã Nam và Nxb Mỹ thuật, 2009.

Parmentier, Henri & René Mercier. 'Eléments anciens d'architecture du Nord Viêt Nam', *BEFEO* XLV, 2 (1952): 285–348.

Paul-Lévy, Françoise & Segaud, Marion. *Anthropologie de l'espace*. Paris: Centre George Pompidou, 1983.

Phạm Hân. *Tìm lại dấu tích thành Thăng Long* [Searching for Traces of Thăng Long Citadel]. Hanoi: Nxb Văn hóa Thông tin, 2003.

Phạm Lê Huy. 'Diện mạo và vị trí địa lý của An Nam Đô hộ phủ thời thuộc Đường' [The appearance and geographical location of the palace of the viceroy of Annam under the Tang], *Nghiên cứu lịch sử* 1 (2012a): 34–51.

_____. Ảnh hưởng mô hình Lạc Dương và Khai Phong đến qui hoạch Hoàng thành Thăng Long thời Lý-Trần' [Influence of the Lạc Dương and Khai Phong model on the planning of Thang Long Imperial Citadel under the Lý and Trần], in *Kỷ yếu Tọa đàm khoa học về khu trung tâm Hoàng thành Thăng Long* [Proceedings of the seminar on the central area of Thang Long Imperial Citadel]. Hanoi, 2012b.

Pham Le Huy ファム・レ・フイ. 'Betonamu ni okeru Annan togo Kō Ben no yōjutsu: sono gensō to shinsō ni tsuite ベトナムにおける安南都護高駢の妖術―その幻相と真相について' [On the sorcery of protector general of Annan Gao Pian in Vietnam: illusion and reality], in *Kodai Higashi Ajia no 'inori': Shūkyō, shūzoku, senjutsu* 古代東アジアの「祈り」―宗教・習俗・占術, ['Prayer' in ancient East Asia: Religion, custom, divination], ed. Mizuguchi Motoki 水口幹記. Tokyo: Shinwasha, 2014, pp. 299–330.

Phạm Lưu Vũ. 'Thăng Long lược phong thủy ký' [Outline notes on the geomancy of Thăng Long], in *Người Hà Nội* [Hanoi People] no. 45, November 2005.

Phạm Quốc Quân. 'Khảo cổ học Quần Ngựa và vấn đề Hoàng Thành Thăng Long' [The archaeology of the Racecourse and the problem of the Imperial Citadel of Thăng Long], *Bảo tàng lịch sử Việt Nam, Nội san Viện Bảo tàng lịch sử* [History Museum intramural bulletin], 1 December 1979: 42–50.

Phan Huy Lê, ed. *Hoàng Thành Thăng Long, Phát hiện khảo cổ học* [The Imperial Citadel of Thăng Long, Archaeological Discovery]. Hanoi: Hội Khoa học Lịch sử Việt Nam, 2004.

_____. 'Vị trí khu di tích khảo cổ học 18 Hoàng Diệu trong cấu trúc thành Thăng Long – Hà Nội qua các thời kỳ lịch sử, *Khảo cổ học* 1 (2006): 5–27. English edition: 'The 18 Hoàng Diệu Street Archaeological Site's Location in the Structure of Thăng Long–Hà Nội Citadel through History', *Vietnam Archaeology* 1 (2006): 31–56.

_____. 'Thành Thăng Long–Hà Nội và di tích Hoàng thành mới phát lộ' [Thăng Long–Hanoi Citadel and the recently discovered Imperial Citadel site], in *Lịch sử và văn hoá Việt Nam, tiếp cận bộ phận* [History and culture of

Vietnam, sectional approach], ed. Phan Huy Lê. Hanoi: Nxb Giáo dục, 2007, pp. 757–810.

———, ed. *Lịch sử Thăng Long Hà Nội*. Hanoi: Nxb Hà Nội, vol. 1, 2010a.

———, ed. *Địa bạ Hà Nội* [Land register of Hanoi]. Hanoi: Nxb Hà Nội, vol. 1, 2010b.

Phan Huy Lê, Nguyễn Quang Ngọc, Tống Trung Tín & Nguyễn Văn Sơn. *Khu Trung tâm Hoàng thành Thăng Long – Hà Nội, Di sản văn hoá thế giới/The Central Sector of the Imperial Citadel of Thang Long – Hanoi – A World Heritage Site*. Hanoi: Nxb Hà Nội, 2014.

Phan Văn Các & Claudine Salmon. *Epigraphie en chinois du Việt Nam/Văn khắc Hán Nôm Việt Nam*. Paris: EFEO & Hanoi: Viện Nghiên cứu Hán Nôm, 1998.

Reinecke, Andreas, ed. *Perspectives on the Archaeology of Vietnam, International Colloquium, Hanoi 29th February–2nd March 2012/Toàn cảnh khảo cổ học Việt Nam, Hội thảo quốc tế, từ 29/2 đến 02/3/2012, tại Hà Nội*. Bonn: LWL Museum for Archaeology Herne, Reiss-Engelhorn-Museen Mannheim, State Museum of Archaeology Chemnitz German Archaeological Institute, 2015.

Schafer, Edward H. *The Vermilion Bird: T'ang Images of the South*. Berkeley: University of California Press, 1967.

Shizunaga Takeshi 靜永健. 'Shiragi bunjin Sai Chien to Tō-matsu setsudo-shi Kō Ben no zen-hansei 新羅文人崔致遠と唐末節度使高駢の前半生', *Bungaku kenkyū* 文學研究 105 (2008): 57–82.

Somers, Robert M. 'The End of the T'ang', in *The Cambridge History of China*, vol. 3, part 1, ed. D. Twitchett. Cambridge: Cambridge University Press, 1979.

Stott, Wilfrid. 'The expansion of the Nan-chao kingdom between the Years A.D. 750–860 and the causes that lay behind it as shewn in the T'ai-ho Inscription and the Man Shu', *T'oung Pao* 50 (1963): 190–220.

Sudō Yoshiyuki 周藤吉之. 'Tō-matsu Wainan Kō Ben no hanchin taisei to Kō Sō totō to no kankei ni tsuite: Shiragi-matsu no Sai Chien no cho *Keien hikkō-shū* o chūshin to shite 唐末淮南高駢の藩鎮體制と黃巢徒黨との関係について —新羅末の崔致遠の著『桂苑筆耕集』を中心として' [Gao Pian's system of regional governorship in Huainan at the end of the Tang and its relationship with the Huang Chao rebels: Centered on the 'Commissioned writings from Cassia Grove by Ch'oe Ch'iwŏn of Silla], *Tōyō gakuhō* 東洋學報 [Journal of Oriental Studies] 68 (1987): 183–218.

Sutton, Donald S. 'A Case of Literati Piety: The Ma Yuan Cult from High-Tang to High-Qing', *Chinese Literature: Essays, Articles, Reviews (CLEAR)* 11 (1989): 79–114.

Tavernier, Jean-Baptiste. *Receuil de plusieurs relations et traitez singulier et curieux de J.B. Tavernier. IV. Relation nouvelle et singulière du Royaume de Tunquin: avec plusieurs Figures & la Carte du Païs*. Paris: Gervais Clouzier, 1679.

Taylor, Keith Weller. *The Birth of Vietnam*. Berkeley: University of California Press, 1983.

────. 'Book review. Nagara and Commandery: Origins of the Southeast Asian Urban Traditions. By Paul Wheatley', *Journal of Southeast Asian Studies* 17, 2 (September 1986): 366–70.

────. 'Surface Orientations in Vietnam: Beyond Histories of Nation and Region', *Journal of Asian Studies* 57, 5 (November 1998): 949–78.

────. 'A Southern Remembrance of Cao Bien' in *Liber amicorum: mélanges offerts au professeur Phan Huy Lê*, ed. Philippe Papin & John Kleinen. Hanoi: Thanh Niên, 1999, pp. 241–58.

Tống Trung Tín. 'Những hiện vật điêu khắc ở Ly Cung' [Sculptures from Ly Cung], *Khảo cổ học* 1 (1981): 49–63.

────. 'Kết quả bước đầu khai quật khảo cổ học' [First results of archaeological excavation], *Xưa Nay* 203–4 (2004): 10–21.

────, ed. *Hoàng Thành Thăng Long – Thang Long Imperial Citadel*. Hanoi: Nxb Văn hóa Thông tin, 2006.

────, ed. *Văn hiến Thăng Long bằng chứng khoả cổ học/Thăng Long Civilisation – Archaeological Evidence*. Hanoi: Nxb Hà Nội, 2020.

Tống Trung Tín & Bùi Minh Trí. *Thăng Long–Hà Nội, lịch sử nghìn năm từ lòng đất* [Thăng Long–Hanoi, a thousand years from under the ground]. Hanoi: Nxb KHXH, 2010.

Tống Trung Tín & Nguyễn Văn Sơn, eds. *Di vật tiêu biểu Hoàng thành Thăng Long 2002–2013/Typical artifacts found in the Imperial Citadel of Thang Long between 2002 and 2013*. Hanoi: Nxb Hà Nôi, 2014.

Tống Trung Tín, Trần Anh Dũng, Hà Văn Cẩn, Nguyễn Đăng Cường & Nguyễn Văn Hùng. 'Khai quật địa điểm Đoan Môn (Hà Nội) năm 1999' [Excavation of the Đoan Môn site (Hanoi), 1999], *Khảo cổ học*, 3 (2000): 11–32.

Tong Zhenzao 童振藻. 'Yuenan Tangdai gucheng kao 越南唐代古城考' [Remains of the Tang walled city in Vietnam], *Yu gong banyue kan* 禹貢半月刊 [Tribute of Yu Fortnightly] 6, no. 11 (1937): 11–5.

Trần Hùng & Nguyễn Quốc Thông. *Thăng-Long – Hà-Nội mười thế kỷ đô thị hóa* [Thăng Long—Hanoi, ten centuries of urbanisation]. Hanoi: Nxb *Hà Nội*, 1995.

Trần Huy Liệu, ed. *Lịch sử thủ đô Hà Nội* [History of the capital Hanoi]. Hanoi: Nxb Sử học, 1960, reprint 2000, Nxb Hà Nội; 2009, Nxb Lao động.

Trần Quốc Vượng. 'Xuân lửa Đống Đa trong bối cảnh văn hóa xã hội đương thời' [The Đống Đa spring of fire in contemporary cultural and social context], in *Trên mảnh đất ngàn năm văn vật*, ed. Trần Quốc Vượng. Hanoi: Nxb Hà Nội, 2000.

Trần Quốc Vượng & Vũ Tuấn Sán. *Hà Nội nghìn xưa* [Hanoi, a thousand pasts]. Hanoi: Sở Văn hóa Thông tin Hà Nội, 1975, reprint 1990.

Trương Quang Hải, ed. *Atlas Thăng Long Hà Nội*. Hanoi: Nxb Hà Nội, 2010.

Twitchett, Denis. 'Tibet in Tang's grand strategy', in *Warfare in Chinese history*, ed. Hans van de Ven. Leiden: Brill, 2000, pp. 106–79.

Verellen, Franciscus. *Du Guangting (850–933): taoïste de cour à la fin de la Chine médiévale*. Paris: Collège de France, 1989a.

———. 'Liturgy and Sovereignty: The Role of Taoist Ritual in the Foundation of the Shu Kingdom (906–25)', *Asia Major* 3rd ser. 2, 1 (1989b): 59–78.

———. '"Evidential Miracles in Support of Taoism": The Inversion of a Buddhist Apologetic Tradition in Late T'ang China', *T'oung Pao* 78 (1992): 217–63.

———. 'Zhang Ling and the Lingjing Salt Well', in *En suivant la voie royale: Mélanges en hommage à Léon Vandermeersch*, ed. Jacques Gernet & Marc Kalinowski. Paris: EFEO, 1997, pp. 249–65.

———. 'Shu as a Hallowed Land: Du Guangting's *Record of Marvels*', *Cahiers d'Extrême-Asie* 10 (1998): 213–54.

———. 'L'ouverture du chenal de la Puissance céleste sous la Chine des Tang: artifice magique ou poudre noire?' *BEFEO* 105 (2019): 229–53.

Viện Văn học. *Thơ văn Lý, Trần* [Literature of the Lý and the Trần]. Hanoi: Nxb KHXH, 1977.

Wang Chengwen 王承文. 'Wan Tang Gao Pian kaizao Annan 'Tianwei yao' yunhe shiji shizheng: yi Pei Xing suo zhuan *Tianwei yao bei* wei zhongxin de kaocha 晚唐高駢開鑿安南「天威遙」運河事蹟釋證－以裴鉶所撰《天威遙碑》爲中心的考察', [A crititcal examination of the traces of the late Tang Heavenly Might Passage canal in Annan breached by Gao Pian, centered on the 'Heavenly Might Passage stele inscription' by Pei Xing], *Zongyang yanjiu yuan lishi yuyan yanjiu suo jikan* 中央研究院歷史語言研究所集刊 [Bulletin of the Institute of History and Philology, Academia Sinica] 81, no. 3 (2010): 597–650.

Wang Gungwu. 'The Nanhai Trade: A Study of the Early History of Chinese Trade in the South China Sea', *Journal of the Malayan Branch of the Royal Asiatic Society* 31 (1958): 82–5.

———. *Divided China: Preparing for Reunification, 883–947*. Hackensack, N.J.: World Scientific, 2007.

Wang Jilin 王吉林. *Tangdai Nanzhao yu Li Tang guanxi zhi yanjiu* 唐代南詔與李唐關係之研究 [Nanzhao in the Tang period and its relations with the Tang dynasty]. Taipei: Hua mulan wenhua, 2011.

Wang Zhenping. *Tang China in Multi-polar Asia: A History of Diplomacy and War*. Honolulu: University of Hawai'i Press, 2013.

Wang Yuanlin 王元林. 'Lun Tangdai Guangzhou neiwai gang yu haishang jiaotong de guanxi 論唐代廣州內外港與海上交通的關系' [Tang Guangzhou's inner and outer harbors and their role in maritime communications], *Tangdu xuekan* 唐都學刊 [Tangdu Journal] 22, 6 (2006): 22–8.

Wheatley, Paul. *The Pivot of the Four Quarters. A Preliminary Enquiry into the Origins of the Character of the Ancient Chinese City*. Chicago: Aldine Publishing Company, 1971.

———. *Nagara and Commandery: Origins of the Southeast Asian Urban Traditions*. Chicago: Geography Department, University of Chicago, 1983.

Woodside, Alexander Barton. *Vietnam and the Chinese Model: A Comparative Study of Vietnamese and Chinese Government in the First Half of the Nineteenth Century*. Cambridge, Mass.: Harvard University Press, 1971.

Xu Haibing 徐海冰. 'Wan Tang zhanluan beijing xia Gao Pian de xintai mingyun yu shige chuangzuo 晚唐戰亂背景下高駢的心態命運與詩歌創作', [Gao Pian's mindset, destiny, and poetic production, against the background of late Tang wartime chaos] *Guangdong haiyang daxue xuebao* 廣東海洋大學學報 [Journal of Guangdong Maritime University] 43, no. 2 (2014): 74–9.

Yamamoto Tatsurō 山本達郎. 'Annan ga dokuritsu-koku o keisei shitaru katei no kenkyū 安南が獨立國を形成したる過程の研究' [A study of the process of the establishment of Annan as an independent kingdom], *Tōyō bunka kenkyūjo kiyō* 東洋文化研究所紀要 [Memoirs of the Institute for Advanced Studies on Asia] 1 (1943): 57–146.

Yamamoto Tatsurō. 'Myths Explaining the Vicissitudes of Political Power in Ancient Vietnam', *Acta Asiatica* 18 (1970): 70–94.

Yu Ying-shih. 'Han Foreign Relations', in *The Cambridge History of China*, vol. 1. Cambridge: Cambridge University Press, 1987, pp. 377–462.

Zeng Liming 曾麗明. 'Han Yu *Nanhai shen Guangli wang miao bei* de lishi yiyi he wenxue jiazhi 韓愈《南海神廣利王廟碑》的歷史意義和文學價值' [The historical significance and literary value of Han Yu's 'Stele to the Temple of the South Sea God Prince of Large Profits'], *Guangzhou hanghai xueyuan xuebao* 廣州航海學院學報 [Journal of Guangzhou Maritime Institute] 21, 4 (2013): 43–5.

Zhang Zengqi 張增祺. *Erhai quyu de gudai wenming* 洱海區域的古代文明 [Ancient civilisations of the Erhai region]. Kunming: Yunnan jiaoyu, 2010.

LIST OF CONTRIBUTORS

Đào Hùng (1932–2013): Historian, former editor of *XuaNay* review, Vietnam History Association.

Đỗ Danh Huấn: Historian, Institute of History, Vietnam Academy of Social Sciences.

Andrew Hardy: Historian, EFEO.

Lê Thị Liên: Archaeologist, administrative officer of the Vietnam Archaeology Association.

Nguyễn Gia Đối: Archaeologist, former director of the Institute of Archaeology, Vietnam Academy of Social Sciences.

Nguyễn Hồng Kiên: Archaeologist, Institute of Archaeology, Vietnam Academy of Social Sciences.

Nguyễn Tiến Đông (1962–2022): Archaeologist, Institute of Archaeology, Vietnam Academy of Social Sciences.

Nguyễn Văn Anh: Archaeologist, Faculty of History, University of Social Sciences and Humanities, Hanoi.

Nguyễn Văn Sơn: Archaeologist, president of the Association of the History of Hanoi.

Phan Huy Lê (1934–2018): Historian, honorary president of the Vietnam History Association, foreign corresponding member of the French Academy of Inscriptions and Belles-Lettres.

Phạm Văn Triệu: Archaeologist, Institute of Archaeology, Vietnam Academy of Social Sciences.

Olivier Tessier: Anthropologist, EFEO.

Tống Trung Tín: Archaeologist, president of the Vietnam Archaeology Association.

Franciscus Verellen: Historian, Professor Emeritus EFEO, member of the French Academy of Inscriptions and Belles-Lettres.

INDEX